Nelson's Annual Youth Ministry Sourcebook

2006 EDITION

AMY JACOBER, EDITOR

NELSON REFERENCE & ELECTRONIC
A Division of Thomas Nelson Publishers
Since 1798

www.thomasnelson.com

Nelson's Annual Youth Ministry Sourcebook, 2006 Edition

Copyright © 2005 by Thomas Nelson, Inc.

Published in Nashville, Tennessee, by Thomas Nelson, Inc.

Book design and composition by Bob Bubnis, Booksetters, Inc., White House, Tennessee.

Jacober, Amy Elizabeth (ed.)

Nelson's annual youth ministry sourcebook, 2006 edition

ISBN 1-4185-0549-8

Printed in the United States of America

1 2 3 4 5 6 7—08 07 06 05

CONTENTS

You can't give what you don't have.

While this book offers lessons, encouragement, articles and resources all in one neat little package, this is not all it will take to minister to your students. In fact, this book provides the least important parts of youth ministry. It will become too easy on busy days to grab this book and read it on the way to church…I mean have it read to you, because, of course, none of you ever reads your lessons in the car! It would also be a mistake to simply look this over a few days before you plan to use it.

Ministering to students is an honor and a privilege. It can also be exhausting and trying. What your students need is a leader who knows and lives the importance of spending time with the Lord. Any of these lessons can be pulled off, but we are called to so much more than that. Before you sit down to prepare for a lesson, spend time letting God love you. Spend time in prayer and in community with other followers of Christ. Spend time wrestling with issues and passages that come up in your own life. Remember and observe the Sabbath, so that you are truly refreshed and not simply busy for God.

Above all, give out of your own life. Give out of the overflow of what God pours into you. These lessons are not meant to be strict rules. They are guidelines. Feel free to use what works for you and to change or drop what does not. Allow God to speak to you through these recommended plans, and, in turn, share with your group. May you be blessed and drawn closer to God as you work with these resources to plan your youth ministry.

It sounds backwards to take care of yourself first. Take a lesson from the airlines and the little yellow oxygen masks they explain at the beginning of every flight. My hope and prayer is that this book is tremendously helpful to you. Even more than that, my prayer is that you fall more passionately in love with the Maker and Savior of the world, Jesus Christ. Your job is to be certain that your mask is securely in place before you begin to take care of others.

Have a good flight!

CONTRIBUTORS

Anna Aven—The junior high director at United Christian Church in Los Angeles, California. She is a graduate of Fuller Theological Seminary.

Fernando (Fred) Arzola Jr.—Raised in the Mott Haven section of the South Bronx, he is deputy chair for the Department of Youth Ministry and Christian Education at Nyack College NYC. He is a Ph.D. candidate in Religious Education at Fordham University's Graduate School of Religion and Religious Education, and holds a Master of Arts in Theological Studies, with concentrations in Peace and Justice, from Maryknoll School of Theology. He is also founder and executive director of the Urban Family Empowerment Center, a faith-based initiative whose mission is to holistically empower urban families.

Rick Bennett—A church consultant in Tampa, Florida, working with the emerging church conversation. Along with his wife, Kristi (his editor), he has planted a church in Boston, assisted in church planting in Houston, and ministered to youth in Virginia, Florida, and Georgia.

Cole Billings—Currently studying youth ministry at Azusa Pacific University. He is a volunteer high school small group leader at Inland Hills Church in Chino Hills, California.

Alicia Claxton—A freelance writer living in Nashville, Tennessee. She serves as a student ministry volunteer at ClearView Baptist Church, and writes small group Bible studies and student ministry materials for churches across the country.

Blaine Clyde— He has been on Young Life staff for fourteen years. His own struggle with dyslexia and a passion for people with disabilities led him to start Open Door in Seattle, Washington. He is currently the area director.

Joyce del Rosario—An urban veteran, graduate of Princeton Theological Seminary and currently an area director for Young Life. While concerned with many issues, her area of interest includes ministry to and with Asian American adolescents.

Calenthia S. Dowdy—Serves on the Youth Ministry faculty at Eastern University. She was born and raised in Philadelphia and has worked in cities most of her adult life. Areas of interest include urban youth cultures, hip-hop, faith, and social justice.

Michelle R. Hicks—A wife, mom to three daughters, and freelance writer. She is a graduate of University of North Texas and Southwestern Baptist Theological Seminary. Michelle has been in ministry while living in California, Washington, Texas, New Mexico, and Florida. She currently resides in Franklin, Tennessee and is involved in lay ministry at ClearView Baptist Church. Michelle first started writing Christian curriculum in 1989 and has not been able to stop. She loves God's Word and wants others to love it too. She loves taking the ordinary things of life and telling God's story.

Amy Jacober—Currently serves as an assistant professor of Practical Theology and Youth Ministry at Azusa Pacific University. She is a graduate of Southwestern Theological Seminary and Fuller Theological Seminary. She also serves on the Mission Wide Committee for Young Life Capernaum.

Dr. Christine Kern—An assistant professor of English at Azusa Pacific University in Azusa, California. She writes fiction and non-fiction.

Sharon Koh—The director of Young Adult and College Ministries at Evergreen Baptist Church of Los Angeles, California. She is a graduate of Fuller Seminary with youth ministry experience.

Ric Lipsey—Currently serves as minister to students at First Baptist Church of Pasadena, Texas, where he has been on staff since June 1997. He is a graduate of Louisiana Tech University and Southwestern Baptist Theological Seminary. Before coming to First Baptist Church, Ric worked with students at churches and camps from California to Florida.

James Miller—The associate pastor at the First Presbyterian Church of Honolulu. He and his wife, Yolanda, have served in youth ministry for a decade and just recently began a youth ministry at home with their new baby girl, Sonoma. He holds degrees from Princeton Theological Seminary and U.C. Berkeley.

Steffen Nelson—When not busy as a Young Life volunteer, he is the president of Objective Medical Assessments Corporation based in Seattle, Washington. He is also on the board of directors as treasurer for Northwest Urban Ministries.

Nick Palermo—The founder and national director for Capernaum Project of Young Life. Capernaum is a ministry to adolescents with special needs. His passion is for all people to know the life changing love of Christ.

Will Penner—He has been a bi-vocational music minister and full-time youth minister in Baptist, Methodist, and Presbyterian churches; he is the editor of *YouthWorker Journal*, a bi-monthly, ecumenical publication for career Christian youth ministers. He and his wife, Christine, are currently the volunteer youth pastors at Westview United Methodist Church in Fairview, Tennessee. He's also a freelance writer and a very popular speaker at youth leader training events and youth retreats, camps, and conferences.

Whitney Prosperi—Makes her home in Tyler, Texas with her family, and contributes to numerous devotionals and magazines. She is a former girls' minister and author of the Bible study *Lifestyle: Real Perspectives from Radical Women in the Bible*. She is currently working on a book about girls' ministry.

Chris Renzleman—A networker extraordinaire. He heads up the northwest area of the Leadership Network. He is also a field representative for Interlinc., a company which seeks to maximize music and media in youth ministry.

2006 CALENDAR

January 1	New Year's Day
January 6	Epiphany
January 15	Sanctity of Human Life Sunday
January 16	Martin Luther King Jr. Day
January 26	Australia Day
February 1–28	Black History Month
February 1	National Freedom Day
February 2	Groundhog Day
February 5	Super Bowl Sunday
February 12	Lincoln's Birthday
February 14	Valentine's Day
February 20	President's Day
February 22	Washington's Birthday
February 26	30 Hour Famine—World Vision
March 1	Ash Wednesday
March 5	First Sunday of Lent; Cinco de Mayo
March 12	Second Sunday of Lent
March 17	St. Patrick's Day
March 19	Third Sunday of Lent
March 20	Spring Begins
March 26	Fourth Sunday of Lent
April 2	Fifth Sunday of Lent; Daylight Saving Time Begins
April 9	Palm Sunday
April 13	Maundy Thursday; Jefferson's Birthday; Passover
April 14	Good Friday
April 16	Easter Sunday
April 22	Earth Day
April 25	Holocaust Remembrance Day
April 26	Administrative Professional's Day
May 4	National Day of Prayer

May 14	Mother's Day
May 20	Armed Forces Day
May 25	Ascension Day
May 29	Memorial Day
June 4	Pentecost
June 11	Trinity Sunday
June 14	Flag Day
June 18	Father's Day
June 21	Summer Begins
July 1	Canada Day
July 4	Independence Day
July 23	Parent's Day
August 6	Transfiguration Day; Friendship Day
September 4	Labor Day
September 10	Grandparents' Day
September 20	See You At The Pole
September 22	Native American Day
September 23	Autumn Begins; Rosh Hashanah Begins
October 1–31	Pastor Appreciation Month
October 2	Yom Kippur Begins
October 8	Clergy Appreciation Day
October 9	Columbus Day
October 16	Bosses' Day
October 22	Mother-in-Law Day
October 29	Reformation Sunday; Daylight Saving Time Ends
October 31	Halloween
November 1	All Saints' Day
November 11	Veterans' Day
November 12	International Day of Prayer for the Persecuted Church
November 23	Thanksgiving Day
December 3	First Sunday of Advent

December 7	Pearl Harbor Remembrance Day
December 10	Second Sunday of Advent
December 16	Hanukkah Begins
December 17	Third Sunday of Advent
December 22	Winter Begins
December 24	Fourth Sunday of Advent; Christmas Eve
December 25	Christmas Day
December 26	Boxing Day; Kwanzaa Begins
December 31	New Year's Eve

WEEKLY
WORSHIP SUGGESTIONS
FOR 52 WEEKS

JANUARY 1, 2006

Golden Revelation

By Amy Jacober

MEMORY VERSE:
The LORD shall reign forever and ever.—Exodus 15:18 (NAS)

Now to the King eternal, immortal, invisible, the only God, be honor and glory forever and ever. Amen.—1Timothy 1:17 (NAS)

SCRIPTURE: Isaiah 52:7–10

LESSON IN A SENTENCE: God, and only God, reigns in the past, in the present, in the future and in all the world!

THE BIG PICTURE (OR WHAT YOU'RE TRYING TO GET ACROSS):
    This is the week of Epiphany. Epiphany traditionally is the celebration of the manifestation of the divine; the incarnation as experienced by the Magi. They experienced the Good News in the flesh. Not only was this spiritual revelation—this epiphany—life changing for the kings who traveled so far, but for all the world for the remainder of history. It was a joyous occasion deserving a celebration.

IN THIS LESSON STUDENTS SHOULD:

- ○ Know that Jesus is not only their personal Lord, but Lord of all.
- ○ Practice praise as an appropriate way to honor Jesus, the King.
- ○ Be encouraged to continue the tradition of revealing to others that Jesus is King.

STUFF YOU NEED:

- ○ Party decorations (as much as you can, anything in gold, bright yellow and white)
- ○ A King's Cake (or some other dessert fit for a party)
- ○ Slips of paper and pens/pencils (for charades)

FOCUS

Decorate the room for a party. This needs to be more than just a streamer or two...think over the top, gold everywhere. Christmas will just have happened, so check out a few sales, pick up some gold garland, gold chocolate coins and whatever else you can find. Have snacks around and music playing.

Teacher's Note: The traditional colors for Epiphany are the same as the colors for Christmas, gold and white. These are to remind us of celebrations, newness, and hope! What could possibly bring more thoughts of newness and hope than a baby?

As each person comes in, hand them at least one slip of paper (if your group is small, hand as many as 3–5). Ask each person to write on this slip of paper the best gift they have every received, but they may not show it to anyone. When it seems everyone is there and they have had a few minutes to write on their papers, split the group into two teams. Collect the papers from each team and trade. It is now time for charades! Go through at least five rounds. Depending on time, you may want to play a few more rounds, but be certain to leave time for discovery, life application, and making it personal!

If you have time and are really into this, offer a King Cake to the winning team.

Teacher's Note: There are many legends around the tradition of the King Cake. It is a staple in New Orleans between Epiphany and Lent culminating in the two weeks prior to Mardi Gras. It is, by tradition, a circle and often twisted (like a cinnamon pastry) to represent a crown. The frosting and sugar sprinkles are in the royal colors of purple, green and gold in remembrance and honor of the three kings who visited the baby Jesus and brought to us Epiphany. Within the cake, tradition has a small plastic baby. This represents the baby Jesus as the three kings discovered the Christ child on Epiphany. While there are many secular traditions that have arisen around Mardi Gras, it holds its roots deep in Europe and the New Orleans version from France in particular. The celebration of the birth and subsequently the life of Christ is celebrated between Epiphany and Lent. The celebration is assured by yet one more tradition; if you are the one to receive the piece of cake with the baby, it is your responsibility to hold the next party.

While you can make a regular cake and simply decorate it in purple, gold and green with the baby in the cake, there is a more traditional recipe at the end of this lesson.

DISCOVERY

PART A (GETTING ADOLESCENTS TO LOOK AT SCRIPTURE FOR THEMSELVES)

Say: This entire party is to celebrate and remind us all of the time when the Magi traveled and found God incarnate! January 6th in the church calendar is known as Epiphany. It is great news for all people, all around the world.

Ask: Why do you think God came to this earth in the form of a man? What kind of reaction does this bring from people?

Break into groups of 3–4. Have each group read Isaiah 52:7–10. While reading, have them consider the same two questions. Why did God come to earth? And what were the reactions of people (look at vv. 8–9)?

LIFE APPLICATION: Jesus came to bring good news of peace and happiness and salvation. The reaction of people was to shout with joy!!

Ask: What makes you shout with joy? If your group is more mature and accustomed to corporate prayer, spend some time in a concert of prayer. Have them shout out praises for Jesus.

If this would be too uncomfortable for your group, ask them in their groups to list the things for which they would praise God. After a few moments, remind them that Scripture tells us where two or three are gathered, He is present. The conversation they just had about praises for God was indeed a prayer!

PART B

Read back over Isaiah 52:7–10.
Read again Isaiah 52:7.

Ask: What does it mean that "God is King."

How does this fit with a worldview that often places Christianity as one of many truths?

What does it mean to read that God is King as opposed to God is my King?

There is a strong trend and has been for several years (if not decades) that has overshadowed the reality that Jesus Christ is King of kings and Lord of lords. That trend has placed the focus on the individual relationship (which is not a bad thing) to the exclusion of the reality (which is a bad thing) that Jesus reigns whether we acknowledge Him or not. This can be a difficult conversation in a pluralistic world. The good news is that even in biblical times, there were believers living faithfully in a pluralistic world.

MAKING IT PERSONAL: Look around the room—this day has been a day of a party, but a party celebrating the King!!! Do you shout with joy realizing this is the King? Do you shout with joy at being invited?

While many of us can say we understand that Jesus is King. . .

Invite each person to spend a few moments pondering how their life might be different if they lived as though they believed this. After a few minutes, invite each person to choose one thing they would like to change in their life as a result of this truth.

DEPENDING ON YOUR GROUP. . .

Close in prayer giving thanks and praise for the happiness and peace brought by God coming to the earth.

Or—close by having a few in your group share how their life would be different if they lived as though they believed God is King.

King Cake Recipe:
King Cake
(From *Southern Living 1990 Annual Recipes*)
1/4 cup butter or margarine
1 (16-oz.) carton sour cream
1/3 c. sugar
1 t. salt
1 pkg. dry yeast
1 T. sugar
1/2 c. warm water (105 ° to 115 °)
2 eggs
6 to 6 1/2 cups all-purpose flour, divided

1/2 cup sugar
1 1/2 t. ground cinnamon
1/3 cup butter or margarine, softened
Colored frostings
Colored sugars

Combine the first 4 ingredients in a saucepan; heat until butter melts, stirring occasionally. Let mixture cool to 105 ° to 115 °.

Dissolve yeast and 1 T. sugar in warm water in a large bowl; let stand 5 minutes. Add butter mixture, eggs, and 2 cups of flour; beat at medium speed with an electric mixer for 2 minutes or by hand until smooth. Gradually stir in enough remaining flour to make a soft dough.

Turn dough out onto a lightly-floured surface, and knead until smooth and elastic (about 10 minutes). Place in a well-greased bowl, turning to grease top. Cover and let rise in a warm place free from drafts, for 1 hour or until dough is doubled in bulk.

Combine 1/2 cup sugar and cinnamon; set aside.

Pinch dough down and divide it in half. Turn one portion of dough out onto a lightly floured surface, and roll to a 28" x 10" rectangle. Spread half of the butter and half of the cinnamon mixture on the rolled-out dough. Roll dough, jelly roll fashion, starting at the long side. Gently place dough roll, seam side down, on a lightly greased baking sheet. Bring ends of dough together and form an oval ring. If you have access to a tiny plastic baby, tuck it into the seam before you seal it. If not, use a large, dried bean. Moisten and pinch the edges together to seal.

Repeat this procedure with the second half of the dough.

Cover and let rise in a warm place, free from drafts, 20 minutes or until doubled in bulk.

Bake at 375 ° for 15 to 20 minutes or until golden. Decorate each cake with bands of colored frostings, and sprinkle with colored sugars.

Makes two cakes.

NOTE: If you prefer, you can replace the cinnamon and sugar inside the roll of dough with a cream cheese filling or a pie filling in the flavor of your choice—just spread it thinly on the center of the rectangle before you roll it up. Popular flavors are blueberry, cherry, and lemon.

Cream Cheese Filling
   1 8-oz. package cream cheese
   1 c. confectioner's sugar
   2 T. flour
   1 t. vanilla
   drop or two of milk

Cream all ingredients together with an electric mixer. Spread on the rolled-out rectangle before rolling it into a ring. You can use cream cheese and a fruit filling if you so desire.

Colored Sugars
   1 -1/2 cups sugar, divided
   1 to 2 drops each of green, yellow, red and blue food coloring

Combine 1/2 cup sugar and a drop of green coloring in a jar. Place lid on jar, and shake vigorously to evenly mix the color with sugar. Repeat with each color, combining red and blue for purple.

Colored Frostings
>   3 cups sifted powdered sugar
>   3 T. butter of margarine, melted
>   3 to 5 T. milk
>   1/4 t. vanilla extract
>   1 to 2 drops each green, yellow, red, and blue food coloring

Combine powdered sugar and melted butter. Add milk (room temperature) to reach desired consistency for drizzling; stir in vanilla. Divide frosting into 3 batches, tinting one with green, one with yellow, and combining blue and red for purple frosting. Makes about 1–1/2 cups.

SONG: "You Are God Alone" by Phillips, Craig and Dean on the album *Let the Worshippers Arise*

QUOTABLE QUOTES:

The kingdom is manifest when God rules in the hearts and social relationships of His people.
> —Donald Kraybill, *The Upside-Down Kingdom*, p. 26

Golden Revelation—Midweek

MEMORY VERSE:
The Lord shall reign forever and ever.—Exodus 15:18 (NAS)

SCRIPTURE: 1 Timothy 1:17

LESSON IN A SENTENCE: God, and only God, reigns in the past, in the present, in the future and in all the world!

FOCUS

OPTION 1—MEMORY VERSE ACTIVITY:

While this may seem rather juvenile, it works! Have enough yellow construction paper or brightly colored gold cardstock ready for at least one sheet per person. At the beginning of the lesson, give each person a piece of paper and share scissors to cut out the shape of a crown. After the crown is cut out, have each person write the Memory Verse on the crown. When they are through with this, give them a few moments to decorate their crown. Be certain to have plenty of markers, glue and glitter, jewels or other decorations to be used. As they are making their crowns, ask what they think it means to reign? (You may need to remind or give a quick summary of Sunday's lesson about Jesus being King of kings.) After they are through, set the crowns aside so that the glue may dry and they may take it home as a reminder of the Memory Verse.

OPTION 2:

King for a day! Tape two large pieces of paper to a wall next to one another. Ask your students to spend a few minutes brainstorming what they would do if they were king (or queen) for a day. Ask them to call these out and write everything down on one of the papers. When they run out of things to say, turn to the second paper. On this sheet write *Offer grace and mercy to everyone.*

How do the two lists compare? Turn to the Bible and see what Scripture has to say about this.

DISCOVERY

Have your students look up 1 Timothy 1:12–17. Ask one student to read this aloud for the group. As you ask them to break into groups of three, pass out a sheet of paper with this same passage printed on it from three different translations. (Try to find translations that truly offer a difference in translation options. Suggested combinations would be NAS, MSG, and NCV; or NIV, NKJV, and MSG.) Take turns in the groups reading this passage in the different translations.

After a few minutes, pass out a blank piece of paper and pen to each group. Direct them to write their own paraphrase of the passage that would fit their lives today. (For example: where it says I am a blasphemer and a violent aggressor, perhaps write: I am a liar and a lazy worker—anything that actually speaks to their lives.)

You know your group best. After a few moments, either ask them to read what they have written in their small group or ask if there is anyone who would be willing to read for the entire group.

Ask: After looking at v. 12, have you ever thought God could consider someone faithful who shared the sins Paul lists?

LIFE APPLICATION: *Ask rhetorically:* Do you think God would consider you faithful?

You've just re-written this passage using your own sins instead of the ones Paul uses. You should also have moved further in the passage to the verses that speak of God's grace, mercy, and desire for all (sinners included!) to be with Him eternally. This is good news! In fact, it is the best news!

Reread v. 17. What does it mean to give honor and glory to God? What does it mean for you personally in your life to give honor and glory to God?

This is the first week of the new year! Many people are making new year resolutions. Invite your students to make a resolution for this year about how they may honor and glorify God. Remember to make this something they can actually do (be realistic). Saying you will honor God in every action, while sounding nice, actually says nothing. Saying that you will do your math homework without cheating is one activity that is specific and attainable.

MEMORY VERSE ACTIVITY

Consider making a memory verse collection. This is quite easy and the first week of the new year is a great time to begin. Use 3 x 5 cards and hole punch the upper lefthand corner. Go to any office supply or hardware store and buy rings to hold together the 3 x 5 cards. As each new week comes, have your students write out the memory verse and add it to their collection on the ring. At the end of the year, they will have a collection of 53 verses on the ring together. Encourage them to carry these in their backpacks or place them somewhere in their rooms where they will be reminded to look at and memorize them. You may want to begin by reminding them of the importance of Scripture memory (Psalm 119:11). If you ask your students to do this, join them! You are their role model and will be blessed as well!

JANUARY 8, 2006

New Beginnings

By Sharon Koh

MEMORY VERSE:
Therefore, if anyone is in Christ, he is a new creation; the old is gone, the new has come!—2 Corinthians 5:17 (NAS)

SCRIPTURE: Matthew 3:13–17

LESSON IN A SENTENCE: We can be excited about our *new* lives in Christ because of all that God wants to do in and through us.

THE BIG PICTURE (OR WHAT YOU'RE TRYING TO GET ACROSS):
New life in Christ is an adventure with many twists and turns in the road. It is unreasonable to expect life to continue on exactly like it "used to be." God intends to do amazing things through our lives as He grows and molds our characters. Some (but not all) of us have a specific event that marks when we began this journey with the Lord. For Jesus, His adult life of ministry began when He was baptized. In the Gospel of Matthew, it was after His baptism that Jesus began to teach and perform miracles.

IN THIS LESSON STUDENTS SHOULD:

- Grasp the idea of "before and after": that our lives should be different before and after we encounter Jesus and allow Him to become Lord of our lives.
- Understand the metaphor of the Christian life as a journey.
- Identify the end goal of this journey as becoming more like Jesus and the process of the journey as fulfilling His purposes for our lives (calling).
- Identify (if they had one) a moment of "calling" when God spoke to them about the purpose of their lives.
- Recognize that, even though there was no specific "moment of calling" in their lives, they are still "called" to the Christian journey—and their task is to figure out what are the specifics of that calling.

STUFF YOU NEED:

○ A movie clip from *The Lord of The Rings I: Fellowship of the Ring*—the scene where the unlikely group of friends decides in Lothlorien to go on the journey, no matter the cost. This was the beginning of the journey (that took three movies and 10+ hours of film to show) that the Fellowship decides to undertake.

FOCUS

Show movie clip (from the discussion where they determine that the ring must be destroyed to the part where they leave the gates of the Elven city to embark on their journey). Speak of the Christian life as a journey that we choose to embark on. For the Fellowship, the goal of the journey was to destroy the ring. What is the end goal of our Christian life and journey?

DISCOVERY

Read Matthew 3:13–16.

Note the context of these few verses in the book as a whole. It is at the beginning of the book (pretty much right after the birth narratives) and before Jesus begins His earthly ministry. The baptism and temptation of Jesus are the two major events that precede His teaching and miracles.

Why did John the Baptist resist baptizing Jesus at first?

Why did John consent to do it in the end?

What did Jesus see immediately after he came up out of the water? (Stop for a moment and picture what "heaven opened" might look like.)

What does God the Father say about Jesus? How does this give Jesus identity?

What is unusual about this statement as a statement of *mission*? (Soon after this, Jesus begins His ministry.)

If this is Jesus' moment of *calling*, what is He being asked to *do*?

LIFE APPLICATION: As Christians, what is our identity before God?

How is the beginning of the Christian life a *new* beginning?

Since this is the moment of calling, what are we called to do or *be*?

Was there a moment in your life when you had a *new beginning* in Christ? If so, what did you believe you were called to be?

God calls us *all* to be children of God, pursuing Christ-likeness as the "end-goal" of the journey, and looking to fulfill His purposes in our lives each day. However, these purposes differ in details. They involve carrying careers and geographical/social locations. What has God *called* you to be *in your life specifically*?

MAKING IT PERSONAL: What are the *specifics* of God's calling on your life? If you're unsure, what are some ways God gives us to help us discern what they are?

Teacher's Note: Note that God claims Jesus as His Son and is "well pleased" with Him *before* His work begins. There is nothing that we, as children of God, *need* to do to earn favor or status before God. Jesus' commission or calling is phrased as an identity. Jesus is *identified* as The Son of God, and God is already pleased with Him—before His ministry begins. Much of this is a "transferable concept" to us—in that, God loves us for who He has made us to be before we start "work" for Him. With that said, it is easy to embrace the calling on each of our lives as a *new beginning*.

January 11, 2006

New Beginnings—Midweek

MEMORY VERSE:
Therefore, if anyone is in Christ, he is a new creation; the old is gone, the new has come!—2 Corinthians 5:17 (NAS)

SCRIPTURE: Isaiah 43:16–21, focus on vv. 19, 21.

LESSON IN A SENTENCE: We can be excited about our *new* lives in Christ because of all that God wants to do in and through us.

FOCUS

Gather students and have them list *signs* of new life. Some of these signs may be associated with springtime (flowers, trees, greenery). Others may be associated with young life (babies, puppies, kittens).

After they are done with this part of the exercise, have the students think about the things that had to *die* or be *removed* to make space for new life. For example, much of the seasons of fall and winter are associated with death and awaiting new life.

Point out that often, death needs to precede life. Old things need to be removed to make space for new things.

DISCOVERY

Read Isaiah 43:16–21 and answer the following questions:

What (vv. 16, 17) gives God the authority to give the commands that follow in the next few verses?

In this passage, God urges the reader to leave behind the "former things." Why would it be important to leave behind the "things of old" before one can embrace the new thing that God is doing in their life?

When God performs a "new thing", what is typically the reaction? (v. 21) Have you found that this is the case in your own life?

LIFE APPLICATION: Read over Isaiah 43:16–21 again. Picture the Lord doing the things mentioned in the first two verses (vv. 16, 17). How does that make you feel? Is this comforting or scary to you? Sometimes it is important to remember what gives God the authority to command us to do things. In addition to His infinite wisdom, He also possesses infinite power.

This can and should evoke both feelings of security and insecurity. That is, it gives us a sense of security that we can trust an all-loving, all-powerful God. However, the fact that He is all-loving and all-powerful does not immediately guarantee that He is safe. God is definitely *not* safe by our standards. He may desire to do dangerous things in our lives.

When have you specifically experienced the need to leave behind "things of old" in your life to make space for God to do a new thing? Was it a rewarding experience? Was the *new* thing something you expected, or did it take you by surprise? How did you respond to God's move in your life?

Read v. 21 again and take some time to thank God for the new things He is doing in your life.

DREAMS THAT MAKE A DIFFERENCE

By Nick Palermo
FOUNDER/NATIONAL DIRECTOR OF CAPERNAUM

I have a Dream.—Martin Luther King

Some men see things as they are and say why? I dream things that never were and say why not?—Bobby Kennedy

As a very young boy I grew up idolizing Martin Luther King and Bobby Kennedy. They touched a sacred place deep inside me that wanted to dream. As I grew older, I came face to face with a world full of ills, pain, and impossible tragedy. While I continued to dream, the world's jagged edged sufferings eroded my belief that any one person could make a difference. The world was a Mount Everest of need and I was a mole hill of resources. What could one person do to make a difference?

An answer began to emerge. . . On a sunny cool fall day in 1980, the answer came in the form of twenty-five kids in wheelchairs rolling towards me on a high school campus. I had never seen that many kids in wheelchairs in one place, or been around any kids like this in my life.

I was a Young Life leader. Young Life is a ministry that befriends High School and Middle School kids. A Young Life leader is a friend who shares the Good News of God's love with kids. But kids in wheelchairs had never been in my mental picture of kids. . .

So of course that crazy God of mine led me to start a Young Life club for kids with disabilities. To say that I was uncomfortable and didn't know what I doing, is a very large understatement. But I had the best teachers in the world—kids with disabilities.

Our club took off and I fell so deeply in love with these precious masterpieces of God. We named it Capernaum, after the incident in Mark 2:1–12, where four friends took their paralyzed friend to Jesus. They blasted through every obstacle to get their friend to Jesus. And it happened in the town of Capernaum.

Before I knew it, the news of what we were doing began to amaze people in Young Life as did Jesus' healing of the paralytic in front of the crowd. The story began to spread as it did with the paralytic.

And just like that, Capernaum began! It sprang up in other cities. More forgotten kids were finding out that God had not forgotten them.

Without my permission, my sneaky God had begun to enlarge my faith and vision. We prayed to find a house for kids that would be a drop-in center. I mentioned it once publicly and a donor came up to me and said, "I love the idea, I'm going to buy the house!"

A friend and I prayed for a million dollars for Capernaum. One year later a donor gave a million dollars unsolicited by me. I prayed for Capernaum to spread beyond our country. Next thing I know, I am receiving a letter from a woman in Kazakhstan stating she has begun a Capernaum Ministry and needs help.

So here I am twenty years removed from that first club; thirty-nine cities and three countries later with Capernaum Ministries. Twenty cities lined up to start. But most importantly of all, twenty years later of kids with disabilities finding out they are loved and valued by God. They have a place and purpose in our world.

I want to encourage you that God can take *anyone* who is willing, and make a difference. The words "can't" and "impossible" must be erased from our vocabulary. Reasoning must be replaced by ridiculous dreaming. What if. . . must replace "how could that happen?"

I love these verses:

> Now Glory be to God who by His mighty power at work within us is able to do far more than we would ever dare to ask or even dream of—infinitely beyond our highest prayers, desires, thoughts, or hopes. May He be given glory forever and ever through endless ages because of His master plan of salvation for the church through Jesus Christ.
> —*Ephesians 3:20–21*(TLB)

> Ask me and I will tell you some remarkable secrets about what is going to happen here.
> —*Jeremiah 33:3* (TLB)

> That is what is meant by the Scriptures which say that no mere man has ever seen, heard or even imagined what wonderful things God has ready for those who love the Lord.
> —*I Corinthians 2:9* (TLB)

So what about you? What dream has God planted in your heart that you've ignored or reasoned away? What's keeping you from pursuing it? If it is a dream from God, no amount of suffering, obstacles, or resistance can stop it.

I have a dream! Do you?

God's Wonderful Creation

By Ric Lipsey

MEMORY VERSE:
Thank you for making me so wonderfully complex! Your workmanship is marvelous—and how well I know it. You watched me as I was being formed in utter seclusion, as I was woven together in the dark of the womb. You saw me before I was born. Every day of my life was recorded in your book. Every moment was laid out before a single day had passed.—Psalm 139:14–16 (NLT)

SCRIPTURE: Genesis 1:26–31; Genesis 2:7; Jeremiah 1:4–5; Isaiah 49:1, 5; Psalm 51:5; Genesis 25:22–28; Psalm 139:13–18; Judges 13:2–5; Genesis 16:11; Isaiah 46:3–4; Psalm 22:9–10; Galatians 1:15; Matthew 1:20–21; Luke 1:41, 44

LESSON IN A SENTENCE: Human life is a precious gift from God.

THE BIG PICTURE (OR WHAT YOU'RE TRYING TO GET ACROSS):
We are God's wonderful creation, but all too often we lose sight of that simple fact. However, this is not only a study of us as individuals, but on us as the human race. We are created in the very image of God and that is an awesome thing to ponder. Life is God's to give and life is not ours to take. Our role is not to take the life of the unborn. Our role is not to take our own life when we see no way out. Our role is not to take the life of the elderly whom we feel are a burden on a family or society. Our role is to protect life and spread the Good News of the giver of new life, Jesus Christ.

IN THIS LESSON STUDENTS SHOULD:

- Be able to explain the importance of human life.
- Be able to locate Scripture to back up their explanation.

STUFF YOU NEED:

- The game of *LIFE*®
- Box of LIFE® cereal

FOCUS

Have a breath-holding contest. Ham it up big. Have practice rounds. Have youth stand up to give their lungs more room to expand. Work your way up to the actual contest by giving them the chance to take several huge breaths.

Now start the contest. The rules are easy. The last person to take a breath wins.

Give the winner a prize. (Either the game or the cereal depending on your budget.)

DISCOVERY

Ask: Is your breath that big a deal? According to a sign seen on the door of a hospital respiratory department, it is a huge deal; "If you're not breathing, nothing else matters."

But why are breath and life such big deals to God's children?

Read Genesis 2:7 and then Genesis 1:26–31.

Breath is important in that it was the breath of God that brought life to Adam, and is God's Spirit that sustains us.

Life itself is important because we are created in the image of God. When life is taken at the hands of another, the image of God is being murdered. Genesis 9:6 (NLT) puts it this way ". . . for to kill a person is to kill a living being made in God's image."

The question still arises though: "When does life begin? Is there life before oxygen fills the lungs and carbon dioxide is exhaled?"

Say: Let's look at some verses in both the Old and New Testaments to see what conclusions we can draw to help us answer that question.

Have students meet individually or in small groups to research the following verses.

O.T. Verses:
Jeremiah 1:4–5; Isaiah 49:1, 5
(God has a plan for each of us before we are born.)

Psalm 51:5
(Life begins at the time of conception.)

Genesis 25:22–28
(Personalities and individuality begin even before birth.)

Psalm 139:13–18
(God watches and cares for us even before we are born.)

"The psalmist surveys his life in four stages: Past, present, future, and before birth, and in all four refers to himself as 'I.' He who is writing as a full-grown man has the same personal identity as the fetus in his mother's womb." (John R.W. Stott)

> Judges 13:2–5
> (Samson was set apart before he was born and God even had his mother alter her diet to care for her unborn child.)

> Genesis 16:11; Isaiah 46:3–4; Psalm 22:9–10
> (In all three verses the unborn child is viewed as alive.)

N.T. Verses:

> Galatians 1:15
> (Paul was chosen by God while he was in his mother's womb.)

> Matthew 1:20–21
> (Joseph was told about Jesus and His role as Savior while still in Mary's womb.)

> Luke 1:15–17
> (The work John the Baptist would do was told to his mother before he was born.)

> Luke 1:41, 44
> (John the Baptist had an encounter with Jesus while they were in their mother's wombs.)

LIFE APPLICATION:

Read Hebrews 13:8.

Ask: How this verse bridges the gap from biblical times to today?

If God does not change, then His view of His children does not change. In other words, He still has plans for us, gives us personality and cares for us before we are born.

Ask: How could you use these verses to help someone who may be considering taking their own life or maybe considering ending a pregnancy?

(If there is a student that you work with who has had an abortion, be sure to assure them of God's love and forgiveness.)

MAKING IT PERSONAL: Read the Memory Verse out loud as a group. Now have students substitute their own names in place of 'me' and 'I' as it is read.

Close in prayer, thanking God for designing us all unique individuals created in His image.

SONG: "More" by Matthew West, from *Happy*
"You Are a Child of Mine" by Mark Schultz, from *Stories & Songs*

God's Wonderful Creation!—Midweek

MEMORY VERSE:
Family of Jacob, listen to me! All you people from Israel who are still alive, listen! I have carried you since you were born; I have taken care of you from your birth. Even when you are old, I will be the same. Even when your hair has turned gray, I will take care of you. I made you and will take care of you. I will carry you and save you.—Isaiah 46:3–4 (NCV)

SCRIPTURE: Isaiah 46:3–4; Exodus 20:13; Job 2:6; 1 Samuel 2:6; Deuteronomy 32:39; Acts 17:24–25, 28; Genesis 2:7; Numbers 16:22; 1 Samuel 31:4; Job 2:8–10

LESSON IN A SENTENCE: From before the cradle to the grave, life is a gift from God and should be treated as such; or, what the Bible has to say about euthanasia.

STUFF YOU NEED:

- The game of *LIFE*®
- Box of LIFE® cereal
- 3 x 5 cards with verse references from discovery section written on them

---

FOCUS

Have students divide into groups and have the use the memory verse to come up with a new commercial using the LIFE® cereal box. Encourage them to find other verses to use in their ads. They could also use the verses from the previous study.

Maybe have a panel of judges award a prize for the most creative commercial.

DISCOVERY

Have the game of *LIFE*® as a visual as you talk about the progression of one's life. There can be some fun discussions as you walk through the winding paths of the game. Notice that the game starts with the decision of career or college. Discuss this point some.

Ask: Does your life really start like the game suggests when you turn 18? Why do you think the game makers don't start their game earlier than that?

Point out some of the highlights of the games and even some of the setbacks. But something stands out as we near the end of the game. There seems to be no more life after retirement.

Ask: Have the makers of our fun little game made another mistake? Are they saying that life doesn't start until college or career and that it ends at retirement? Why is there no more fun and exciting life events, like the birth of grandchildren, teaching a Sunday school class, or packing up the RVs with some friends to go on an extended mission trip with friends?

God did not design us to quit life at a certain age. He made us to be like the drum-beating bunny who keeps going and going and going until we can't go no more. This is the one life we've got and we are to make every day count for our Lord.

In the last lesson we looked at what the Bible says about life and the unborn. Today we'll be looking at what God's Word has to say about life, and the elderly, and sick, and those that society says is of no use to them.

If you are talking about taking the life of your pet that is suffering, you would say that Fluffy is being "put to sleep." The same act for a human being is called euthanasia. But can we take the same action for a person who is created in the image of the one true God?

The word euthanasia actually means "happy death." It is also called "mercy killing," "physician-assisted suicide" and "deliverance."

Since Dr. Kevorkian has been in jail, there has not been much talk in the media about euthanasia lately. However, the doctor is up for parole next year (2007) and along with it the release of the remake of a 1976 movie concerning the subject, being produced by the folks that brought us *The Matrix*. (We will soon be talking more about this controversial topic.)

The movie's title is *Logan's Run* and the tag line for the 1976 version sums up the whole premise of the movie: "Welcome to the 23rd Century: A perfect world of total pleasure, with just one catch. . .The only thing you can't have in Logan's world is your 30th birthday. Unless you run away."

It is the story of a guy named Logan who wants to live past 29 and the people he is running away from—government officials who are attempting to euthanize them. It sounds crazy, but there are people right here in 2006 who are trying to take death into their own hands.

The Bible even mentions euthanasia. For instance, in the middle of Job's affliction he is encouraged by his wife to "Curse God and die!"

(Job 2:8–10) In 1 Samuel 31:4, Saul pleads for a "mercy killing" but is refused it out of fear.

Let's look at what Scripture says about taking the life of someone rather than leaving the timing up to God.

Hand out 3 x 5 cards with the following verses written on them and have them answer the following questions.

Where does life come from? What is the source?

"But Moses and Aaron fell face down on the ground. 'O God, the God and source of all life,' they pleaded. 'Must you be angry with all the people when only one man sins?'"—Numbers 16:22 (NLT)

Did life just happen? Are we all just happy accidents?

"Then the Lord God took dust from the ground and formed a man from it. He breathed the breath of life into the man's nose, and the man became a living person."—Genesis 2:7 (NCV)

What keeps human life going? What is the sustaining factor?

"The God who made the whole world and everything in it is the Lord of the land and the sky. He does not live in temples built by human hands.

This God is the One who gives life, breath, and everything else to people. He does not need any help from them; he has everything he needs.

We live in him. We walk in him. We are in him.' Some of your own poets have said: 'For we are his children.'"—Acts 17:24, 25, 28 (NCV)

Who is in control of when someone actually lives and dies?

"Now you will see that I am the one God! There is no god but me. I send life and death; I can hurt, and I can heal. No one can escape from me."—Deuteronomy 32:39 (NCV)

"The LORD sends death, and he brings to life. He sends people to the grave, and he raises them to life again."—1 Samuel 2:6 (NCV)

What does the following passage say about who has say over the ending of a life?

"The Lord said to Satan, 'All right, then. Job is in your power, but you may not take his life.'"—Job 2:6 (NCV)

What does God call euthanasia?

"You must not murder anyone."—Exodus 20:13 (NCV)

LIFE APPLICATION: *Ask:* Looking at the above verses, what do you feel God's take on euthanasia is?

How does this study change your view of the sanctity of life?

MAKING IT PERSONAL: Have the group read the Memory Verse out loud while inserting their name in the appropriate place.

"I have carried [name] since [he/she] was born; I have taken care of [name] from [his/her] birth. Even when [name] is old, I will be the same. Even when[name] hair has turned gray, I will take care of [name]. I made [name] and will take care of [name]. I will carry [name] and save [name]."
—Isaiah 46:3–4 (NCV)

Close in prayer, thanking God for His continued provision and care for life.

JANUARY 22, 2006

Make the Call!

By Cole Billings

MEMORY VERSE:
But you, when you pray, go into your room, and when you have shut your door, pray to your Father who is in the secret place; and your Father who sees in secret will reward you openly.—Matthew 6:6 (NKJV)

SCRIPTURE: Matthew 6:5–6

LESSON IN A SENTENCE: God calls His followers to one-on-one communication with Him through prayer.

THE BIG PICTURE (OR WHAT YOU'RE TRYING TO GET ACROSS):
    It is common knowledge that God seeks an intimate relationship with every one of His followers. Communication is an essential aspect to any relationship between two people. Our relationship with God is no different; it requires one-on-one communication to develop in a healthy manner. God instructs us to meet Him through prayer. Prayer is the vehicle in which we draw close to God. We are called to pray to God in private, where the true rewards are found. These rewards may be answers to prayer or the relationship that is developed through the one-on-one communication with Him. Often we come to God in the presence of others, yet we fail to ever be alone with Him. However, we are called to meet God alone, in the presence of Him and only Him. We will examine communication with God and try to understand how we can truly receive the rewards that come from prayer.

IN THIS LESSON STUDENTS SHOULD:

Understand that:
- Prayer is between you and God.
- God calls us to spend time alone with Him.
- Intimacy with God comes through time alone with Him.

STUFF YOU NEED:

○ Bible
○ Movie (*Meet the Parents*)
○ CD player or band to play the song "Secret Place."
○ Construction paper and markers
○ Overhead projector, white board, or large paper (optional)
○ Television, DVD player or VCR

FOCUS

To get the students' attention you will show a clip from the movie *Meet the Family*. Show the clip in which Greg prays at the dinner table with his girlfriend's family. After you have showed this clip, ask the students a couple of questions in regards to the clip.

Suggested Questions:
○ Who is Greg praying to?
○ Is Greg trying to impress anyone during this prayer?
○ Is this an intimate time between Greg and God?

DISCOVERY

Ask the students to break into groups of 5–7, sitting in a circle on the floor or around a table. Have them open their Bibles (if they have one) to Matthew 6:5–6. If they do not have one they can simply listen or follow along with a friend. Have a volunteer from each group read aloud through the passage, vv. 5–6. If possible, display these questions on a white board, large piece of paper, or on an overhead projector. If not, you can just ask the questions orally. Give the students five minutes to discuss these questions.

Questions:
1. Would you ever pray on a street corner? Why or why not?
2. Who gives better rewards, humans or God?
3. Why do you think God asks us to pray alone in our rooms?

Teacher's Note: The hypocrites described in v. 6 refer to the Pharisees. These were the religiously educated of the time. A synagogue was a place of prayer. The Pharisees would pray in the synagogues or on the street corners, not necessarily for God's recognition but for man's. Communicate this to the students if it seems necessary.

Explain that God is seeking a personal relationship with all of us. Prayer is simply the telephone, email, or text message system that God has given for us to reach Him. This system is much more sacred though. Christ wants a clear line of communication with you, and only you. When we choose to be alone with God in prayer, He recognizes our dedication or efforts and rewards us for it. If we come to God alone, our reward through prayer comes from heaven; if we only come to God in the presence of others, our rewards are only seen and given by those around us. Each group will now play the game *Telephone*. One person will make up any prayer request that they want. (Make sure that it is a long prayer request). They will whisper it to the person to the left of them. Then that person will whisper it to the person to the left of them, and so on until they reach the last person. The last person will then say, out loud, what they have heard. If the game works the way it should, the original prayer request will be totally different from what the last person says. After the game ask the students to discuss these questions for a few minutes in their groups.

Questions:

How could this game relate to our prayer life with God?

What seems to happen when we don't communicate one-on-one with God?

Once again, when we come to God in private we will receive the rewards that God has intended for us, like it says in v. 6. One of these rewards is an intimate relationship with Christ.

LIFE APPLICATION: Distribute three pieces of construction paper and markers to each student. Ask the students to draw three pictures, one that represents something that may be cutting their communication off with God, another picture that will help them remember to spend time alone with God, and lastly a picture that represents intimacy with God in their own lives.

Teacher's Note: Give the students the option of taking these pictures home with them, or allowing their leaders to keep them for them. This activity will help the student apply what they have discovered to their own life. It will also remind them throughout the week what they thought and discussed during this study. This would be a great time to get the band or CD player into place.

MAKING IT PERSONAL: Now that the students understand that we have to apply ourselves to God's Word, it's time to fully reflect and put into action what we have learned about prayer.

Before you ask these questions make sure that either the band or the CD player is ready.

At this time read Matthew 6:6 out of *The Message* Bible, "Here's what I want you to do: Find a quiet secluded place so you won't be tempted to role-play before God. Just be there as simply and honestly as you can manage. The focus will shift from you to God, and you will begin to sense his grace."

These are the student's instructions during the song. Make sure that all of the students spread out; ask them to try to find the "secret place" in their heart where it is just them and God. Tell them that the song they are about to hear is called "Secret Place". Begin the music.

Teacher's Note: During the song, have your leaders roam throughout the room making sure no one is talking or distracting anyone else.

After the song is finished and all are done praying, invite the students to take 10 minutes each day for the next week where they can be alone, away from all distractions. Challenge them to be alone with God in prayer for this time, coming before God just as they are, with a heart that is real before Him. Close the night with prayer.

Teacher's Note: Make sure to tell your students that if they need any prayer, the leaders will be available to pray with them after the service. Designate as many leaders as you can, to stay for a few minutes after service to pray with students or answer any of their questions.

Make the Call!—Midweek

MEMORY VERSE:
But you, when you pray, go into your room, and when you have shut your door, pray to your Father who is in the secret place; and your Father who sees in secret will reward you openly.—Matthew 6:6 (NKJV)

SCRIPTURE: "If we don't know how or what to pray, it doesn't matter. He does our praying in and for us, making prayer out of our wordless sighs, our aching groans. He knows us far better then ourselves."—Romans 8:27–28 (MSG)

LESSON IN A SENTENCE: Although it is hard to know how or what to pray, God knows our needs and His Spirit will guide our hearts in prayer.

STUFF YOU NEED:

- 2 blindfolds
- Objects to create a simple obstacle course. (e.g. cones, chairs, bean bags)
- *The Message* Bible (optional)
- Overhead projector, whiteboard, or paper (optional)

FOCUS

It's game time. Split the group into two teams, each team on opposite sides of the room. For each team set up a short obstacle course, nothing too technical, just objects placed throughout each team's half of the room. There will be one person from each team who will be blindfolded; once they are blindfolded their teammates will have to direct them through the obstacle course using only their words. All team members have to stay outside of the obstacle course as their blindfolded team member tries to make their way around each object. You can repeat this activity two or three times using different blindfolded team members. Allow 10–15 minutes for this game. After the game is finished leave the teams together. Have each team discuss these questions.

SUGGESTED QUESTIONS:
Was it hard to direct the person who was blindfolded? If so, why?

Was it hard to make it through the obstacle course when you were blindfolded? If so, why?

Teacher's Note: This game is supposed to have a direct correlation with our prayer lives. At times we are the blindfolded, we don't know how or what to pray. The teammates that were guiding the blindfolded, represent God. The point is that it is OK if we are not sure how or what to pray, God can see the path ahead of us, He knows us better then we know ourselves, and His Spirit will guide and direct our prayer life. Make sure that your leaders understand the purpose of this game.

DISCOVERY

Bring the entire group back together. Read Romans 8:27–28 out of *The Message.*

Teacher's Note: If you don't have a copy of *The Message,* these verses are at the top of the first page. If possible, have these verses on an overhead projector or somehow visible so the students can read along. Read through twice.

Ask the students:

1. How the passage might relate to the game that they had just played?
2. Who God might be if He would have played?
3. Who they would be if they had to be part of the game?

Teacher's Note: If the students are not making the connection, try to guide them through the link between the game and someone's possible prayer life.)

4. If they have ever felt like the blindfolded person in their prayer life?
5. If it has been hard to know what to pray to God this week?

MAKING IT PERSONAL: Does the fact that we don't know exactly what to say to God make it impossible for God to hear us? No. Is it bad that it's hard to trust in a Spirit to guide our prayer life sometimes? No. Is it hard to believe that God could really know everything that I need, even better then I know? Yes. These are all hard questions, but the fact of the matter is that all of these questions are answered and confirmed by God in Romans 8:27–28. God never tells us exactly how or what to pray, but we can be sure that His Spirit will prompt us on what to pray. We can also be sure that God has called us to spend one-on-one alone time with Him.

Ask the students: Where does my prayer life fit into these questions? What active steps can I take (if I haven't already) to start spending more alone time with God? Ask each student to reflect upon these questions for a few minutes. Before you close the night in prayer, ask each student to ask God for direction in their prayer lives, for His Spirit to pray in them, and to thank God for knowing us better then we know ourselves. Close the night in prayer, praying that each student would spend more alone time with God and trusting that He would guide their hearts in prayer.

Give Me a Break!

By James Miller

MEMORY VERSE:
If the LORD doesn't build the house, the workers are working for nothing. If the LORD doesn't guard the city, the guards are watching for nothing. It is no use for you to get up early and stay up late, working for a living. The LORD gives sleep to those he loves.— Psalm 127:1–2 (NCV)

SCRIPTURE: Exodus 20:8–11

LESSON IN A SENTENCE: God has designed us to spend a day in rest and worship every week.

THE BIG PICTURE (OR WHAT YOU'RE TRYING TO GET ACROSS):

God created the world in six days, and on the seventh He rested. In the same way, God has designed our lives to function in a cycle of work and rest. God commands in the fourth of the Ten Commandments that we take a day each week for rest without work. Jesus furthermore promises rest as a blessing that comes from following Him. The Scriptures even say that sleep is a gift that God gives to the people He loves!

There are some practical and simple ways that we can remember the Sabbath and keep it holy, taking time to rest, reflect, and redirect our lives. Homework and sports don't have to conquer every day! Instead, we can learn to spend one day per week remembering the perfection of creation and worship, reliving a day in Eden.

IN THIS LESSON STUDENTS SHOULD:

○ Understand the biblical basis for the Sabbath.
○ Analyze why Sabbath-keeping is a challenge.
○ Make practical plans to take a day of rest during the week.

STUFF YOU NEED:

○ Paper and pens
○ Printed discussion questions from the Discovery section
○ Music and or video images of nature scenes for the Application section

FOCUS

Create a day planner schedule of your typical day. Using lined paper, put times down the left hand side, starting at whatever time you wake up, and then listing each hour after that until the time you go to bed. Insert all of the activities you typically do in any given week, including school, homework, sports and activities, time with family and friends, meals, etc. At the bottom, create a checklist of things you need to finish before bed today. Put boxes beside each one to be checked off.

How does it feel to look at all of this? What does God think of your many activities? Is everything on here essential? Do you think people are more or less busy than they used to be? How would you know if you were doing more than God wanted you to?

DISCOVERY

Divide into groups of four or more and discuss the following questions. However, each person is to play a certain role in the discussion. Have one person read the text, someone else read the discussion questions below, and someone else be responsible for answering each one first. Most importantly, each group should assign someone else to just listen to everything without comment. Make these questions available either on printed sheets or on a markerboard that is visible to everyone.

Questions for Discussion:
How well do Christians keep this commandment? Why?
Why do you think God commands a day of rest?
What are things we could do with a Sabbath day?
What would be things to avoid?
Do you think you could take a day off from all work every week? What would make it hard? What would be the benefits?
For the person who is just listening, how does it feel to not have to be responsible for this activity? Do you feel the need to do something? Is it relaxing to just listen? How is your experience in this activity like the experience of having a Sabbath day?

TEACHER AID: Effective teaching usually includes elements of reflection on the teacher's personal experience. While you can teach a lesson on Sabbath-keeping without taking a Sabbath day in your own week, you are liable to be far more effective if you can make reference to your own personal habits. You can teach your class what you know, but you can only recreate what you are. Make a point of taking a day off from your own week for rest and worship and share the experience with your class. Be honest about your own struggles with spiritual disciplines, so that they don't feel intimidated by them.

LIFE APPLICATION: Have the group spend five minutes in quiet. Tell them specifically that they should not talk or use their phones during this activity. Play soft music or show images of nature scenes in the background if you'd like, but nothing with lyrics or words.

When they're finished with the activity, ask them the following questions.

Where does your mind go? Do you feel relieved or stressed? Why? How easy is it to concentrate? How much is your mind distracted by the things you need to do? What would you rather have been doing? What would it have felt like to do this for a full day? Why does God want us to rest?

MAKING IT PERSONAL: Look back at the day planner you created in the first activity. Mark out something that you would be willing to drop in order to make more time for God in your weekly schedule. Pick something else that you do regularly and decide how you can accomplish it in less time than it usually takes. Pray with a friend about how you will make this happen.

QUOTABLE QUOTES:

"Labor is a craft, but perfect rest is an art."
[Abraham Joshua Herschel, *The Sabbath.* New York: Farrar, Straus, and Giroux, 1951, p. 14]

CONNECTIONS: The idea of taking a day of rest appears throughout the Scripture. It begins in Genesis 2:1–3, with God's own pattern of work. In the Ten Commandments (Exodus 20:8–11 and Deuteronomy 5:12–15), God gives a direct command that we are to take a Sabbath day. More clear instructions are given in Exodus 31:12–18. Psalm 127:1–2 poetically promises rest as a gift. Finally, Jesus Himself says that rest is a consequence of following Him (Matthew 11:28–30). On the other hand, Jesus models that keeping the Sabbath is not to be legalistic (Mark 2:23—3:6). Finally, if you reconstruct the last week of Jesus' life, it seems that one day is missing, a day for which no events are recorded. It may be that Jesus honored the Sabbath and did no work, even knowing He had only a week to live.

Give Me a Break!—Midweek

MEMORY VERSE:
If the LORD doesn't build the house, the workers are working for nothing. If the LORD doesn't guard the city, the guards are watching for nothing. It is no use for you to get up early and stay up late, working for a living. The Lord gives sleep to those he loves.— Psalm 127:1–2 (NCV)

SCRIPTURE: Matthew 11:28–30

LESSON IN A SENTENCE: God has designed us to spend a day in rest and worship every week.

FOCUS

Using two sheets of poster paper, have students create several lists. One list should be titled, "Things to Do." Explain that they should list on it everything they need to get done this week. The second list should say, "Free Time." Tell them to write everything they would do if they had a free day this week. Give them time to cover both sheets with ideas.

Now ask, "If I cancelled our meeting tonight, which of these two lists would you do? Why?" Give them a few minutes to discuss their priorities.

DISCOVERY

Read Matthew 11:28–30.

In groups of three or four, discuss the following questions together:
What makes it hard to take these promises seriously?
Why might Jesus be concerned with our levels of work activity and rest?
What images of God do you have that might make you think He doesn't want you to rest?

LIFE APPLICATION: Make plans to set aside a day each week to be your Sabbath day. What kinds of things could you do on that day that would be truly restful? What kinds of things would count as work? If it helps, ask your parents ahead of time if you can have a day without specific responsibilities at home as long as you can take care of them the day before.

Sometimes it is tempting to turn our rest time into a moment of catch-up work. If this is a temptation for you, put whatever reminds you of work in a backpack on the day that you have chosen to be your Sabbath. If you feel tempted to work—whether it's homework, housework, or whatever—instead of taking it out of the backpack, put the backpack on. Walk around in it for a while and remember Jesus' promise to give you a light burden to carry.

Try and return to a day of rest without work. Remember that God both commands and promises it in Scripture.

FEBRUARY 5, 2006

Mine all Mine?

By Amy Jacober

MEMORY VERSE:
The earth belongs to the Lord, and everything in it—the world and all its people.—Psalm 24:1 (NCV)

SCRIPTURE: 1 Chronicles 29:10–16; Luke 19:13

LESSON IN A SENTENCE: God has given not only all we possess but the great privilege and responsibility to figure out what to do with it.

THE BIG PICTURE (OR WHAT YOU'RE TRYING TO GET ACROSS):

It's easy to get caught up in what we do not have, compared to others. This can become so consuming that we forget to be thankful for what we do have. Even more, we forget that what we have is only ours temporarily, to be used wisely. This goes for everything we have. The idea of using something until it is worn out (as opposed to out of style) is almost unheard of! The idea of recycling or taking care of the earth has been relegated to a wacky, tree-hugging, New Age perspective. Actually using our time and resources wisely instead of wasting them is rarely discussed and almost never taught. Of course the term for this is stewardship. . .and it goes way beyond giving the 10% tithe. Being a good steward of all that God has given you is hard work. This work however both honors God and is completely worth it!

IN THIS LESSON STUDENTS SHOULD:

- Define stewardship.
- Learn that everything they have comes from and belongs to God.
- Identify a few concrete ways they may honor God with stewardship.
- Discover the joy that can come from God's perspective on possessions.

STUFF YOU NEED:

○ Clothes pins (enough for at least 5 per person, see Focus
  Option #1)
○ Large pieces of paper (butcher paper or tear sheets)
○ Markers
○ Pre-cut paper people (see Memory Verse Activity)

FOCUS

OPTION 1:

Give each person five clothes pins. The object of the game is to give
away as many as possible! In an area with clear boundaries, set your
students free to run around and try to attach their pins to anyone else.
(*Hint for the leaders*—The sides and backs of shirts or hoods work best,
as you are less likely to feel the pin being attached.)

After 5–10 minutes, call time and see who has the least pins and
who has the most pins. Feel free to play more than once if your students
are still into it.

Ask: What was it like to give away all of your pins? Did any of you
try to get pins in spite of the directions? Can you think of any other
time in your life when you are asked to give away all that you have?

Let's see what God has to say about this. . .

OPTION 2:

Break into groups of 2–3 and give each group a large piece of paper
and a marker. Have each group make a list of all the things they think
the perfect household should have. What are all of the things, in the
ideal world, they would hope to own as an adult? Give a few minutes
for them to create these lists and then ask each group to share. When
they are done, tape the lists on a wall clustered together.

Look back over the lists and name off several items and then ask
why? Why do they want to own all of this stuff as adults?

DISCOVERY

Have one of your leaders read 1 Chronicles 29:10–16 nice and
loud!!

Ask each group to reread the entire passage. Verse 14 poses a question—ask each group to come up with the response that would be given
by either David (remember he was king!) or his people (remember the
Israelites were wealthy and tremendously blessed at this time!)

In reality, no one, not even a powerful king in a powerful nation, has anything to offer that does not come from God!

Verse 15 talks of the Israelites being like foreigners and strangers on this earth. What does this mean?

Teacher's Note: 1 & 2 Chronicles cover much of the same history as 1 & 2 Samuel and Kings. The Chronicles, commonly accepted to have been written by Ezra, were at one time assumed to have been one scroll. They offer what is commonly seen as a priestly perspective (as opposed to the prophetic perspective of Samuel and Kings). David has assembled all of the officials, royals, and military in Jerusalem to let them know he would not be building the temple. (For more detail on this read 1 Chronicles 28.) David was the king of Israel. While a great man, he knew his limitations and where he had strayed from God. The passage for this lesson follows directly his letting the officials know that it would be Solomon, his son, and not himself who would see the building of the temple. Still, David rejoices and acknowledges that all he has, all Israel has, is not from their own efforts, rather from God alone.

LIFE APPLICATION: Okay—let's be honest—is it easier to spend your own money or your parents' money? Why? (Really push this with your students—of course it is easier to spend someone else's money.

You have just read that David was rejoicing and reminding his people that ALL they have, ALL of their good fortune, comes from God. They are able to be generous because in reality, they are not giving away anything that is really theirs anyway—they are being good stewards of what God has given to them.

Ask: What does it mean to be a steward of something?

If you are met with blank stares, offer a quick understanding of being a steward. It is someone who looks after or keeps that which has been entrusted to his or her care.

Pass another large piece of paper out to each group. This time, ask them to come up with a list of everything they own. (If you have an older or more mature group you can nuance this by asking them to list possessions as well as skills, talents, relationships, and resources with which they have been blessed.) If you did option #2 under Focus, ask them to compare the lists of what they have now with what they hope to have. Draw attention to the fact that even now they have a lot!!!

OPTIONAL DISCUSSION (this will only work for older/mature groups):

This is a great lesson to point out that we all have more than we realize. Remind your students of others around the world who indeed have only one or two outfits and struggle day to day to eat. Even in this country, there are families who struggle for basic nutrition and housing not to mention any extra possessions or health care. Ask how this perspective helps them to deal with what they do or do not have.

Ask: Do you think these things have come from God? Why or why not?

Would it change what you do with them if you believed that?

What other questions does this raise for us if God indeed has given all that we have? How does this impact your understanding of giving generously, knowing that everything you have belongs to God anyway?

MAKING IT PERSONAL: Have each person choose one thing they currently own (this can be a possession or something more abstract, like time, being good at math, etc.) Have them brainstorm with their small group how they could become a good steward of what God has given to them, starting with this one thing. How can they begin to give generously from what God has given to them? Close in prayer, asking God to remind everyone that all we have comes from Him.

MEMORY VERSE ACTIVITY

At the end of your time together, offer your students a few moments of quiet to think through one thing they can identify as being from God. As you are doing this, cut a chain of paper people (nothing fancy needed—just so it looks like a person). You should be able to get four of these per standard sized paper. As you hold up the chain, say the memory verse. Give each person present one of the paper people and ask them to write the memory verse on the person.

SONG: "All I Need" by Bethany Dillon on the Album *Bethany Dillon*

Q U O T A B L E   Q U O T E S :

Life begets life. Energy becomes energy. It is by spending oneself that one becomes rich.

—Sarah Bernhardt

We make a living by what we get but we make a life by what we give.

—Winston Churchill

Mine all Mine!?—Midweek

MEMORY VERSE:
The earth belongs to the Lord, and everything in it—the world and all its people.—Psalm 24:1 (NCV)

SCRIPTURE: Luke 19:12–26

LESSON IN A SENTENCE: God has given not only all we possess, but the great privilege and responsibility to figure out what to do with it.

FOCUS

Play a game of bigger and better! This is a kind of door-to-door scavenger hunt. Split into groups of 2–6. Be certain you have an adult leader with each group. Give each group something small like a penny. The object of the game is to trade the penny for something bigger and better. You keep trading until time is up and the groups return to the meeting. Give approximately a 45 minute time limit. (The actual amount of time is unimportant but be certain they have enough time without this becoming the only thing for which they have time.) It may help to tell the leaders what block or apartments their group is to go to, so the entire group does not go to the same place. When the groups return, have them share what they have brought back. Have a prize for the group with the biggest, best item!

DISCOVERY

Use the passage of Luke 19:12–26 as the script. As this has already been a chaotic active time, it would be best to have four leaders prepared with this ahead of time. There are three main characters and a narrator in this passage, the master and two servants, with several others as bystanders or witnesses. Make at least 4 copies of this passage. Highlight the four parts respectively. Have the narrator begin the story with the nobleman and servants reading each of their parts. At the end, ask your students if they can summarize what they have just heard.

Have the students reread this one more time from their own Bibles.

LIFE APPLICATION: Remind your students that the last time you were together you talked about stewardship.

Ask: How does this same concept apply to this lesson?

What does this mean for how wasteful we can be with all that God has given to us?

You have just had an experience of taking something small and doing something with it to get something bigger and better. While this was just a silly game, God has given each of us possessions, talents, relationships, skills, and resources that He not only wants us to use, but expects us to invest. We are not intended to simply receive for the rest of our lives.

Reread v. 26. What do you think this means? Does it seem fair or consistent with what you know of God?

Think back through the story you have just heard. You may not have been given money to invest, but you have plenty of other things to offer. In pairs, discuss what God has given to you and one concrete way you could invest this. (This may be difficult for some of your students. Help them out by suggesting that even if they don't have money to give, they can volunteer their time as an after-school soccer coach, they can tutor someone at school, they can offer to babysit for free, etc. Help them to identify the many ways to invest what God has given to them.)

FEBRUARY 12, 2006

Truth to Tell

By James Miller

MEMORY VERSE:
So Jesus said to the Jews who believed in him, "If you continue to obey my teaching you are truly my followers. Then you will know the truth, and the truth will make you free."—John 8:31–32 (NCV)

SCRIPTURE: 1 Corinthians 13

LESSON IN A SENTENCE: God intends for us to express the truth in love when we speak to each other.

THE BIG PICTURE (OR WHAT YOU'RE TRYING TO GET ACROSS):

Valentine's week is a time in which a lot of people are thinking about l-u-v! However, as much as this topic conjures up thoughts of passion, romance, and chocolates, the Bible makes a unique connection between love and truth. Love rejoices with the truth, and those who know the truth are set free to love. In this study, students will learn that love and truth must go side-by-side, like a couple holding hands.

False images of love are very popular and tend to distort truth. Movies and media portray love as without consequence and without effort. Students will need to learn to break out of some of these caricatures of true love.

IN THIS LESSON STUDENTS SHOULD:

- Learn to seek love that is based in truth.
- Learn to proclaim truth with love.
- Learn to identify authentic and unauthentic types of love.

STUFF YOU NEED:

- A lot of newspapers and magazines, and perhaps a recording of some TV commercials for the first Focus activity option
- Several pairs of scissors, at least one for every three students

○ For the second Focus activity option, you will need a sheet of paper and a pen for every four students
○ Everyone will need Bibles
○ For the Life Application section, you will need to place large pieces of poster paper on the walls of the room with words on them like "school, government, parents, friends, drugs, church." Each student will need a pen.

FOCUS

Choose either Option 1 or 2.

OPTION 1: For larger groups

Using magazines, newspapers, or recorded TV commercials, look for advertisements that say something about love. Cut them out. Turn to a neighbor and describe what they suggest about love.

Say: There are laws that govern what is called "truth in advertising," stating that advertisers must tell you the truth about their product. Do you think these ads would meet a "truth in advertising" requirement based on what they say about love? Tell your neighbor where the ads are misleading. Discuss:

Are people convinced by ads like these?

What do you know about love that is different than what appears in these ads?

Say: Today we'll talk about speaking the truth in love. This means finding things that are worthwhile to say and saying them in the right way.

OPTION 2: For smaller groups that know one another

In groups of four, list everything you can say that is true of everyone in your group. Avoid redundancies like "we all have eyes, ears, noses," etc. Write them down. You have four minutes.

Count how many items you have.

Now circle everything on that list that you love about yourselves. How many are left?

Say: Today we'll talk about speaking the truth in love. This means finding things that are worthwhile to say and saying them in the right way.

SONGS: "I Will Be Here" by Steven Curtis Chapman
"Love Song" by Third Day

DISCOVERY

Read 1 Corinthians 13. Discuss:
   Why does love rejoice with the truth?
   In what other ways is this passage related to truth-telling?
   How do truth and love work together?
   In what ways is it unloving to be dishonest? Can you give an example?
   Name everything you think of when you hear the word "lying." Compare and contrast your description of lying with the description of love in this passage.

LIFE APPLICATION: Have various words printed on sheets of paper on the walls, including "School, government, parents, friends, drugs, church," and whatever else you deem appropriate for your group. Give each student something with which to write. Have students mill around the room writing truthful, loving descriptions of these things underneath them. Encourage them to think about what God thinks of these things and how God would describe them.
   When they've finished the activity, ask the following questions: Is it hard to say something that is both loving and truthful? Why or why not? Which comes more easily? Why might God want us to speak the truth in love? In what situations will that be most difficult for you personally? Are there times when it comes naturally?

MAKING IT PERSONAL: Create an ad campaign for your church or youth group. Make sure it meets the "truth in advertising" requirement. Tell people about God's love and the love of your church.
   Think about these things: Where is God's love most apparent in your church? Who are some loving people you have met in that context? What kind of love are teenagers looking for? What do they settle for in its place? What could you tell them that would entice them to give up false kinds of love for the real love that God offers?

MEMORY VERSE ACTIVITY: Try wearing someone else's glasses for a day, or wear sunglasses when you normally wouldn't. How does this change your view of the world around you? How would it change your view of the world to look through God's eyes for a day? How would it change the way you interacted with people? Think about the fact that God wants you to see the world with truth and love the way He does.

SERVICE OPTION: Create a Valentine's truth e-card. If you've never seen one, an e-card is just like a card you'd send in the mail, but you send it by e-mail, along with music, graphics, and a personal note from you. Using a site that allows you to create e-cards for free (like www.hallmark.com), create a Valentine card that tells loving truth to someone you know. In it, list all of the good things you can about that person as a way of encouraging them.

Teacher's Note: This would be a great time for you to send an encouraging note to individuals in your group or to send one to your entire group. Since this can be their service project, your note can also serve as a reminder for them to send a note to someone else!

Q U O T A B L E   Q U O T E S :

For though we love both the truth and our friends,
piety requires us to honor the truth first.
—Aristotle, *Nicomachean Ethics*, bk. 1, ch. 6,
trans. by Terence Irwin (1985).

Truth to Tell—Midweek

MEMORY VERSE:
So Jesus said to the Jews who believed in him, "If you continue to obey my teaching you are truly my followers. Then you will know the truth, and the truth will make you free."—John 8:31–32 (NCV)

SCRIPTURE: Genesis 27:1–41

LESSON IN A SENTENCE: God intends for us to express the truth in love when we speak to each other.

FOCUS

Have candles available for everyone in the room. Light a large, central candle and read the memory verse, John 8:31. Invite students to come forward one at a time with their candles. As they do, they should say something that is true about God or quote a Scripture verse that is important to them. Depending on what is best for your room, they should then light their candle and either return to their seat or place the lit candle next to the center candle. When all candles are lit, explain how telling the truth is like walking in God's light (1 John 1:5–7).

DISCOVERY

Break into groups of five. Read the passage with one person for each part: Jacob, Esau, Rebekah, Abraham, and the narrator. Read the text together.

When you are finished, discuss these questions:

What came out of Jacob's lie? How did he benefit? What did he lose?

Relate an experience in which you experienced the consequences of a lie. What did you gain or lose?

Is it more easy or difficult to tell the truth in love? Why?

Are there challenges to telling the truth in love?

APPLICATION: Think about the times that you are most inclined to lie and what you get out of lying. Think about the kind of person that you become when you tell lies. Think about the false image of yourself that you present to others when you lie.

Get a dry erase marker and a mirror. Draw over your own reflection in the mirror whatever you think lying turns you into, like a mask. Be creative. When you're finished, as you erase the drawing, think about how the truth makes you free and brings you into the light of God.

WORK ETHIC OR WORKAHOLISM?

By Will Penner
EDITOR, YOUTH PASTOR

I grew up in Meridian, Texas—a tiny town of less than 1,400 people, where if a man didn't have dirt under his fingernails and dust all over his boots, he seemed a bit out of place. Most of my friends drove tractors and combines on their family farms well before they could legally drive a pickup truck on the public highways. And because we went to a small school, most of us were involved in a lot of different extracurricular activities at once. I even marched in the band at halftime in my football uniform.

All of my friends worked like crazy, so it didn't seem odd to me that every day after football practice, I would work at the grocery store until closing time, then head across the street to clean the bathrooms, take out the trash, and sweep and mop my parents' hardware store. It was simply a way of life.

On Sundays, we never had any kind of athletic practice, band rehearsal, debating meet, or even an FFA meeting (Future Farmers of America—and yes, I was in that, too). On Sundays, the grocery store was open, but only for a few hours, and I rarely had to work then. That was our day to slow down a bit. We went to church, and I went to youth group. And the rest of the day was spent with family and friends having all kinds of fun—some redeemable, some mischievous.

Then and Now

Almost a decade later I was the youth pastor at a church in Brentwood, Tennessee's wealthiest suburb, and the landscape was very different. Most of the time, parents worked themselves silly trying to create an affluent lifestyle that would offer all of the best opportunities for their children. They were constantly on the go, and so were their kids. There was a busy-ness to their lives that seemed to exhibit a strong work ethic, which I appreciated; but lying underneath the surface, I sensed something else.

For these parents, hard work was also a way of life, but, I think, for very different reasons. The adults of my childhood believed hard work was good for a person's soul; they also recognized that it was good for the community. It seemed many parents in my new community believed in hard work primarily because it would be good for their bank accounts.

In Meridian, adults around me were always challenging me to try new things, to wear many different hats. So I participated in journalism, math, and drama competitions, but also shop class, vocational agriculture, and even home economics. I led the church choir my junior and senior years, was active in the youth group, and preached every time we had a youth-led Sunday. Even in sports, I got to play football, basketball, tennis, and run track. I wasn't an expert at any of that stuff (in fact, I stunk at some of it), but adults in the community appreciated seeing kids active in things, and my parents valued the well-roundedness these varied experiences brought.

In Brentwood, it wasn't uncommon for kids to be involved in a single travel sports club that practiced year-round, often seven days per week. They spent most weekends in a different state at one tournament or another, and rarely did entire families spend a full day, or even an evening all together at the same time. I was simultaneously hailed and ridiculed as our youth ministry calendar filled up. Many loved having something else to keep their kids "busy and out of trouble," and others were angry with us for giving their kids "one more thing" to have to choose from, diverting them from the more important purposes of their chosen extracurricular endeavor.

Time to Be Human

There are benefits, I guess, to being an expert at something. Goodness knows, if my wife had a heart attack, I wouldn't want the person repairing a valve in her bypass to be somebody who just barely got through medical school because class time interfered with frisbee golf. And I know it's awful, but I'd probably care less about the surgeon as an individual than I would about his or her function as it would relate to the health of my wife. The unfortunate thing is that we all seem to relate to one another this way in every area of our lives.

Most of us know a great many people in our lives, but we have very few deep, thriving relationships with people we value as individuals over function. And that, I think, is sad.

As a result, most of us too often spend energy in ways that aren't ultimately beneficial to our own health or to the well-being of our families and communities—including our church communities. We spend our energy doing things that will either make us a lot of money or gain us a lot of prestige—or put us into a good position to later get more money or prestige. Without realizing it, we try to earn the favor of God and others. We do that because we don't feel okay just being human; in order to feel worthy, we have to measure ourselves against others.

We find ourselves chasing our tails, wondering what it's really all about. We're not sure where we're going, but at least we know we're getting there quickly. Is it any wonder our students are often overwhelmed and busy as they follow right in our footsteps?

Church Busy-ness

Even churches reward busy-ness more than they reward stillness. They seek crowds over solitude, honor high-energy over silence, and prefer activity to rest. Most people judge our ministries, whether we're paid staff or volunteers, not based on the quality of our relationships with God but by the activity that can be found in our ministries.

The truth is that our relationships with God are pivotal in our effectiveness in ministry, not afterthoughts. If we busy ourselves with programmatic and administrative tasks without attending to our own souls, our effectiveness will diminish and we set ourselves up for burnout.

We must differentiate our own discipleship with our youth ministry function. How well we do in retreat planning, fund raising, or small group leadership is just that: it's how we're doing at performing those specific tasks. In and of themselves, they don't define how well our youth ministries are ushering students into deeper relationships with Christ. And they darn sure don't equate with our own worth as disciples of Christ.

So what do we do now?

Earning Our Place

I think it's great for us to work hard, for hard work is good for the soul and good for the community. In fact, it's easy to miss the fact that the first part of the Fourth Commandment talks about working six days, not five—something I don't hear in many sermons. But we also need to take just as seriously the resting part of the Sabbath Commandment. A body cannot run long without physical rest. And neither can a spirit. We are more than our functions, and so are our students. God loves us because of who God is, not because of what we can do for God.

Theologically, we know we can't earn our salvation—but it doesn't keep us from trying We may not verbally preach a works-based doctrine to our youth, but our actions can.

Resting from our work isn't just about taking a vacation day, though that's a good thing to do as well, from time to time. Frankly, if we don't find some rest in our faith—specifically in the knowledge that God's love transcends what we do or don't do, and what our kids do and don't do—then there's something wrong with our theology. We mustn't be anxious about earning God's favor. We can't earn it, no matter what; it's already been bestowed.

If we're busy trying to be top-notch youth workers in order to earn the favor of God or others, then, well, we need to knock it off. Whether we're paid staff or volunteers, we need to be faithful to fulfill whatever job description we've agreed to (or work to change the description if it's unreasonable, or be faithful to God's calling us elsewhere if it's unreasonable and unchangeable); that's being a good steward of the task we've been assigned.

Remember the Sabbath, and keep it holy.

FEBRUARY 19, 2006

Materialism / Consumerism

By Rick & Kristi Bennett

MEMORY VERSE:
It is worth nothing for them to have the whole world if they lose their souls.—Mark 8:36 (NCV)

SCRIPTURE: Matthew 19:16–26

LESSON IN A SENTENCE: How we look at our possessions (past, present, future) is a test of our commitment to Christ or to the world.

THE BIG PICTURE (OR WHAT YOU'RE TRYING TO GET ACROSS):

Like the Rich Young Ruler, each student has a decision to make regarding their "stuff" and Christ. As Americans, most students in any group would be considered rich by the world's standard. As C. S. Lewis said, "Nobody who gets enough food and clothing in a world where most are hungry and cold, has any business to talk about 'misery'."

Jesus understood that the Ruler would be seen as a good person by his outward appearances, but his loyalties (which cannot be seen as easily as other behaviors) were not to Christ and the Scriptures. Jesus and His disciples had no homes, and the disciples were sent out with no extra possessions (Luke 9:1–6). To follow Christ, the man would have to be willing to give away everything and live in community with these other men, with no financial security. He would have to make the same decision that Matthew had, when he gave up his security to follow Jesus.

Jesus knew this young man would have to be willing to give up his identity as a rich man to become a follower of Jesus. Each of us has a similar decision to make. We must ask ourselves if our identity is wrapped up in the stuff we have, the security we have, the money we have (or hope to have one day). If it is, then it is impossible to follow Christ.

IN THIS LESSON STUDENTS SHOULD:

- Have questions to ask themselves regarding their connections to their "stuff."
- Know the story of the Rich Young Ruler.
- Begin to question their own connection to their possessions and identity in Christ.

STUFF YOU NEED:

○ VCR and copy of *Mosquito Coast* for Option 1
○ Butcher paper or chalkboard
○ Markers or Sharpies
○ Poster board (for Option 2)
○ Scissors
○ Glue/tape

FOCUS

Choose either Option 1 or 2.

OPTION 1: High School

If you have access to a VCR, try to find the film *Mosquito Coast*, starring Harrison Ford, from 1986.

In one of his diatribes against modern consumer society, the Father (Allie Fox), played by Harrison Ford, says this:

"We eat when we're not hungry, drink when we're not thirsty. We buy what we don't need and throw away everything that's useful. Why sell a man what he wants? Sell him what he doesn't need! Pretend he's got eight legs and two stomachs and money to burn. It's wrong! Wrong. Wrong. Wrong."

Even if you are unable to find the film, use this quote as a conversation starter. Ask the students,

"What do you eat when you are not hungry or drink when you are not thirsty?"

"What do you buy that you do not need?"

"What do you feel pressured into buying that you know you do not really need?"

"Why?"

OPTION 2: Junior High (or Active)

Gather ads from magazines and a Sunday newspaper. Split into groups of 4–5 students each. Give poster board with a line dividing it into two halves, some scissors, glue/tape. Ask the students to put on the left side ads of things they think are really necessities in life, and on the right side things that the ads make them want but they don't need. Let the groups report on their findings. Then ask: What do you want that you don't really need? What do you want to buy or have your parents buy for you, that you only want so that you can "keep up with your friends"?

**Be sure to give a time limit (10 minutes or so) to this activity so that it does not eat into the teaching time.

DISCOVERY

Read Matthew 19:16–24 as a whole group.

Ask for students to give their opinions of Jesus' challenge to this young man.

Ask: "Did this seem fair?"

Ask: "Why do you think Jesus asked this man to sell everything?"

Have you ever bought a cola or snack in a machine? Have you ever had the snack get stuck on its way down? You stick your hand in there and feel the snack. However, you cannot remove your hand with the snack. It is stuck. You have a decision. You can either hold on to the snack and stand there all day, or you can release your hand, leaving the snack behind.

Jesus saw this young man like the person unwilling to release the snack to free himself. He was holding all he owned tightly and refused to let go of it. He would be unable to join Jesus' followers as long as he held tightly to his possessions. Jesus did not give this requirement to everyone, but he saw this young man putting his identity and loyalty in these possessions. Also, if he chose to be a disciple of Christ, in the context of Jesus' day, he would have no place to sleep and could have no ties keeping him from his task. Jesus knew this man's possessions would be his alternative god.

Jesus knows that money and possessions can have a tight grip on each person. He wants each person to hold these possessions with a loose grip, able to drop them at any time if they get in the way of the person's relationship with Christ.

Regarding v. 24, there has been some debate regarding this verse. However, all agree that the main thrust is that a camel is the largest animal in Palestine. The contrast is powerful. The largest thing must go through the smallest opening. This is impossible.

An interesting point for us may be that if it is so difficult for a rich man to enter heaven, then we should hold our possessions loosely, so we may not have the difficulty of the rich young man.

Teacher's Note: Jesus spoke on money and possessions more than any other topic, according to the New Testament. Of the 38 parables, an astonishing 17 are about possessions. Possessions are mentioned 2,172 times in Scripture—three times more than love, seven times more than prayer and eight times more than belief. The Bible takes possessions very seriously. In fact, worship of money and stuff is a violation of the First Commandment.

LIFE APPLICATION: Have the students split up into groups of 3–4 and answer the following questions: (If you chose Option 2, you will probably have less time, so feel free to pick and choose among the following suggestions.)

1) What pressures do you feel on yourself to have certain material possessions because of what other people at your school/work have?

2) What about time? Do you feel like you give up so much time that you don't really have much energy left for "spiritual" matters? If so, what things are you doing that may not be necessary? What things could you add to your list that would be more along the lines of what Jesus would want you to do?

3) Why do you think Jesus said it is so difficult for a rich man to get into heaven? Can you see anything in your own life that might be making it difficult for you to follow Jesus the way He wants you to?

4) What would the world look like if Christians took seriously Jesus' command to the young ruler in v. 21 to give away everything and follow Him? What if we did that? What would that look like?

5) If it's unrealistic right now for us to do exactly what Jesus said in v. 21, what are some ways we can make a start in the right direction? What practical things can we implement in our own group? At school?

MAKING IT PERSONAL: Pass out 3 x 5 index cards to each student and have them write down what is keeping them from following Jesus, or competes for their loyalty to Him—possessions, lack of time, etc. Then have them write down one thing they could give up (material good or something that eats up too much of their time) so they are able to follow Jesus and to "store up their treasure in heaven."

Going Deeper: To push the students into action, encourage them to bring the possession they wrote down to the following week's session, and have a box that students can put stuff in and then donate it to a local charity/children's home, etc.

MEMORY VERSE ACTIVITY

On the back side of the card where they wrote down things they could give up, write the Memory Verse for the week.

As they spend the week with the card, ask them to look at those things competing for loyalty and turn the card over to focus on the Memory Verse.

SONGS: "Material Girl" by Madonna ("We are living in a material world and I am a material girl")—*negative and funny, it could be a good intro to the lesson*
"Throw it All Away" by Toad the Wet Sprocket—*positive and powerful*
"Treasures in Heaven" by Burlap to Cashmere—*straight from Scripture*

CONNECTIONS: Colossians 3:5 tells us that materialism is actually idolatry. Greed is seen as a destructive force (James 4:1–3; 1 Timothy 6:7–10).

EXTRA EXTRA!: According to many experts, advertising is becoming more and more difficult to resist. It is everywhere we turn. It is in our schools, on our buses, hidden in television shows, on boxes of cereal, and in bathrooms. Teaching students to be aware of advertising is integral to resisting its power. Point out advertising and marketing to your students. Ask them to make a conscious effort to notice where they see it and to make light of it when they see it in odd places.
These quotes point out advertising's power upon us:

"Advertisers regularly con us into believing that we genuinely need one luxury after another. We are convinced that we must keep up with or even go one better than our neighbors. So we buy another dress, sports jacket or sports car and thereby force up the standard of living. The ever more affluent standard of living is the god of twentieth century North America and the adman is its prophet."
—Ronald J. Sider,
Rich Christians in an Age of Hunger, 1977

"Advertising tries to stimulate our sensuous desires, converting luxuries into necessities, but it only intensifies man's inner misery. The business world is bent on creating hungers which its wares never satisfy, and thus it adds to the frustrations and broken minds of our times."
—Archbishop Fulton Sheen (1895–1979),
Lift Up Your Heart, 1942

"Our present culture, however, specializes in inflaming endless lust for possessions with advertisements that constantly convince us that we need more (particularly to create the ease we have never found). The marketers don't tell us much about their products, but they spend a great deal of energy (and enormous amounts of money) appealing to our fears and dreams. Thus, the idolatry of possessions plays to the deeper idolatry of our selves—and in an endlessly consuming society, persons are always remaking themselves with new belongings."

—Marva J. Dawn,
A Royal "Waste" of Time, 1999

QUOTABLE   QUOTES :

In the last twenty-five years alone, new inventions and improvements have utterly transformed the way we live. Personal computers and fax machines, cordless phones and wireless speakers, e-mail and other hi-tech, labor-saving conveniences have revolutionized our work and home life. Yet have they brought us the peace and freedom they seemed to promise? Without realizing it, we have become dulled, if not brainwashed, in our eagerness to embrace technology. We have become slaves to a system that presses us to spend money on new gadgets, and we have accepted without question the argument that, by working harder, we will have more time to do more important things. It is a perverse logic.

—Johann Christoph Arnold, *Seeking Peace*, 1998

When I walk into a grocery store and look at all the products you can choose, I say, "My God! No king ever had anything like I have in my grocery store today."
—Bill Gates quoted in *Parade Magazine*, 14 July 2002

A house is just a pile of stuff with a cover on it.
—George Carlin

Materialism/Consumerism—Midweek

MEMORY VERSE:
It is worth nothing for them to have the whole world if they lose their souls.—Mark 8:36 (NCV)

SCRIPTURE: Matthew 6:19–24

LESSON IN A SENTENCE: How we look at our possessions (past, present, future) is a test of our commitment to Christ or to the world.

FOCUS

When students come together, have a brainstorming session and come up with a list of what they want out of life. If they have trouble, give them examples such as what kind of career, house, etc. Then give everyone a piece of paper and have them write down what they each want out of life, making the list as long as they wish.

DISCOVERY

Read through Matthew 6:19–24 as a group.

Ask these questions (if possible, use a chalk board to write down answers):

1. Can you name some "earthly treasures"?
2. What are some positives about earthly treasures?
3. Other than reasons given in v.19, what are some negatives about earthly treasures?
4. What are heavenly treasures?
5. How do you gather these treasures?
6. Can you give some examples of v. 21 when you look at adults or other students?
7. What do you think v. 24 means for you right now, and the life decisions you make as you become an adult?

LIFE APPLICATION: Have students pair up and share their lists. In light of the Scripture just studied, what would they change about what is on the list now? How do the things on their list either help them in following Jesus or impede them from it?

EXTRA! EXTRA!: Philip Yancy tells the story of Willie Stokes, Jr, a young gambler living on the south side of Chicago. Stokes "attracted local attention when the family had an auto-body shop outfit his coffin as a Cadillac Seville, complete with trunk and front grille, windshield and dashboard, silver spoke wheels, working headlights and taillights, and Stokes' vanity license plate. Newspaper photos showed the embalmed gambler, like a display in a wax museum, sitting at the steering wheel of his coffin-car in a hot-pink suit, with five hundred-dollar bills between his thumb and forefinger."—from *Rumors of Another World,* p. 209.

FEBRUARY 26, 2006

Economic and Spiritual Poverty

By Fred Arzola

MEMORY VERSE:
They all gave out of their wealth; but she, out of her poverty, put in everything. . .—Mark 12:44a (NIV)

SCRIPTURE: Luke 6:20; Matthew 5:1

Luke: Blessed are you who are poor,
             for yours is the kingdom of God. (NIV)

Matthew: Blessed are the poor in spirit,
             for theirs is the kingdom of heaven. (NIV)

LESSON IN A SENTENCE: Poverty is both an economic and spiritual condition.

THE BIG PICTURE (OR WHAT YOU'RE TRYING TO GET ACROSS):

There are two types of poverty: economic and spiritual. While the first type of poverty is experienced externally, the second type of poverty is experienced internally. Conversely, while economic wealth represents the economy of the kingdoms on earth, spiritual wealth represents the economy of the kingdom of heaven.

In "this" world, the economic poor are often pitied or looked down upon. However, in God's kingdom, the economic poor are lifted up, shown compassion and even have special treatment—"for yours/theirs is the kingdom of heaven."

Interestingly, the economic poor are often spiritually rich. For many poor people, their faith may be their greatest, and only, asset. Conversely, the economically wealthier have to deal with unique spiritual challenges, such as materialism, consumerism, greed, and even the exploitation of the poor.

Of course, both need Christ. We all do!

The Bible says, "For the love of money is a root of all kinds of evil. Some people, eager for money, have wandered from the faith and pierced themselves with many griefs" (1 Timothy 6:10). Notice, it does not say that money in and of itself is evil. We must be careful not to judge a person who has obtained financial blessings through hard work or through a rightful inheritance. Being wealthy is not sinful. In fact, many Christian churches and organizations often rely on the generosity of wealthier people or foundations for financial support. We cannot say the wealthy are sinful, on the one hand, yet ask for their money on the other hand. This is hypocrisy. Quite frankly, it is doubtful many poor people would deny a generous financial gift out of fear of losing their faith!

Nevertheless, we must be honest. There are many unique ethical and spiritual challenges for those who are wealthier. Wealthy Christians have an obligation and responsibility to assist the poor. Overwhelmingly, it is the rich who oppress the poor. It is the wealthy corporations, economic systems and structures that often create or perpetuate poverty on a macro level. It is the rich who are at the center of power and the poor who are at the margins. In this world, it is the rich who are the powerful. This is why we must pray with and for our wealthier sisters and brothers. Wealthier Christians need to develop strong support systems, accountability relationships, and spiritual disciplines in order to deal with the temptations, passions, ethical dilemmas, and greed which frequently exist in the world of wealth.

Jesus says, "The poor you will always have with you" (Matthew 26:11 NIV). But, he also says the very disturbing words, "I tell you the truth, it is hard for a rich man to enter the kingdom of heaven. Again I tell you, it is easier for a camel to go through the eye of a needle than for a rich man to enter the kingdom of God" (Matthew 19:23–24 NIV).

But there are also those whom we refer to as the middle class. This group is neither poor nor rich. They are often burning the candle at both ends, working long hours, trying to live a decent life, paying the rent, taking care of their children, keeping their healthcare, maintaining their bills, etc. While this group is not economically poor, many middle class families often fear of one day becoming economically poor. And while they are not rich, they often get pulled into the seductive temptations of wealth. For middle-class teenagers, the stress on their parents to maintain a middle-class life—and middle-class image—may not be appreciated. Furthermore, the unique social pressures and spiritual challenges to live a holy life make an honest and open discussion on economic and spiritual poverty an absolute necessity.

A serious attempt must be made to help teenagers, especially middle-class and upper-class teenagers, stand in solidarity with their poor sisters and brothers. While not making middle-class and upper-class teenagers feel shamed, they need to learn to appreciate the privilege that God has allowed them to hold, as well as the responsibility to confront economic injustice and poverty.

While a strong financial portfolio may certainly be a blessing, this does not guarantee spiritual wealth. We must have an open and honest discussion on the realities of both economic poverty and spiritual poverty, and how we may be able to address both issues.

IN THIS LESSON STUDENTS SHOULD:

○ Address economic poverty and the struggles of the poor.
○ Address spiritual poverty as a related, yet distinct, reality.
○ Raise the awareness of middle-class/upper-class Christian teens regarding the privilege and their unique place as it relates to economics, and develop a deeper sense of spiritual and fiscal responsibility.

FOCUS

The teacher asks the following provocative questions:
Is it a sin to be wealthy?
Do people choose to be poor?
Do wealthier Christians have an obligation to assist the poor?
Are poorer people holier or more spiritual that wealthier people?
Are wealthier people holier or more spiritual that poorer people?
Why are certain groups poorer than other groups?
Can you be economically rich and spiritually poor?
Can you be economically poor and be spiritually rich?
Can you be economically rich and spiritually rich?
Can you be economically poor and be spiritually poor?

DISCOVERY

Have one student read Luke 6:20, and another read Matthew 5:1.
There are five points that are important when looking at both the Lucan reading and the Matthean reading
First, these sayings in the Christian tradition are called "The Beatitudes." The word "beatitude" comes from the Latin, meaning "blessing." As usual, Jesus turns over the common beliefs in the first century as well as today. How can being poor be a blessing? While Jesus recognizes that according to this world's standards, the rich and the spiritual leaders have their blessings, ultimately it is the poor and those who are struggling with poverty of spirit who will experience the unique blessings of the kingdom of heaven.
Second, in the Lucan passage, Jesus addresses the economically poor. We see the poor have a special place in God's heart. While God

loves all people, the poor are in need of special help. Are you economically poor? God stands with you in your poverty. Do you know someone or a community living in poverty? Jesus understands how it feels to live among the poor.

Third, in the Matthean passage, Jesus addresses those poor in spirit. We have all experienced moments of spiritual poverty. This does not mean that we must live a life of misery. However, life is painful. There will be times in our lives when our spirits will feel very poor, painful, and lonely. Jesus offers us a word of hope and encouragement. He reassures us that the pain of spiritual poverty will not last forever—"for yours/theirs is the kingdom of heaven."

Fourth, after reading the Lucan and Matthean passages, we see the uniqueness of both economic poverty and spiritual poverty. A person who is economically poor may be spiritually rich. However, this person may also be spiritually poor. In fact, there may be few worse and harsher global experiences than being both economically poor and spiritually poor. While economic poverty may rob a person of material things, spiritual poverty robs a person of hope and meaning. A combination of these poverties is profoundly depressing.

A person who is economically wealthy may be spiritually rich. What a blessing and privilege and responsibility. However, this person may also be spiritually poor. Ultimately, it is spiritual wealth that matters. For both the economically poor and wealthy, joy comes from within. Jesus says, "What good is it for a man to gain the whole world, yet forfeit his soul? Or what can a man give in exchange for his soul?" (Mark 8:36–37 NIV).

It is important to appreciate both poverties. Economically poor people struggle with day-to-day realities. "Will I have enough to feed my children?" "Will I have enough to pay the rent?" "I can't afford health care." Parents often feel terrible shame not being able to provide for their families with basic essentials. Even buying a new pair of jeans or sneakers becomes a significant financial burden.

Yet, for those who may not be economically poor, they too struggle with temptations, passions, selfishness, loneliness, ethical dilemmas, pride, greed, etc. Are you spiritually poor in your life right now? What do you need to do to become spiritually wealthier?

There is one final point. Jesus says, "Not everyone who says to me, 'Lord, Lord,' will enter the kingdom of heaven, but only he who does the will of my Father who is in heaven" (Matthew 7:21 NIV). Whether one is rich or poor, we are all sinners. We all need Jesus Christ. We must all repent from our sins and confess that Jesus Christ is Lord. Economic wealth will not guarantee us heaven, but neither will economic poverty. Only our faith in Jesus Christ will assure us of participation into the economy of heaven. Are you spiritually poor in your life right now? Commit (or re-commit) your life to Jesus (again) right now. This is the only wealth that ultimately matters.

LIFE APPLICATION: Have the teens decide how they can make a difference in dealing with poverty in their community or local vicinity.

Teacher's Note: Make sure the youth ministry is contextually engaged. It should not only be limited to sending money to an organization dealing with these issues. While this may certainly be one aspect, this should be supplemental to a hands-on activity.

Process as a large group. Or break into small groups and return to the large group.

Gather as a large group to process suggestions. Encourage an open and honest discussion without having to reveal confidential names or issues.

These issues should be listed on the board.

Follow the "Justice Cycle" explained in Week 22—Theme: Justice.

MAKING IT PERSONAL:

Teacher's Note: Questions for poorer students

If you are economically poor, how does this influence or impact your faith?

How would your faith be different if you were wealthier?

What can economically poor people learn from the spiritual struggles of wealthier Christians?

What are some things you can do now to strengthen your economic situation in the future?

Teacher's Note: Questions for wealthier students

If you are economically wealthier, how does this influence or impact your faith?

How would your faith be different if you were poorer?

What can economically wealthier people learn from the struggles of poorer Christians?

What are some things you can do now to prevent spiritual poverty?

QUOTABLE   QUOTES:

There is much suffering in the world—physical, material, mental. The suffering of some can be blamed on the greed of others. The material and physical suffering is suffering from hunger, from homelessness, from all kinds of diseases. But the greatest suffering is being lonely, feeling unloved, having no one. I have come more and more to realize that it is being unwanted that is the worst disease that any human being can ever experience.

—Mother Teresa

WEB CONNECT:

World Vision—www.worldvision.org

Mission: A Christian relief and development organization dedicated to helping children and their communities worldwide reach their full potential by tackling the causes of poverty.

Bread for the World—www.bread.org

Mission: A nationwide Christian citizens' movement seeking justice for the world's hungry people by lobbying our nation's decision makers. BFW Institute seeks justice for hungry people by engaging in research and education on policies related to hunger and development.

Economic and Spiritual Poverty—
Midweek

MEMORY VERSE:
They all gave out of their wealth; but she, out of her poverty, put in everything.—Mark 12:44a (NIV)

SCRIPTURE: Mark 12:41–44 (NIV)

> [41]Jesus sat down opposite the place where the offerings were put and watched the crowd putting their money into the temple treasury. Many rich people threw in large amounts. [42]But a poor widow came and put in two very small copper coins, worth only a fraction of a penny.
> [43]Calling his disciples to him, Jesus said, "I tell you the truth, this poor widow has put more into the treasury than all the others. [44]They all gave out of their wealth; but she, out of her poverty, put in everything—all she had to live on."

LESSON IN A SENTENCE: Poverty is both an economic and spiritual condition.

FOCUS

Review what the teens decided to do this past Sunday in order to make a difference in dealing with poverty in their community or vicinity.

Continue to follow the "Justice Cycle" as explained in Week 22 (Theme: Justice). Review and process the "Examination" and "Plan" components.

By the end of today's session, the group should have an initial date for the "Action" component," in order to implement the plan.

DISCOVERY

There are three points that are important when looking at today's reading.

First, Jesus places more value on the spirit or motive of giving over and above the amount of giving. The woman who gave the two coins was not only poor, but was also a widow. During the time of Jesus, widows had very few resources. The fact that she gave, represents a spiritual wealth which is truly amazing. It is always humbling to see the poor take care of the poor. Remember, the poor live with the poor. When you give money to the church or a worthy cause, do you do so with a generous spirit? Honestly speaking, is your financial giving sufficient based on your current financial resources and circumstances or should you give more?

Second, Jesus recognizes when you give from your poverty rather than your wealth. Again, the spirit of the giving is surely more important than the amount of the giving. However, it is reasonable to expect those with more money should give more money. There is a profound connection between "giving" and "poverty." Economically, this is obvious. But, to give when one is in spiritual poverty or spiritual pain is also a truly amazing gift. To continue to give—whether in treasures, talents or time—when one is experiencing spiritual poverty, reflects a depth of spiritual maturity. How often when we are going through tough times, do we hide our treasures, talents and time until we "feel" better? Yet, to continue to be a blessing in the lives of people even in the midst of spiritual poverty, reflects what it means "to give from your poverty." This is the spirit of the "wounded healer." Like Christ, we carry crosses in our lives, yet we are called to continue to serve and sacrifice for one another, even unto death. Do you give from your poverty or from your wealth? Is your giving sacrificial or from your surplus?

Finally, Jesus uses ordinary moments to teach extraordinary principles. The disciples received a powerful lesson about the spiritual life, yet Jesus was not preaching a sermon or formally teaching. He was simply sitting and looking at the people. Leaning to His friends, He shared His reflection. We, too, should seek and look out for teaching lessons that come informally through God's world. Learning does not necessarily come from the classroom or a formal teacher. What can God's creation tell us about life, whether good or bad? What wisdom can we learn from each other? What do people learn from you? Do you teach things that are life-giving? If not, why not? Explain.

LIFE APPLICATION: Are you struggling with spiritual poverty in your life? What are three things you can do to increase your spiritual wealth?

Does poverty create righteous anger in your heart? Explain. If not, why not?

What is your part or contribution to addressing poverty to the Justice Cycle?

Is there anything in the lesson with which you disagree? Explain?

What does poverty mean to you?

Why would some Christians "feel" uncomfortable speaking about poverty?

Do your teenage friends live in a world primarily of economic poverty, spiritual poverty or both? Explain.

MARCH 5, 2006

One Way (Cults)

By Michelle Hicks

MEMORY VERSE:
Jesus answered, "I am the way and the truth and the life. The only way to the Father is through me."—John 14:6 (NCV)

SCRIPTURE: 2 Corinthians 11:1–6; 1 Timothy 1:3–7; 2 Timothy 4:3–5; 2 Peter 2:1–3

LESSON IN A SENTENCE: Although the world may claim many different ways to finding and knowing God, Jesus is the one true way.

THE BIG PICTURE (OR WHAT YOU'RE TRYING TO GET ACROSS):

In secular culture today it is popular to be tolerant. People advocate a tolerance that suggests all religions are equally valid. It is suggested by many that it is no different if one worships Allah, Buddha, Hare Krishna, or Jesus Christ. However, Jesus never presented Himself as one option among a multitude of spiritual leaders. The focus of this lesson is to help students recognize a cult. It is not meant to degrade any group of people or religious groups. Instead, it is to make students aware of groups of people that gather around and follow a specific person or that person's misinterpretation of the Bible. This lesson is to help students recognize when people or belief systems contain major deviations from historic Christianity and the Bible.

IN THIS LESSON STUDENTS SHOULD:

- Be able to define what is considered a cult.
- Discover what the Bible says about false teaching and deceptive philosophies.
- Begin determining whether their belief system is based on biblical Christianity.

STUFF YOU NEED:

- Masking tape
- Playing cards
- Radio
- Cotton balls

○ 12 poster boards
○ Markers
○ Paper
○ Pens

FOCUS

Choose either Option 1 or 2. Be certain to watch your time and not get carried away with this part of the lesson.

OPTION 1: Junior High

Before the lesson, use masking tape to divide your classroom into four sections. Designate the areas as hearts, diamonds, clubs, or spades. As students arrive give them one card. Explain that all students are to stay within their team's area and only talk to the people who have the same type card. However, secretly explain to those with hearts that they are to move around and try to convince students from other teams with different playing cards to join them in the heart section. Continue playing until all students have arrived and had a chance to play the game.

State: The hearts were assigned to try and get others to join their team. Just like it was difficult for them to get you to move to their team, it is hard for us to convince people with a different worldview or religious background to leave their way behind to follow Jesus as a Christian. Today we will look more at the difference in biblical Christianity and other belief systems.

OPTION 2: High School

Before the lesson, review your local radio stations and the types of music they play, and create a list to use in this activity. As students arrive arrange them into two teams. Explain that you are going to scan through the radio stations, staying on each station for about 2 seconds. The teams are to guess the type of music represented. For example, Top 40, rock, country, jazz, talk radio, Christian, and so forth. The first team to give the correct answer gets 100 points. Enlist a student or another volunteer to keep score. Scan through at least 8–12 radio stations if possible. Announcing the winning team and then add: It takes only a few seconds for most of us to recognize and identify different types of music on the radio. Our ears are trained to recognize the various musical styles and we are quick to stop scanning when we find the style we like best. Unfortunately, most of us do not have the same ability when it comes to recognizing information that does not line up with biblical Christianity. Sometimes we are able to recognize false information and untruth and sometimes we are not. God wants us to know Him so well, to know the truth about Jesus and the Bible, that we will be able to recognize false and wrong information quickly before it becomes part of our belief system.

DISCOVERY

Create four teams. Assign each team one of the following passages: 2 Corinthians 11:1–6; 1 Timothy 1:3–7; 2 Timothy 4:3–5; or 2 Peter 2:1–3. Instruct teams to read their Scripture and then plan a way to creatively present it to the large group. Teams may act out the Scripture, use drawing and symbols, write a song, and so forth to creatively present their Scripture. Set a time limit and then when teams complete their assignments, allow them to share their presentations. Discuss their findings and use the following questions as a guide:

In 2 Corinthians 11:1–6, how is Paul's servant-attitude being distorted by the false apostles?

How is Jesus distorted by their message?

1) In 1 Timothy 1:3–7 what were some of the problems plaguing the church?

2) How do you think Timothy felt being left in charge of a situation like this?

3) In 2 Timothy 4:3–5, what does it tell us about some people's beliefs?

4) What is our challenge when we hear false teachers and information?

5) In 2 Peter 2:1–3, what does Peter say about false teachers?

6) Why do people follow false teachers and become involved in cults?

What is a cult?

Explain that a cult is defined as a "system of religious beliefs and rituals" or a religion considered "unorthodox, extremist, or false." Also, a cult is defined as a "great devotion to a person, idea, object, or movement." [Source: www.merriam-webster.com and www.dictionary.reference.com] Point out students will face many different people and belief systems during their lifetime. Sometimes those belief systems will be confusing to you or cause you to doubt your faith.

Create a large square on the floor using masking tape. Create two more lines to divide the square into four equal parts (like a game of four-square). Lead students to form their four teams again. Scatter cotton balls evenly in each quarter of the square. At your signal, instruct each team to blow the cotton balls out of their square and into another. After about one minute, stop the activity and have students look at the cotton balls on the squares. *Continue:* Look where the cotton balls landed. Although you blew away some, you still have cotton balls in your team square. Doubts and questions in the Christian life will often be like the cotton balls. You get rid of some only to find you have more that took their place. Instead of becoming discouraged by the things you do not understand, try to focus on the things you do understand. When learning about cults or even hearing someone talk about their beliefs which differ from yours, keep your focus on the things you understand about biblical Christianity and Jesus. Call on a volunteer to read John 14:6 aloud. Remind students that Jesus was specific in saying He was the only way to the Father. Today's lesson will compare other beliefs against that truth from Scripture.

Teacher's Note This lesson is not the time to debate the accuracy of the Bible, whether or not students believe the Bible, and so forth. If students begin those types of questions and/or statements, explain that in this lesson you will take at face value Jesus' statement in John 14:6 and compare other information to biblical Christianity. Remind students that you are available to discuss this information and differing viewpoints with them at another time one-on-one or in a small group. Also, if possible have additional resources, books, pamphlets, websites, etc. available for students to do further research.

LIFE APPLICATION: Write Jehovah's Witness, Mormon, Unification Church, Islam, Hinduism, Baha'i World Faith, Hare Krishna, Buddhism, Transcendental Meditation, Scientology, Wicca, and New Age on twelve different posters and place them throughout the room with markers at each one. Direct students to walk around to each poster and to write down things they know about each of the different cults and religions. When students complete the posters, review what each one says about the following:

1) What is this cult or religion's source of authority?
2) Who or what do they consider God?
3) Who is Jesus to them?
4) Who is the Holy Spirit or do they acknowledge the Holy Spirit?
5) What happens according to this belief system after death?
6) How does a person get into heaven based on their beliefs?

Say: The key question we want to explore is: how do these beliefs differ and/or compare with biblical Christianity? Use the following information to help answer the questions above based on biblical Christianity:

Biblical Christianity says the Bible, both Old and New Testaments, is to be our source of authority. God is Triune—that means one God in three Persons, not three gods; Father, Son, and Holy Spirit. Sometimes this can best be explained by thinking of an egg—there is the egg yoke, egg white, and the egg shell. All three create the egg.

Biblical Christianity also says Jesus is God the Son. He is fully God and fully man. Jesus is the only way to the Father, salvation, and eternal life. The Holy Spirit is the third person of the Trinity. He comforts, guides, teaches, and fills Christians. After death believers go to be with Jesus. Jesus' bodily resurrection guarantees believers they will be resurrected and receive new immortal bodies. Those who are not believers will suffer the torment of eternal separation from God. To get into heaven one must believe Jesus died on the Cross for their sins and physically rose again. This is the way sinful people are forgiven by God. This salvation is by God's grace, not by doing good works.

MAKING IT PERSONAL: Remind students they do not need to know every detail about every other cult or religion in the world. When they hear different information that contrasts with biblical Christianity, encourage them to ask the person one or more of these questions:

1) What do you mean by that?

2) Where did you get your information?

3) How do you know that is true?

4) What happens if you are wrong?

Explain that sometimes people are only repeating what they have heard or been taught. They may not be aware of the inconsistencies or untruths that relate to that belief system or cult. Encourage students to always compare information they are given with the Bible. Sometimes information given out by cults may sound like it is a quote from the Bible when in fact they have distorted the Scripture.

Distribute paper and pens to students. Ask students to write out their beliefs on the sheet of paper. Challenge them to include any Scripture references that support their beliefs. Encourage students who do not have much to write down, to begin questioning and digging deeper as they study the Bible and learn in Bible studies like this one. Close in prayer asking God to help students continue to evaluate their belief system this week. Pray students will begin to recognize any deception or false information they are receiving from others.

One Way (Cults)—Midweek

MEMORY VERSE: Jesus answered, "I am the way and the truth and the life. The only way to the Father is through me'"—John 14:6 (NCV)

SCRIPTURE: Colossians 2:6–8

LESSON IN A SENTENCE: God wants us to receive and follow Jesus, not deceptive philosophies and false teachings.

FOCUS

Ask students if there is anyone who would like to try juggling three tennis balls. Allow students to show off any juggling talent. Then group students in teams of six or more. Ask each team to form a circle and explain they will do group juggling. Give them one tennis ball and instruct them to toss the ball underhanded within their circle. Ask them to establish a pattern so that each person in the group receives the ball only once. The ball cannot be tossed to the person on their immediate right or left. Allow the teams to practice their pattern several times. Once the teams feel they have established a juggling pattern, add in two more balls.

Discuss these questions after team juggling:

1. How well did your juggling team do and why?
2. What did you have to watch and pay attention to as you did the team juggling?
3) What are some ways we watch out for one another as a group?

Explain that God wants students and churches to watch out for one another and take care of one another. One of the ways we can do that is to be aware of any deception or false teaching we hear or are exposed to in our community or wherever. Just like we worked together to do the team juggling, God wants us to work together to build one another up and stay connected to Him. And He wants us to encourage each other and hold one another accountable as we stay connected to Him and avoid false teachings.

DISCOVERY

Call on a volunteer to read Colossians 2:6–8 aloud. Distribute paper and pens to students. Ask students to write Colossians 2:8 in their own words. Allow volunteers to share their translations. Discuss the following questions:

1) As you look at Colossians 2:6–8, what words or phrases mean the most to you?

2) What warning is this passage giving us?

3) What deceptive philosophies or false teaching have you heard this week?

4) How did you respond to that false information?

5) How are you displaying to others John 14:6—that Jesus is the way, the truth, and the life?

LIFE APPLICATION: Remind students of the cult study on Sunday. Discover how many students were exposed to those belief systems during the week thus far. Call on students to share additional information they learned about the different belief systems that contrasted with biblical Christianity. Instruct students to find a partner to participate in a role-play. Explain that one person is supposed to be a cult member and the other person is to share biblical Christianity with the cult member. The student who is the cult member may choose any belief system that opposes biblical Christianity. Allow students to practice sharing their beliefs and faith with one another through this process. Be sure students role-play in both positions. Discuss the importance of setting a good example of kindness and acceptance to people of other belief systems. Explain that one does not need to believe the same way or accept their beliefs in any way; however, it is important to begin a relationship with that person if we ever want to be able to share our faith with them. Close in prayer. Allow students to share the first names of people they know who are being led astray or deceived by a cult or false belief system. Pray specifically by name for these people. Continue to encourage students to share their faith with their friends during the week and to invite them to church.

PRACTICAL HELP FOR REACHING THE

GIRLS IN YOUR YOUTH MINISTRY

By Whitney Prosperi
WRITER/AUTHOR

If your youth group is like most in the country, more than half the members are females. For some this may be good news, while others find it a challenge. If you're a man in youth ministry—or a woman for that matter—how do you effectively reach and minister to the growing number of girls in today's youth group?

Years ago, when the concept of youth ministry was just in infancy, designating someone to minister to youth was novel and hip. Today many churches not only recognize this need, they have equipped someone to serve in this vital ministry. But the idea of lumping all youth together, female and male, and assuming they have the same needs and interests, is past. Today's youth face unprecedented challenges and unique sets of temptations. Is there a way to minister to both males and females while also focusing on the distinctive needs of each? While I agree that males are equally important, in the following we'll look at some creative ways to reach the females in a youth group.

Girls' Council

A friend in youth ministry thought of this idea. At a sleepover with the girls in her youth group, she cast the vision for a girls' council that would represent the girls as a whole. She let the females in the youth group nominate and vote for the council, stressing that it wasn't a popularity contest, but a serious spiritual responsibility. She allowed for a certain number of girls per grade, which was determined by the size of her youth group. The girls would serve on the council for a year and be held to a certain standard of behavior that they agreed upon beforehand.

If you're a male, you will want to designate a female to meet with the council and then keep you updated. If you're a female, this will actually be a perfect vehicle for discipling a small group of young women. The council can meet weekly for prayer, accountability, and planning. Not only is there a serious level of discipleship taking place, but it also allows for the person in charge to get a "pulse" on the girls in the youth group. It trains girls for leadership and shows them that there is a lot more to ministry than what people see. By taking part in planning and praying for events, they will take ownership of their youth group and learn about ministry. This council will be helpful in evaluating whether the programs in your youth ministry are meeting girls where they are. It will also give you a female perspective with which to bounce off ideas.

Mentoring

As you know, you can't meet with every student on a personal level on a regular basis. There is not and never will be enough time. This is exactly why you need to equip other capable, godly adults to pour into the lives of your students. Why not train others who will serve as mentors to the young women in your youth group? You may want to appeal to the youth volunteers and Sunday school teachers in your ministry. Another good place to find mentors is in the adult Sunday school classes. There may be some older "empty nesters" just looking for a place to invest. Or there may be singles or college students in your church who have the time and energy to pour into a student's life. As with all volunteers, you will want to screen them properly and thoroughly. Pray over your list of qualifications and then start asking around.

You will want to lay out the exact specifications and purpose of these mentoring relationships before kicking off your program. Clearly lay out your expectations before your mentors. Do you want them to go through a Bible study or book with the student? Do you want them to simply meet for friendship and prayer? Will they serve together in some capacity?

Next match up students who are interested in being mentored, with trained mentors. You may want to have a party where the mentor and student meet. Plan some things that will help conversation start in a relaxed atmosphere. You will probably want to meet with your mentors on a semi-regular basis for feedback and updates. While some of these relationships may just be for this season of a student's life, others could last a lifetime.

Girls only, please

Depending on your gender, you may never have had the experience of attending a sleepover for girls. If you have, you know one thing—girls are different when there are no boys around. They are much less guarded and more themselves. They are more apt to let you "in." For this reason it's important that every now and then you plan something just for the girls in your youth group. If you're a guy, you may want to ask a sturdy volunteer with a heart for young women to be the point person for these events. Chances are she'll look forward to this time with just the girls, listening to them and learning more about who they are.

Don't panic! This doesn't have to be the infamous sleepover or even an elaborate event. Just make sure it's something that appeals to girls and that allows for conversations to happen. For this reason, a movie may not be the best choice. Some ideas would be nights out at a fun restaurant, dinner at a volunteer's house, serving together, outdoor activities and sports, or playing games. Or you could even plan a small retreat at a house, campsite, or hotel. This could be a night for not only building relationships; it could provide a time away from the distraction of boys where girls could hear from God's Word and worship. You could ask someone to share a talk on an issue that relates especially to girls, and could even ask local businesses to donate some supplies or gift bags for the event.

Every time you plan an event for just the girls, it does two things. It shows them that they are valuable to the ministry and, more importantly, to God. Next, it gives them an opportunity to deepen relationships with each other, older godly females and with the Lord. A "girls only" event could even be a point of life-change for some girls in your youth ministry. You never know.

Girl Groups

Girls love to talk, as we all know. They love to share ideas and hear from each other. Why not capitalize on this and start some groups within your youth ministry? You may want to offer girls a Bible study, accountability group, service group, or even a support group led by a professional in your church. Ask God to provide the leadership for these groups and then offer the girls some choices. Some may want to go through a particular book or simply meet to pray for their campuses.

Whatever you do, don't try to lead all of these groups. In fact, you probably won't want to lead one at all. You may simply want to meet with the leaders and provide curriculum choices, prayer support, and encouragement. You will also want to drop in on these groups once in a while to show your support for the leader and hear what the girls are sharing.

As you know, girls love relationships and community. By providing girls' groups, you are offering them a way to get these needs met, while also growing in their walk with Jesus. These groups may even prove to be a vital tool for outreach, since girls may feel more comfortable asking their friends to come to a Bible study or support group that meets at a house rather than a church building.

Equipping others

Obviously if you are a man, it would be a good idea to pass on some of these ideas to a trusted woman who will help you minister to the girls in your youth group. As you know, if you're a male you must be cautious to not be alone with girls or be too involved in their issues. It's absolutely vital that you find someone to help you reach girls and counsel them. It is protection for you, and of course beneficial for the females in your youth group. Start to pray that God will bring you godly women who will partner with you in ministry. Find ways to equip these women to minister to the girls in your youth group, and then watch Him do more than you can ask or imagine.

MARCH 12, 2006

To Be or Not to Be...
In Community

By Amy Jacober

MEMORY VERSE:
Do not merely look out for your own personal interests, but also for the interests of others.—Philippians 2:4 (NASB)

SCRIPTURE: Acts 4:32–37

LESSON IN A SENTENCE: We are a communal people.

THE BIG PICTURE (OR WHAT YOU'RE TRYING TO GET ACROSS):

God never intended that any person walk this life alone. While different personalities require different amounts of interaction, we all need one another. Sometimes this is for pragmatic help, sometimes just for fun! Many of our students, many of us for that matter, can be surrounded by people all of the time and still feel lonely. God offers the model for community within the Triune Godhead. We were made to be with one another. Faith, in recent years, has come to be thought of and discussed as a private matter. Scripture talks of praying in a closet so as not to boast, but more frequently it says to find others, to share your beliefs, to build relationships. Our faith is to be worked out by the way we live, and the way we live is to be in community.

IN THIS LESSON STUDENTS SHOULD:

- Consider the idea of Christian community.
- Discuss the connection between possessions, money and community.
- Be encouraged to live a life generous with the abundance with which they've been blessed.
- Recognize that we all are needy at times.

STUFF YOU NEED:

- 3 x 5 cards, cut in half (Option 1)
- Markers
- Toilet paper (Option 2)

○ Small prize for winning team (Option 2)
○ Poster board
○ Tape

FOCUS

OPTION 1:

Give each student ten cards (cut 3 x 5 cards in half to be 2½ x 3). Tell them to write their ten most valuable possessions on each, but not to show them to anyone else. Talk them through the following sequence.

Discard two into the center of the group. (If you have a large group, have them break into groups of 6–10.)

Give two to the person on their left.

Trade three with the person across from them.

Discard one.

Have the person on your right, draw a card from your hand and discard it.

Have the person on your left, draw a card from your hand and discard it.

Look at the remaining five cards in your hand. Set aside what you would consider to be the most valuable possession remaining.

Ask if they would rather sell or give up the four remaining in their hand for the good of the group or their one most valuable possession.

Have them discuss what they would choose and why this would or would not be difficult.

OPTION 2:

Break into two teams, large teams are just fine! Line up across a room or if you need more space, go outside to a field or a safe spot in the parking lot. Line up each team facing one way where you can put your hands on the shoulders of the person in front of you. This is just to get you lined up the correct way, you needn't keep your hands on one another's shoulders. Give each team a roll of toilet paper. Be certain to have extra rolls on hand for when there is a break in the paper. Have an over-under relay where the first person hangs onto the end of the paper and passes it over his head to the person behind. The next person passes it under her legs to the person behind and so on. Once you get to the end of the line, send the paper back to the front. Go back and forth until the entire roll is gone! If the paper breaks during one of the passes, the game starts all over. Offer the team that wins a small prize to celebrate their unity in working together!

Teacher's Note: Some areas are more affluent than others. While we all own something, if you are in an area or working with a group and know that possessions are sparse, be sensitive if you choose this option. You may want to lower the number to five cards or discuss what we do have to offer if not money or material goods.

DISCOVERY

Ask: What if you were given everything you ever needed? How would this change your life?

Break your teams into smaller groups to read through the Scripture.

Tell each smaller group that they are to be a part of a marketing team. Give them a posterboard and markers. Their ad campaign is to revolve around the following passage, Acts 4:32–37.

Have each team take turns presenting their poster. Tape these up around the room.

LIFE APPLICATION: *Ask:* What things are easy to share?

Verse 32 says that the people were united, of one mind. They were so united in fact that they considered all they had to be for the common good. This is a really hard way to live, even for the most generous of people. Discuss whether you think it still means this literally today or not.

Verse 34 says that there was no needy person among them. Discuss what the world would be like if there was no one left needy.

Ask: Do you think it would be comforting to know that if you ever found yourself in need, that you would be cared for? How would you ensure that no one took advantage of this system? Would you ever be tempted to take advantage of it?

Discuss who you think are the needy of the world right now.

MAKING IT PERSONAL: *Say:* We all have more than we realize. Likewise, we all need other people more than we like to admit. Living on either extreme does not honor God nor help to build community. Even Jesus asked for water when He was thirsty.

In pairs, take a few moments to consider where you are blessed and where you have need. Pray for one another that God may show you specifically a way that you can offer what you have to better the community. Pray also that you are open enough to ask for help when you need it.

SERVICE OPTION: You just spent time a few weeks ago looking at issues of materialism and poverty. Some of you may have even participated in the 30 Hour Famine. Caring for others is certainly helped by events. It is, however, more than that; it is a lifestyle. Consider finding a way to build up your immediate community on an ongoing basis. This may be by taking a monthly rotation serving at the emergency shelter, writing letters to missionaries, or tutoring at the local grade school. This needn't be costly—give from what you genuinely have to offer.

SONG: "Raised in Harlem" by Hero on the CD *Hip Hop 2005*

QUOTABLE   QUOTES :

This is the duty of our generation as we enter the twenty-first century—solidarity with the weak, the persecuted, the lonely, the sick, and those in despair. It is expressed by the desire to give a noble and humanizing meaning to a community in which all members will define themselves not by their own identity, but by that of others.

—Elie Wiesel

Rain does not fall on one roof alone.

—Cameroonian Proverb

To Be or Not to Be...

In Community—Midweek

MEMORY VERSE:
Do not merely look out for your own personal interests, but also for the interests of others.—Philippians 2:4 (NASB)

SCRIPTURE: Matthew 22:34–40

LESSON IN A SENTENCE: We are a communal people.

FOCUS

Bigger than/Smaller than
Divide into two teams. Have each team create a list of ten items. Write next to each item if it is a *what*, a *where* or a *who*. Assign a keeper of the list for each team. Each team will send one person to the keeper of the list, to be told the item they must describe and try to get their team to guess. They may not use the actual word nor any word using that word. To make things a little more interesting, the clue is only able to be delivered in a statement saying: It is bigger than——and smaller than——. For example, if the item is the Eiffel Tower: It is bigger than a croissant and smaller than the Empire State Building. It is bigger than a tree and smaller than France. Award the winner by timing each turn and adding the cumulative time, rewarding the lowest time. Alternatively, give each group two minutes to guess and award a point for each item they are able to guess.

We tend to live much of our life this way. Looking for what is bigger than what we currently have, and avoiding what is less than or smaller. Jesus is quite clear on what He considers to be the biggest when it comes to commandments.

Ask: What commandment do you think He considers to be the greatest?

DISCOVERY

In teams of four, read Matthew 22:34–40. Ask them to discuss what stood out to them.

While they are reading, write the following questions on a dry erase board.

Why were the Pharisees asking questions of Jesus? (They were trying to trap Him. You may want to point out times when we try to trap or outsmart God.)

What does it mean to love God with all your heart, mind, and soul? Is it possible to love someone with only one or the other of these?

What does it mean to love your neighbor as yourself?

This passage is certainly about loving God, but it is also about loving each other, not to mention ourselves. We are often encouraged to sacrifice all that we have for the sake of others. Christians are taught to consider themselves as nothing in order to elevate others. This is not at all what Jesus said. In fact, He said it was one of the greatest commandments to love others as you love yourself.

Have you ever thought that taking care of yourself actually helps you to be in a healthy place to care for others? We do need to be careful to not be selfish and only look out for ourselves, but neither are we called to ignore ourselves. It's a little like the oxygen masks that you hear about every time you fly. If you are flying with a child, you are instructed that you must put on your mask first. If you don't take care of yourself, you may not be able to take care of either of you. This passage is a little like that—as you love yourself, you are able to love others.

LIFE APPLICATION: Finding the balance between arrogance and self-loathing can be more difficult than most like to admit, especially in the adolescent years. Even students who come across like they have it all together have doubts, and things about themselves they simply do not like. God does not want us to think too highly of ourselves. The flip side of that coin is that it is not His desire that we dislike or hate ourselves, either. As we experience His love, we are able to love ourselves and others.

Give each student a penny.

Say: Arrogance and self-deprecation are two sides of the same coin, this however is not the coin God wants us to have. The other side of a healthy love for self is love for others. This is not only what God desires, but what He commands. Take this coin and put it in your pocket. Let this be a reminder of the healthy balance God requires.

MARCH 19, 2006

Truth and Consequences

By Michelle Hicks

MEMORY VERSE:
For the wages of sin is death, but the gift of God is eternal life in Christ Jesus our Lord.—Romans 6:23 (NIV)

SCRIPTURE: Ecclesiastes 7:20; Romans 6:20–23; Romans 10:9–10; Ephesians 2:1–5; 1 John 2:15–17; Romans 6:1–2

LESSON IN A SENTENCE: Sin will bring spiritual death to the person who does not ultimately come under the lordship of Jesus.

THE BIG PICTURE (OR WHAT YOU'RE TRYING TO GET ACROSS):
Although we don't always want to admit it, we all sin. We all do things that disobey God and His plan for our lives. We make mistakes, accidentally and/or intentionally, that hurt our relationship with God and with other people. Even though we may classify some sins as worse than others, God views sin equally. God sees sin as sin. The result of this sin in our lives is eternal death and separation from God. However, the good news is that through God's grace, He has provided a way for us so that we do not eternally suffer the consequences of our sin. That way is by believing Jesus died on the Cross for one's sins and receiving the gift of eternal life by living and trusting Jesus as one's Savior and Lord.

IN THIS LESSON STUDENTS SHOULD:

○ Be able to define and explain sin and the consequences of sin.
○ Identify excuses we make for the sin in our lives.
○ Begin to recognize and take responsibility for the sin in our lives and the consequences of that sin.

STUFF YOU NEED:

○ Masking tape
○ Chalkboard
○ Poster board and markers
○ 3 x 5 cards
○ Pencils/pens

FOCUS

Choose either Option 1 or 2. Be certain to watch your time and stay on track during this part of the lesson.

OPTION 1: Junior High

Ask all the boys to stand in a single file, shoulder to shoulder, and link arms at the elbow. Arrange the girls into two teams. Explain that the girls will play a game of tug-of-war, except instead of pulling a rope they will pull the line of guys. At your signal, start the game. Depending upon how long it takes the girls to pull the boys apart, you may want to play the best of two out of three games. After completing the tug-of-war games, call the group together in a circle. Discuss how the guys felt being pulled in two different directions. Allow the girls to share how they felt, knowing they needed to pull one way to win but instead they were being pulled in the opposite direction. Allow students to respond. Point out that just like a game of tug-of-war, we sometimes feel like we are being pulled in different directions. Sometimes we are pulled when we are trying to decide between right and wrong. Also, many times we are struggling between what we know God wants us to do, and our own selfish desires. Depending upon our choices, we will face consequences to our actions.

OPTION 2: For Active, Physical Learners

In advance, use masking tape to create a target on the floor of the room. In the bull's eye circle, in the center, spell out the word "sin" with masking tape. Make sure you have at least two outer circles building upon the bull's eye.

As students arrive, explain that this lesson is on sin and the consequences of sin. However, before getting into the main portion of the lesson, explain that you want students to rate various sins. Point to the center or bull's eye of the target and explain that this center circle represents the worst sin possible. The other circles that come out from the target represent different degrees of sin. The farther you are from the bull's eye, the lesser the sin. Direct students to stand outside the target and then move inward according to the level of sin from the statements you read aloud. Read from the following list or make up statements of your own:

Writing answers on your hand for a test.

Running a yellow light in your car.

Spreading rumors about someone though you know the information is false.

Lying to your parents to keep yourself out of trouble.

Taking money from your family members' purses or wallets.

Robbing a bank.

Running a yellow light and hitting and killing someone on a bike.

Spreading harmful information about someone even when the info is true.

Hiding the truth about a painful past experience.

Driving over the speed limit.

Ask: Is driving over the speed limit a sin? Does it make a difference if you drive 5 miles over or 25 miles over the limit? *State:* Although we may rate some sin or breaking of the law worse than others, according to God's standards, all sin is sin. God views all sin equally. We may have differing opinions on what is right and wrong, but God's standard is the only true and unchanging way to live. Let's discover more about sin and the consequences of sin in our lesson today.

DISCOVERY

Ask: What is sin? Allow students to respond and then explain that sin is any attitude or action that disobeys God. Sin is missing the mark of God's will by choices we make and because of our own human weakness. Direct students to form five groups. Assign each group one of the following passages to read, and then present to the group what it says about sin: Ecclesiastes 7:20; Romans 6:20–23; Romans 10:9–10; Ephesians 2:1–5; 1 John 2:15–17. After groups study the Scripture and then present their information on sin, direct their attention to a chalkboard or poster board with the following questions:

1) Why are we unable to do the right thing all the time?

2) What are our two choices as sinners?

3) How can we be released from sin?

4) What does it mean to be dead in our sins?

5) Why do Christians need to reject the world's values?

Say: These verses and how we answered some of the questions confirms we are all sinners. We all have done things that disobey God and what He wants for our lives. However, God wants us to turn from that sin and trust Him. He wants us to have the best life possible and to do what it takes so we do not continue to sin and suffer the consequences of that sin. Many people continue to sin even after they are believers, because they do not believe that a loving God would really punish them. But in Romans 6:1–2 God lets us know He does not want us to make excuses for our sin. Call on a student to read aloud Romans 6:1–2. Explain that Paul says God's great grace is not an excuse for us to keep on sinning. His grace and forgiveness does cover our sin, but only if we ask for that grace and forgiveness and then turn away from sin.

LIFE APPLICATION: On poster board, make a list of the common excuses people use to justify or explain their sin. Remind students that no matter how many excuses we make for our sin and no matter how good those excuses sound, the fact remains that our sin is still disobedience to God. Distribute 3 x 5 cards, one per student. Encourage students to write or draw symbols to represent present sin in their lives that they need to address. Once again explain that sin is any actions or attitudes that are disobedient to God. Ask students to reflect on the excuses they have made to justify these sins.

Say: We all must make the choice, whether we will continue to live with sin in our lives or live a life obedient to Christ.

MAKING IT PERSONAL: *State:* There will always be consequences to our sin. For Christians and non-Christians there are consequences for actions and attitudes that disobey God. There are different steps we can take to claim responsibility for our sin. List the following steps on a chalkboard or poster board.

1) Admit to God and yourself that you are a sinner.

2) Believe Jesus died for you to provide forgiveness for your sins.

3) With your words and actions, live placing complete trust in Jesus as your Lord and Savior.

4) Decide that you are dead to your sins because Christ died for them.

5) Take responsibility for the present sin in your life and eliminate it.

6) Correct any hurt relationships or other problems your sin has caused.

7) Be a part of an accountability group and pray for one another.

Ask: What do you need to do to accept responsibility for your sins and their consequences? Direct each student to take a few moments reflecting on this. Close in prayer asking God to help students to begin or continue living obediently to His laws and His ways.

Teacher's Note: Be sensitive to students who do not seem to understand the concept of sin. Be available to talk with students who have questions about their relationship with Christ.

QUOTABLE QUOTES:

Forgiveness is the final form of love.
                    —Reinhold Niebuhr [www.brainyquote.com]

Truth and Consequences—Midweek

MEMORY VERSE:
For the wages of sin is death, but the gift of God is eternal life in Christ Jesus our Lord.—Romans 6:23 (NIV)

SCRIPTURE: Romans 6:15–18

LESSON IN A SENTENCE: We can be set free from sin as we follow and obey God daily.

FOCUS

Before the session, make a huge mess in the room. Throw paper on the floor, turn over chairs, and so forth. As students arrive don't say anything about the room and do not give instructions for them to clean up the mess. Instruct students to write on a large sheet of paper placed on the floor in the center of the room the things that most hinder them and distract them from living the way God wants them to live. Observe the students (if anyone) who take the initiative and begin cleaning up the room. After ample time, call the group together. Review their list and then point out the mess around the room.

Ask: How many of you were distracted by the mess in the room? Why did it bother you? Explain that like the messy room, we are surrounded by things that try to hinder and distract us from focusing on God and what He wants us to do. Point out the students who chose to clean up the room instead of writing their answers on the paper.

Say: If we are not focused and slaves to God, we can easily become slaves to the things that surround us and demand our time. We will constantly be surrounded by people who are involved in sin or doing things that disobey what God wants for them. God wants us to learn to be set free from sin and the distractions that hinder us from following and obeying God daily.

DISCOVERY

In pairs, read Romans 6:15–18 and answer the following questions:
1) If Paul were around today, what would he say we were slaves to?
2) What is the result of slavery to sin?

3) What are our choices when it comes to serving and being slaves?

4) What are the benefits of being a slave to God?

5) What do you think or how do you feel about being a slave to God?

LIFE APPLICATION: Remind students of the lesson on Sunday. Explain that although it sometimes may be difficult to choose between right and wrong, often we know the difference and simply refuse to make the right choice. Our selfishness and slavery to sin overrides our desire and willingness to obey God and be a slave to righteousness. In those situations we will eventually pay or experience the consequences of our sin.

Display a bag of unpopped microwave popcorn. Explain that when we sin and are slaves to sin, we often are like the bag of popcorn. Nothing happens to us so we think that the sin is maybe not so bad after all. What really happens is that our sin simply stays packaged away for a while. Display a bag of popped microwave popcorn.

State: Eventually our sin grows bigger and bigger and we cannot avoid the consequences. Although we may try to make excuses, our sins have taken over. Our sin is unmanageable and we can see that we are slaves to sin. As we learned in our lesson on Sunday, God wants us to recognize our sin and take responsibility for it. He wants us to ask and receive His forgiveness and learn how to live as slaves to righteousness so that sin does not control us any longer.

Invite students to join you in a "popcorn" prayer. Ask students to share one word or thought related to the lesson on sin and its consequences. They may choose to voice words such as "grace," "thankful," "forgiveness," or share words related to sin they need to turn from to reconcile their relationship with God. After the prayer, be available to those students who may want to talk more about the consequences they are dealing with because of past mistakes and sin in their lives.

CONNECTIONS: There are many Scriptures that relate to sin. As you focus on sin and the consequences of sin, be sure to give equal time and balance to the great grace and forgiveness of God. Here are some additional Scriptures you may choose to have students look up and read, or give them a list to take home and read during the week: Numbers 32:23; Psalm 51:2; Psalm 119:11; Isaiah 1:18; Matthew 1:21; Luke 11:4; John 1:29; Romans 3:23; Romans 6:23; 2 Corinthians 5:21; 1 John 1:9.

Clean and Clear

By Sharon Koh

MEMORY VERSE:
For the Word of God is living and active. Sharper than any double-edged sword, it penetrates even to dividing soul and spirit, joints and marrow; it judges the thoughts and attitudes of the heart. Nothing in all creation is hidden from God's sight. Everything is uncovered and laid bare before the eyes of him to whom we must give account.
—Hebrews 4:12, 13 (NIV)

SCRIPTURE: Ezekiel 2:8—3:3

LESSON IN A SENTENCE: The Bible is God's precious Word—a gift—given so that our lives might be changed forever if we internalize it.

THE BIG PICTURE (OR WHAT YOU'RE TRYING TO GET ACROSS):
   Many Christians today take the Bible for granted because it is so readily available. However, at a time when the Bible was not in print and available in every hotel room and bookstore, the Word of God had to be spoken through the prophets by His Spirit. It is at these times of genuine encounter with the Word that we find ourselves unable to stay the same anymore.

IN THIS LESSON STUDENTS SHOULD:

- Recognize that the Word of God is something to be treasured and taken very seriously. The reason that God does not speak through the prophets as much in our day is that His Word is now available in the Scriptures for all to access.
- Identify the Word of God as something to be internalized and studied thoroughly.

STUFF YOU NEED:

- Laundry detergent
- Laundry softener
- Water
- Transparent container

FOCUS

This simple demonstration illustrates the work of the Word of God in our lives.

Fill the container with water.

Pour a little detergent in and mix until bubbles form on the surface of the water and it appears cloudy. *Say:* "This container represents our minds. The cloudiness is representative of our thoughts."

Hold an equal portion of softener over the container, and say: "This represents the Word of God. Notice how it affects our lives."

Pour and mix. (Water should clear up—suds and cloudiness disappear.)

Say: "We are *cleansed* by the Word."

DISCOVERY

Read Ezekiel 2:8—3:3

God gives Ezekiel unusual instructions. What does He ask Ezekiel to do?

What does Ezekiel's consumption of the scroll represent? Why did it taste "sweet as honey" to him?

LIFE APPLICATION: Get into smaller groups and discuss the factors that make it difficult to study the Word of God. "Difficult to understand"? "Boring"? "Dry"?

What are some ways that one can address these difficulties?

Teacher's Note: This is a difficult lesson to teach because one can only *talk* about the Word of God changing and cleansing lives so much before students feel like they've already heard all that we have to say. The key is to use this lesson as an introduction to more in-depth study of the Bible. Most of the time, if one approaches the Scriptures asking the Holy Spirit to reveal and to speak through the *living* Word of God, He will. Other times, it is simply a discipline that we must undertake out of appreciation for this gift that God has made available to us. These are the two points that you want to make clear, either by explicitly saying them or demonstrating them.

MAKING IT PERSONAL: Have you experienced a time when you were listening to or studying the Bible and the words on the pages just seemed so applicable to your life at the time? If so, why?

Have there been other times when reading the Bible just felt empty and dry? When this happens, what is a good way to view these times? What is a good way to deal with them?

If there were any differing characteristics between the ways you read the Bible each time, what were they?

What makes something precious or valuable in our lives? (Cost? Rarity?) What would it take to make the Word of God more precious in your life?

Clean and Clear—Midweek

MEMORY VERSE:
For the Word of God is living and active. Sharper than any double-edged sword, it penetrates even to dividing soul and spirit, joints and marrow; it judges the thoughts and attitudes of the heart. Nothing in all creation is hidden from God's sight. Everything is uncovered and laid bare before the eyes of him to whom we must give account. —Hebrews 4:12, 13 (NIV)

SCRIPTURE: Matthew 24:35

LESSON IN A SENTENCE: The Bible is God's precious Word—a gift—given so that our lives might be changed forever if we internalize it.

FOCUS

Ask the students to share an experience when an authority (teacher? parent?) in their lives has gone back on a promise. For example, has anyone ever experienced a teacher forgetting a quiz or a parent forgetting how long a punishment is in effect? Some of these will be good stories (punishment waived) and others will be not-so-good stories (promises unfilled). Enjoy sharing experiences with one another.

DISCOVERY

Read Matthew 24:35. If you have more time, you may want to read it in the context of Matthew 24. In this chapter, Jesus is speaking of a time to come—when all things will come to an end. It is in *this* chapter that Jesus makes the statement, "Heaven and earth will pass away, but my words will not pass away." How does the framing of this verse (within this chapter) help you reframe the statement?

LIFE APPLICATION: Earlier, we talked about how the Word of God *cleanses* us when we internalize it. With that in mind, how does it feel to know that the Word of God will *never* pass away? What does that tell us about the work that God is doing by changing and redeeming our lives?

APRIL 2, 2006

Authority Figures

By Whitney Prosperi

MEMORY VERSE:
Obey your leaders and act under their authority. They are watching over you, because they are responsible for your souls. Obey them so that they will do this work with joy, not sadness. It will not help you to make their work hard.—Hebrews 13:17 (NCV)

SCRIPTURE: Romans 13:1–7; Colossians 3:22–25

LESSON IN A SENTENCE: Submission to God and the authorities He has placed over us brings the benefits of freedom and joy.

THE BIG PICTURE (OR WHAT YOU'RE TRYING TO GET ACROSS):
God has placed authority figures in our lives to teach us how to obey Him. When we submit to these authorities we are honoring God because the Bible teaches that all authority is from Him. When we disobey our parents, teachers or the "laws of the land" we disobey God and choose sin.

The way students work at their job, talk to their parents, and do their homework is all a part of submitting to authority. Honoring the authorities that God has placed over us brings freedom from the fear of punishment. It also offers joy that comes with obeying God.

IN THIS LESSON STUDENTS SHOULD:

- Identify the authorities God has placed in their lives.
- Evaluate whether or not they honor these authorities.
- Recognize areas where they need to change their actions and attitudes so they can honor authorities God has placed over them.

STUFF YOU NEED:

- Pens/pencils
- 3 x 5 cards
- Chalkboard/chalk or dry erase board and markers

FOCUS

Show students pictures of several convicted felons or notorious people who have broken the law. Ask them to tell you what they have in common. Point out that the thing they all have in common is their disrespect for the authorities God has placed over them.

DISCOVERY

Read Romans 13:1–7 as a whole group. Explain that God has placed authorities in our lives for our protection.

Ask: If there were no authorities what would our world be like: Your town? Your school? Your family?

If there were no authorities, there would be complete anarchy and no one would be safe from anyone else. No one would know the guidelines and deadlines by which we would live. Quite simply, life as we know it would not exist.

Point out that v. 1 teaches that the authorities over us are directly from God. Although we may not like to hear that, it's true. He has placed parents, teachers and government leaders over us for our own good.

Ask: What does v. 2 teach happens when we rebel against the authorities over us?

God gave us our parents to teach us how to obey and submit to Him. When we were young we learned the meaning of "no" and "yes" and experienced consequences for our behavior. This trained us to later respond to God in obedience.

Reread v. 5. What part does conscience play in submitting to authorities?

Read v. 7. To whom do you "owe respect" and "owe honor"? In what ways can you pay what you owe?

Now break students into small groups of 4–7. On a 3 x 5 card, write Colossians 3:22–25 and the following questions. Encourage them to answer these questions among themselves while you go from group to group listening in on some of their answers.

Since we do not have slaves in our modern day culture, how can you translate this to apply to you?

How can you "obey your masters in everything"?

Why is it more important that we obey when no one is watching than when they are?

What can you do "as working for the Lord" in your daily life?

Discuss a time when you received consequences for not submitting to authority. What lesson did you learn?

Teacher's Note: God longs for us to serve Him, not because we fear bad consequences, but because of our sincere devotion to Him. Be sure to stress that while God does punish us for disobedience, He is fully loving and always ready to take us back when we mess up. He longs to restore us to a right relationship with Him and with others in our lives. We never need to fear coming to Him with a repentant and honest heart.

LIFE APPLICATION: Consider our model for submission, Jesus Christ. On a chalkboard or dry erase board make a list of the ways Jesus chose to submit to His Heavenly Father's plan.

Now read Hebrews 12:1–4 as a whole group.

Say: Jesus, although He was God Himself and all-powerful, chose to submit Himself to death on a cross so He could redeem mankind back to Himself.

Ask: How can you model Christ's submission in your own life?

Ask: If we can't submit to the earthly authorities we can see, then how do we expect to submit to God that we can't see?

Choose a student to read Ephesians 6:1–3.

Ask: What promise is given if we obey our parents?

Now read Acts 5:29. This verse tells us that the only way we are to disobey authority is if they ask us to do something that goes against God's Word.

Ask: Can you think of an instance where you would need to go against an authority and it would be the right thing to do?

Say: While this would be a rare occasion, there may be a time in your life when you will need to do this.

MAKING IT PERSONAL: Now hand out an index card to each student. Ask them to make a list of the authority figures that God has placed in their lives. Encourage them to think of as many as possible, even including the principal at their school.

Now ask them to take a few minutes alone and think of ways that they can honor the authorities God has placed over them. Have them write down these tangible actions next to each authority's name.

Now ask students to think of ways they may have disrespected someone who is in authority over them. Encourage them to apologize to that person this week.

Lastly, tell them to think of any role of authority they hope to fill one day. Have them write that down on the back of the card. Remind them that the best leaders are those who submit to the authority over them. Just look at the example of Jesus Christ!

Connections: If you have time, look at some verses that talk about the submission of Christ. Reflect with students on how amazing it is that the God of the Universe humbled Himself to become a lowly man. (Philippians 2:5–8; Hebrews 5:8)

SONGS: "Here I Am to Worship" by Matt Redman

MEMORY VERSE ACTIVITY

Challenge students to write this verse out on a piece of paper they will see everyday. Below the verse ask them to write the name of one authority figure in their life that they want to learn how to submit to better. When they work on their Memory Verse, ask them to pray for their relationship with this person.

Authority Figures—Midweek

MEMORY VERSE:
Obey your leaders and act under their authority. They are watching over you, because they are responsible for your souls. Obey them so that they will do this work with joy, not sadness. It will not help you to make their work hard.—Hebrews 13:17 (NCV)

SCRIPTURE: 1 Peter 2:18

LESSON IN A SENTENCE: Submission to God and the authorities He has placed over us brings the benefits of freedom and joy.

FOCUS

Ask students to define what it means to be submissive in their own words. Have them share different situations where submission is necessary. You may want to start the conversation with sharing the example of a soldier following the orders of his commander. For the survival of the entire company, a soldier must learn to submit to authority. Otherwise he will risk failing in the mission—and possibly endangering his own life and the lives of others. Encourage students to share their ideas with the group and then discuss each of the ideas.

DISCOVERY

In pairs, read 1 Peter 2:18 and answer the following questions.

1) Since we don't have slaves in today's culture, how does this command translate to you personally?

2) Why do you think the passage added the phrase "with all respect"? Is it possible to obey without showing respect?

3) Why do you think we should obey even if we are in an unfair situation?

4) Does this passage teach that we are to be "human doormats"? Explain your answer.

LIFE APPLICATION: Think of the different "masters" in your life. In what ways does showing them respect mean you are really respecting God?

Have you ever been treated unfairly? Maybe it was a call you thought was wrong in competition or a decision your parent made. How did you respond? How do you think Jesus would have responded in the same situation? Spend some time praying that you would choose to honor the authorities in your life the next time something like that happens.

Palm Sunday

By Amy Jacober

MEMORY VERSE:
But Jesus answered, "I tell you, if my followers didn't say these things, then the stones would cry out."—Luke 19:40 (NCV)

SCRIPTURE: Luke 19:28–44

LESSON IN A SENTENCE: Jesus regularly defies what is expected.

THE BIG PICTURE (OR WHAT YOU'RE TRYING TO GET ACROSS):

It is Palm Sunday!! In many churches, today is a day to celebrate, albeit with hesitation. Living on this side of the Cross we know what is coming just a few days after the triumphal entry. Still, we commemorate Jesus riding a donkey into Jerusalem knowing garments and the branches of trees were spread all along His path. Many expected a king to arrive with pomp and circumstance. Jesus chose a donkey. Most people are joyous in the midst of a celebration, especially when they are the one being honored. While Scripture says nothing of Jesus' mood or how He received the attention, it does offer some insight through words commonly attributed to Him. He responds to Pharisees that if His people did not cry out, the rocks would. Unexpected! Even more, as He saw the city, He wept over it and lamented. Most guests of honor enjoy the celebration and at least temporarily suspend sobering words. Not Jesus; His heart and concern overrule any manner of decorum.

IN THIS LESSON STUDENTS SHOULD:

- Hear for the first time or become reacquainted with the triumphal entry.
- Identify reasons they, too, could praise God for miracles.
- Grapple with the idea that if they do not praise, rocks will cry out.
- Learn more of Jesus' concern for people as He laments over the city.

STUFF YOU NEED:

- ○ Large piece of paper
- ○ Tape
- ○ Markers
- ○ Notebook paper
- ○ Pens/pencils
- ○ Rocks (for Memory Verse Activity if you have no rocks nearby)

FOCUS

OPTION 1: Graffiti Wall

Have a large piece of paper taped to a wall where you meet. Have many brightly colored markers on hand. As students arrive, hand each a marker and ask them to write on the graffiti wall at least one thing they either identify as a miracle, or as something really good in their life for which they can praise God. They may need a little help—a miracle needn't be walking on water. It can be as simple as the realization that they woke up this morning breathing! It can be as extreme as a sibling being healed from a serious illness. Nothing is too small or too big. Once they have all had a chance to contribute something, ask if they have spent time praising God for these? If they say no, why not? If they say yes, ask what that means to them?

OPTION 2: Bad Situations?

Break into groups of 3–4. Ask each group to write two or three bad situations. Encourage them to be as creative as possible (and yet still appropriate)! You may need to give a few examples to get them going. This can be anything from trying to dye your own hair and having it turn a horrible color or fall out, to something more serious like finding out that you are seriously ill. After each group is done, have them trade. The new task is to find at least one positive in the midst of that really bad situation. Go around the room and have each group offer their bad situations with the positive (the reason to praise God). These can be as silly as they like!

Say: While it is easy to get caught up in our own worlds and with what seems to be going wrong, there is always a reason to praise God!

DISCOVERY

Ask: Who knows the story of Palm Sunday? Have one or two people re-tell this story to the best of their ability. Once they have told the story, invite them to turn to Scripture for themselves.

Have each of your students turn to Luke 19:28. Ask a strong reader in your group to read Luke 19:28–38.

Jesus' followers believed He was the Messiah for whom they had been waiting. He was to be the King of kings! How would you have expected a king to enter into the city? Read back over this passage. How did Jesus enter? How would this impact what people may have thought of Him?

What expectations do we place on wealthy or prestigious people today? How do we receive them if they do not behave as expected? Do you think you would recognize Jesus if He entered your town today?

Once you have the first part of this passage explained, break into groups of 4–5.

Have each group read Luke 19:39–40.

Ask: What does this mean to you? What do you think happens if you are silent? Is praising God a privilege or a responsibility?

Read Luke 19:41–44.

Ask each group to summarize this in their own words.

Teacher's Note: This section of Scripture is often passed over. Your students may be a bit confused as to what it means, let alone what to do with it. You know your students best! Let their spiritual maturity determine where you spend the most time. While this is a day associated with celebration, reality is that Jesus was on His way to be crucified. This was not hidden to Him, He knew exactly why He was going to Jerusalem and what was about to happen. As your students read the lament of Jesus over Jerusalem, point this detail out. While this passage may seem obscure, it is clear Jesus' heart breaks for the city of Jerusalem. On the way to His own crucifixion, Jesus is still weeping for others.

LIFE APPLICATION: *Whew! For a story that is often familiar, you just covered a whole lot!*

Ask: What are some of the things we can learn today from this story? (You will surely come up with other things and probably many more!)

1) Jesus does not come as expected.

2) If we don't cry out/praise God, someone else or something else will!

3) Jesus weeps over those who do not recognize Him.

Jesus was lamenting over Jerusalem as He was approaching the city. If Jesus were to be approaching your city or town today, what would He say?

MAKING IT PERSONAL: We still have the opportunity to praise God!

We all have reasons to praise God. Even in the darkest and hardest of times! Have a closing time of thanks and praise.

Thanks = thanking God for something He has done in your life.

Praise = praising God for who He is. This is a subtle nuance but it allows us to be aware of what God is doing in our lives, but not to make our praise dependent upon that. Job chose to praise God as He lost everything. We, too, are called not to curse God when life is not going well, but to praise Him. If we do not, the rocks will cry out!

MEMORY VERSE ACTIVITY

Send your students outside for a few moments to find a rock. Strongly suggest it needs to be at least the size of a walnut, no larger than a tennis ball. (If you do not meet in an area where you have rocks easily accessible, gather rocks before you meet and bring them.) Have markers ready to write reference for the Memory Verse, Luke 19:40. Invite students to take their rock home and place it somewhere they will see it every day as a reminder to praise God daily!

EXTRA EXTRA!! I have now heard this phrase so often and in so many different situations that I have no idea where it began! Babbie Mason first introduced it to me, and I would guess countless others. Regardless of where it originated, it still holds true and is a great reminder of praise, even in the darkest of times!

Here is the phrase. . .

God is good, all the time. And all the time, God is good.

It was often said as a call and response…

Leader: God is good
Response: all the time.
Leader: And all the time,
Response: God is good.

This is a great way to end a meeting!!

SONG: "Indescribable" by Chris Tomlin, on the album *Arriving*

QUOTABLE QUOTES:

If you accept the expectations of others, especially negative ones, then you will never change the outcome.
—Michael Jordan

Passion Week—Midweek

MEMORY VERSE:
But Jesus answered, "I tell you, if my followers didn't say these things, then the stones would cry out."—Luke 19:40 (NCV)

SCRIPTURE: Luke 22:1–13; Exodus 12:1–13, 42

LESSON IN A SENTENCE: Jesus regularly defies what is expected.

FOCUS

As your students walk in, have music playing quietly and let them know this day is going to be different from most others. They are free to talk, but today is not a day with wild crazy games. Explain that this is the week of the Passion. While this word is used in many ways, within a Christian context it refers to the week of the Crucifixion.

Have several representations of the Lord's Supper around the room. These can be pictures (check art books or the Internet), carvings, statues, or any representation you can find. You may want to set out paper and markers or watercolors and allow your students to create their own representations as well.

Have your students gather in groups of 2–3 around each representation. Give them 10–15 minutes to talk with each other about what they see. (This will be a stretch for many of them—it is not often that teenagers are asked to look at art and discuss what they think. There is no right or wrong answer. You can expect giggles as a natural response to being nervous or feeling like they do not know what they are doing.)

Another way to do this if you do not have access to several art books or representations of the Lord's Supper, is to create a power point presentation. Do a search using "Last Supper", "Lord's Supper", "Communion" or "Eucharist". The Internet is full of images of famous and not so famous depictions of the Last Supper. Choose a few images and discuss them as a group.

Teacher's Note: While we spend a great deal of time as youth workers creating fun and creative environments to learn about following Jesus, do not be afraid to have a more serious, sober environment. There is something powerful and authentic about setting a different tone when we are in the season that defines us as a people. Adolescents value authenticity. It is appropriate to observe the seriousness of the Crucifixion and the Passion.

DISCOVERY

You've just spent time looking at images of the Last Supper. But what led up to this? And what does it all really mean?

Divide into groups. Have half of the groups look up Luke 22:1–13, the other half look up Exodus 12:1–13, 42. Ask each group to read their passage and be prepared to retell it in their own words.

Ask the groups with the Exodus passage to go first. After they are through summarizing, ask the whole group:

According to this passage, what, exactly is the Passover? Why do you think the Israelites were told to continue to observe this?

Ask the groups who looked at Luke 22:1–13 to summarize their passage.

What was being celebrated by Jesus and His disciples according to this passage?

What does Passover have to do with the week of the Passion?

Teacher's Note: In some of your traditions, tomorrow is Maundy Thursday. In Latin, maundy means commandments—the Thursday of commandments. Tomorrow the Last Supper is celebrated in preparation for Good Friday. The Last Supper wasn't just a random meal the night before the Crucifixion. Jesus was following the Jewish tradition of the Passover meal with His disciples. Honoring the Israelites being spared and the Exodus as God saved His people.

LIFE APPLICATION: We spend a lot of time talking about the Crucifixion and Resurrection all year, but in particular at this time. Understanding the Passover helps us to understand what Jesus has done for us even more. He was the final Passover lamb. When we celebrate the Last Supper, we are remembering His sacrifice.

What can you do this week to remember what Jesus has done for us? What Jesus has done for you?

Look back at the Memory Verse. If you do not cry out, the rocks will. Close with a few moments thanking God for what He has done and praising Him for who He is.

Easter

By Amy Jacober

MEMORY VERSE: Jesus said to her, "I am the resurrection and the life; he who believes in Me will live even if he dies, and everyone who lives and believes in Me shall never die. Do you believe this?"—John 11:25–26 (NASB)

SCRIPTURE: 1 Peter 1:1–9

LESSON IN A SENTENCE: Our hope is found in the resurrection of Jesus Christ.

THE BIG PICTURE (OR WHAT YOU'RE TRYING TO GET ACROSS):
Resurrection Sunday! If it weren't for this day, we would not be assembled together. It is around the Passion of Christ that our faith is centered. It encompasses unconditional love and sacrifice, miracles, and faith. It is the full expression of God's work of reconciliation in the world. While the resurrection was a one-time event, God's love is eternal. In that we can rejoice! The icing on the cake is that not only are we able to be born again by His mercy, but He offers joy beyond belief. It is so easy to take this lightly. This is so fundamental to who we are as followers of Christ, that we can forget how revolutionary this really is! Slow down, celebrate the resurrection. Take a few moments to realize just how eternally life-changing this is!

IN THIS LESSON STUDENTS SHOULD:

- Be reminded of the central truth of the Christian faith.
- Celebrate the Resurrection of Jesus.
- Reflect on how Easter impacts their own lives today.

STUFF YOU NEED:

- Construction or drawing paper (Option 1)
- Crayons, colored pencil and colored chalk (Option 1)
- Tape (Option 1)

FOCUS

OPTION 1: pictures of Easter

Give each person a piece of construction or drawing paper as they walk in. Have tables set up with crayons, colored pencils, colored chalk, or any other art supplies you have available. Today is Easter. Invite each person to draw what they understand Easter to be or how it impacts them. This can be really concrete—like a picture of an empty tomb, or abstract—like colors and images the Resurrection evokes. If you have several visitors today, retell the story of the Crucifixion and Resurrection of Jesus to give a starting place. As people complete their pictures, hang these around the room. Ask each person to offer a short explanation of what they have drawn.

OPTION 2:

Show a clip of the Crucifixion *and* Resurrection to your students. You can get this from a variety of films including *The Jesus Film* or *The Passion of the Christ*. Preview the clip beforehand and take note of how long it runs.

After watching the clip:

Ask: Do you think that we today are really able to understand someone resurrecting from the dead?

How does this fact make being a follower of Jesus so different from every other religion in the world?

Is there anyone today for whom you would be willing to knowingly be tortured and die? Do you know of anyone who would do such a thing for you?

DISCOVERY :

Read 1 Peter 1:1–8 aloud with the entire group. Reread this from a few translations.

Ask your students to close their eyes and reread it one last time. While you are reading it this last time, ask them to really listen and see if there is a word or a phrase that seems to stick out. Have them turn in their own Bibles to read this passage for themselves. Spend some time talking about these words and phrases. What is God saying. . .what do these words mean. . .why do you think these phrases stand out?

Hand out 3 x 5 cards and have them write the word or phrase on one side of that card.

LIFE APPLICATION: It is the Resurrection of Jesus that brings a living hope. This hope is not intended only for the future, but for now. We have a hope through the Resurrection that offers an inheritance fit for royalty. And that is just what we are, children of the King through adoption.

Ask: In what does the world seek to find hope? How does this measure up with what this passage says?

MAKING IT PERSONAL: Ask: In what do you seek to find hope? How does this fit with the passage we read? How does this fit with the word or phrase that stood out to you? You may want to have your students share in partners or with the group.

MEMORY VERSE ACTIVITY

Have each person write John 11:25–26 on the opposite side of their card. Explain that this is Jesus speaking and asking a direct question.

Spend a few moments reflecting on the specific word or phrase that stood out to them as it relates to the memory verse. Jesus asks a direct question: Do you believe this? Give your students a few moments to consider their response. Close in prayer, praising God for who He is and thanking Him for what He has done.

SONG: "Song of Repentance" by Jacob's Well on the CD *You Are Better*

Check out www.jacobswellmusic.com to learn about this band and where to buy this CD.

QUOTABLE QUOTES:

And He departed from our sight that we might return to our heart, and there find Him. For He departed, and behold, He is here.

—St. Augustine

Earth's saddest day and gladdest day were just three days apart!

—Susan Coolidge

Easter—Midweek

MEMORY VERSE:
Jesus said to her, "I am the resurrection and the life; he who believes in Me shall live even if he dies, and everyone who lives and believes in Me shall never die. Do you believe this?"—John 11:25–26 (NASB)

SCRIPTURE: John 11:1–27

LESSON IN A SENTENCE: Our hope is found in the Resurrection of Jesus Christ.

FOCUS

Divide into groups of six. Give each group two or three rolls of duct tape. Find a clear space on a wall for each team. Be certain the walls you choose are not delicate where the paint will easily peel! Have each group choose one member they will duct tape to the wall. Have that person stand on a chair and then tape away! When they are out of tape, pull the chair away and see which team's player is able to stay on the wall the longest. This is a great one for pictures!

Every day we put our trust in the craziest of things. We take what is precious and often use something as simple as duct tape to protect it and believe it will be safe. We do the same kinds of things with our spiritual life. As long as it looks like it's been covered a lot and it holds together for the short term, we are satisfied. When it begins to fall apart, we just stick on another piece of tape. Jesus wants us to stop trying to patch together our spiritual lives and to place our trust entirely in Him.

DISCOVERY

In the same groups, read John 11:1–27.

Have each group summarize what they read. (Most likely they will focus on the main story of Lazarus, Martha, and Jesus.)

Reread vv. 24–27.

Ask: What did Martha mean when she talked about the resurrection on the last day?

What did Jesus mean when He responded saying He was the resurrection?

How did this change Martha's understanding?

Martha says to Jesus that this wouldn't have happened if He had been there. Why did Jesus say it was in His plan to not be there?

LIFE APPLICATION: Life is often hard. We are told from the time we are little, that if we ask, it will be given to us. That if we so desire, God is right there with us. Yet this time, Jesus says it is better that He was not there with His close friends.

Ask: What things are going on in the world right now that make you question where God is? How does this impact your faith?

Reread vv. 14–15. Jesus says He is glad He was not present, so that they may believe. Why would Jesus not want to be present in order to help them believe? Wouldn't it make more sense to be fully present, physically visible, in order to help them believe?

We are much like Martha and Mary. We cannot see Jesus and at times it seems He is far removed from this world. But He is not. He is involved and present. His ways are not our ways. Our hope comes in the Resurrection, and this has already happened.

Walk your students through a guided prayer. Invite each one to find a quiet place in the room where he or she will not be disturbed. Have them close their eyes and say the following.

Martha was talking directly to Jesus. She came to Him heartbroken that her brother had just died. Jesus is not angry or frustrated. He is full of compassion and patience with her. Imagine that you were talking directly to Jesus. (pause) Where are you? What does it look like? What does it smell like? (pause) What is Jesus like? Can you see what He is wearing? What is His mood? (pause) What is the first thing you would like to tell Jesus? (pause) How does He respond? (pause) If He were to say directly to you that He is the resurrection and the life, that if you believe in Him you will never die…how does this make you feel? Are you nervous or excited? Anxious or worried? (pause) Imagine that Jesus asks you directly "Do you believe this?" How do you respond? (pause) How does Jesus react to your response? (pause) It is now time to step away from this conversation. Imagine that you are saying good-bye to Jesus. How does this make you feel? (pause) Jesus says that He loves you and that He will always be with you.

We have hope because of the Resurrection. Martha was heartbroken and mourning but chose to still believe. Just like Martha, even when we do not see or cannot completely understand, we can choose to believe.

APRIL 23, 2006

Worship

By Alicia Claxton

MEMORY VERSE:
"Yet a time is coming and has now come when the true worshipers will worship the Father in spirit and truth, for they are the kind of worshipers the Father seeks."—John 4:23 (NIV)

SCRIPTURE: Psalm 34:1–3; Psalm 95:1–7; John 4:23

LESSON IN A SENTENCE: Authentic worship is a lifestyle of discovering and responding to the magnificent revelation of God.

THE BIG PICTURE (OR WHAT YOU'RE TRYING TO GET ACROSS):

There are numerous misconceptions in the church today about what "worship" is. Many believers define worship as a particular segment of the church service or the service itself. Still others would describe it as a feeling or an emotion that leads them to do certain things like raise their hands or close their eyes. The danger of these misconceptions is that countless people (including students) are walking away with an inadequate and skewed perspective of worship. True worship is not limited to a particular action, place, or length of time— it is a lifestyle. Worship is our humble response to the magnificent revelation of God. He reveals Himself in many ways—through His Word, through music, through prayer, through creative initiatives, through creation itself. His desire for us is that we recognize Him in every aspect of our lives and that we respond to the glory of His presence.

IN THIS LESSON STUDENTS SHOULD:

- ○ Recognize misconceptions about worship.
- ○ Learn what authentic worship looks like.
- ○ Focus on their own personal worship time.

STUFF YOU NEED:

- ○ Several bottles of Coke and Pepsi, paper cups (see Focus: Option 2)
- ○ Index cards

○ Pens
○ Materials for stations (see Making It Personal): suitcase, rocks, sharpie markers, wooden cross, thumbtacks, butcher paper, blank paper, Lego®'s, old fashioned timers with sand

FOCUS

Choose either Option 1 or 2. Be certain to watch your time and not get carried away with this part of the lesson!

OPTION 1:

Have students divide up into groups of 5–6 people and play a round of *Two Truths and a Lie*. Students will take turns telling three things about themselves—two of their statements will be true and one will be false. The others in the group must vote on which statement they believe is false. Give them 10 minutes to play this game. Encourage students to come up with things no one would know about them.

TRANSITION TO DISCOVERY by saying: "The object of the game is to try to hide a lie between the truth—to try to manipulate your words and facial expressions so that those around you can't tell when you are being truthful and when you are not. Now think about times in your life when you have played this same game here at church—times when you have been going through the motions in your heart, but making those around you believe you had it all together spiritually. Tonight we will be talking about authentic worship—through this study we will discover the joy of worshiping God with all our heart, soul, mind, and strength. We should also remember that God sees our hearts and knows when we are really worshiping Him and when we are just going through the motions. His desire for us is to understand the purpose and power of authentic worship."

OPTION 2:

Invite your students to participate in a Coke/Pepsi Challenge (or any other taste test type activity). Divide the room by putting the *Coke* fans on one side and the *Pepsi* fans on the other. Set up two tables (one table for each side of the room) with small paper cups and drinks. Write *Coke* or *Pepsi* on the bottom of each paper cup so you will know which is which, but students will not be able to read it. Have students step up to a table and take one cup of each soda. See if they can distinguish one from the other.

TRANSITION TO DISCOVERY by saying: "The object of this activity is to try to distinguish the real thing from an imposter—for those of you who really like *Coke*, nothing else compares no matter how similar it may look (the same goes for those of you who are loyal to *Pepsi*). Tonight we are going to talk about authentic worship. In this study we will discover that once we have experienced the power of God's presence and tasted the joy of true worship, then our hearts will never again be satisfied by anything less."

DISCOVERY

Open this time with a word of prayer.

Ask your students to describe what worship means to them. After a few minutes, invite them to open their Bibles and read what God's Word has to say about worship.

1) Why should we worship?

Have a student read Psalm 95:1–7a, then discuss the following questions.

Q: According to these verses, why should we give thanks, honor, praise, and adoration to the Lord?

A: Because He is worthy! He is above all others—He is our Maker, our God, our Savior, our King, etc.

Q: What words or phrases stick out most to you in these verses? Why?

A: open-ended

2) How should we worship?

Continue looking at Psalm 95:1–7 as you discuss the following question.

Q: According to this passage, what are some ways we can worship God?

A: Sing to the Lord; shout aloud; come before the Lord to give Him thanks; exalt Him with music and song; bow down, kneel before Him in reverence.

Now look at John 4:23 and discuss the following question.

Q: How should we worship the Lord according to this verse?

A: "In spirit and in truth"...our worship should come from a regenerated spirit (a spirit that recognizes the Lord) and a sincere heart.

3) When should we worship?

Have a student read Psalm 34:1–4, then discuss the following questions.

Q: What does "extol" mean?

A: It means to lift up or exalt.

Q: Based on v. 1, how often does the writer (David) exalt and praise the Lord?

A: All the time... "praise will always be on my lips."

According to these passages, we should worship the Lord for Who He is and for what He has done in our lives. Because He is holy and worthy, we should always be able to find a reason and a way to worship Him (all day, everyday).

Teacher's Note: Students may have questions about worship styles. It is important to help them understand that different people will respond to God in different ways. We see in the example of David that he used music, poetry, dance, prayer, praise, etc. in his worship. The litmus test for what is acceptable worship is found in John 4:23—we must worship Him in spirit and in truth. True worship must focus ON HIM and bring glory TO HIM.

LIFE APPLICATION: Ask students to think about some of their most memorable worship experiences (camp; during times of trouble; after a specific prayer was answered; etc.). Have a few students share their experiences.

MAKING IT PERSONAL: Set up several stations around the room or throughout several rooms if your space is limited. At these stations, place instructions for what students are to do while they are there. Each station should incorporate elements of worship and give students a chance to experience God in a personal way, while in a corporate setting (in a room full of other students experiencing similar moments of worship). This activity can take 15–20 minutes, depending on how many stations you set up. Preface this time by telling students to take a few minutes to pray and ask God to prepare their hearts for a time of creative worship, then invite them to start their journey when they are ready. Ask them to respect each other by limiting the amount of people at each station to three or four.

Examples of initiatives/challenges for each station:

Place a suitcase (medium to large suitcase), rocks (all shapes and sizes) and sharpie markers at one station. Instruct students to think about the "burdens" they pack up and carry around with them each day and then read Psalm 55:22 (NIV): "Cast all your cares on the Lord and He will sustain you; He will never let the righteous fall." Invite them to consider giving those burdens over to the One who is strong enough to carry them. If they desire to trust God in this area, instruct them to write their burden(s) on a rock and place that rock in the suitcase as they leave this station.

Place a wooden cross (large), index cards, pens and thumb tacks at one station. Instruct students to consider the sacrifice that Jesus made so that we might have fellowship with God through Him. Encourage them to write down words of gratitude on an index card and place the card somewhere on the cross (using the thumbs tacks).

Place a large sheet of butcher paper on the wall or floor and markers at this station. Instruct students to write down prayer requests. When they have done that, encourage them to spend a few minutes praying over the requests of others that they see on this sheet.

Place a stack of Lego®'s at this station (make a large wall out of the Lego®'s). Instruct students to think about the things they have allowed to come between them and their relationship with God (i.e. other relationships, desire to please people more than Him, a busy schedule, etc). Encourage them to spend some time in prayer asking God to remove the wall they have built. Invite students to take a Lego® off the top of the wall and keep it as a reminder.

Place several old fashioned timers (with sand in them) at this station. Instruct students to turn over a timer and watch the sand fall for a minute. Challenge them to consider how they spend their time on an average day—do they practice a lifestyle of worship throughout their day or do they waste precious time on meaningless things? Encourage them to spend some time in prayer asking God to teach them how to make the most of the time they've been given.

Place a sheet of paper with the Memory Verse on it (John 4:23), pens and index cards at this station. Instruct students to think about what it means to worship God in spirit and in truth. Encourage them to evaluate whether or not they worship God openly and honestly and with all of their heart. Challenge them to write John 4:23 on an index card and take it with them.

You can come up with countless variations or object lessons for this activity. Limit the number of stations so that students can make it around to all or almost all of them within the allotted time. Play soft music in the background.

MEMORY VERSE ACTIVITY

The Making It Personal activity above incorporates the Memory Verse for this lesson. Remind them to take the index card with the verse written on it and put it in a place where they will see it often.

CONNECTIONS: God's Word is full of examples of and instruction for true worship. Challenge students to study David's lifestyle of worship as found in passages such as Psalm 5:7; Psalm 8; Psalm 19:14; Psalm 27:4; Psalm 40:1–10; Psalm 84.

SONGS: "Unaware" by Mercy Me, from the album *Undone*
"Seeing You" by Matt Redman, from the album *Facedown*
"Facedown" by Matt Redman, from the album *Facedown*

QUOTABLE   QUOTES :

My father always told me, "Find a job you love and you'll never have to work a day in your life."

—Author: Jim Fox

QUOTABLE QUOTES:

A person will worship something, have no doubt about that. We may think our tribute is paid in secret in the dark recesses of our hearts, but it will out. That which dominates our imaginations and our thoughts will determine our lives, and our character. Therefore, it behooves us to be careful what we worship, for what we are worshipping we are becoming."

—Ralph Waldo Emerson

Worship—Midweek

MEMORY VERSE:
Yet a time is coming and has now come when the true worshipers will worship the Father in spirit and truth, for they are the kind of worshipers the Father seeks.—John 4:23 (NIV)

SCRIPTURE: Psalm 51:16–17; Romans 12:1

LESSON IN A SENTENCE: Authentic worship is a lifestyle of discovering and responding to the magnificent revelation of God.

FOCUS

Divide students into groups with 3–4 in each group. Give each group a sheet of butcher paper and markers. Instruct some of the groups to create a mural of images that represent what they think of when they hear the word "sacrifice." Instruct the rest of the groups to create a mural of images that represent "worship." Don't give them too much direction. Let their own thoughts and creativity inspire them. Give them 5–10 minutes to work on this. Have each group present their mural and share some insight on their work. TRANSITION TO DISCOVERY by asking students how "sacrifice" relates to "worship." Point out any correlation you see in the different murals they have created.

DISCOVERY

Open this time with a word of prayer.

Have a student read Romans 12:1 and then discuss the following questions:
   Q: What does Paul urge us to offer as a sacrifice?
   A: Our bodies—which represents self-sacrifice (offering all of ourselves).
   Q: What does Paul state is the motivation for this sacrifice?
   A: God's mercy—in light of all the grace and mercy He has given us.
   Q: What makes this sacrifice holy and pleasing to God?
   A: It is motivated by God's mercy; it is a sacrifice of self for the sake of true worship.

Have a student read Psalm 51:16–17 and then discuss the following questions:

Q: What kind of sacrifice is David referring to in v. 16?

A: The sacrificial system where the blood of an animal was offered on the altar for the sins of the people.

Q: Why does David say, "You do not delight in sacrifice...?"

A: The need for a sacrificial system came as a result of sin; the ritual of sacrifice was a constant reminder of the sin that separated us from God.

Q: According to v. 17, what kind of sacrifice pleases God?

A: Self-sacrifice motivated by a repentant spirit and a humble heart.

Once sin entered the world, sinners could no longer worship God without first bringing a sacrifice. Only the blood of our perfect sacrifice, Jesus Christ, could completely atone for our sin and allow us to once again worship God with heart, soul, mind, and strength. When our worship is authentic, we are motivated by His mercy and compelled to offer ourselves as a living sacrifice—to be used for His glory.

LIFE APPLICATION: Challenge students to think about what they are willing to offer God in view of His mercy. Open an area somewhere in the room that can serve as an altar and invite students to spend some time with the Lord as they worship and respond to His presence.

CONNECTIONS: To better understand the amazing privilege we have to worship God through Christ, have students compare how worship was conducted under the Old Covenant (OT sacrificial system) to how we worship under the New Covenant. The best place to find this comparison is in Hebrews 9 and 10.

APRIL 30, 2006

Freedom

By Michelle Hicks

MEMORY VERSE:
You will know the truth, and the truth will set you free.—John 8:32
(HCSB)

SCRIPTURE: Galatians 5:1–14

LESSON IN A SENTENCE: It is for freedom that Christ has set us
free.—Galatians 5:1 (NIV)

THE BIG PICTURE (OR WHAT YOU'RE TRYING TO GET ACROSS):

   Unfortunately, many students see Christianity and following Christ
as a huge list of do's and don'ts. They see obedience and submission as hin-
drances to living a full life, instead of possibly being a way to experience
the most abundant life possible. This lesson is to help students identify
with an example of the early New Testament Christians and their struggles for freedom as new believers. Students will recognize that often we
trade one form of bondage for another. However, Jesus' desire for us is
that we experience a level of freedom that is abundantly more than we
could imagine. It is freedom from unforgiveness, guilt, shame, lies, deceit,
pride, and more. Through this lesson, students will begin determining and
planning steps they will take toward greater freedom in Christ and giving Him total authority and control in their lives.

IN THIS LESSON STUDENTS SHOULD:

- Acknowledge the desire to do things or make decisions
  on their own and by their own power.
- Identify things that hinder freedom in Christ.
- Determine steps they will take toward freedom in Christ.

STUFF YOU NEED:

- Masking tape
- Paper
- Pencils
- Strips of paper
- Stapler/staples
- Markers

FOCUS

Choose either Option 1 or 2. Be certain to watch your time and not get carried away with this part of the lesson.

OPTION 1: Active Group

Before the lesson, use masking tape to form a large letter V on the floor. Each line of the letter will be approximately 15 feet in length. Create an angle so the ends of the lines are not more than 10 feet apart.

As students arrive, instruct them to choose a partner they trust who is approximately the same height. Ask partners to stand opposite each other at the narrow end or bottom of the letter V. With their arms raised above their heads, instruct students to place their palms together. Caution them to avoid interlocking fingers or grasping hands. Partners will slowly walk along the lines of the letter V, gradually leaning in and relying on each other's support. The object is to walk to the end of the line or the top of the V with one person on either side while still touching. However, if a pair begins to feel uncomfortable or like they may fall, they can stop.

After all the students complete the activity, *ask:*

How would you complete this activity if you never touched another person? (*You would simply walk the lines and never touch another person. You would reach the end of the letter V and be farther apart from the person than when you started.*)

What difference does the touch make in this activity? (*You stay connected to the person. It is more difficult in some places but you work together and depend upon another person. You rely upon one another and support one another.*)

Explain that like this activity, there are times when we just want to do things on our own. We don't want to lean or depend on anyone. Often we call that wanting our freedom. However, other people like the security of depending upon someone else. They like to feel connected and supported by others. They experience a freedom in knowing they are connected and supported. In today's Bible study we will look at what causes us to pull away from relationships physically, emotionally, or mentally, when we want freedom. Also, we will see how sometimes freedom comes when we experience connection and support from others.

OPTION 2: Reflective Activity

As students arrive, arrange them in groups of 8–12. Instruct students to sit one behind the other to form a line with their team. Explain that the person in the back of the line will begin the game by using his finger to draw a simple design on the back of the person in front of him. That person tries to replicate the design by drawing it on the person in front of her, and so on up to the first person in the line. The person at the front of the line will draw the design on a sheet of paper of what he thinks was drawn on his back. Compare the original design drawn at the back of the line with the drawing.

For this first round of drawings, have teams race one another to see who finishes first. You may use designs of your choice or use ideas from the following: a star, a car, a flower, and so forth. After the first relay, compare designs drawn by each team. Discover which team was closest to the original design.

Ask: What might help your team draw something closer to the original design? (*Allow responses. Draw slower and don't worry about finishing first. Concentrate on the drawing. Do the right thing and try harder. Close your eyes and focus on the drawing on your back.*)

Continue with the activity, however, this time do not make it a relay. Compare and contrast the results of this round with the previous game.

Ask: How is the game different when you focus on the task, even though you still cannot see the drawing?

Does this type of activity cause you to feel a sense of freedom or a lack of freedom? Why?

Say: Often when we are told what to do or how to do something, it takes away that our sense of freedom. Many people think that is what life is like for Christians. They see a list of do's and don'ts and wonder why anyone would want that for one's life. In today's Bible study we are going to look at how freedom is a big part of the Christian life.

DISCOVERY

Distribute strips of paper and markers to students. Ask them to write down the things that "weigh them down" or burden them in any way. Write one answer per strip of paper. For example, one strip might say "homework" while another says "anger." Allow students to write down as many items as they wish on the strips of paper. Then instruct students to create a paper chain from the strips of paper using a stapler. Students may keep their own individual chain or join their chain with others.

Read Galatians 5:1–14 as a large group and then discuss the following questions:

What does "freedom" mean to you?

What does it mean to be free in Christ?

Explain that Paul wanted his listeners to hear and understand "the purpose of Christ's work was to set Jews free from the curse of the law and to allow Gentiles to enjoy the same liberation by breaking their chains to disobedience and sin." [Source: Scot McKnight, *The NIV Application Commentary: Galatians*, (Zondervan Publishing House, 1995) 242.] For Paul, freedom is a major theme and goes to the heart of the gospel. God sets us free through Christ and in the Spirit, so that we can love God and others. He wants the Galatians to realize his main point that being in Christ is living in freedom. Living in freedom meant not being caught up in the Mosaic Law that demanded circumcision for the early Christians. They were putting the law before Christ. Today, for us, living in freedom means not being caught up in anything that hinders us from putting Christ first in our lives.

Direct students' attention to their chains made earlier. Encourage them to think about the things they wrote down and how many of those things hinder them from putting Christ first in their lives.

LIFE APPLICATION: Explain that there was a lot of confusion among the Galatians. Many people had left one form of "slavery" to find themselves in bondage to other forms of slavery. Instruct students to find a partner. Explain that as you read the following statements students will form frozen statues that represent their reactions and emotions.

Read aloud and give students time to react as a frozen statue:

You broke off your relationship with someone who took a lot of your time (*frozen statue*). Now you find yourself in a similar relationship again, only with a different person (*frozen statue*).

You've made a decision to quit lying or deceiving your parents (*frozen statue*). You just got grounded for telling the truth (*frozen statue*).

You made a commitment to go on the summer mission trip with your church (*frozen statue*). Your grandmother just gave you $100 for your birthday (*frozen statue*).

Point out that sometimes when we finally make the decision and commitment to do the right thing living as a person free in Christ, we still find ourselves clinging to the old chain. Like the first example where the person decides to break off a relationship that takes so much time that Christ is definitely not first—then later finds herself in the same type of relationship and back in bondage. Although all relationships are not unhealthy, a relationship that pulls you away from Christ instead of drawing you closer, may not be the best choice.

In the second example of being honest and then being grounded, although it may not appear to be freedom, think about the freedom this person now experiences. He does not have to lie or keep up with what lies he has told others. There is nothing to hide. He becomes free from guilt and shame.

Much like the third example, when a person is living in freedom with Christ, he or she may experience freedom in a whole new way. Although many people might want to spend birthday money on themselves and for their own wants and needs, there is a new level of freedom one experiences when one chooses to indulge and serve others with one's resources. The final verse in the Scripture study today is Galatians 5:14 (NIV), which states: "The entire law is summed up in a single command: 'Love your neighbor as yourself.'" When we use our freedom to love others and give to them, we become free from all the things and stuff that weigh us down and hinder our relationship and freedom in Christ.

MAKING IT PERSONAL: Call on students to stand in a circle with the connected paper chains. Counsel that there are several choices we make if we are going to choose freedom in the Christian's life. Ask the following questions and encourage students to break a link in the paper chain if they are choosing freedom in each situation:

Will you choose to be real, honest, and open, or continue to be someone you are not? Will you choose to be a fake and hide behind a mask or tell the truth?

Will you choose to remain bitter and hold grudges, or will you choose to forgive others and yourself?

Will you choose to rebel against God in your life and reject His authority, or will you choose to submit to God and trust that He wants the best for you?

Will you choose to remain prideful and try to do things on your own, or will you humble yourself and place your confidence in God?

Will you stay trapped in bondage to sin and the things that pull you away from Christ, or will you choose to break free trusting Jesus for freedom?

Draw attention to the number of paper chain links broken. Tell students that the broken chains are a visual reminder of how Jesus can set them free from things that hinder and hurt them. Encourage students that when they doubt their freedom in Christ or feel weighed down by the things of the world, to read Scripture. Call on a volunteer to read John 8:32 aloud. Instruct students to take one strip of the broken chain link and write the memory verse on it to keep at home or in their locker. Close in prayer by assigning prayer partners for students to have during the next week. Instruct students to pray with their prayer partner about one thing they want to change or do this week to experience more freedom in Christ.

MEMORY VERSE ACTIVITY

Instruct students to form groups of three. In small groups challenge them to make up hand motions, a song, a rap, or use other symbols to help them memorize John 8:32. After a few moments allow teams to say the Memory Verse aloud for the other groups.

CONNECTIONS: There are many Scriptures that relate to freedom. Here are some additional verses you may choose to have students look up and read, or give them a list to take home for further study during the week. Additional Scripture:

Leviticus 26:13; Isaiah 61:1; Jeremiah 34:8; 15–17; Luke 4:18; Acts 24:23; Romans 8:21; 2 Corinthians 3:17; Galatians 2:4; James 1:25; James 2:12; 1 Peter 2:16.

Freedom—Midweek

MEMORY VERSE: You will know the truth, and the truth will set you free.—John 8:32 (HCSB)

SCRIPTURE: Isaiah 61:1–4

LESSON IN A SENTENCE: Jesus is our way to freedom.

FOCUS

Ask students if anyone has ever seen live or on TV the musical *Stomp*. Explain that *Stomp* is an all-percussion musical performance. Explain that students will create their own "stomp" routine making sounds and noises. In a circle allow each student to add a rhythm sound to the routine. Distribute brooms, trash can lids, drumsticks, pencils, and so forth if you want it to be really loud. However, students can clap, snap, whistle, and make other sounds for the same effect. After everyone in the circle is part of the routine, stop and allow students to work in small groups to create additional routines. Conclude the activity by saying: we all like the freedom to be creative and sometimes as individuals we live out the saying "he walks to the beat of a different drum." Our natural tendency is to do things our way, on our time, by our power, so that we stay in control. And although that may appear to mean we have a lot of freedom, we are all a slave to something. Discuss the things that people become slaves to in our society. This Bible study continues Sunday's theme and study of freedom.

DISCOVERY

Arrange students into four teams and assign each team one verse from Isaiah 61:1–4. Distribute paper and pens to students and instruct each team to create a TV news report on their verse. Encourage students to be creative. For example, v. 1 might be an interview with Jesus or v. 3 might be a story about a different twist on a funeral or graveside service. After ample time, allow teams to present their verses in news report form to the large group. Make sure the teams present in order of their verses. When students finish their presentations, discuss the following questions:

1. What is the good news in v. 1?
2. What stories from Jesus' ministry do you think of when you read vv. 1–3?

3. What is the year of the Lord's favor? What does that mean?

4. How will God change mourning and grieving according to v. 3?

5. What does v. 4 promise us?

6. What if the rebuilding is physical or material? What if it is spiritual?

7. What is one way you want to see God bring you freedom?

LIFE APPLICATION: Write the following statements across a chalkboard or on four separate sheets of paper:

1. Ways we can seek God's guidance and experience freedom in Christ.

2. Why I feel freedom in Christ.

3. Why I do not feel freedom in Christ.

4. Something I can do to gain more freedom in Christ this week.

Instruct students to move around the room to each statement and write their answer below each one. When students complete all four statements, read the various answers aloud. Invite students to share other thoughts or insights if they wish during this time. Read Isaiah 61:1–4 again. Point out that in v. 1 we can sum up "to proclaim freedom for the captives" with Jesus is our way to freedom. We will not experience the true freedom that God is trying to give us until we turn our lives over to Jesus. That means trusting Him with every area of your life and allowing Him to set you free from the things that hurt you and your relationship with Him. Close in prayer asking God to give students wisdom as they pursue and experience freedom in Christ. Pray students will not abuse their freedom in Christ, but will responsibly use their freedom in Christ for the plans and purposes He has for them.

Discouragement (God does have a plan)

By Ric Lipsey

MEMORY VERSE:
"For I know the plans I have for you," says the LORD. "They are plans for good and not for disaster, to give you a future and a hope." —Jeremiah 29:11 (NLT)

SCRIPTURE: Jeremiah 29:11; Matthew 16:18; John 10:10; James 1:17; Romans 8:28; Psalm 91:9–16; Ephesians 2:10; 2 Corinthians 4:17–18; John 16:33

LESSON IN A SENTENCE: In times of discouragement we can be confident that God is near.

THE BIG PICTURE (OR WHAT YOU'RE TRYING TO GET ACROSS):
We are all busy. There is no time to slow down. The pace is frantic. There is tremendous pressure to perform and produce results. These used to be just the lives of adults, but now it is the lives of the teenager to whom we minister. When life seems to get out of hand we get frustrated and discouraged. When life gets to that point, we all need to know that even when we feel that we have lost control, God has not and He has a plan for our lives.

IN THIS LESSON STUDENTS SHOULD:

- Understand that God has a purpose for their lives.
- Know that even in times of discouragement, the Lord has not left them alone.

STUFF YOU NEED:

- A Bible marked with the verses for your "reader"
- Money (one dollar bills in an amount divisible by 5, 20, 25, 40, etc.; the more you use, the more impact is made. By the way, you will not get this money back, so budget accordingly.)

FOCUS

Play "Everybody Hurts"—song or video by R.E.M. from the album *Automatic for the People*—1992

Ask: Even though this song is older, do the words carry some amount of truth to them?

Say: In John 16:33 (Don't actually read the verse here, save the whole verse for the Making It Personal section) Jesus isn't candy coating it here, folks. He flat out tells us that there will be hard days ahead, and in most cases they will be accompanied by discouragement.

Ask: What are some areas where we face discouragement?

DISCOVERY

Ask if there is anyone who has had a discouraging week? Have the first person to raise their hand tell of their source of discouragement.

Say: When we face times of discouragement, God still wants His children to be faithful, and even more than that, He wants to bless them.

(If this student agrees to take part in the rest of the Bible study, she will receive the cash you have. Put the cash in bundles of five to distribute throughout the study.)

Ask the same student if she would mind being your assistant Bible teacher for the rest of your time. Assure her that in the midst of a discouraging time she will leave blessed for her faithfulness.

(It would be helpful to have a Bible marked and color coded to make finding the verses easier on the student. That way you can say "Turn to Matthew 16:18, it's marked with the blue paper," etc.)

Have your assistant sit on a stool in front of the group.

Say: Even though God does not cause times of discouragement and trouble in our lives He does use them and He still has a plan for the lives of His children. And don't forget that you will be blessed for your faithfulness.

Have your assistant read Jeremiah 29:11.

"For I know the plans I have for you," says the LORD. "They are plans for good and not for disaster, to give you a future and a hope." (NLT)

Say: We are going to break this verse into five parts and find some words of encouragement for my assistant.

PART 1:

For I know the plans I have for you (While your assistant is reading, walk around her and one by one scatter the first bundle of dollar bills on her. Let the money lay where it falls and accumulate until the end of the lesson.)

Have your assistant read Mathew 16:18.   (Simon to Peter)

Say: Jesus is telling Simon that he has some life-changing plans in store. Plans that even include a name change to Peter. Just as Jesus had plans for Peter, He also has big plans for all who claim the name of Christ. Even if you feel that you do not have much to offer, remember that God uses ordinary people to do extraordinary things.

PART 2:

They are plans for good (Scatter the second bundle of bills around the assistant while she is reading).

Have your assistant read John 10:10.

Say: Satan's plan is to destroy you and render you completely ineffective for the kingdom. On the other hand, Jesus' plan is to give you the most incredible life you can imagine. Jesus wants you to have a full and amazing life here on this earth right now, as well as eternal life with Him in heaven. Now this life will still have its ups and downs, but we can trust in the plan He has for us to be a good one.

Have your assistant read James 1:17.

Say: We are assured that every, not just some, but *every* good thing we have, is a gift from God our Father. We may think that we have worked hard to get something materially or accomplish some award, but in all actuality even the ability to do the work is an incredible gift from God.

God wants your whole life so He can do something extraordinary with it.

PART 3:

not for disaster (Scatter third bundle of bills around the assistant while she is reading).

Have your assistant read Romans 8:28.

Say: Now we know that bad times will come, but we know that they will not destroy us. God never promised that He would deliver us from the storms of life, but He does promise that He will be with us through the storms when they come. And according to this verse, He uses the tough times to ultimately bring good to our lives.

Have your assistant read Psalm 91:9–13.

Say: God is telling us that when we are discouraged He is our refuge. We can run to Him for strength and support and He will give us power.

PART 4:

to give you a future (Scatter fourth bundle of bills around the assistant while she is reading).

Say: God sees the big picture of our lives. A pastor in Texas says our life is like a parade. We view the parade from street level, where we can only see the float, marching band, or clowns in their little cars that happen to be right in front of us. God, however, views the parade of our lives from the highest skyscraper along the parade route. He sees the beginning and the end, along with everything in between. God sees it all, but we only get to see the here and now.

Have your assistant read Ephesians 2:10.

Say: The plans that God has for his "Masterpiece" (NLT) are not haphazard and last minute. They were thought out before you were a twinkle in your parents' eye. Before the earth was formed, God had a plan for you. WOW!

PART 5:

and a hope. (Scatter fifth bundle of bills around the assistant while she is reading).

Say: God wants us to see that there is hope in the midst of our discouragement. Hope even when nothing seems to be going our way. In Christian symbolism, hope is represented with an anchor. Hope, in a sense, anchors our faith when the storms of life come our way.

Have your assistant read 2 Corinthians 4:17–18.

Say: God assures us that the discouragement we face is nothing compared to the blessings He has in store for us. (Make sure, in light of the visual money illustration, that you mention that God may choose, more often than not, to bless us in many other ways rather than financial: i.e. health, peace, salvation of friends and loved ones, heaven).

Have your assistant read Psalm 91:14–16 to follow the last point made.

Thank your assistant for her help, allow her to pick up the cash scattered around her and let her return to her seat.

MAKING IT PERSONAL: *Say:* At the beginning of our meeting we listened to the song by R.E.M. and we heard a true statement, "Everybody hurts, sometimes." The statement is true, but there is little comfort there. The only comfort that is offered is that of our friends who also hurt. Now listen to a song that says the same thing with a little more hope.

Play: "Bound To Come Some Trouble" (By Rich Mullins from the Rich Mullins Reunion Album, *Never Picture Perfect.* Also on the album: *The Countdown Magazine Remembers Rich Mullins*)

Now read all of John 16:33.

Say: Jesus tells us that in the midst of our discouragement, He has overcome. We need the comfort of our friends, but what we have in Christ is victory!

Close in prayer, thanking God for the victory we have in Christ. Thank Him that He has a plan for each of His children that is meant to prosper them.

Invite students back for the mid-week study. Let them know that in this lesson the discouragement that was discussed is everyday stuff—that just happens as we live our lives, with no fault of our own. Next time we will look at the story of Jonah to find out what to do when the discouraging times are brought about *by* us.

SONG: "Sit with You" by Dennis Jernigan

Discouragement (God does have a plan)—Midweek

MEMORY VERSE:
"For I know the plans I have for you," says the LORD. "They are plans for good and not for disaster, to give you a future and a hope." —Jeremiah 29:11 (NLT)

SCRIPTURE: Jonah 1:1; 2:2–4; 10; 3:2–3; 1 John 1:9

LESSON IN A SENTENCE: Sometimes we enter times of discouragement brought on by our going against the plan God has for us. (I apologize in advance for the grossness of the study, but on some strange level it works!)

STUFF YOU NEED:

- ○ Cans of either tuna or sardines (depending on how tough your youth are)
- ○ Trash can for the weak stomachs in the group
- ○ Prize for the winner

FOCUS

Start off with a fish eating contest. Make it as wild and entertaining as possible. See who can eat the most sardines in a given time, or who can finish off the can first (that is up to you.) If you want to be kinder, have the youth eat a can of tuna.

Say: This gross display sets the stage for a great story in the Bible about a guy who found himself in a very discouraging place. The sad thing about the story is that he would not have been put in the situation if he had followed the plan God had for him in the first place.

We will look at an acrostic that can help us when we may find ourselves in a similarly discouraging situation that we have caused, all by getting out of step with God's plan. If you have not figured it out yet, we are looking at the story of Jonah and the whale.

DISCOVERY

Let's start our study with our friend Jonah and ask the question; "what can we learn from his discouraging and very fishy predicament?"

In chapter 1 of the Book of Jonah we see God giving Jonah a very specific assignment. Go to Nineveh. However, that is not what Jonah wanted to hear, because Nineveh was a very wicked city. (Nahum goes into more detail concerning the wickedness of the city if you want to go farther in the study.) So our boy jumps on a ship and heads in the other direction. God whips up a storm on the sea, which causes all on board to panic and seek some reason for the storm. Jonah knew he was the cause and spoke up.

This leads us to the word VOMIT. How does Jonah handle this discouraging turn of events? Let's dive in.

Give me a "V."
  Verify the source of the Problem.
  Read: Jonah 1:12

Jonah knew that he was the source of the turbulence at sea. He knew that his sin was affecting those around him, and he chose to help his shipmates out. He told them to throw him overboard.

Sometimes our disobedience not only affects us, but it can also affect others. We need to recognize that sometimes we are the cause of our problems, and even the problems of others.

As Jonah is floating out in the water a large fish (whale) swallows him up where he now has some time to think. He realizes what needs to be done.

Give me an "O."
  Open your mouth—call out for help.
  Read: Jonah 2:2

There comes a time when we must own up to our mistakes and confess our sin. The good news here is found in 1 John 1:9 where God tells us that when we ask for forgiveness He will give it to us.

Jonah repented and God heard his cry for help, and he chose to. . .

Give me an "M."
  Move as the Lord leads (Go with the flow).
  Read: Jonah 2:10

When Jonah was vomited out of the fish's belly, he hit the ground running toward Nineveh. That is a pretty good picture of repentance. We are heading in the opposite direction God desires for us to go, we realize our disobedience, ask for forgiveness and head in the direction God wanted us to be heading in the first place.

Now what did our friend do next?

Give me an "I."
  Intend to get back on track.
  Jonah 2:4

Even while in the fish Jonah knew what had to be done. He determined to return to a life honoring to God and not return to his current path of disobedience. We, too, must decide to follow God for the entire journey of our lives, without getting distracted by our own agenda.

Now when Jonah was (and we are) back on track, he did what he was told to do and that was to. . .

Give me a "T."
   Tell others about your Deliverer (and theirs).
   Jonah 3:1–10
   Jonah now gets about the business God had for him, and an amazing thing happened—the wicked people of Nineveh are saved from the wrath of God.

LIFE APPLICATION: *Ask:* Can you think of any discouraging times in your life that you caused? Can you see God's hand leading you to restoration?

Maybe you are in one of those self-induced times of discouragement right now. What you need to do is, like Jonah did, Verify the source of the problem, Open your mouth—call out for God's help, Move as the Lord leads, Intend not to go back, and Tell others of your God.

MAKING IT PERSONAL: Thank God that He hears us and responds, forgives and restores us, no matter where we are.

SONG OR VIDEO: "In The Belly Of The Whale" by Newsboys from *Jonah: A VeggieTales Movie*—Original Movie Soundtrack or Video from the DVD

Sacrificial Strength

By Amy Jacober

MEMORY VERSE:
A wise son makes his father happy but a foolish son disrespects his mother.—Proverbs 15:20 (NCV)

SCRIPTURE: Exodus 2:1–10

LESSON IN A SENTENCE: Even when we don't realize it, mothers make sacrifices for their children.

THE BIG PICTURE (OR WHAT YOU'RE TRYING TO GET ACROSS):
We have all been significantly impacted by a woman (and sometimes many!). While we may also fight, be frustrated with, annoyed, or embarrassed by our mothers, grandmothers or aunts at one time or another, reality is that a mother stands by her children long after most others have moved away. What is often overlooked is what mothers have given up to be in the lives of their children. Dreams, hopes, career aspirations, and material goods all take a backseat to a mother's focus on caring for her children. The amazing part is that there are even some women who take this role of mothering beyond their own biological children. They become foster moms, mentors, and yes, even youth leaders! Women have a significant role in the wellness of the community. This Sunday is the day we remember that and seek ways to honor them for what they do all year long.

IN THIS LESSON STUDENTS SHOULD:

- Learn of the sacrifices women made to protect and nurture Moses.
- Consider ways their own mothers and/or women in their lives have sacrificed for them.
- Have the opportunity to express thanks to their own mother.
- Be encouraged to imitate the sacrificial actions when they consider their own futures.

STUFF YOU NEED:

- ○ Straws—at least 10 per group
- ○ Masking tape—1 roll per group
- ○ Eggs—1 per group
- ○ A ladder or some high location from which you can drop the caged eggs
- ○ Prize—for the group whose egg survives the greatest height (a crème egg makes a good prize for this one)
- ○ Notecards
- ○ Pens/pencils

FOCUS

OPTION 1: Egg Drop

Break into teams of 2–4. Give each team at least ten straws, one roll of masking tape and one egg. Instruct each group to build a container to offer the best protection to their egg as it is dropped from the top of a ladder to the ground (or whatever place of great height you are able to find). The goal is to create a cage that keeps the egg from breaking. Give 10 minutes or so and then set off to see who is able to offer the most protective container. Give a prize to the group that is able to create the container that protects their egg from the greatest height.

Ask: Have you ever thought of your own life being protected? What things in your own life have been like the straws and tape—things that have come around you and protected you when you would have otherwise been hurt or worse?

OPTION 2: Mother's Share

Ask two or three mothers to share part of their story. Be certain you know these women and have talked with them beforehand. While there are many ways their stories could be shared, ask them to focus on what they sacrificed to become mothers, or sacrificed as their children grew up. Ask them to also share a few realistic moments of having to rely on God, as they realized they were in over their heads and simply did not know the best way to parent. If the women are comfortable, open this up for a Q & A time.

Some students will come from loving, healthy homes. Others will be in difficult situations of either stress, abandonment or frequent arguments. Either way, in the teenage years it is most common to see the situation from their own point of view. To hear that a mother worried she was doing the wrong thing, or felt out of control, can help to put some perspective on relationships, and open conversations for extending grace and understanding when their own situation is not as ideal as they would like it to be.

Teacher's Note: There has recently been a great deal of research regarding the relationships between parents and their children. While the father becomes more significant in the teenage years, the mother's importance does not wane. That said, she also becomes the target of struggle and animosity. This can be a confusing time, not only for her children, but for her as well. It is not a bad idea to mention to your students that mothers are still people and can get their feelings hurt. They need to hear once in awhile that they are appreciated and loved.

DISCOVERY

Read Exodus 2:1–10.

Ask: Who are the main characters in this passage?

On a dry erase board at a focal point in the room, make a column for each person named. (Be certain they include Moses' mother and Pharaoh's daughter. You may also include Moses and his sister, but for this time the two women are the focus.)

Write down each thing you think the characters sacrificed in order to protect Moses.

Ask: Could you ever imagine giving up your child in order to be certain he or she was going to be safe and have a better life? Would this be an easy or a difficult decision?

Most of the time when we think of Moses, we rush past this part of his story. He is a great patriarch and has shaped so much of our faith and traditions. There was, however, a time when he was still a baby and a boy, when he needed to be protected and nurtured.

Exodus 2:1–10 offers a glimpse of at least three women who sacrificed for Moses.

He could not have made it without them, without God working through them.

Teacher's Note: The word mother was used in a broader context than we typically use it today. It could be used in reference to grandmothers, ancestors, any female superior in age or wisdom. Mother could also be used symbolically in reference to the true church, the kingdom of Judah, any capital city, or the earth. All of this to say, mother was not a default position for someone who had nothing to contribute to the community or world. She was exalted, important, and necessary for the survival and nurturance of the world.

LIFE APPLICATION : Moses' mother had to sacrifice her son to save his life. Pharaoh's daughter sacrificed her flexibility and stood up to her father to save the life of the baby floating in the river.

Break into small groups, ideally with a leader in each group.

Ask: What women have sacrificed for you? How?

Assuming somehow we could still have babies, what would the world be like without mothers?

If your group is open, go around the group and ask each person to say one thing they appreciate about their own mother, grandmother, or caretaker. You may need to encourage this for those who are currently in a fight with their mother, or for those who are truly in difficult home situations. Try to help them find at least one positive thing or one way they can recognize their mother has sacrificed for them.

Say: You've just heard about some amazing women.

Ask: What ways can you see yourself imitating their sacrificial spirit in your life now? What about in the future?

MAKING IT PERSONAL: Pass out notecards to each person. Give a few minutes for each person to write a note to their mother. Encourage them to say, in their own words, what they appreciate about their own mom. Tell them to give the card to their mom when they see her.

SONG: "Homesick" by Mercy Me, on the album *Undone*

QUOTABLE   QUOTES :

My mother is a walking miracle.

—Leonardo DiCaprio

May 17, 2006

Sacrificial Strength—Midweek

MEMORY VERSE:
A wise son makes his father happy, but a foolish son disrespects his mother.—Proverbs 15:20 (NCV)

SCRIPTURE: Matthew 12:46–50

LESSON IN A SENTENCE: Even when we don't realize it, mothers make sacrifices for their children.

FOCUS

Have each person write down the names of at least three famous people on separate slips of paper. They may be famous in any category—biblical characters, pop culture, history, etc. Once these are written, collect the slips of paper in a bucket. Have the people in your group partner up. In a circle (or two or three if your group is really large—twenty people in one circle is just fine, as that is only ten teams.) Have one person from the first team draw one of the slips of paper. In two minutes or less, the person who drew the slip of paper must try to get the other person to guess the name they drew, without saying the name or spelling it out. Once either the person has guessed or time has expired, pass the bucket to the next team. Each team gets a point for every name they are able to successfully guess before the time runs out.

Ask: What made a name easy or difficult to guess? Could you always recognize the clue your partner was trying to pass?

DISCOVER

Family can be hard to define. For many of us we think of the nuclear family—mom, dad, and siblings. You may include grandparents, aunts, uncles, and cousins. For some, friends become like family.

Read Matthew 12:46–50. Write these questions on a board or say them to the group.

Ask: How do you think it made the disciples feel to be called brothers and sisters?

How do you think Jesus' biological mother and brothers felt at hearing this?

What would it mean to you to have other believers consider you as close as family?

How would this change the way you live? Why or why not?

Do you think Jesus meant this for just then, or does this apply today?

LIFE APPLICATION: Look at the memory verse, Proverbs 15:20. Was Jesus showing disrespect when He asked who was His mother? Was He denying the woman who raised Him?

In the last lesson we looked at women who sacrificed for you. Technically, any time anyone takes the time to pour into you, to listen to you, to teach you, or help you, they are sacrificing their own selves for you. They might rather just be quiet or talk to their own friends or take care of their own errands—but they choose to be with you.

We've all had teachers or neighbors or women at the community center or church who have taken time for us. Think of one woman who has significantly poured into your life, whom you would like to imitate.

Just like you have people who have filled those roles of mentor—of being a spiritual brother, sister or mother—you are called to do the same.

Ask: What have you learned and what would you like to pass on?

Close, thanking God for family, both biological and the ones He has provided through relationships.

MAY 21, 2006

Vocation—What's Our Job?

By Alicia Claxton

MEMORY VERSE:

For we are God's workmanship, created in Christ Jesus to do good works, which God prepared in advance for us to do.—Ephesians 2:10 (NIV)

SCRIPTURE: Genesis 1:27; Psalm 18:32–35; Psalm 139:13–16; Zephaniah 3:17; Galatians 3:26–28; Ephesians 2:10

LESSON IN A SENTENCE: Our purpose in this life is to bring honor and glory to God. No matter what vocation we pursue, we must see it as an opportunity to fulfill our greater destiny.

THE BIG PICTURE (OR WHAT YOU'RE TRYING TO GET ACROSS):

As children we dream about what we'll be when we grow up: a doctor, a lawyer, a preacher, a professional athlete, a superhero. Raised in a society that defines people by what they do, it's no wonder we are obsessed from a young age with finding the right vocation. Even as believers we get caught up in the pursuit of success. We tend to departmentalize our lives (personal life, professional life, and spiritual life) so we can better manage our time and our efforts. The truth is, we were not created to climb a corporate ladder or compete in a virtual rat race. We were created to glorify God. Our identity is IN Christ, not in a title or on a resume. There is great freedom when we discover our purpose is to live and work as unto the Lord.

IN THIS LESSON STUDENTS SHOULD:

- Discover that their value is based on who they are IN Christ and not on what they do for a living.
- Be reminded that God has a plan for their lives.
- Learn to pursue opportunities/vocations that fit the abilities and gifts God has given them.

STUFF YOU NEED:

- Pens
- Index cards (see Option 1)
- Large sheets of paper or dry erase boards (see Option 1)
- Butcher paper, markers, glue sticks, magazines (see Option 2)

FOCUS

Choose either Option 1 or 2. Be certain to watch your time and not get carried away with this part of the lesson!

OPTION 1:

Give each student an index card and have them write down what they dreamed of becoming as a child (i.e. doctor, lawyer, professional athlete, etc.). Take up cards and put them in a hat. Ask for a volunteer to come up and draw a card from the hat. Play charades—have the student act out the "occupation" until someone guesses it correctly. Give bonus points if someone can guess whose childhood dream was just acted out. As an alternative to charades, you can also play this game like Pictionary®, using a large sheet of paper or dry erase board and dividing students into teams.

TRANSITION TO DISCOVERY by saying, "We all have dreams for our lives. . .some are childish dreams that we grow out of, while others linger and challenge us to strive for certain goals. Having the ambition to pursue our dreams is healthy as long as we remember that God created us to be eternally significant, not just temporarily successful. He is the One who breathes into us the passion to pursue excellence, but His dreams for us reach far beyond an occupation or earthly prize. He desires that we define ourselves by who we are IN Him and that we strive to glorify Him in all we do."

OPTION 2:

Have students create a mural of pictures and words that describe who they are. Roll out a large sheet of butcher paper and provide students with a stack of magazines (make sure they are age and gender appropriate), scissors, glue sticks, and markers. Have students write their name somewhere on the paper and use that space to place pictures or words that best describe them. Set a time limit of 10 minutes for this activity.

TRANSITION TO DISCOVERY by saying, "When we are asked to describe ourselves, we usually think first about our hobbies, our personalities, our families, etc. What we also need to think about is who we are IN Christ—understanding our value and significance in this life begins there."

DISCOVERY

Open with prayer. Divide students into four groups and give each group a topic to study. After sufficient time, bring them back together and have groups share what they learned.

VALUE

Group 1 should read Psalm 139:13–16; Zephaniah 3:17 and answer the following questions:

1. According to Psalm 139:13, what part does God play in our lives from the very beginning?

2. What evidence can you find in vv. 13–16 that God loves us and wants the best for us?

3. In Zephaniah 3:17, what does it say God will do for His children?

4. What does it mean when it says He will "take great delight in you?"

5. According to these verses, is our value to God based on anything we do or accomplish? What is it based on?

IDENTITY

Group 2 should read Genesis 1:27 and Galatians 3:26–28 and answer the following questions:

1. According to Genesis 1:27, in whose image have we been made?

2. We believe all of creation was made by God, so why is it significant that we were made in the image of God?

3. According to Galatians 3:26–28, when we are born again we are baptized into _____, clothed with _____ and one in _____.

4. How does our new identity IN Christ affect how God sees us?

5. How should the fact that we have been created in the image of God and are now identified with Christ affect how we see ourselves?

PURPOSE

Group 3 should read Jeremiah 29:11 and Ephesians 2:10 and answer the following questions:

1. What does Jeremiah 29:11 say about God's desire and purpose for His children?

2. What does Ephesians 2:10 say we've been created to do?

3. Who prepares and equips us for that work?

4. What examples can you think of from your own life where God equipped you for a special purpose?

SUCCESS

Group 4 should read Psalm 18:32–35 and answer the following questions:

1. What are some ways God has helped David (the writer) according to these verses?

2. Based on what you know about David, would you consider him to be a great man?

3. Who does David give the credit to for his greatness (end of v. 35)?

4. The phrase "You stoop down to make me great" implies that God is a personal God who is involved in our daily lives. Can you think of examples from your own life when God has stooped down to give you victory, to sustain you and to help you succeed?

Teacher's Note: Many teenagers today feel pressure to follow certain career paths or to achieve great success in order to prove their worth. They are growing up in a culture that defines people by what they can DO and not by who they ARE. Once out of college, they can expect to hear the question, "what do you do for a living" as many or more times than "how are you" or "what's your name." In this career driven society, we need to help our students understand that they are valuable to God and to the body of Christ no matter what occupation they choose.

LIFE APPLICATION: Ask them to share their thoughts on the following questions:

1. Do you feel pressured to make decisions about your future career? If so, where is that pressure coming from—parents, peers, yourself, etc.? How do you respond to that pressure?

2. For those of you who have a job right now, do you enjoy working, or is it something you dread? Why do you think that is?

3. Do you think there is such thing as the perfect job?

4. Why do you think it's important to understand your value and identity before making decisions about your vocation?

MAKING IT PERSONAL: Remind them of the Focus activity you did at the beginning of this lesson.

If you followed Option 1: Ask them to think back on the career they put down as their childhood dream. Is that dream still alive, or has it faded over the years? If God were to allow that dream to come true, how could they use that occupation to bring Him honor? Remind them that no matter what they do in life, they are called to do it in such a way that God is glorified.

If you followed Option 2: Roll out the sheet of butcher paper that they decorated with descriptions of themselves. Ask them to consider the personality traits, family heritage, hobbies, and passions God has given them. Encourage them to thank God for creating them with those unique qualities. Remind them that God has a purpose for them and desires to use their uniqueness for His glory.

MEMORY VERSE ACTIVITY

This is a relatively simple verse to memorize, so it would be fun to mix things up a little as they learn it. Try to find someone in the church or community who can teach your students this verse in sign language or in another language such as Spanish or French. Doing this type of activity will give your students a greater appreciation for the words and will reinforce memorization.

CONNECTIONS: There are many verses in the Bible that deal with work—how and why we should work, how we should treat those we work for, etc. Encourage students to look up verses like Ephesians 6:5–9, Colossians 3:22–24, and 1 Thessalonians 4:11–12.

SONGS: "This Mystery" by Nichole Nordeman, from the album *This Mystery*
"The Greatest Story" by Avalon, from the album *Avalon*

QUOTABLE QUOTES:

God has called the laity to be his basic ministers. He has called some to be "player-coaches"...to equip the laity for the ministry they are to fulfill. This equipping ministry is of unique importance. One is appointed to this ministry by the Holy Spirit; therefore it must be undertaken with utmost seriousness. This is a radical departure from the traditional understanding of the roles of the laity and the clergy. The laity had the idea that they were already committed to a "full-time" vocation in the secular world, [and] thus they did not have time—at least, much time—to do God's work. Therefore they contributed money to "free" the clergy to have the time needed to fulfill God's ministry. This view is rank heresy. If we follow this pattern, we may continue to do God's work until the Lord comes again and never fulfill God's purpose as it ought to be done.

—Author: Findley B. Edge

Vocation—What's Our Job—Midweek

MEMORY VERSE:
For we are God's workmanship, created in Christ Jesus to do good works, which God prepared in advance for us to do.—Ephesians 2:10 (NIV)

SCRIPTURE: 1 Samuel 16–18 (various Scriptures); 1 Chronicles 25:1–8; Psalm 78:70–72

LESSON IN A SENTENCE: Our purpose in this life is to bring honor and glory to God and no matter what vocation we pursue, we must see it as an opportunity to fulfill our greater destiny.

FOCUS

Set up a mock job fair in the room before students arrive. Have tables for different occupations and place object lessons or items of interest at each table—if possible, have adults who are in these fields at the table to answer questions. Instruct students to visit as many tables as they are interested in within the allotted time (10–15 minutes). Examples of job fair tables:

MEDICAL FIELD—place the game *Operation*® at this table and let students interested in medicine take turns playing.

BUSINESS— place the game *Monopoly*® or *Life*® at this table and let students play.

SPORTS— place some handheld video games at this table and let students play.

ART—place sheets of paper and paint at this table and let students create.

MUSIC—place instruments at this table and let students enjoy.

VIDEO— place video equipment at this table and let students take turns recording or editing footage.

After the time is up, bring everyone back into a large group and ask students to share about a profession they are interested in.

TRANSITION TO DISCOVERY by saying, "Think about the first table you walked over to. What made you go there first? What makes certain jobs/careers more interesting to us than others? We tend to lean toward tasks that we are more naturally inclined to excel in, or ones where our personality traits are assets. There's good reason for that. God made us with certain traits, talents, gifts and passions so we could fulfill His unique purpose for our lives."

DISCOVERY

Open with a word of prayer.

Using the example of David, help students see how God will use our talents, character traits, and experiences to bring Him glory in whatever task He calls us to.

DAVID—THE SHEPHERD

Q: According to 1 Samuel 16:11–12, where was David when Samuel came to anoint him as the King of Israel?

A: Out in the fields tending to his flock.

Q: Based on 1 Samuel 17:32–37, how did David's experience as a shepherd prepare him for the battles he would face later in life?

A: He fought off wild animals to protect his sheep; his time as shepherd helped him to build his physical strength as well as his courage in battle.

Q: Based on Psalm 78:70–72, how did David's experience as a shepherd prepare him to be the King of Israel?

A: The qualities that made him a good shepherd (protector, guide, provider, comforter), helped him to lead the nation of Israel.

DAVID—THE SONGWRITER/MUSICIAN

Q: According to 1 Samuel 16:14–23, what door was opened for David because of his musical talent? Do you think this experience was significant to David's future?

A: He was invited to play for King Saul—to comfort the king with his music. This was significant because it gave David an opportunity to serve in the palace where he would later rule.

Q: Based on 1 Chronicles 25:1–8, how did David's love of music effect the worship services of his time?

A: He was able to incorporate music in a new way in the temple.

DAVID—THE WARRIOR

Q: According to 1 Samuel 18:5, how did David's time as a warrior prepare him to be king?

A: He served with passion and achieved success—he earned the respect, authority, and favor of Saul and the people.

LIFE APPLICATION: God used David's talents, his passion, and his experiences to accomplish eternally significant things. God had a plan for David's life, but it was bigger than him becoming the King of Israel—it was about him becoming a "man after God's own heart." Each step of David's journey helped shape his character and allowed him the opportunity to glorify the Lord!

Ask students to prayerfully consider the journey they are on right now. Are they allowing God to use their talents, passions, and experiences for His glory, or are they pursuing their own ambitions? No matter how young they are, God can use them right now—they don't have to wait until they are given a greater span of influence or responsibility (such as in college or in their career). Challenge them to pursue God and allow Him to direct their steps today, tomorrow, and forever.

CONNECTIONS: The Bible is full of examples of how greed and the pursuit of selfish ambition can hinder God's work in our lives. Have students study some of the following examples: Matthew 6:19–24 (Treasures in Heaven); Luke 12:13–21 (the Parable of the Rich Fool); Luke 18:18–25 (The Rich Ruler).

SONGS: "Meant to Live" by Switchfoot, from the album *The Beautiful Letdown*
"This is Your Life" by Switchfoot, from the album *The Beautiful Letdown*

RAP MUSIC, HIP-HOP CULTURE

AND ITS USEFUL FUNCTIONS

By Calenthia Dowdy
ASSISTANT PROFESSOR OF YOUTH CULTURE

Rap music can be traced as far back as Africa; it is rooted in African storytelling and drumming. Africa's tribal poets, musicians, and oral historians were called "griots," the original rappers. They rapped or told stories about what was going on in the village as it related to family life, social conditions, and politics. But in America we trace rap music back to the early 1970s in the Bronx, New York City. It began as an underground fad that no one knew would eventually grow to become a mainstream, multi-million dollar industry and subculture. Today that subculture is called "hip-hop." Rap music and hip-hop culture recently celebrated thirty years of thriving and evolution. The genre has changed a great deal over the decades, but it continues to entertain and challenge the masses, especially the church.

Just as the original African rappers focused on family life, social conditions, and economics, twentieth-century rappers started out doing that very same thing. Youth rapped about what was going on in their communities. It was the mode through which young urbanites told the world their stories. One such story was called *The Message*, by Grand Master Flash and the Furious Five, and was released in 1983. It describes life and conditions of poverty in an urban municipal housing project:

> *Broken glass everywhere,*
> *People pissin' on the stairs,*
> *you know nobody cares*
> *I can't take the smell, can't take the noise,*
> *Got no money to move out, I guess I got no choice*
> *Rats in the front room, roaches in the back,*
> *Junkies in the alley with a baseball bat*
> *I tried to get away but I couldn't get far,*
> *'cuz a man with a tow truck repossessed my car.*
> *Don't push me 'cuz I'm close to the edge,*
> *I'm trying not to lose my head, Uh huh ha ha ha*
> *It's like a jungle sometimes,*
> *It makes me wonder how I keep from goin' under...*
> *A child is born with no state of mind,*
> *Blind to the ways of mankind*

God is smilin' on you but he's frownin' too,
Because only God knows what you're goin' through
You'll grow in the ghetto livin' second-rate,
And your eyes will sing a song of deep hate
The places you play and where you stay,
Looks like one great big alleyway

Bein' used and abused to serve like hell,
'til one day, you was found hung dead in the cell
It was plain to see that your life was lost,
You was cold and your body swung back and forth
But now your eyes sing the sad, sad song,
Of how you lived so fast and died so young so...
Don't push me cuz I'm close to the edge,
I'm tryin' not to lose my head...

The Message offers a vivid and painful depiction of young life and
its ultimate demise resultant from growing up in an urban ghetto.
Early rap music often served as a tool for telling these sorts of stories.
Stories of the lives of oppressed people rarely seen or acknowledged.
They are the invisible underprivileged, hidden away in pockets of
despair where others are privileged by not having to see them or feel
their pain. Early rappers had a function similar to Old Testament
prophets like Isaiah, Amos, Micah, and Jeremiah. They prophesied
about the impoverished and unjust life conditions of oppressed people
like orphans, widows and strangers in their community:

> They sell the righteous for a pair of sandals. They trample on
> the heads of the poor as upon the dust of the ground and
> deny justice to the oppressed
> —Amos 2:6–7 (NIV)

> All are greedy for gain; prophets and priests alike, all practice
> deceit. They dress the wound of my people as though it were
> not serious. "Peace, peace," they say, when there is no peace.
> —Jeremiah 8:10–11 (NIV)

> If you really change your ways and your actions and deal
> with each other justly, if you do not oppress the alien, the
> fatherless or the widow and do not shed innocent blood in
> this place, and if you do not follow other gods to your own
> harm, then I will let you live in this place, in the land I gave
> your forefathers forever and ever.
> —Jeremiah 7:5–7 (NIV)

Today rap music has become overly commercialized, mostly serving as global entertainment. Unfortunately much of hip-hop culture

and rap music has moved far away from its primary historical purpose. But in place of that it has created something that even the church has had a difficult time creating and sustaining. That is, the ideal of diversity within unity under the Lordship of the one Christ. Hip-hop has bridged many youth divides under the banner of hip-hop. These young people can be found in all ethnic groups, cultures, and countries. It is an international phenomenon crossing social classes, metropolises, suburbs, ex-burbs, and tiny rural regions. With this understanding, it is important for youth leaders to recognize that hip-hop and rap music are not exclusive or unique "problems" that only urban American youth workers must deal with. Hip-hop culture shapes a way of life for young people, from what they wear, to how they may be encouraged to think and act. It is more than music; it is a culture, and the culture of choice for many young people today.

Teaching young people about hip-hop's roots can help open up a broader understanding of an holistic gospel message for our youth; a gospel message that includes both a focus on personal piety and structural justice. To be clear, this is not a call to a social gospel, rather it is a call to a whole gospel. One that also embraces the prophetic social ministry of Jesus as He reached out to the poor and oppressed "least of these" around Him (see Matthew 25). Hip-hop developed out of a vacuum left by the church as it neglected social justice and focused solely on personal salvation and piety.

What happens when the church neglects its prophetic responsibility to speak on behalf of poor and oppressed communities? What happens when the church becomes a mirror reflection of social power structures only looking out for its comforts and wealth? God fills in that void with other willing voices, voices that will make the church uncomfortable, and point fingers at its silent slumber.

After hip-hop artist Tupac Shakur was murdered in 1996 at the age of 25, Reverend Willie Wilson agreed to hold a memorial service for the slain rapper in his Washington, D.C. church. It drew youth from across the city who were lost and bewildered about Tupac's murder. In his eulogy Wilson said, "hip-hop artists in many instances are the preachers of their generation, preaching a message which, too often, those who have been given the charge to preach prophetic words to the people have not given.... The Tupac's of the world have responded and in many instances have reflected... *if you don't speak out, then the rocks will cry out...* I think in a real sense these pop artists are the rocks that are crying out with prophetic words." (Dyson 2001, 202) For Wilson, Tupac was the prophet for young people. Just as it was for Israelite prophets, so it has been for hip-hop youth, the prophet is he or she who speaks on behalf of those silenced by structural evil. In many ways, rapper Tupac Shakur was a post-industrial urban prophet. He spoke these words in 1991:

What we need to do as a community is start
taking control back of our communities,
I understand there's always gonna be drug dealing
I understand there's always gonna be violence
but we just need to regulate it,
so that we can at least have like a peaceful zone.
...and no matter what these people say about me,
my music does not glorify any image.
My music is spiritual if you listen to it.
... If you listen to it....
I just try to speak about things that affect me
And about things that affect our community.
I always been a fighter,
always been a soldier,
always been a struggler.
Can't nothing stop me but death itself.
People are resilient, we're very strong.
—Tupac Shakur, 1991 (2-Pac 4Ever)

Young people need to know that God loves the city and is at work redeeming it. Through the Bible and through an understanding of hip-hop's true roots, He calls young people as change agents and fighters against injustice in suffering communities. He calls them to "Seek the peace and prosperity of the city to which I have carried you...Pray to the Lord for it, because if it prospers (thrives), you too will prosper."—Jeremiah 29:7 (NIV)

References

The Bible, New International Version

Dyson, Michael Eric. *Holler if You Hear Me: Searching for Tupac Shakur*. New York: Basic Civitas Books, 2001

Grand Master Flash and the Furious Five, *The Message*, Audio recording, 1982

Trinity Home Entertainment, 2-Pac 4Ever, Interview on Video: VHS Footage, 2003

MAY 28, 2006

Holistic Ministry

By Fred Arzola

MEMORY VERSE:
If we say we love God yet hate a fellow believer, we are liars. For if we do not love a brother or sister whom we have seen, we cannot love God, whom we have not seen.—1 John 4:20 (TNIV)

SCRIPTURE: Luke 4:14–21 (TNIV)

> [14] Jesus returned to Galilee in the power of the Spirit, and news about him spread through the whole countryside. [15]He was teaching in their synagogues, and everyone praised him.
>
> [16]He went to Nazareth, where he had been brought up, and on the Sabbath day he went into the synagogue, as was his custom. He stood up to read,[17]and the scroll of the prophet Isaiah was handed to him. Unrolling it, he found the place where it is written:
>
> [18]"The Spirit of the Lord is on me, because he has anointed me to proclaim good news to the poor. He has sent me to proclaim freedom for the prisoners and recovery of sight for the blind, to release the oppressed, [19]to proclaim the year of the Lord's favor."
>
> [20]Then he rolled up the scroll, gave it back to the attendant and sat down. The eyes of everyone in the synagogue were fastened on him. [21]He began by saying to them, "Today this scripture is fulfilled in your hearing."

LESSON IN A SENTENCE: As Christians, we are called both to share the good news of Jesus Christ AND to social action.

THE BIG PICTURE (OR WHAT YOU'RE TRYING TO GET ACROSS):
Jesus tells us the greatest commandment is to "Love the Lord your God. . . AND Love your neighbor as yourself." (Luke 10:27). Many Christians tend to forget the conjunction "and." When using the word

"and," this implies the second part or the sentence is equal in importance to the first part. As 1 John 4:20 (TNIV) states, "If we say we love God yet hate a fellow believer, we are liars."

For many Christians, we tend to separate these two components. This tends to create two Christian camps: In the first camp, there are the spiritually active Christians who are engaged in worship and discipleship, but not committed to social action. In the second camp, there are the socially active Christians who are engaged in social justice activities, but are not committed to biblical discipleship and holiness. As Christians, we are called to a third Camp: engaged in personal, spiritual, and social transformation in Christ.

It is also important to note, there is a difference between charity and justice. Giving people fish to eat is charity. Teaching people how to fish so they may eat for the rest of their lives is justice. This involves a three step process: 1) recognizing that people are suffering—physically and spiritually; 2) challenging Christians to ask the radical question, "Why are these people suffering and treated unjustly?" and 3) requires Christians to actually become engaged in social justice teaching, equipping and empowering those who are poor and marginalized.

Holistic Ministry is the call to share the Good News of Jesus Christ and be engaged in social action.

IN THIS LESSON STUDENTS SHOULD:

- Understand that all Christians are called to share the Good News of Jesus Christ and be engaged in social action.
- Understand that Christians' social justice is distinct from what is commonly understood as social justice.

STUFF YOU NEED:

- Community demographics and statement of needs of the local church or youth ministry
- Blackboard/whiteboard/flip board
- Chalk/marker

FOCUS

OPTION 1:

The teacher asks, "What are the three biggest social problems, concerns, or issues for teenagers in our community?"

Break into small groups to process.

Gather as a large group to process, and encourage an open and honest discussion without having to reveal confidential names or issues.

These issues should be listed on the board.

OPTION 2:

Distribute the community demographics and/or community statement of needs. (These may be obtained through www.census.gov or check with your local chamber of commerce.)

The teacher highlights significant points in the data: Total population, race, gender, economics, youth, foreign born, single head of household, education, health, crime, unemployment, etc.

The teacher asks, "Based on these demographics, what are the three biggest social problems, concerns, or issues for teenagers in our community?"

Break into small groups to process.

Gather as a large group to process, and encourage an open and honest discussion without having to reveal confidential names or issues.

These issues should be listed on the board.

DISCOVERY

Read Luke 4:14–21.

One student reads vv. 14–15

A second student reads vv. 16–17

A third student reads vv. 18–19

A fourth student reads vv. 20–21

There are three things in the story above that are very important for us to understand as Christians engaged in holistic ministry.

First, it says Jesus was "in the power of the Spirit." As Christians, we, too, are "in the power of the Spirit." While there are many good and wonderful people who are involved in helping others, as people "in the power of the Spirit," we offer not only social help, but the love and message of Jesus Christ. For the poor and marginalized, we see them both as people in need and as people with dignity. They are created in the image of God and are eternally valuable to Him. Are you "in the power of the Spirit?"

Second, this is the first time in Jesus' ministry that He publicly declares His Messiahship. Whenever a leader speaks for the first time, it is always an important event. He or she is casting a vision towards the future. By saying "Today this scripture is fulfilled in your hearing," Jesus is telling his listeners: *the kingdom of God that you have been waiting for has now begun.* This is the good news that we as Christians are to share with our friends and with the world. Jesus is saying, "Heaven has now arrived on earth." This is the good news. Are you sharing the good news?

Finally, what makes this story even more significant is that Jesus declares His Messiahship by reading a message of justice from the prophet Isaiah. This was very radical in the first century—and is still very radical today! As usual, Jesus turns over the rules of etiquette. How does Jesus publicly initiate His Messiahship? By combining the spiritual and social dimension, "preach good news to the poor. . .proclaim freedom for the prisoners. . .recovery of sight for the blind. . . release the oppressed. . .proclaim the year of the Lord's favor."

Teacher's Note: If the youth ministry is located in a middle-class or upper-class setting, these words tend to be very upsetting. Remind the teens that, of course, God loves all people equally. Then share this image, *"If you had two children, one was healthy and one was very sick, which would you love more?"* Allow them to struggle with this question and process responses.

Here is a suggested response. *"Of course you would love them both equally. But the child who is sick and weak is in need of more care. While everything you have is for both children, you may have to spend more time and energy with the sick and weak child. Jesus says, "It is not the healthy who need a doctor, but the sick" (Mark 2:17 NIV). This is the same with the church. While the church loves all people, it needs to take care of the sick, the weak, and the most vulnerable. If the church does not take care of these people, then who will? It is our call as Christians—to love God AND to love our neighbor. Do you take care or stand up for the teens and people in your life who are weak and vulnerable?*

Based on this story, there are three ingredients for holistic ministry: the power of the Holy Spirit, the good news of Jesus Christ, and social action.

MAKING IT PERSONAL:

Teacher's Note: *Ask the following questions, and invite the teens to reflect quietly for a moment.*

Do you see the poor and marginalized as people with dignity created in the image of God? If not, why not? Explain.

Do you see the poor and marginalized as your mother, father, sister, brother, son, or daughter? If not, why not? Explain.

Do you interact with the poor and marginalized? If not, why not? Explain.

Do you share a message of hope with the poor and marginalized? If not, why not? Explain.

Do the poor and marginalized see Christ in you or not? If not, why not? Explain.

Do you love the poor and marginalized? Are you scared of them? Do you hate them? Explain.

Do the people in your community who are poor and marginalized see your church and/or youth ministry as a place of love or judgment? Are they welcome to your church or youth ministry?

LIFE APPLICATION/SERVICE: Take a look at the list on the board.

Decide, as a group, which one of the social issues listed the youth ministry is willing to address.

Teacher's Note: The youth ministry can solve all the problems. Make sure they select one issue that is important to them, but is also an issue that can realistically be addressed. It must, however, be something local that requires the students to get contextually engaged.

Process as a large group. Or break into small groups and return later to the large group.

Follow this format:

Identification:	Identify a specific social problem affecting your community.
Examination:	Critically examine why this problem exists in your community.
Plan:	Explore and list ways the youth ministry may address this Issue.
Action:	Implement your plan.
Evaluation:	Evaluate the plan, celebrate the joys, plan for the future.

QUOTABLE   QUOTES:

I must admit that I was initially disappointed in being so categorized.

But as I continued to think about the matter I gradually gained a bit of satisfaction from being considered an extremist. Was not Jesus an extremist for love— "Love your enemies, bless them that curse you, pray for them that despitefully use you." Was not Amos an extremist for justice—"Let justice roll down like waters and righteousness like a mighty stream." Was not Paul an extremist for the gospel of Jesus Christ—"I bear in my body the marks of the Lord Jesus." Was not Martin Luther an extremist—"Here I stand; I can do none other so help me God." Was not John Bunyan an extremist—"I will stay in jail to the end of my days before I make a butchery of my conscience." Was not Abraham Lincoln an extremist—"This nation cannot survive half slave and half free." Was not Thomas Jefferson an extremist—"We hold these truths to be self-evident, that all men are created equal." So the question is not whether we will be extremist but what kind of extremist will we be. Will we be extremists for hate or will we be extremists for love? Will we be extremists for the preservation of injustice—or will we be extremists for the cause of justice? In that dramatic scene on Calvary's hill, three men were crucified. We must not forget that all three were crucified for the same crime—the crime of extremism. Two were extremists for immorality, and thusly fell below their environment. The other, Jesus Christ, was an extremist for love, truth, and goodness, and thereby rose above his environment. So, after all, maybe the South, the nation and the world are in dire need of creative extremists.

—Martin Luther King Jr.
Letter from a Birmingham Jail

WEB CONNECT:

Evangelicals for Social Action—www.esa-online.org
Mission: To challenge and equip the church to be agents of God's redemption and transformation in the world.

ESA pursues this mission through:

○ Reflection on church and society from a biblical perspective
○ Training in holistic ministry
○ Linking people together for mutual learning and action.

Network 9:35—www.network935.org
Mission: To nurture and strengthen local congregations, pastors, and lay leaders who are committed to and engaged in holistic mission by offering materials, developing new channels of communication, and researching what congregations most need to increase their holistic ministry.

Holistic Ministry—Midweek

MEMORY VERSE:
If we say we love God yet hate a fellow believer, we are liars. For if we do not love a brother or sister whom we have seen, we cannot love God, whom we have not seen.—1 John 4:20 (TNIV)

SCRIPTURE: John 2:13–19 (TNIV)
^{13} When it was almost time for the Jewish Passover, Jesus went up to Jerusalem. ^{14}In the temple courts he found people selling cattle, sheep and doves, and others sitting at tables exchanging money. ^{15}So he made a whip out of cords, and drove all from the temple courts, both sheep and cattle; he scattered the coins of the money changers and overturned their tables. ^{16}To those who sold doves he said, "Get these out of here! Stop turning my Father's house into a market!" ^{17}His disciples remembered that it is written: "Zeal for your house will consume me." ^{18}The Jews then responded to him, "What sign can you show us to prove your authority to do all this?" ^{19}Jesus answered them, "Destroy this temple, and I will raise it again in three days."

LESSON IN A SENTENCE: As Christians, we are called both to share the good news of Jesus Christ AND to social action.

FOCUS

Review the social issue identified in the Justice Cycle this past Sunday.

Continue to process the "Examination" and "Plan" components.

By the end of today's session, the group should have an initial date for the "Action" component, in order to implement the plan.

DISCOVERY

This week, we have focused on the theme of justice. Specifically, we have examined "holistic ministry." Holistic ministry is a philosophy of ministry which teaches we are called both to share the good news of Jesus Christ AND to social action.

Perhaps no other image of Jesus' response to injustice is as passionate as the image in John 2:13–19. Here, Jesus enters the temple courts and sees what He believes is a desecration of God's house. In keeping with the Passover tradition, the marketers were selling cattle, sheep, and doves for sacrifices of sins. The spiritual significance of sacrificing animals to appease God surely would irritate Jesus, although He would have been familiar with this tradition as a Jew Himself. However, the visual of marketers in God's house financially profiting from the vulnerability, guilt, shame, and pain of people who desire forgiveness from God, infuriated Jesus. Undoubtedly, Jesus recalled the words of the ancient Hebrew writings, psalmists, and prophets:

> Does the LORD delight in burnt offerings and sacrifices as much as in obeying the voice of the LORD? To obey is better than sacrifice, and to heed is better than the fat of rams.
> —1 Samuel 15:22 (NIV)

> Sacrifice and offering you did not desire…burnt offerings and sin offerings you did not require…I desire to do your will, O my God, your law is within my heart.
> —Psalm 40:6–8 (NIV)

> You do not delight in sacrifice, or I would bring it; you do not take pleasure in burnt offerings. The sacrifices of God are a broken spirit; a broken and contrite heart.
> —Psalm 51:17 (NIV)

> To do what is right and just is more acceptable to the LORD than sacrifice.
> —Proverbs 21:3 (NIV)

> "The multitude of your sacrifices—what are they to me?" says the LORD. "I have more than enough of burnt offerings…I have no pleasure in the blood of bulls and lambs and goats…Stop bringing meaningless offerings! Your incense is detestable to me…They have become a burden to me; I am weary of bearing them…Your hands are full of blood; wash and make yourself clean…Stop doing wrong, learn to do right! Seek justice, encourage the oppressed. Defend the cause of the fatherless, plead the case of the widow. Come now, let us reason together." says the LORD.
> —Isaiah 1:11–18 (NIV)

> This is what the LORD Almighty, the God of Israel, says: "Go ahead, add your burnt offerings to your other sacrifices and eat the meat yourselves! For when I brought your forefathers out of Egypt and spoke to them, I did not just give them

commands about burnt offerings and sacrifices, but I gave them this command: Obey me, and I will be your God and you will be my people. Walk in all the ways I command you, that it may go well with you."

—Jeremiah 7:21–23 (NIV)

For I desire mercy, not sacrifice and acknowledgement of God rather than burnt offerings.

—Hosea 6:6 (NIV)

With what shall I come before the LORD and bow down before the exalted God? He has showed you, O man, what is good. And what does the LORD require of you? To act justly and to love mercy and to walk humbly with your God.

—Micah 6:6, 8 (NIV)

In the Christian tradition, we often refer to this scene as "righteous anger." That is, anger is recognized as a "right" and "good" thing because it is a primal response to an injustice. In this case, Jesus' anger is in response to an unjust attitude to the house of God, and, therefore, to God Himself.

There are five things about the story that are very important to understand in order to reinforce our understanding of holistic ministry.

First, Jesus recognized an injustice. From the moment Jesus walked in to the temple, He recognized there was something wrong. He recognized that what He saw contradicted the teachings of the Scripture. There was no respect for God. And there was no compassion for God's people. Do you recognize the injustices around your community?

Second, He used a tool to fight injustice. Jesus made a whip out of cords. This image surely eliminates any presumptions that Jesus was "soft" or a pushover. Like Jesus, we, too, are called to be humble and meek, but not weak. As a Christian, especially when confronting injustice, we must be strong—spiritually, emotionally, and intellectually. In the struggle for justice, it may even require sacrificing our lives. Jesus used what He had at the moment. What gifts and tools do you have that can be used to fight injustice? What gifts and tools has God given you that can be used for social action?

Third, He turned over the tables. This is a call to arms to become engaged in social action. Jesus did not just recognize the injustice solely with His eyes and heart. He became involved, in a small yet dramatic way, to make a statement. This is scary. Sometimes, when you stand up for people in the name of God, "the powers" that cause the injustice feel threatened and resentful. Be meek but be strong. Do you become involved when you recognize injustice, or do you stand on the sidelines watching it happen?

Fourth, He challenged the marketers. When Jesus turned over the tables, He made a radical statement against economic and systemic injustice. But Jesus went one step further. He looked into the eyes of the marketers and said, "Get these out of here! Stop turning My Father's house into a market!" Not only was He challenging "the system," but He challenged the very people who profit from this unjust system. It is one thing to say, "This system is racist." It is another thing to say, "You are racist." It is one thing to say, "What is happening here is wrong." It is another thing to say, "You are wrong." Sometimes, we have to challenge people directly. Of course, we want to do this in a way that honors God and uses wisdom. This is always difficult and uncomfortable, but when engaged in social action, often necessary. Are you willing to speak up against injustice, even confronting unjust people?

Finally, Jesus offered a new paradigm. When Jesus said, "Destroy this temple, and I will raise it again in three days," He offered a new worldview, a new way of looking at things. When we are involved in holistic ministry, we must always offer a paradigm of hope and love rooted in Christian faith. As Christians we are not called to be involved in random acts of social engagement. The change we hope to initiate should always be geared towards a greater unfolding of the kingdom of God that is consistent with biblical principles.

Our society often promotes issues and causes that are viewed as socially just, but these issues and causes are not always consistent with the teaching of God's Word. Authentic holistic ministry and true biblical justice cannot promote issues that contradict God's Word. Many Bible-believing Christians involved in social justice may be challenged or even mocked for not fighting all so called "progressive" or "justice" causes. But Christians involved in holistic ministry must be faithful to God's Word while engaged in God's world.

LIFE APPLICATION: Does injustice create righteous anger in your heart? Explain. If not, why not?

1. What are three things you can do to become a more just person?

2. What is your part or contribution to the Justice Cycle?

3. Is there anything in the reflections with which you disagree? Explain?

4. What does justice mean to you?

5. What are your thoughts about holistic ministry?

6. Why would some Christians "feel" uncomfortable with holistic ministry?

7. Why would some Christians "feel" comfortable with holistic ministry?

JUNE 4, 2006

Not by Might

By Amy Jacober

MEMORY VERSE:
Not by might nor by power, but by My Spirit says the LORD Almighty.—Zechariah 4:6b (NIV)

SCRIPTURE: 2 Corinthians 3:1–6

LESSON IN A SENTENCE: It is better to live in the Spirit than in our own power.

THE BIG PICTURE (OR WHAT YOU'RE TRYING TO GET ACROSS):

We are taught from early on that we are to take care of ourselves. To be responsible and rely on our own resources. Everywhere you look there are self help books, magazines and TV shows. We work really hard at being powerful in order to look out for #1. God interrupts this kind of thinking and offers something different. What He offers is a new heart, freedom from the law, and His unending love for you. We don't have to fight for His attention or guidance. He is closer than most of us realize.

IN THIS LESSON STUDENTS SHOULD:

- ○ Learn about a few characteristics of the Holy Spirit.
- ○ Differentiate between their own human power and the power of God.
- ○ Distinguish the Holy Spirit as working on who we are on the inside.

STUFF YOU NEED:

- ○ Paper, and lots of it! At least a ream or two
- ○ Foam noodles for the pool, cut in half (at least 3, more if your group is large)

FOCUS

OPTION 1:

Get several foam noodles for the swimming pool (these should be easy to find at any grocery or drug store). Cut them in half so they are

2 ½–3 feet long. Form a circle by connecting hands and spreading out. Start with two people in the center, giving each a foam noodle. The object of the game—try to hit the other person. Once a person has been hit, she hands the noodle to someone else in the group. After a few minutes, add extra players in the center. Depending on how large your circle is and how many noodles you purchased, have 6–10 people in the center. End this game while they are still having fun and before it gets out of hand.

Ask: What made someone able to survive in the center?

OPTION 2:

Ask for three or four of your strongest students to come to the front. Tell them, you are going to have a little contest to see who is the strongest! Start with just a single sheet of paper and ask them to rip it. Next hand each person a stack of ten. Continue to increase the stacks by increments of ten until they are unable to rip the stack. If someone cannot continue, ask him or her to sit down. Once the increment of ten becomes too much, increase by only five and then one at a time until you are able to declare a winner. Make a big deal out of how strong and powerful they are!

DISCOVERY

Ask: How many of you would like to be more powerful? What do you think it would take for you to be more powerful? What do you think the Holy Spirit might have to do with this?

Teacher's Note: There is no answer in particular here. It is not often that most churches discuss the Holy Spirit at all. By beginning the Discovery section with this question, you are already guiding your students to be thinking in this direction when they read the Scripture.

Read 2 Corinthians 3:1–6 as an entire group. After you have read through this once, ask your students to reread this in groups of 4–5.

Pay close attention to vv. 5–6.

Ask: From where does our adequacy come? Do you agree or disagree? What about times you have worked really hard for something? What if anything comes from yourself?

Teacher's Note: Verse 6 speaks of the letter killing, but the Spirit giving life. The letter is in reference to the letter of the law. If you live in a legalistic way, death comes. This may not be a physical death, but a spiritual and emotional death will come. The Spirit brings life out of legalism. There is always the possibility of applying this passage incorrectly, living as though anything is fair game, as though no rules whatsoever apply. As your students wrestle with this passage, offer guidance to develop a healthy perspective of avoiding legalism and walking in the Spirit.

LIFE APPLICATION: *Ask:* What is legalism?

Give each group a piece of construction paper and a marker. On one side, have them write down behavior they would consider to be legalistic. On the other side, have them write an alternative behavior that would reflect living in the Spirit.

Ask: Why is it easier to live under legalism than under the Spirit?

Spend some time really trying to look at legalism. It often looks like the perfect Christian life on the outside, yet the inside is unrecognizable to God. This can be a huge threat to many Christians. Legalism offers clear-cut boundaries, checklists to determine when a person is doing well or not. Scripture, however, tells us that we are not to live by the letter, rather by the Spirit.

Ask: What is the difference between living in your own power and living in the power of God? How can you know the difference?

MAKING IT PERSONAL: Reread v. 6. What does it mean to you that the Spirit gives life?

What would your life look like if you actually believed this? If you were open enough to allow the Holy Spirit to free you from legalism and truly live? The Holy Spirit works on the inside. Instead of requiring legalistic behavior, behavior flows from the changes taking place in our heart and soul.

Spend a few minutes in silence. Invite each person to consider one specific way their life would be different if they really lived by the Spirit instead of the letter. Close in prayer, thanking God for the gift of His presence.

CONNECTIONS: Check out Galatians 5:1 for a further look at the freedom that comes as a result of walking in the Spirit.

SONG: "I'll Fly Away" by Jars of Clay on *Redemption Songs*

QUOTABLE QUOTES:

The Holy Spirit, object of faith, is also an object of prayer: we must not only pray that we receive the Holy Spirit. We must pray to him.

—Karl Barth

Not by Might—Midweek

MEMORY VERSE:
Not by might nor by power, but by My Spirit says the LORD
Almighty.—Zechariah 4:6b (NIV)

SCRIPTURE: Ezekiel 36:25–28

LESSON IN A SENTENCE: It is better to live in the Spirit than in
our own power.

FOCUS

Have a glass nearly full of milk sitting in a bowl (the bowl must be
large enough to catch the spills). Have a second glass with equally as
much or a little more, filled with corn syrup. Tell your students they
must figure out how to replace the corn syrup for the milk without
touching the milk glass. They may get creative so remind them to not
make a mess!! The easy solution, with the glass of milk sitting in the
bowl, pour the corn syrup into the glass. Corn syrup will displace the
milk. Without ever touching it, the milk will spill out and the corn
syrup will fill the glass.

Ask: How is this experiment like the Holy Spirit and our nature?

When the Holy Spirit comes in, it takes up residence. In fact so
much so, that our own sin nature is pushed away!

DISCOVERY

Print out this passage one verse at a time. Depending on the size
of your group, make enough copies where you will have each person
read at least one verse (this would mean reading the entire passage several times). For example, if you have eight people in your group, have
one person read v. 25, the next reads v. 26, the third reads v. 27, the
fourth reads v. 28 and start over, with the fifth person reading v. 25, the
sixth reading v. 26, etc. If you have a larger group, split into groups of
twelve and go through the same process.

You will have just heard the same passage several times.

Ask: After listening, what stands out to you?

Have you ever thought about God replacing your old heart and
spirit with new?

LIFE APPLICATION: God's Spirit displaces ours when we let Him in.
Just like the corn syrup pushed the milk right out, God's Spirit fills us
and cleanses us from the inside.

We've all had experiences of having our thoughts totally consumed by something—upcoming party, a crush on someone, a looming test!

Ask: What times can you remember finding it hard to concentrate because you had something consuming every thought?

ANCIENT CONNECTION: It is very difficult in our world filled with noise, to hear or sense the presence of the Holy Spirit. One way to attempt to bridge this gap is in a centering prayer. This is most likely unlike any prayer to which you have been accustomed. There is no prayer to memorize, no phrase to repeat, in fact no words to be lifted up at all! It involves choosing a word or an image that allows you to focus on God (like Father, Abba, king, love, lion, or a heart). The word or image does not matter, as long as it is meaningful to you. Focus on this word or image. Other thoughts will creep in; don't get frustrated, rather just refocus and settle in. The object of this prayer is not to speak to God or even to hear a specific message, rather simply to be in His presence. Not unlike those times when you are with the most intimate of friends and words are not necessary, it is simply being in the presence of one another that is so fulfilling. Ideally, this takes 20 minutes or so. This can seem intimidating at first! Start small and build up! For a much more in-depth explanation see either http://www.contemplativeoutreach.org or *Soul Shaper: Exploring Spiritual and Contemplative Practice in Youth Ministry* by Tony Jones.

JUNE 11, 2006

Two Sides, Same Coin

By Amy Jacober

MEMORY VERSE:
And he said to them, "Go into all the world and preach the gospel to all creation."—Mark 16:15 (TNIV)

For I am not ashamed of the gospel: for it is the power of God for salvation to everyone that believeth; to the Jew first and also to the Greek.—Romans 1:16 (ASV)

SCRIPTURE: Luke 24:1–11; Mark 16:1–13; Mark 4:1–9

LESSON IN A SENTENCE: We have the privilege and responsibility of sharing the gospel with the world.

THE BIG PICTURE (OR WHAT YOU'RE TRYING TO GET ACROSS):
Sharing the gospel with the world is not an option for Christians. What this looks like and how this is interpreted has been debated for centuries. Regardless of where you land on your understanding of sharing the gospel, it cannot be ignored. It is a great privilege, a great blessing, that God has made room for us to join Him in His work of reconciling the world to Himself. This privilege and responsibility are really two sides of the same coin—one does not exist without the other. Fortunately, it is not our job to "save" anyone. It is our job to share, to preach, to witness in all its varied forms of communication. The really tricky part is that we will often be misunderstood. No one likes to feel like a fool or to be misunderstood, especially teenagers!! In God's ultimate wisdom, He warns us up front. We are to share—some people will get it, others will not. That part is not our concern. Sharing the gospel is. I love when Paul is writing to the Corinthians and declares that he planted, Apollos watered, but it is God who causes the growth (1 Corinthians 3:4–9). This principle is still true today. We may be misunderstood, but we also know that God works all things for good—even when we can't see it!

IN THIS LESSON STUDENTS SHOULD:

○ Recognize the call of God to join Him in the work of sharing the gospel.
○ Be able to articulate what the gospel is.

○ Understand that it is both a privilege and a responsibility to share the gospel.
○ Connect sharing the gospel with the role of a missionary.

STUFF YOU NEED:

○ Pre-made game board for Option 2
○ Prizes
○ A poster or several strips of paper with missionary jobs written on it/them

---

FOCUS

OPTION 1: Missionary Jobs

Students may not be aware of all of the things you can do as a missionary. Do a little research and compile a list of the variety of jobs available for missionaries. This will include ESL teachers, radio broadcasting, coaches, preachers, art directors, medical professionals, chaplains, surfers, youth workers, and musicians to name a few!

Point these occupations out around the room. Ask your students if they see anything they may want to do later in life.

Ask: Can you imagine any way where these jobs can be used in missions?

OPTION 2: Top 10 Countdown

Create a pre-made game board before your students arrive. This can be done on either a dry erase board or using paper taped to the wall. Make a list of the top 10 things people like to share. Feel free to use the following examples, or if you know of examples that fit your group better, use those.

Pizza	Websites
Vacation pictures	E-mail addresses
Birthdays	Movies
Clothes	Secrets
Music	Good news

Once these are up on the board or wall, cover each with a strip of paper that will be easy to rip away. Be certain to keep a numbered list, so you are able to remove the strip covering the answer if it is guessed.

Get six volunteers, three per team. Ask the memory verse from last week to determine which team goes first. Ask both teams the question: What are the top 10 things people like to share? Allow the first team to guess, one player at a time. (They may consult with one another, but only one person at a time is to answer.) Once they have missed twice, play moves to the other team. Continue play until all of the top 10 list is revealed. Offer the team with the most points a prize. Ideally, have enough for them to share with everyone. You may suggest this, but ultimately it is that team's choice.

DISCOVERY

Divide your entire group into three. Give each group one of the following passages and questions.

GROUP #1

Read Mark 4:1–9.
Who is telling this story?
Who is the sower?
What are the three types of soil?
What is this parable really about?

GROUP #2

Read Mark 16:1–13.
Who came to the tomb early in the day?
What were they told?
Did they tell anyone what they had seen? (see v. 8, 10)
Did the disciples believe her?
To whom else did Jesus appear?
Did they tell anyone?
How was the news they told received?

GROUP #3

Read Luke 24:1–11.
Who came to the tomb?
What did they experience?
To whom did they report what they had experienced?
Were they believed?

After giving each group a few moments, ask each to report what they found.

Ask: What do these stories have to do with each other?

LIFE APPLICATION: These three passages show different perspectives of the same concept. The first, a parable, tells the principle of sharing the good news regardless of how it is received. We are to "sow seeds" everywhere. What the ground is like, is irrelevant to what we are to do.

Did you notice anything in particular about the account of the women and the disciples as they shared the news of the resurrection of Jesus? Even His own followers did not believe at first!

Ask: Could you ever imagine refusing to share what you had just experienced if you just talked with the two angels in the tomb?

Would this be difficult for you to believe?

What parts of your relationship with God do you tend to share?

What about God do you think is difficult for most people to believe?

Think back over the passages you have just read. For what part of sharing the gospel are you responsible?

Teacher's Note: Many of us, as well as many of our students, have been raised in a climate encouraging the sharing of the gospel. The problem is that we have been made to feel inadequate if we don't share in a way that is immediately recognized and received by others. Those who knew Jesus, those who were His closest of friends, even missed it at first. Our only job is to share in joyful response. The rest is up to the Holy Spirit.

MAKING IT PERSONAL: *Ask:* What parts of your relationship with God do you find difficult to believe?

What parts of your relationship with God are difficult for others to believe?

For those who are followers of Christ, sharing your story is a great way to share the gospel. Sharing the gospel in your daily life is no different than the calling of a missionary.

Get in groups of 2–3 to close. Pray for one another, asking God to guide your words as you seek opportunities to honor the privilege and responsibility of sharing the gospel. Pray that God may make it clear if He is calling anyone in your group to fulltime missions as a lifetime vocation.

SONG: "The Space Between Us" by Building 429, on the album *The Space Between Us*

SERVICE PROJECT: There are missionaries all over the world. Most often they are heard of only when there is a tragedy somewhere, or as a rather removed part of a regular addition in your church bulletin or newsletter. Check into missionaries supported either by your denomination, church, or through agencies like World

Vision or ServLife. Missionaries love to know the body of Christ is supporting their work. Either choose to pray for the contact person/people and spend some time writing letters, or choose to adopt the missionaries, sending monthly letters, cards, and care packages. E-mail has done wonders for being able to keep in touch quickly over a great distance.

QUOTABLE QUOTE:

Salvation is a work of God for man, rather than a work of man for God.

—Lewis Sperry Shafer (1871–1952)

I used to ask God to help me. Then I asked if I might help Him. I ended up by asking Him to do His work through me.

—James Hudson Taylor (1832–1905)

Two Sides, Same Coin—Midweek

MEMORY VERSE:
And he said to them, "Go into all the world and preach the gospel to all creation."—Mark 16:15 (TNIV)

For I am not ashamed of the gospel: for it is the power of God for salvation to everyone who believeth; to the Jew first and also to the Greek.—Romans 1:16 (ASV)

SCRIPTURE: Philippians 2:9–11

LESSON IN A SENTENCE: We have the privilege and responsibility of sharing the gospel with the world.

FOCUS

OPTION 1: *The Mission* (movie)
Rent the movie *The Mission* with Robert DeNiro. It's a full-length film and would take the majority of your time, if not a little longer than usual. It is a film that shows a repentant man who becomes a missionary in a remote part of the world. It's a difficult film for many reasons. While it offers a very stereotypical presentation of a missionary in a jungle, it also offers great insight for a group discussion. It is a heavy movie with a difficult ending. It shows both the courage of early missionaries and the risks.

Questions may include:

1. What is your overall gut reaction?
2. Do you think DeNiro's character was worthy of being a missionary?
3. What did he do well?
4. What did he not do well?
5. Was his missionary work worth it in the end?

If you choose this option, before you dismiss for the night, read Philippians 2:9–11. Pray for those who are sacrificing their very lives all throughout the world in order that every knee should bow—that every person would be reconciled to God.

OPTION 2: History Lesson

We have a long legacy of missionaries in our history. At times they have been amazingly brave and sacrificial people. At other times, our missionary efforts have left us colonizing and wreaking havoc on indigenous cultures. Either way, it is good to know our past. Check with your pastor to see if your church has any program for educating about missionaries from the past or present. If not, check out a few websites and choose one or two to share with your group. There are many websites available for such research. http://www.wholesomewords.org offers the biographies in detail of many past missionaries. Print the information and distribute this to small groups of your students. Encourage them to try to imagine the details of the story as it unfolds.

If you have a group that you know cannot tolerate this much reading and research, work with your leaders to present one or two mini-plays. Choose one or two of the missionary biographies prior to the time of your lesson. To the best of your ability, recreate costumes, tell the history as though it is your story you are telling. If they served in another country, try to find a snack that would be indigenous to that location.

Say: From the time of Christ, there have been people willing to go. These people, in obedience to God's command, would go to the ends of the world to share the gospel. This was often at great cost to themselves personally.

DISCOVERY

Read Philippians 2:9–11.

Ask: What does it mean to you that every tongue will confess? That every knee will bow? The verse says this is for everyone. Do you think this is for everyone or are some people excluded?

LIFE APPLICATION: We are all called to share the gospel. Every one of us is privileged to take part in God's work reconciling all people to Himself. We do this through following Jesus and sharing the gospel, both with the choices we make in our lives, and the words we choose to clarify those choices.

We've looked at some missionaries from the past and discussed a few in the present.

Invite each person present to pray for career missionaries and ask God to work in their lives that they may be open to hear His call to missions if it is His will.

EXTRA! EXTRA!: Before your study, do an Internet search on the 10/40 window. Type this into a search engine to learn the most up-to-date information. Share this with your group for a little insight into missions today!

LOOKING AHEAD: So this is quite early but, better safe than sorry!

November brings the International Day Of Prayer for the Persecuted Church. You will be looking at the idea of persecution at that time. Go ahead and look through some of the online resources now. There are even videos, maps, and free monthly newsletters you can begin to receive and use now.

Check out www.persecutedchurch.org. You will find many links to organizations concerned with this issue. If you scan the Voice of the Martyrs website, you can find various videos and newsletters. Also check out www.idop.org. This site has many downloads to help in preparation for the day of prayer, including lessons, devotions, and maps. As some of the materials may take time to get to you, go ahead and order them now to be certain you are prepared come November!

JUNE 18, 2006

Training Our Children in the Way They Should Go—What It Takes to Be a Father

By Amy Jacober

MEMORY VERSE:
God is in his holy Temple. He is a father to orphans, and he defends the widows.—Psalm 68:5 (NCV)

SCRIPTURE: Matthew 1:18–25

LESSON IN A SENTENCE: Fathers put the interests of their families above their own.

THE BIG PICTURE (OR WHAT YOU'RE TRYING TO GET ACROSS):
The impact of a father can hardly be overstated. Fathers contribute a great deal to their families and the community as a whole. Fathers also sacrifice and have to make choices every day that put their families first. Children are told in Scripture to not curse their parents. Fathers must be intentional as their children enter adolescence. Where mom has been the primary caregiver for most younger children, fathers gain a position of importance when they enter the teenage years.

IN THIS LESSON STUDENTS SHOULD:

- Think of Joseph as a father who put the needs of his family above his own.
- Understand that a man can be kind and self-sacrificing.
- Consider imitating these same self-sacrificing characteristics for their own future.
- Have a chance to thank their own fathers or other men in their lives for giving so much.

STUFF YOU NEED:

- Balloons (Option 2)
- Shaving cream (Option 2)
- Razors/spoons (Option 2)

FOCUS

OPTION 1: Fathers Share

Ask two or three fathers to share part of their story. Be certain you know these men and have talked with them beforehand. Encourage them to balance their struggles in trying to learn how to be a good father while encouraging the young men in your group to take this responsibility seriously when the day comes. Ask them to also share a few realistic moments of having to rely on God, as they realized they were in over their heads and simply did not know the best way to parent. If the men are comfortable, open this up for a Q & A time.

During the teenage years, research shows a great significance of the relationship with the father. Your students may not be able to put this into words, but their relationship, or in some cases lack of relationship, is very important. It is helpful to hear from a father how he was nervous or excited or worried as he learned the best ways to care for his children. You know your group best. You will also want to be sensitive if you have some students who have particularly difficult relationships or non-existent relationships.

OPTION 2: Rite of Passage (Jr. High)

Fathers are instrumental in helping their sons move through a few rites of passage. One of these is shaving! In honor of Father's Day, recreate this with your group. The difference is that you will be shaving balloons! Ask for five volunteers to participate. Lay a sheet on the floor beneath their feet. Have a wastebasket nearby to catch the shaving cream. Give each person a balloon and a handful of shaving cream. Once they have covered their balloon, hand each a razor to "shave" their balloon. Give the first one to finish a prize.

Teacher's Note: Carefully consider if it is wise to place razors in the hands of your students. If not, you can find play razors in the toy store or even accomplish the same thing with a spoon to scrape off the shaving cream.

DISCOVERY

Break into groups of 3–4. Ask each group to storyboard Matthew 1:18–25. Storyboarding is what is done for films and TV when the scenes are being considered. Each group will need either several sheets of paper, or a paper large enough to create several frames. Have them draw roughly, stick figures are fine, and include what they understand to be happening in their own words.

After several minutes, begin with one group and ask them to explain their first frame. Ask the second group to explain the next frame and so on until the entire passage is covered.

Be sure to ask if anyone had anything different in the way their group covered the story. While each group is reading the same passage, it is not unusual for different perspectives to be offered.

LIFE APPLICATION: Summarize the basic story again.

Ask: Were Mary and Joseph married yet?

What do you think you (or one of your friends) would do today if you found out your fiancé(e) had cheated on you and now you could be responsible for the baby?

What did Joseph sacrifice to stay with Mary?

To whom was Joseph being obedient? (not Mary. . .to God!)

Joseph was Jesus' earthly father. How difficult do you think that would have been?

Obviously Joseph sacrificed a lot. What can you think of that your father has sacrificed for you or your family?

Spend a few moments in your small groups thinking of all the sacrifices men may have to make in order to be better fathers. Which of these actions is something you would like to imitate in your future? Which of these actions is something you can imitate right now?

MAKING IT PERSONAL: Dads are often overlooked. They don't tend to get candies or flowers, cards and hand-drawn pictures; these are most often given to moms.

While this may sound silly or cheap, invite your students to make a coupon for their father on this day. These are not the "I will mow the lawn for free" kind of coupons. Rather, encourage them to be creative and make a coupon for something they can share with their father. This may be a movie, a game of hoops, washing the cars together, or whatever. Fathers don't need more things. What they need and want is time with their children, even their growing adolescent children.

Pray, thanking God for the blessings that so many fathers, grandfathers, uncles, and other men have been in the lives of your students.

SONGS: "Nothing Without You" by Bebo Norman, on the CD *Try*
"Thank U" by Rachel Washington, on the CD *Spiritually Unpredictable*
You can find this CD at www.rachelwashington.com.

QUOTABLE   QUOTES :

By the time a man realizes that maybe his father was right, he usually has a son who thinks he's wrong.
—Charles Wadsworth

You've got to do your own growing, no matter how tall your grandfather was.
—Irish Proverb

What It Takes to Be a Father—
Midweek

MEMORY VERSE:
God is in his holy Temple. He is a father to orphans, and he defends the widows.—Psalm 68:5 (NCV)

SCRIPTURE: Deuteronomy 27:16; Ephesians 6:4

LESSON IN A SENTENCE: Fathers put the interests of their families above their own.

FOCUS

Good Father/Bad Father

This is an improv game that is a take-off from the idea of good cop/bad cop. Ask for two volunteers from your group. They needn't be guys, but it will help if they are not shy and can think on their feet. Begin by giving them scenarios to which they will respond. The catch is they must decide who will be the good father and who will be the bad father. Use the following as examples of the pattern:

Your child has broken curfew. . .

Good Father—I would say their curfew is made an hour earlier for the next month.

Bad Father—I would lock my child in the closet.

Your child dyes his hair without your permission. . .

Good Father—I would assume that now that he is taking responsibility for his own hair, he can now pay for his own shampoo and haircuts.

Bad Father—I would pin him down and shave his head.

Feel free to create a few of your own. Once your students get the pattern, ask them to offer scenarios as well. You may want to trade volunteers after a few turns to give several people a try.

There are no hard and fast rules about what makes a good father or a bad father. We can, however, recognize that some are better than others.

DISCOVERY

Read Deuteronomy 27:16.
Ask: Does this seem fair?

What does it mean to be cursed?

How do you think God would want us to understand this today?

Read Ephesians 6:4.

Ask: How does this shed light on the passage in Deuteronomy?

In what ways can a father provoke his children?

Does the action of the father excuse your response, or does God hold you accountable for your actions as well?

What can we learn about the relationship God intends between a father and his children from these passages?

LIFE APPLICATION: Have students break into groups of four.

Have each group write a job description for a father. Be certain they include specifics of what they consider the role of a father to be. Once they have done this, ask for a description of the perfect father. What characteristics would they desire?

Have a discussion on what it means to be a father. Consider expectations from culture, society in general, gender stereotypes, and your church tradition.

God is our heavenly Father. We often understand God through the images we have of our own fathers. Many men seek to imitate Christ as a way of learning to be a good earthly father. Jesus was no wimp! Neither was He arrogant, domineering, nor oppressive. He was loving and gentle, wise and loyal. He spent time teaching and caring for others and did not neglect His own family.

Finding the balance to be a good father can be hard. The rewards however are priceless.

Race Relations

By Amy Jacober

MEMORY VERSE:
Therefore be imitators of God, as beloved children.—Ephesians 5:1
(NASB)

That Scripture says "anyone" because there is no difference between
those who are Jews and those who are not. The same Lord is the Lord
of all and gives many blessings to all who trust in him.—Romans 10:12
(NCV)

SCRIPTURE: John 4:7–30, 39–42

LESSON IN A SENTENCE: God loves all people equally, regardless
of race, and calls us to do the same.

THE BIG PICTURE (OR WHAT YOU'RE TRYING TO GET ACROSS):
We have come a long way from the days of civil rights.
Unfortunately there is still much more work to be done. Racial tensions
still run high in many parts of our country. We may no longer have
public spaces with signs out front that read "Whites Only," but we
functionally live this way. By no means are Caucasians the only ones
to discriminate. All over this country, all over this world, those of differing races and communities fight to varying degrees with one
another. The church contributed a great deal both to prejudicial behavior and to the elimination of this in the past. It should still be the church
leading the way toward racial reconciliation. Talk with your students
now as we truly see the kingdom of God for all people.

IN THIS LESSON STUDENTS SHOULD:

- Learn why it was so scandalous for Jesus to talk with this
  woman.
- Put themselves in the place of this woman to gain understanding of oppressed groups.
- Learn of God's perspective as she becomes the first
  female evangelist.
- Name ways racism exists today.
- Identify ways to stand up to racial discrimination as it
  exists today.

STUFF YOU NEED:

○ A list of situations (Option 1)
○ A coloring book (Option 2)
○ Crayons, box of all one color and at least one box of a variety (Option 2)

FOCUS

OPTION 1: Bridges and Bombs

In all relationships our words and actions can serve to build things up or to tear things down. When it comes to cross-cultural issues, this tends to be magnified. This activity is about building bridges to create better relationships, or dropping bombs that create all kinds of problems. Often, neither is done maliciously. Being more aware of issues, however, will help to have more bridges than bombs.

Have your students get in pairs. Ask each pair to come up with one bridge and one bomb for the different situations. The following are just examples with possible responses; feel free to come up with your own examples, allowing your students to come up with responses.

An Asian American family provides dinner for the youth group. It is a noodle dish you do not recognize. *Bridge*—I've never tasted this. It looks good and I love trying new things. *Bomb*—I've never tasted this. It looks weird!

Your group meets at the home of a Samoan family. You are asked to leave your shoes at the door. *Bridge*—Take your shoes off without arguing or fussing. You may ask why, but truly out of curiosity, not with an attitude. *Bomb*—No way!! Wear your shoes right into the house and ignore the request of the family.

You are driving to camp and each person gets a turn choosing music. The first person chooses hip-hop. *Bridge*—This has never been my favorite, but I'm willing to give it another try. What do you like about it? *Bomb*—This music is a bunch of no-talent garbage. I can't stand it!

There is a new girl visiting for the summer. She is from a small town and talks of raising horses and listening to country music. *Bridge*—What is your home like? How are you adjusting to this place for the summer? *Bomb*—Do people go to school and wear shoes where you're from?

Remind your students that bombs are not good things. They may get carried away trying to be funny and end up missing the point, or worse, really hurting someone else present. Teasing and making fun of others is often a relational humor not shared by all.

What we say or do can be offensive; what we say or do can build bridges.

OPTION 2: Crayons

Give each person a page from a coloring book. It may seem a bit childish, but chances are it has been so long since they have colored, they will go along with you. Tell your students you have boxes of crayons to share. Ask some manner of trivia questions to give away the first box. (This would be a good time to ask who knows the Memory Verse from the previous week.) Once you have your first student, show two boxes of crayons. One has only one color while the other box has a variety. You can purchase boxes of crayons from school supply stores in all one color, or piece one together by borrowing from the children's ministry. Ask which box your student would like to have to take back to his or her table.

Your student should choose the one with a variety of colors and think it is stupid to offer one that has only one color.

This is a simple object lesson. Just like it is better to color pictures with many colors and our world would be boring if it had only one, it is better that God made variety in people. The world would not only be much less interesting if we all looked alike and came from the same background, but we would be missing facets of the image of God required by including everyone in the world.

DISCOVERY

Have your leaders prepare ahead of time to offer this passage as a sketch. You will need Jesus, a woman, a narrator, and a small group of men. If possible, have the lines memorized. This is taken from the New Century Version. If you like, choose another translation or write your own sketch that communicates the same story in a modern setting.

JOHN 4:7–30, 39–42

Narrator:	When a Samaritan woman came to the well to get some water, Jesus said to her,
Jesus:	Please give me a drink.
Narrator:	(This happened while Jesus' followers were in town buying some food.)
Woman:	I am surprised that you ask me for a drink, since you are a Jewish man and I am a Samaritan woman.
Narrator:	(Jewish people are not friends with Samaritans.)

Jesus:	If you only knew the free gift of God and who it is that is asking you for water, you would have asked him, and he would have given you living water.
Woman:	Sir, where will you get this living water? The well is very deep, and you have nothing to get water with. Are you greater than Jacob, our father, who gave us this well and drank from it himself along with his sons and flocks?
Jesus:	Everyone who drinks this water will be thirsty again, but whoever drinks the water I give will never be thirsty. The water I give will become a spring of water gushing up inside that person, giving eternal life.
Woman:	Sir, give me this water so I will never be thirsty again and will not have to come back here to get more water.
Jesus:	Go get your husband and come back here.
Woman:	I have no husband.
Jesus:	You are right to say you have no husband. Really you have had five husbands, and the man you live with now is not your husband. You told the truth.
Woman:	Sir, I can see that you are a prophet. Our ancestors worshiped on this mountain, but you Jews say that Jerusalem is the place where people must worship.
Jesus:	Believe me, woman. The time is coming when neither in Jerusalem nor on this mountain will you actually worship the Father. You Samaritans worship something you don't understand. We understand what we worship, because salvation comes from the Jews. The time is coming when the true worshipers will worship the Father in spirit and truth, and that time is here already. You see, the Father too is actively seeking such people to worship him. God is spirit, and those who worship him must worship in spirit and truth.
Woman:	I know that the Messiah is coming. When the Messiah comes, he will explain everything to us.
Jesus:	I am he—I, the one talking to you.
Narrator:	(men from town begin to come up, woman moves towards them.) Just then his followers came back from town and were surprised to see him talking with

a woman. But none of them asked, "What do you want?" or "Why are you talking with her?" Then the woman left her water jar and went back to town. She said to the people,

Woman: Come and see a man who told me everything I ever did. Do you think he might be the Christ?

Narrator: So the people left the town and went to see Jesus. Many of the Samaritans in that town believed in Jesus because of what the woman said:

Woman: He told me everything I ever did.

Narrator: When the Samaritans came to Jesus, they begged him to stay with them, so he stayed there two more days. And many more believed because of the things he said. They said to the woman,

Crowd of men: First we believed in Jesus because of your speech, but now we believe because we heard him ourselves. We know that this man really is the Savior of the world.

Ask: What did you just see happen?

Did anyone catch that Jesus was a Jew and the woman a Samaritan? Why is this a big deal?

How did Jesus treat the woman?

Was this Samaritan woman capable of sharing the gospel?

LIFE APPLICATION: We all have prejudices. These are pre-judgments based on stereotypes or limited experience. Prejudices are a fact of life. What you do with them is not. When you allow a prejudice to impact your behavior or treatment of someone, this is discrimination.

Ask: What stereotypes exist for different people groups?

What stereotypes exist at your school?

Have any of your students experienced discrimination? If yes, ask if they would be willing to share that story with the group.

Jesus clearly did not discriminate. It was not only socially unacceptable for a Jew to associate with a Samaritan, but Jesus ignored all social boundaries by talking with an unclean woman who was also of a different race.

Ask: In what ways do you think people are still kept from doing things based on their race?

The Samaritan woman became the first female evangelist. She went and told the men in her town about Jesus. Scripture even says it was because of the words of this woman that many Samaritans believed in Jesus.

Brainstorm concrete ways you can work as a community to speak out or act out against discrimination. This may include cutting out racial slurs or jokes, including a variety of foods or music to better represent your community, etc. Brainstorm concrete ways this can be taken into school, sports, music, or any other activity in which your students may be involved.

Teacher's Note: Different parts of the country have varying degrees of diversity. Even in diverse areas discrimination still exists. For those in less diverse areas, you may need to work a little harder to drive this lesson home, as it may not be readily before your eyes; but it is still a struggle in this country.

MAKING IT PERSONAL: Ultimately choosing to be aware of our prejudices and ways we discriminate is a choice each individual must make. Think through your daily life. How can you intentionally work to better understand the problem of discrimination, or what changes do you need to make?

Pray, thanking God for the diversity He has created and that His people may better come together to reflect the kingdom.

SONG: "Diverse City" by TobyMac, on the CD *Welcome to Diverse City*

QUOTABLE QUOTES:

Everyone is a prisoner of his own experiences. No one can eliminate prejudices—just recognize them.
    —Edward R. Murrow, TV broadcast, 31 December 1955

CULTURE CONNECTION: Check out the movie *Guess Who?* A modern day remake of the film *Guess Who's Coming to Dinner?* If you consider showing this with your group, it is a great discussion starter but be warned, there are lines that will be found objectionable to some churches. You may want to prescreen this and determine if it would make a good movie night for your group or not.

Race Relations—Midweek

MEMORY VERSE: Therefore be imitators of God, as beloved children.—Ephesians 5:1 (NASB)

That Scripture says "anyone" because there is no difference between those who are Jews and those who are not. The same Lord is the Lord of all and gives many blessings to all who trust in him.—Romans 10:12 (NCV)

SCRIPTURE: Romans 10:8–13

LESSON IN A SENTENCE: God loves all people equally, regardless of race, and calls us to do the same.

FOCUS

Chalk drawings
Give each student a piece of sidewalk chalk. Give them time to draw, create, and just have fun. After a few minutes, tell them you are going to have a contest to see who can draw the best picture. The only catch is that they can only use one piece of chalk. No sharing! Call time and let the judging begin!!

Look at all the drawings and then declare all of the green (or blue or red or whatever color you choose) drawings as the best, regardless of whether they were actually the best or not. Give a prize to each person who used a green piece of chalk. If you have the budget, try to make it something they would actually want like a movie ticket or old camp shirt.

Ask: How does it feel to know only those who drew with green won?

Is anyone annoyed? Why or why not?

Do you think it ever happens in real life, that people get different treatment based on nothing more than the color of their skin?

DISCOVERY

Read Romans 10:8–13.
With what do we usually associate this passage? (with talking about salvation)

What does this passage tell us about who is to be saved?

What is the difference between a Jew and a Greek?

Of whom is Jesus Lord?

LIFE APPLICATION: This passage tells us that Jesus is Lord of all people, all Hispanics, all African Americans, all Pacific Islanders, all Caucasians, all Asian Americans, all Native Americans, not to mention all Mexicans, Canadians, French, Koreans, Ghanaians, Iranians, and all people of all the world. He is Lord!

If Jesus is Lord of all and desires all to be saved, how much more should we be treating all people as equals. Salvation is the greatest gift ever. Jesus desires that the kingdom includes all the people He has created.

Read Ephesians 5:1.

We can't save anyone. How can we practically imitate Christ as He shows no partiality for race?

Consider practical ways to imitate Christ in your everyday life.

Say: There are Christians who still believe separation is the right thing. How would you address this issue if it were in your community? How is this supported or refuted in the Scriptures you have read?

Just like it was unfair to judge the drawings based only on color, it is unfair when we judge others based only on color. God is grieved when we treat others poorly. He is grieved when we treat others like dirt or non-humans, based on prejudices.

Whatever you have done to the least of these, you have done to Me.

MUSIC IN TODAY'S TEEN CULTURE AND AS A TOOL IN MINISTRY

By Chris Renzelman
N.W. REGIONAL COORDINATOR,
NATIONAL NETWORK OF YOUTH MINISTRIES

Do you have an iPod yet? How about satellite radio? Okay, a cassette player? What? You have an 8 track? Wow! You know that vinyl's made a comeback? Good thing you saved yours, or at least your folks' collection. However, you might have noticed that most of them are played a bit different than what was considered normal. Yes, the times change, but some of the good old music is still around and fun to listen to, no matter how it's delivered.

Music remains one of the most powerful forces in our lives. Music motivates, comforts, communicates, and most of all makes you feel. Music is exhilarating, whether it was created last week or penned by candlelight during the 18th century. A single song can take you on a journey, awaken your senses or inspire you to action. Nothing triggers an emotion as quickly and completely as music. Music has a powerful impact on all our lives and with the rapid changes in how we receive and listen to music, more people of all ages are listening to a broader selection of music than ever before.

Recent research by two different groups found that the average teen in the average youth group spends 21–28 hours every week listening to music. Behind sleep and school, this could be the largest dedication of time in a student's life. My own teenager's school allows students to listen with head phones during class, except when the teacher is talking. Whether it's active or passive listening, music has surrounded us. While giving these stats during a recent seminar, I was interrupted by a student saying that was not true, at least in his life, because he listens to music 7 hours a day or about 50 hours a week. Now factor in survey work done among youth, revealing that approximately 80% of an average youth group listens 100% to mainstream music. By combining these statistics, we see we have some heavy influencing going on. Now that's not necessarily bad. However, if you take a look at which songs make the top ten on any given week (www.top20lyrics.com or www.azlyrics.com and other recommended sites, found when you scroll down their web page) you should definitely have a question about the potential influence these most-listened to songs have on their listeners. Now compare this 21+ hours to the approximately 3 hours each week that teens are attending youth groups. One has to question who is having the greater impact on the thinking and belief system of today's teens. Fortunately there are other positive influences in most teens' lives. Some of that influence is contemporary Christian music. Check out the lyrics found at www.christianrocklyrics.com; it doesn't take long to see that there is indeed a difference of content in the lyric message. So, how do we raise the quality of message in the music kids listen to?

You've probably heard that 90% of solving a problem is identifying it. So the other 10% is gonna be easy, right! Hardly. There are several challenges to be addressed. Here are some of them.

1. There is a constant stream of new music being released into the air waves.

2. The genre of music is so expansive that few can be continually on the cutting edge of it all.

3. Who has the time to check all this out?

4. Peers have great influence on what is being listened to.

5. Then the statement; "I don't listen to the lyrics, I just like the music." (*Listening or not, the words are still getting through. Watch students lip the lyrics when a song plays or they tell you not to listen to this song because you won't like it. They know what's being said more often than not.*)

6. Did I say burning songs off the Internet or from other CD's? (*No! We are not going to discuss that here, it would take too much time to unpack all the perspectives.*)

7. Seems that we are in the thick of a spiritual battle when it comes to mind influence.

Above all else, guard your affections. For they influence everything else in your life.
—Proverbs 4:23 (TLB)

You could list a few more challenges I'm sure, like volume and beat issues. Howard Hendricks, a respected Christian Education professor, states that *"Music is the most controversial issue in the church today."* That being true, let's go to some thoughts and resources packaged to help you address this challenge.

First realize that *music can help your students in their growth spiritually.*

How can a young man keep his way pure? By living according to your word. I seek you with all my heart; do not let me stray from your commands. I have hidden your word in my heart that I might not sin against you.
—Psalm 119:9–11 (NIV)

Love the Lord your God with all your heart and with all your soul and with all your strength. These commandments that I give you today are to be upon your hearts. Impress them on your children. Talk about them when you sit at home and when you walk along the road, when you lie down and when you get up. Tie them as symbols on your hands and bind them on your foreheads. Write them on the doorframes of your houses and on your gates.
—Deuteronomy 6:5–9 (NIV)

How about: *"and you shall listen to them on your MP3/iPod, and on your car stereo, and your CD & DVD players. . ."* (i.e. *places where you will spend "mind" time and where they can impact you to think about the Lord in the right way.*)

Secondly, clarify what are your personal convictions regarding music and its viability in ministry. Include: Lifestyle of Artists, Lyrics, Music Style. Interact (not react) with teens on all these issues. Here are some websites that might help you in this process. You don't have to agree with all their points of support or concern, but it helps to hear them.

*Al Menconi (www.almenconi.com)

"Today's music is one of the most powerful vehicles to the minds and emotions of our young people. Al Menconi is a much-needed voice for them and their parents. He is biblical, relevant, and offers positive solutions."— From Tim LaHaye (co-author of the Left Behind Series) and Beverly LaHaye (Concerned Women for America founder)

*Phil Chalmers (www.truelies.org)

" 'every kid in America needs to hear this presentation'. . .His style and content is the best I've ever heard on the subject"—Jim Burns, PhD.; President, YouthBuilders

*Solid Sounds (www.solidsounds.org/song—detail.php?sid=35) is produced by Back to the Bible, a non-denominational Bible-teaching ministry that has been teaching God's Word all over the globe for decades.

*Mark Matlock's Wisdom Works Ministries www.planetwisdom.com reviews movies and music (see side bar tabs found at website).

*Focus on the Family's review is found at http://www.pluggedi-nonline.com/index.cfm.

Here's an additional resource site with a lot on it: www.christian-rockersonline.com.

Want to know more about the artists themselves? These sites should help. http://www.ccmcom.com/ Contemporary Christian music www.interlinc-online.com. Click top tab "Artists"

http://dir.yahoo.com/Entertainment/music/news—and—media/mag-azines/ several choices here.

Learn to be a fruit inspector asking, "What is the impact of this specific artist and their music on my life and my kids?" Does it result in a deeper love walk with God? Are certain styles wrong? How far is too far? What about fashion, hair styles, piercing, tattoos, beat, etc. We each have to figure out where we stand on these matters. Spend time studying the Scriptures; not only is it good input, but it will also give you some handles on all these questions. *(If you would like a free study guide called "Issues of Right or Wrong" send me an e-mail requesting a copy to the address at the bottom of this article.)*

Be proactive. Provide good alternatives to what students might be listening to. You can do this by going to live concerts. Here are two websites letting you know when and where the concerts are happening. www.ccauthority.com or www.itickets.com

Provide a lending library, teach lessons that are built around many of the current new release Christian songs and written by active youth leaders. A membership with interlinc's Youth Leader Only brings you the latest from several artists. Details can be found at www.interlinc-online.com or by calling 800-470-3101. Work with others; Church Leadership and Parents.

- Understand that you are a person with responsibility and often under authority
- Become a student of what your leadership's convictions are regarding music.
- Educate for good thinking and communication regarding positions adopted.
- Show the results from cultural adaptation; Billy Graham and Luis Palau are just two respected older generation ministers who saw the need to bridge the gap.
- Provide resources, several have been listed in this article. Here's another site: www.cpyu.org (Center for Youth/Parent Understanding). It serves as a great youth culture site; there is a lot here. Click the side bar "Youth Culture Hot lists" and see the music list, then tour the site for a whole lot more on other issues.

Realize that music is an art form. The purpose, setting, and meaning might not be easy to interpret at first glance. But as you interact with teens along the journey, everyone will grow through the experience.

If you would like a downloadable copy of this article, so that you don't have to retype all the web links, send an e-mail with a note requesting this article to crenz@networknw.org.

Thanks for being on the cutting edge with kids for the kingdom's sake!

JULY 2, 2006

The Meaning Is Missing

By Anna Aven

MEMORY VERSE:
He has made everything beautiful in its time. He has also set eternity in the hearts of men; yet they cannot fathom what God has done from beginning to end.—Ecclesiastes 3:11 (NIV)

SCRIPTURE: Acts 17:16–34; Luke 10:2–3; Romans 1:20; Ecclesiastes 3:11; Psalm 139.

LESSON IN A SENTENCE: Instead of approaching pop culture as either "good" or "bad," we can recognize the search for God in pop culture—a search that enables them to write the message, but not understand the meaning, until we point them to the connections to Christ.

THE BIG PICTURE (OR WHAT YOU'RE TRYING TO GET ACROSS):
When Jesus sent out His disciples, "Then He said to them, 'The harvest truly is great, but the laborers are few; therefore pray the Lord of the harvest to send out laborers into His harvest. Go your way; behold, I send you out as lambs among wolves'" Luke 10:2–3 (NKJV). The comparison may be grim—lambs to wolves—but notice that the disciples are being sent out *among* these wolves. The command is to "go" and not "stay." The direction is "out" not "in." Only by engaging culture do we as Jesus' disciples fulfill this timeless command to preach the gospel. The longing is there, and as the P.O.D. song "Sleeping Awake" says, "The message is written, the meaning is missing." It is up to us to go into culture, and connect the dots so that the world can see our Christ as their Savior as well.

IN THIS LESSON STUDENTS SHOULD:

- ○ Understand that there is much in culture that speaks truth and reflects a search for God.
- ○ Understand that they can appreciate culture as art, but also realize that it provides a perfect jumping off point for conversation about God, without being awkward.

Teacher's Note: Doing this preparation the week before you do this lesson will make it much more powerful: Ask your students what is the number one song they are listening to. You could just pass around a couple of sheets of paper with the words "Title" and "Artist/Band" on them and ask each student to write down one song. Then, go listen to the ten most popular ones that your group brings up and identify themes, find Scriptures that correspond to those themes, and have them ready for the "Making It Personal section."

Examples of how to do this from songs that have been popular in the past:

"I'm With You," Avril Lavigne, *Let Go*, connects to Acts 17:23, which could be rephrased like this: "You've said you're looking for someone to help you figure out life and show you where home is. Well, I can tell you about the Person you're talking about, even though you don't know who it is."

"Somewhere I Belong," Linkin Park, *Meteora*, connects to John 14:1–6; 10:10, which can be paraphrased together in terms of the song like this: "You're hurting, needing to heal and find somewhere that you belong. Well, I [Jesus is talking here] have prepared a place for you, a place beyond your wildest imagination, and I've come to give you a full life. If you're wondering how to get to this place, the way is clear: I am the way, truth and life, so if you know Me, you know the way."

SONG: "Sleeping Awake" by P.O.D. from the *Matrix Reloaded* Soundtrack and/or find the lyrics and create a handout with the lyrics on one side and a blank space for reflection/journaling on the other.

Paper or index cards with the verses that you read in the Discovery section on them. Put one verse per card so that multiple students have an opportunity to contribute by reading.

FOCUS

Ben Moody, who was one of the founders of Evanescence (though he's no longer with the band), explained the rationale behind the band's music like this: "We're very sincere about what we do. There's so much prepackaged teen angst these days in music. That's not us. We're not trying to sell an angle, we're just here writing from our heart." What was the result of this authenticity? A platinum album. How does our approach to the gospel in our culture today differ from Evanescence's approach? Too often we're still trying to sell an angle and not speaking from our heart. If we approach culture with the assumption that people are searching for truth and are captivated by the pursuit of this mystery, then the connections from culture to Christ will suddenly become apparent.

DISCOVERY

This section requires several Scripture passages. It may be helpful to pass out paper or index cards to student volunteers and have them ready with the passages. Looking at current movies and music from this reveals what art and literature throughout the ages reveal: a search for something real. People can see just enough to chase something, though most of the time, they do not know what they are chasing.

Read Romans 1:20 (NKJV) "For since the creation of the world His invisible attributes are clearly seen, being understood by the things that are made, even His eternal power and Godhead, so that they are without excuse."

If people can see these invisible qualities of God through creation, then it makes sense that—even if they don't realize that what they're seeing is God—they see enough to give them a longing for the infinite. For God "has also set eternity in the hearts of men; yet they cannot fathom what God has done from beginning to end" (Ecclesiastes 3:11 NIV). Instead of setting up actual idols (as in figures to represent a god) as the people did in Paul's day, the people in our day chase all kinds of personal success and satisfaction, from wealth and fame, to pleasure, to various forms of religion. Paul looked around at the vast array of idols available to the people in Athens and found a way to address them, starting with their culture and an altar with an inscription: TO THE UNKNOWN GOD. He said, "for as I was passing through and considering the objects of your worship, I even found an altar with this inscription: TO THE UNKNOWN GOD. Therefore, the One whom you worship without knowing, Him I proclaim to you" (Acts 17:23 NKJV).

By taking a careful look at the objects of worship in our culture today, we can find a connection between their search and our faith. We have to present them with our story as it relates to their story. P.O.D.'s lyrics in "Sleeping Awake", the *Matrix Reloaded's* theme song, are reminiscent of Romans 1:20:

Can you see it? The writing, Can you tell me what it means? Translate the symbols, Enigma Expressions keep questioning me. The message is written, the meaning is missing.

People can see the message. We have to be the ones who connect it to the meaning for them. Read all of Acts 17:16–34 and observe how Paul moves from the connections in their culture to the gospel.

LIFE APPLICATION: *Say something like:* "I don't have to tell you that pop culture is the language we speak. We're constantly discussing movies, music, and so forth with friends. We put lyrics to songs in our away messages, in our journals, and so forth to express how we're feeling when we can't quite figure out how to put it into words."

Now is a good time to pass out the sheets with the P.O.D. lyrics on them. Ask students to journal reflect on what the writer of the song is trying to get across. If you have access to the song itself, you could play it while your students think about it.

MAKING IT PERSONAL: Group brainstorm: ask students what song lyrics they've recently seen friends use to represent emotions or something that they're going through. Ask them what the point is that their friend is trying to get across, by putting up the song lyrics. *Ask:* What longings do these songs express? Allow time for answers. In what ways do these songs express needs for help, a longing for something they can't quite explain? Now you can bring up the songs you've researched the week before and show how there are themes that connect. See teacher's note for ideas of how to do this.

Now that we've looked at themes from songs and how they connect to our friends' lives, let's think about this in terms of our lives. It's so easy when we're emotional to go stick on a song that expresses what we feel. And there's nothing wrong with this. However, most of the time, that's where we stop. If our heart is breaking, we listen to songs about broken hearts, and think, "hey, there's someone out there that feels the same way that I do." And yet we forget that there is One that knows all about us because He fashioned us, and ultimately is the One who knows what's going on and can get us through whatever it is that we're facing.

Read Psalm 139. You can do this as a reflective time with students' eyes closed, or you could put it up on a slide, or pass it out on sheets of paper and have everyone read it together. I suggest you dim the lights, and if you have a reflective instrumental track to put on softly in the background, it would create a more reverent atmosphere.

WEB CONNECT: http://www.ministryandmedia.com has discussion questions for music and movies (requires a membership).

EXTRA! EXTRA!: There is a discussion about God going on in popular culture in which the church is not engaged and is often unaware. . . The Gospels were written "for the people." Educated Greeks in the first century communicated in Attic Greek, a high cultural form that excluded many. But the writers of the Gospels preferred Koine Greek, a "street-level" language that communicated to the masses. We must get back to that street-level discussion. . . People of faith need to become conversant with. . . the new literacy, and join the new conversation.— Craig Detweiler and Barry Taylor, *A Matrix of Meanings: Finding God in Pop Culture,* (Grand Rapids: Baker Academic, 2003), p. 23.

The Meaning Is Missing—Midweek

MEMORY VERSE: He has made everything beautiful in its time. He has also set eternity in the hearts of men; yet they cannot fathom what God has done from beginning to end.—Ecclesiastes 3:11 (NIV)

SCRIPTURE: Acts 17:16–34; Luke 10:2–3; Romans 1:20; Ecclesiastes 3:11

LESSON IN A SENTENCE: Instead of approaching pop culture as either "good" or "bad," we can recognize the search for God in pop culture—a search that enables them to write the message, but not understand the meaning, until we point them to the connections to Christ.

STUFF YOU NEED:

○ Movie: *Signs*

FOCUS

Ask: Have any of you seen the movie *Signs?* If yes, ask for a quick summary. If no, offer the following as a set up of the summary.

Here we have what seemed to be ostensibly billed as an "Alien" movie. All of the scenes in the trailers gave no real clue as to what the meat of this film would end up being. Once we view the actual film, we find the lead character is an ex-minister (Graham) who lost his faith over his wife's death. Because of who Graham is, the movie is riddled with interactions with people over why he isn't a minister, questions about God, questions about the end of the world. All this packed into a movie where we only ever see one alien. This isn't a movie about the presence of aliens and what that does, but rather, it is a movie about the presence and absence of God and what that does. The aliens are a device. In some ways, the threat could have been something other than aliens; however, the "other-worldliness" of aliens lends itself to the discussion of the supernatural.

In the movie *Signs*, the little boy, Morgan, says of the crop signs: "I think God did it." *Clip: START: 00:03:42 END 00:05:38 (Chapter 2 of DVD).* It is interesting that an abnormality is assumed to be divine. Also, it is interesting to note that the writers put these words in the mouth of a child.

DISCOVERY

Read Psalm 19:1–4.

Ask: What are the implications of her statement in light of Psalm 19:1–4? Why is it hard for some people to connect the incredible world we see around us with God's hand? Is it easier as a child to think that God is responsible for things that we see? Why or why not?

(Possible answers to these questions include observing that in the movie it is OK, at least for a child, to assign supernatural things to God, and that as the passage for this week says, "The heavens declare the glory of God. . ." Yet people in general don't see the heavens as pointing to God because acknowledging God as creator has moral implications; yet a child might be able to point that out, because a child is not as likely to cognitively reason away the felt or observed presence of God, as an adult is).

LIFE APPLICATION: *Clip: START: 00:20:35 END: 00:21:25 (Chapter 5 on DVD).* The newscaster says of the crop signs appearing all over the world: "Either this is one of the most elaborate hoaxes of all time or else. . .It's for real." (Setting: First news report of crop signs all over the world.) Interesting that when such a phenomenal occurrence takes place there are only two options that remain: (1) it's an extraordinarily elaborate hoax, or (2) it's true. Disprove the hoax and you're left with the truth. How can we relate this to our understanding of God? God has been credited with being a fictional character meant to make weak people feel better. Yet so many people are involved in some sort of religion—a fact which tends to point to the idea that people in general believe in some sort of "higher power." This general feeling is too elaborate to be a hoax. How does this concept shed light on our belief in Jesus, and how might a story like this fit into your own personal story when sharing about your relationship with Jesus?

MAKING IT PERSONAL: Lead singer of Evanescence, Amy Lee, makes a comment on their purpose as a band. "The point of this whole record and band is to let people know that they're not alone in dealing with bad feelings, or pain, or anything that they go through," says Lee, who pens most of the words. "That's life and that's human. They're not alone, and we're going through it, too."

Reflect with your students how this quote shows what people need. They don't need to be smacked over the head with a Bible in an effort to convert them. They need to know they aren't alone, and that someone cares. We have to demonstrate the love of God before we can talk about it.

JULY 9, 2006

What Does the Bible Really Say about Drinking?

By Amy Jacober

MEMORY VERSE:
Wine and beer make people loud and uncontrolled; it is not wise to get drunk on them.—Proverbs 20:1 (NCV)

SCRIPTURE: Ephesians 5:15–21; Proverbs 23:29–33

LESSON IN A SENTENCE: God does not approve of drunkenness because He cares for us.

THE BIG PICTURE (OR WHAT YOU'RE TRYING TO GET ACROSS):

Drinking is a huge issue with teenagers. Whether they have tried drinking or not, the images, commercials, and messages are all around. Drinking is glamorized in music, movies, and television. The impact of being drunk however is neglected. Different denominations hold different positions on alcohol. Talk with your pastor to best determine how to handle that question with your students. What this lesson does offer is a look at what Scripture says. Realistically, if your students are not twenty-one, it shouldn't be an issue. This argument, however, rarely helps. Educate your students not only on the negative effects of alcohol and drugs, but on what Scripture actually says. Giving facts and tools to wrestle with their own understanding can go a long way in decision-making and internalizing choices, rather than just being told what to do with no explanation.

IN THIS LESSON STUDENTS SHOULD:

- Learn that God does have an opinion on drunkenness.
- Identify ways being drunk impacts their body.
- Discuss the principles that can be applied to drugs as well.
- Develop a plan to avoid drunkenness and/or drug use.

STUFF YOU NEED:

○ Paper
○ Pens or pencils
○ Butcher paper (Option 2)
○ Markers (Option 2)

FOCUS

OPTION 1: Name that slogan

Split into teams of 3–4. Give 2 minutes and ask each team to come up with as many slogans for alcoholic beverages as they can. (This is not to promote alcohol, rather to point out how prominent this is in our society. Even for those who say they are not impacted, it is often a surprise how aware they are of its presence.)

Have them share their lists.

Ask: Were any of you surprised at how many of these you knew?

Why do you think it is that these were so easy to name?

OPTION 2: Butcher paper draw

Tear sheets that are at least 6 feet long from a roll of butcher paper. Have your students get in groups of four, choosing one student to lay on the paper and be traced using markers. Once you have their silhouette, have them draw in features, clothes, etc. Next tell your students you are going to be looking at alcohol and drugs and their impact on our bodies. Have them label, to the best of their knowledge, how alcohol and drugs impact different parts of their bodies. For example, they may point to eyes and say they turn red, they may point to feet and say they don't walk straight, or they may point to the head and say the mind is distorted for reflex times and decision making. Encourage them to really think of everything that is impacted.

OPTION 3: Testimony

Stories are amazing ways for people to connect. Many students have been warned against drinking or drugs before. They also know that the Bible warns against this as well. What they may not know is how easy it is to slide from trying something, to allowing it to ruin your life. If you know of someone in your community who has alcohol or drug addiction in their past and is now sober, invite them to share their story. Ask them to focus on the ease with which a person can go from trying something or experimenting, to addiction. If they are comfortable, invite your students for a Q & A at the end.

DISCOVERY

Break into groups of three. Give each group a sheet of paper divided into two. On one side, write what God wants us to do, and on the other side what God wants us to avoid according to Ephesians 5:15–21.

Ask: How strong of an argument for or against drinking do you think this passage makes?

How do you think Christians have come to the place of being so strong against drunkenness?

Now turn to Proverbs 23:29–33.

Ask: Is this still a good description of a drunk today?

If yes, how? If no, how would you change it?

What message does this passage send about drinking?

What does the comparison with a serpent mean?

LIFE APPLICATION: Two passages have just been read regarding drinking.

Ask: How is drinking viewed today?

If we know there are so many negative things that can come with it, why is drinking still such a problem?

What about drugs? The Bible does not address every drug we have today directly. Do the same principles apply?

Make a list on a dry erase board of all the reasons you think people try drinking, or continue to drink, even when they know it is illegal and not good for you. (These may include rebellion, curiosity, self-medication, fun, etc.)

Ask: Do you think God is just trying to keep us from having fun or make rules for no reason?

How do we balance this with God's warning that sorrow, complaints, wounds, red eyes, hallucinations, and perverse thoughts come with drinking?

Teacher's Note: If you are comfortable, this would be a good time to enter into a discussion of the laws of our country. Scripture warns against drunkenness for anyone. It does not say to never drink. Many students are frustrated or feel lied to when they have been told that the Bible says to never drink. When they make the connection of being lied to in this area, they wonder where else they have been taught lies. This does not mean that it is OK for teenagers to drink. The law states that you must be twenty-one years old. Until they are twenty-one, this is a non-issue. They will however be confronted with alcohol many times before turning twenty-one. This lesson is about looking honestly at what Scripture says regarding drinking, and guiding students to wise choices.

Make a plan as a group of ways to avoid getting drunk. This needs to go beyond just saying don't drink. How, specifically, can you avoid being in situations where you will be tempted to be drunk or try drugs?

MAKING IT PERSONAL: *Ask rhetorically:*

Have you ever been tempted to be drunk or try drugs?

How could you use the plan created?

Today's Memory Verse is Proverbs 20:1. I have yet to meet the person who wants to be known as a fool, but I have known plenty of people who act the fool.

Getting drunk or doing drugs is foolish. It breaks God's heart, but not because He is mean and judgmental. Rather, He knows how much this will mess you up.

Pray for your students that God may give them wisdom in making choices when faced with alcohol and drugs.

SONG: "Jesus Walks With Me" *(radio version)* by Kanye West, purchase the single, radio mix

QUOTABLE   QUOTE:

Drinking makes such fools of people, and people are such fools to begin with, that it's compounding a felony.

—Robert Benchley

What Does the Bible Really Say about Drinking?—Midweek

MEMORY VERSE: Wine and beer make people loud and uncontrolled; it is not wise to get drunk on them.—Proverbs 20:1 (NCV)

SCRIPTURE: Luke 21:33–36

LESSON IN A SENTENCE: God does not approve of drunkenness because He cares for us.

FOCUS

Izzy Dizzy

This is a relay race. Break into teams of 6–10. Find an area large enough for running. Have the teams line up behind a line. At least 20 yards away, have a baseball bat for each team. Have one person holding the bat and being the official counter, as students run around the bat. Begin the race by having the first person in each team run to the bat, place their forehead on the bat while the end of the bat is on the ground, and run in ten circles. Once the circles have been run, send the person back to his or her team. Once they have crossed the line, send the second player. Keep going until the entire team has gone.

Teacher's Note: Your students will be dizzy after circling the bat. It may seem easy to run back to the group but place a few spotters around (people to help guide) to be certain your dizzy runners do not run into each other!

You may have some students who become extremely dizzy after this. Keep some water on hand and be certain to allow time sitting down for recovery.

Ask: Why was it so hard to run in a straight line?

While we just did this in a game, can you imagine making yourself feel this way on a regular basis by choice?

What other things are hard to do when you are really dizzy?

DISCOVERY

Jesus is not going to care if you are simply dizzy from running around. He does care if it is from drinking. So much so that He warns against this.

Read Luke 21:33–36.

Questions:

v. 33—Jesus said a long time ago that His words would not pass away. But the world has changed a lot since then. Do you think these words still mean something to us today?

v. 34—What does it mean to be on guard? How do we avoid being wasted and/or drunk?

v. 35—Do you think this is a temptation that can come to anyone?

v. 36—Are you supposed to have to do this on your own?

LIFE APPLICATION: *Ask:* Why do you think Jesus warns us?

What would it be like to be wasted or drunk in front of Jesus?

Teacher's Note: Verse 34 says the day will come suddenly like a trap. This can be misunderstood if you only look at the few verses mentioned here. In context, Jesus is talking about His return. He is warning to not be caught wasted or drunk when He returns. Since we do not know when His return will be, we must be on guard at all times.

Jesus cares enough for us to not try and trick us, but to offer plenty of warning.

Think of a time when someone warned you about something coming up—this could be to avoid a teacher who wasn't fair, or to tell you about traffic to avoid. It doesn't need to be anything major, just a time when you avoided something bad because of a warning.

Jesus' warning to avoid being drunk falls in this same category. He knows what is best for us and the heartache that can come. He tells us to not be wasted or drunk—not to keep us from having fun, but because He loves us and cares for us.

EXTRA! EXTRA!: The origins of Alcoholics Anonymous began with a Christian perspective. The language of the 12-step program makes this very evident. If you think it would be appropriate, share this with your students, letting them know the most successful program to break addiction was created with God in mind.

JULY 16, 2006

Good News-ism

By James Miller

MEMORY VERSE:
But before people can ask the Lord for help, they must believe in him; and before they can believe in him, they must hear about him; and for them to hear about the Lord, someone must tell them.—Romans 10:14 (NCV)

SCRIPTURE: Matthew 28:16–20

LESSON IN A SENTENCE: You are the most influential Christian many people will ever know.

THE BIG PICTURE (OR WHAT YOU'RE TRYING TO GET ACROSS):

People who are not Christians find out about Christians in all sorts of ways. The media tells us about the scandalous failures on the part of religious leaders. Atheistic scholars will take every opportunity to make fun of Christianity, while scholars who are also believers may be timid about proclaiming their faith openly in the academy. Politicians vie for our votes by claiming to be as close to God as we are. The only authentic experience of Jesus that most people will get, comes from the people we know. That means that when you become a Christian, you may be the most influential Christian your friends ever meet. Between the media, the politicians, the schools, and you, you are the best impression of Jesus many people will ever get.

IN THIS LESSON STUDENTS SHOULD:

- Learn the importance of sharing their faith with their friends.
- Think about how to answer hard questions.
- Pick out someone with whom to share.

STUFF YOU NEED:

- For the Focus activity, you will need enough paper and pens for everyone.
- For the Option 2 of Making It Personal, you will need a candle for each person in the room.
- Bibles

FOCUS

OPTION 1:

Game: This game is called "Missionaries." Have students line up on one end of a field or gymnasium. Two students, the "missionaries," stand in the middle of the room and yell, "Go!" The line of students then tries to run to the other side of the room without getting caught. If the missionaries tag them, they join the missionaries and try to tag others.

OPTION 2:

Break into groups of 2–3. Have each group pick an object that people normally wouldn't buy (like a coin, or air, or lint) and develop a sales pitch for it. Using paper and pens, draw up a proposal in images of how you would sell it. Give each group a few moments to present their sales pitch and tape their proposals on the wall around the room.

DISCOVERY

Read the text.

Have several people question what was read in the text as though they are doubting or challenging what was said. At the same time designate one or two people to defend it. Depending on your group, choose either biblically mature students, or you may need to have a leader in the role of defending what is being read.

Ask: Is it difficult to defend what you're saying? Why or why not?

When you are asked about your beliefs, do you find it hard to answer questions?

Why do you think God brings people into your life to ask you hard questions about the faith?

What do you do when people ask you questions about what you believe that you cannot answer?

Why might they pick you to ask?

What makes you most anxious about the possibility of being asked about your faith?

LIFE APPLICATION: Get into groups of about four people. Think about someone you could invite to faith. Without naming the people, discuss what they want, what you have to offer, and what might prohibit them from coming to faith. Talk about how you might explain the faith to them.

After several moments of your students working this out for themselves, ask them to share with the whole group. If they are stuck, or simply as another method of explaining faith, offer the following—

Here are three easy steps to consider:

1. Don't argue, just tell your story.
2. Think about how the gifts that Jesus offers meet the needs this person has.
3. Be confident about saying "I don't know" when you need to, but always add, "but I'll find out."
4. Remember, you may be the most important Christian they ever meet.

MAKING IT PERSONAL:

OPTION 1:

Split into pairs. Think of someone at your school with whom you really want to share your faith. Again without naming them, pray for these people, for one another, and for God to guide the timing and your words.

OPTION 2:

Offer prayer for the people who brought you to faith. As you think of someone, light a candle for each. You can have one candle in the center of the room and invite people to light from that one. Remember that each of these people let their light shine before you (Matthew 5:16) so that you would know Jesus.

Teacher's Note: It is priceless to be able to tell a story of inviting someone to faith. This is the chance to model what you want your students to recreate. Only if you model it will they imitate it.

SERVICE OPTIONS: Have students write a one-page explanation of Christianity and design it with their best computer graphics and creativity. Gather them at the church for a mailing day and have each student mail to five of their friends.

Good News-ism—Midweek

MEMORY VERSE:
But before people can ask the Lord for help, they must believe in him; and before they can believe in him, they must hear about him; and for them to hear about the Lord, someone must tell them.—Romans 10:14 (NCV)

SCRIPTURE: Romans 1:7–12

LESSON IN A SENTENCE: You are the most influential Christian many people will ever know.

FOCUS

Think of the many things for which you can be thankful. Usually we only compile this list at Thanksgiving. Take some time to come up with the most meaningful things in your life for which you're thankful, and not just personal belongings.

Now think of someone whose faith has made you thankful. It might be a pastor or youth leader, a parent or a friend. Think about who was most influential in leading you in your faith.

Using a pen and paper, write them a brief note telling them why you're thankful for their faith. You need only send this if you're comfortable doing it, but take time to write the note in any case.

DISCOVERY

Read Romans 1:7–12.

Discuss the following questions:

Why do you think Paul is so excited about someone else's faith?

How do we benefit from someone else's faith?

How do others benefit from our faith?

Who are the specific people in your life who will benefit from your faith?

LIFE APPLICATION: Before a football game, teams will often play what is called a "scrimmage," a practice game to go over skills and maneuvers. We're going to do the same thing in the area of evangelism.

Break into pairs. Each person in the pair should share either how they became a Christian, or why they think Jesus is important. It is important to include a description of the differences they think Jesus makes in their lives. It's OK to give each other ideas and suggestions.

When you're finished, think about whether or not you could share that same information with someone else you know who is not a Christian. Plan a strategy for how you might introduce the topic of faith in a conversation with them.

If you know your group has students who are not Christians, ask the group to share in pairs what they understand about their own personal story with Jesus. Encourage them to be honest. They may even have more questions than stories to tell!

At the end, have one last group model what this kind of sharing looks like. Be certain to choose a pair you know are indeed Christians. After they have finished modeling for the group, ask one of them to pray for each person in the room, that they may know Jesus; and for those who already do, that they may find the words to talk with their friends about being a follower of Christ.

JULY 23, 2006

Light in Our Darkness

By Sharon Koh

MEMORY VERSES:
God, the blessed and only Ruler, the King of kings and Lord of lords, who alone is immortal and who lives in unapproachable light, whom no one has seen or can see. To him be honor and might forever. Amen. —1 Timothy 6:15b–16 (NIV)

When Jesus spoke again to the people, he said, "I am the light of the world. Whoever follows me will never walk in darkness, but will have the light of life."—John 8:12 (NIV)

SCRIPTURE: John 9

LESSON IN A SENTENCE: Jesus is the Light of the world—He illumines the spiritual darkness of human lives.

THE BIG PICTURE (OR WHAT YOU'RE TRYING TO GET ACROSS):
Without Jesus, we are spiritually blind—like the man in John 9 is physically blind. The man in the story finds himself healed so that "the work of God might be displayed in his life." (John 9:3) Likewise, when we encounter Jesus and allow Him into our lives, we are healed from sin and the darkness it brings—so that the work of God might be displayed in our lives.

IN THIS LESSON STUDENTS SHOULD:

- Observe the properties of light in action. (i.e. light cannot be "unseen" in a dark room when it is present. Its presence is unmistakable.)
- Learn Jesus' claim that He is the Light of the world.
- See human lives as *dark* because of sin and death since the Fall.
- Understand that Jesus is the light that pierces that same darkness.

```
STUFF YOU NEED:
```

○ A room that is as dark as possible (If your meeting is at
night, this is easier to obtain).
○ Students with cell phones (Nowadays, this isn't too difficult to find at all).

FOCUS

Turn off the lights and allow students to sit in the dark for a while.

Say, "this darkness represents the natural state of humankind. For
all people, sin and death have introduced deep darkness into life."

Then tell the students to turn on their cell phone lights and wave
them in the air. You'll notice that the phone LED lights appear *very*
bright in the dark. Let the students know that the light is representative of who Jesus is in our lives: It pierces the darkness, and it is unmistakable when the light is present in the darkness.

DISCOVERY

Read John 9 and answer the following questions:

What is the reason *that Jesus gives* as the cause for the man's blind-
ness? What did He mean by this?

What does Jesus claim about His identity in v. 5?

Why did the Pharisees insist that Jesus was not from God? What
was their basis for this claim?

What was the controversy surrounding the statement that Jesus
had to be a sinner? What was the counter-argument?

Why did the (ex-) blind man's parents refuse to answer the questions directly?

What does the (ex-)blind man say is remarkable about the Pharisees'
accusations?

Read the discussion that Jesus and the man have in vv. 35–41.

Why was it easy for the man to believe and then begin to worship
Jesus?

LIFE APPLICATION: It was easy for the man to worship Jesus even after
the unpleasant encounter he had with the Pharisees, because he knew
what he had experienced. It was relatively simple to him—he was blind
and then he could see (v. 25). The *light* that Jesus claimed to be had pene-
trated his life in a real and tangible way. It was a physical healing.

In a more abstract way, how is Jesus, the Light of the world, able to
make an encounter with Him just as unmistakable?

MAKING IT PERSONAL: Have you ever encountered Jesus in a way that is unmistakable? What do you remember best about that experience? Has it changed your life? How so?

Teacher's Note: It is impossible for there to be light in a room without it reaching to the far corners of the room. It simply spreads out for all to see. Likewise, Jesus cannot be touching a person's life without His presence being unmistakable. Our objective in this lesson is to make that much obvious, and then to help students identify times in their lives when Jesus' presence was unmistakable.

QUOTABLE   QUOTES :

In the history of humanity there are no civilizations or cultures which fail to manifest, in one or a thousand ways, this need for an absolute that is called heaven, freedom, a miracle, a lost paradise to be regained, peace, the going beyond history...There is no religion in which everyday life is not considered a prison; there is no philosophy or ideology that does not think that we live in alienation...Humanity has always had a nostalgia for the freedom that is only beauty, that is only real life, plentitude, light.

—Eugene Ionesco

Light in Our Darkness—Midweek

MEMORY VERSE:
When Jesus spoke again to the people, he said, "I am the light of the world. Whoever follows me will never walk in darkness, but will have the light of life."—John 8:12 (NIV)

SCRIPTURE: Genesis 1:1–5

LESSON IN A SENTENCE: Jesus is the Light of the world—He illumines the spiritual darkness of human lives.

FOCUS

"Sardines in the Dark" can be a fun game to play, if students are careful not to move too quickly through the darkness. This is how it works: One person is sent to hide. The others wait for 1 minute or so, and then proceed, in the dark, to find the first person. If and when they find that person, they simply hide with them.

The game should result in fewer and fewer people walking around in the dark (as they find the group that is hiding). It also gets a lot more difficult for the group to stay hidden as it grows in size.

After a few rounds of this game, allow students to play it with flashlights (or cell phone lights). Help them to notice that the "order" of everyone hiding together comes more quickly when they were using light. The light helped to organize the chaos in the darkness.

DISCOVERY

Read Genesis 1:1–5. Allow the students some time to picture a "formless void". What kind of chaos existed before God spoke? If possible, allow them to picture this in a dark room. (Something about dark rooms helps one to picture fearful chaos without much trouble.)

Read Genesis 1:1–5 again. Where was God in this scene? (You'll find that He was present both before and after the act of creation.)

Notice how little effort it took for God to create light. He simply spoke it into existence! However, this light began the process of organizing the darkness—it pierced the darkness as the first thing to be created.

Take some time to allow students to notice how the creation of light began the creation process over the next five days.

LIFE APPLICATION: Have you ever felt like there is unbearable darkness and chaos in your life? What were the circumstances that surrounded such a time? Could you have described it as a "formless void" within you?

God wants to allow His light to penetrate your darkness. What are some ways that His light could enter into your life? How have you observed God's light in the world around you?

THE POWER OF THREE

By Joyce del Rosario
AREA DIRECTOR, YOUNG LIFE

My parents always remind me that I was independent from the very beginning. I wanted to sleep in my own bed at an early age, I wanted to pour my own milk, I wanted to do it all—*all by myself.* "All by myself" is great when growing up, but it can make adulthood very difficult, especially when one's adulthood includes being in full-time youth ministry.

Over the past ten years of part-time, full-time, church, and para-church youth ministry, I have found this to be true: we are made to be in relationship. From the beginning God began in relationship. "We must make man in our image." The triune God existed in relationship and created for relationship. According to God it was not right for Adam to be alone and so he made Eve that they might be in relationship. There is power in relationship. There is creativity in relationship. There is wholeness in relationship.

Giving yourself away to kids every day can be a depleting experience. We youth workers are often like water reservoirs, tapped into when needed. When a young person experiences great tragedy, they often come to us youth workers for counsel, hope, and a word of comfort that everything will indeed be alright. DRIP. When a young person struggles with life changing decisions about school, family, drugs, sex, they turn to us (well, that's the hope at least). DRIP. When a parent finds themselves exacerbated by their teenager's sudden taste for everything not having to do with them, they turn to us. DRIP. When the pastor, church elders, and deacons want to see progress in the youth department, they turn to us. DRIP. We give. Drip. And we give. Drip. Drip. Drip.

I have heard many times that the average ministry lifespan of a youth worker is three years. For an urban youth worker like myself, the lifespan is shortened to two. We give all that our spiritual reservoirs can hold. Judging by the average lifespan, many of us are giving until the proverbial well runs dry. So how does one last in such a demanding call? How does one live off the Living Water? The answer is found in relationship.

I'm not an expert on relationships. I haven't studied the long term effects or researched the exact kinds that are draining and beneficial.

All I can do is share with you two relationships that have carried me through the last ten years of my ministry life and will probably carry me through many more.

When God called me to youth ministry I knew He wasn't kidding. I knew it would be for the long haul. I also knew that I had better equip myself properly from the very beginning if I was to do this right.

At the beginning of my ministry journey I didn't have very many Christian friends. I was a senior in college and had many great and wonderful friends, but not many who shared the same beliefs and values. So I prayed. I prayed that God would provide me with Christian friends. I knew God would answer my prayers, but I didn't realize what an impact those friendships would make.

I remember being at a Fall Kickoff retreat for the volunteer Young Life leaders in Seattle. We were at our camping property called Club Malibu in British Columbia, Canada. When we entered the cabins, people began throwing their bags in one room or another. In our scramble to find just the right roommates without overtly looking picky, I threw my bags in the room with two girls who had shared in a small group Bible Study with me for the past year, Beth and Jeri. Kimi also put her bags in the room. From that moment on it was an instant connection.

Kimi joined our small group that met weekly at our mentor's house. Our mentor, Connie, set the tone for our friendship. She would make us dinner and we would share how our weeks went, over soup and homemade bread. Over the years through graduations, marriages, babies, moving out of state, and other life changes, our group of five became a group of three.

Almost ten years later, Jeri, Kimi and I still meet every week for dinner. We tried to keep the same structure as our earlier years of dinner, sharing, Bible study, and prayer. But it became apparent what was most important to us during these times. It was sharing. Intentionally sharing. Honest sharing. Open sharing. We meet every week possible over dinner for an average of four to five hours.

I'm often asked what could we possibly talk about for four hours every week? It's not that we're particularly chatty or even overly detailed about our sharing. It's just that we share everything. Over the years we've talked openly, honestly, and confidentially about family, friends, ministry, work, calling, school, finances, sex, politics, dreams, aspirations, and our relationship with Christ. We ask each other the difficult questions. We alert each other when we see one sliding into temptation. We cheer for one another when someone does well. We cry for one another. We pray for one another.

I believe that what makes our times together so fruitful is intentionality and honesty. Without those two elements we could easily be very strong acquaintances. Being intentional about sharing our lives and the events of our past week has changed the way I ask, "How are you?" At our weekly dinners we ask the question and sit for hours listening to the response. It's a gift to take time and really listen to each other. And it's a gift to be able to freely be honest about my response. I often think, "No one really wants to know how I am." But at these weekly dinners I can be honest about everything and I know they truly want to know how I am.

We've had other friends comment on the strength of our friendship. The three of us have very different personalities, different interests, different callings. We don't spend a lot of time with each other outside of these weekly dinners (much to our dismay). We don't dress alike or act alike or talk alike like many long time friends often do.

What we do have is a commitment to keeping our friendship sacred. Our weekly meetings have become such a part of our lives we get restless when too much time passes without seeing each other. We feel the impact when we miss a week or two of meeting. Our times together have become a part of our overall mental health.

I've found myself making mental notes throughout the week about moments and thoughts I want to share when we meet again. We have a commitment to asking each other the tough questions, even if it risks making the other person defensive or mad. We have a commitment to sharing the intimate details of our lives that most people would never dream of sharing outside their homes.

Our relationship has been difficult many times. We've witnessed one another struggle through very ugly moments and rejoiced with one another through the most beautiful ones. We've cried many tears together, most of which no one else will ever see. We've admitted our weaknesses and lifted up one another's strengths. Our transparency with one another has been transforming to me personally, and to my understanding of others. It is reality at its absolute finest.

If anyone were to ask me how I can give and give to so many kids on a daily basis, I would answer: "I have relationships that give to me".

JULY 30, 2006

Let the Church Be the Church

By Amy Jacober

MEMORY VERSE:
Let us hold firmly to the hope that we have confessed, because we can trust God to do what he promised. Let us think about each other and help each other to show love and do good deeds. You should not stay away from the church meetings, as some are doing, but you should meet together and encourage each other. Do this even more as you see the day coming.—Hebrews 10:23–25 (NCV)

SCRIPTURE: 1 Corinthians 12:12–27; Hebrews 8:10; Matthew 6:33; 1 Corinthians 3:9; Ephesians 2:19–22; Revelation 21:2; 2 Timothy 2:3–6

LESSON IN A SENTENCE: Church is not an outdated idea, it is God's desire.

THE BIG PICTURE (OR WHAT YOU'RE TRYING TO GET ACROSS):
The church is the plan, a gift God designed for His followers. It is not often, however, that we view it this way. There is a lot of talk that church might be outdated. In such a busy world, believing in Jesus and even having that impact how you live your life, is fine. When it comes to joining a community, when it comes to really sharing your life with others, suddenly there are reservations. There is a common thought that following Jesus is fine as long as it doesn't interrupt my life. Of course, there is also the reality that humans have done all manner of awful things in the name of the church over the years. It may be that there is good reason some people are willing to have a relationship with Jesus but are leery of organized religion and some Christians. This lesson is all about being reminded that in spite of any of the ways that people have messed up the church, this is still the desire of God, that His people be together.

IN THIS LESSON STUDENTS SHOULD:

○ Realize organized religion is not a creation of humans.
○ See more than one perspective of what the church is.
○ Learn of God's desire for His followers to be the church.
○ Discover that they too have been created to be a part of the church.

STUFF YOU NEED:

- ○ Clay/dough (Option 1, it will be less expensive if you make this from scratch but you will need to do it ahead of time.)
- ○ Cardboard squares (Option 1)
- ○ Wet wipes (Option 1)
- ○ Paper, 6 rectangles or squares, 2 triangles, 1 cross or steeple (Option 2)
- ○ Tape (Option 2)
- ○ Pens, crayons, markers, etc.
- ○ Cardstock cut into strips the size of bookmarks

FOCUS

OPTION 1: You are the potter. . .

For today, your students are the potters. Either buy clay or make homemade (see recipe below).

Break into teams of four. Give each team a significant amount of clay, at least three containers if you are buying it, or at least three sandwich bags worth if you make it.

Ask each team to sculpt the church. Let them be as creative as they like! You may want to have pieces of cardboard on which they are building so that you can move them later, and prevent them from becoming permanent fixtures on your tables. Hand out wet wipes afterwards to clean hands, chairs, and tables. After they are done, set all of the sculptures on the same table. Ask each team to explain their sculpture.

DOUGH RECIPES:

Option #1

Mix all of these ingredients together until they are the consistency of dough. Add food coloring at the end, mix together with dough to create colors. Store colors separately in sandwich bags.

1 c flour
½ c salt
1 T cream of tartar
¼ c water
1 T oil
food coloring, to personal preference

Option #2:

Mix all of these ingredients together until they are the consistency of dough. Store colors separately in sandwich bags.

1 c flour
½ c salt
½ c water
3 T oil
1 package of Kool Aid for color and scent

We all have different ideas of what the church is. Some will create a building…very concrete. Others may make many people and have them standing together. Try to avoid declaring one as right or wrong.

OPTION 2: Church Montage

Break into eight teams. If your group is large, make two and break into sixteen groups. Give each team a word, a sheet of paper and something with which to draw and color. The words to be used are body, people, kingdom, building, bride, soldier, athlete, and farmer. Ask each group to create a representation of the word you have given. Don't necessarily tell them yet that you are looking at different understandings of the church. Let them be as creative as possible with the limited information. Once they are through, have each group show what they have drawn and collect the papers.

Have two of the sheets of paper in the shape of triangles. After you collect the papers and tape them to the wall, use six of the sheets to make a rectangle and the remaining two to come together in the shape of a roof. Place a cross or steeple you have cut out ahead of time on top.

Ask: Did anyone realize you were all drawing the same thing? How can this be?

DISCOVERY

Give each group the passage to read that matches the picture they have just created.

1 Corinthians 12:12–27—the church as body
Hebrews 8:10—His People
Matthew 6:33—Kingdom of God
1 Corinthians 3:9; Ephesians 2:19–22—God's building
Revelation 21:2—The bride of Christ
2 Timothy 2:3–6—A soldier, an athlete, a farmer

Ask: How can all of these be describing the same thing?
What do these passages mean?
What does it mean for the church to be both a bride and a soldier? Which of these seems to contradict?

LIFE APPLICATION : *Ask:* Which ones do we emphasize, if not in words, at least functionally?

How would we approach church differently if we took all of these perspectives into account?

There are many people today who say they have no problem with Christianity; in fact they say they are followers of Jesus. The problem according to many is organized religion. What does this mean?

Spend a few moments and look at what the church does well and where the church needs to improve. Draw a line down the center of your dry erase board and write the pros on one side and the cons on the other.

Church is clearly God's idea. . .it was not created by people.
People, however, can twist what God has created.

Ask: What is our responsibility, as being a part of the church, to seek to be what God desires?

How do we keep from giving up on church when people can make such a mess of it?

MAKING IT PERSONAL: While your students may not have a choice right now whether they attend church or not, there will come a day when they do choose.

Look back at the different perspectives you covered.

Ask: What would make you want to be a part of a church community?

What would make you not want to be a part of a church community?

Do any of these seem to not fit how you have always understood church?

God desires that you are a part of a church. In a world where it often does not matter where you are or what you choose, the Creator of the universe states that He desires, not only wants, a relationship with you, but that He wants you to have relationships with others. He wants to care for you and to give you a place to care for others.

Give each student a strip of cardstock cut to the size of a bookmark. As you close thanking God for His church, have each person write down the eight words that help to offer God's description of His church.

SONG: "This Is Your Life" by Switchfoot on the CD *The Beautiful Letdown*

QUOTABLE   QUOTE :

Baseball is like church. Many attend, few understand.
—Leo Durocher (1906–1991)

Let the Church Be the Church—Midweek

MEMORY VERSE:
Let us hold firmly to the hope that we have confessed, because we can trust God to do what he promised. Let us think about each other and help each other to show love and do good deeds. You should not stay away from church meetings, as some are doing, but you should meet together and encourage each other. Do this even more as you see the day coming.—Hebrews 10:23–25 (NCV)

SCRIPTURE: Acts 2:42–47

LESSON IN A SENTENCE: Church is not an outdated idea, it is God's desire.

FOCUS

Describe your perfect church. Ask your students to write down everything they think would have to be present to be the church you would want; leave out no detail.

Spend some time really wrestling with this. Invite your students to debate, agree, or disagree, but to think! Most likely you will not come upon a point of complete agreement.

If your students just go along with everything said or offered, encourage them to really think this through. A few possible questions may be: Could church exist with no music? What about a building, is it necessary? Should the building be simple or ornate? What is the difference between a church and a group of Christian friends who get together? Is the church for believers to be discipled, or to share the gospel with non-believers?

DISCOVERY

Read Acts 2:42–47.

According to this passage, what are the marks of the church?

Make a list on a poster board of these marks.

This seems like an impossible list!!

Ask: What could ever keep a group of people together to actually be able to live this way? Do you really think they were united in one mind?

What about the verse that says they sold all they had so that they could share all they had? Is this a literal understanding, or something else?

LIFE APPLICATION: *Ask*: How did the church we designed earlier match with the description of the church in Acts?

How would this church look different if it were really imitating Acts 2:42–47?

How would this youth group look different if we were really imitating Acts 2:42–47?

Go through the marks of the church. Choose at least one, and set a goal to achieve this and specific steps to move you toward that goal.

Teacher's Note: As best as you can, facilitate a discussion around this idea. If you have a younger or more immature group, this can be difficult. Pray that God guides this conversation. A growing trend is that people identify with loving Jesus, but despise organized religion. The problem is that once we abandon each other in the church, not only are we no longer obeying the commands of God, but our faith and lives are not being supported as God intended. Truly understanding the church as coming from God, and not an institution full of hypocrisy and legalism, opens the doors for authentic community.

Inside Renovation

By Amy Jacober

MEMORY VERSE:
I no longer call you servants, because a servant does not know what his master is doing. But I call you friends, because I have made known to you everything I heard from my Father.—John 15:15 (NCV)

SCRIPTURE: Matthew 17:1–13

LESSON IN A SENTENCE: Authentic friendship from God always leaves its mark on our lives.

THE BIG PICTURE (OR WHAT YOU'RE TRYING TO GET ACROSS):
We live in a world that is busy and crowded yet people are lonely all of the time. Today we consider two emphases. The first is Transfiguration Sunday, the Sunday we remember Jesus taking His close friends to a mountain and meeting with Moses and Elijah. It is fitting that Jesus included His close friends in such an excursion. This is also Friendship Sunday. We are not meant to walk this life alone. Jesus has called our attention to this time and again. So much so that He Himself says that we are His friends. He does not want us to be alone. Even in times of feeling abandoned by all or surrounded by lots of people but having no connection, Jesus calls to us and desires to be an intimate part of our lives. He wants us to know we are wanted and loved. It is impossible to be in the presence of someone who genuinely loves you and not be impacted. It is impossible to be in the presence of Christ and not be changed.

IN THIS LESSON STUDENTS SHOULD:
- Learn about the Transfiguration.
- Recognize how important friendship is to Jesus.
- Recall times they have been changed by friends in their lives.
- Be encouraged to hang out with Jesus, making Him a part of their daily lives.

STUFF YOU NEED:

- ○ Celery (Option 1)
- ○ Glasses or cups large enough to hold a stalk of celery (Option 1)
- ○ Food coloring and water (Option 1)
- ○ Sheets or towels, 3 (Option 2)
- ○ Make-over materials (Option 2)

FOCUS

OPTION 1:

Set out cups of water and stalks of celery around the room. Invite pairs of students to choose their color of food coloring or created color, and saturate the water. Right at the beginning of your time together, set the stalks of celery in the water. Within the hour the color will go into the celery and tint the spines.

After the color has begun to show, point out the stalks of celery as they change.

This is a lot like us when we spend time with Jesus. If you are in His presence, you will be different. It just happens. We spend so much time trying to be like Christ, when realistically we will be like Him if we are with Him all of the time. By the end of your hour, the color should be all the way up the spines of the celery.

Ask: How does this object lesson show what the Christian life is like?

OPTION 2: Not So Extreme Makeover

Tell your students you are going to host the Not So Extreme Makeover right here today! Ask for six volunteers, three sets of partners. (Be certain you choose students who will take this well. Keep in mind students who may have to go to work directly after.) Have each set of partners decide who is the one to receive the makeover, and who is to give the makeover. Once this has been decided, drape the recipient with a towel or sheet to keep their clothes from being ruined. Seat the partners next to one another, where everyone can see them. On a table nearby have hairbrushes, gel and make-up, enough for three people to use. As you begin, ask each make-up artist to stand behind their partner for a before-look. Just before they begin, tell them they must do the entire make-over from behind and blindfolded!

Talk your students through the make-over. Instruct them when to do hair and when to move to make-up. (This is so the process does not drag on forever.) You may need to serve as an assistant and hand them their supplies as they are blindfolded.

Have your students vote for the best make-over! Offer a small prize to the partners who win. (Be certain to allow the three who were "made-over" to run to the washroom and get cleaned up.)

Ask: So how do you think the transformation went? Anyone else ready to be in the presence of one of these three to get a little change?

DISCOVERY

Split into groups of 4–6. Have each group read and storyboard Matthew 17:1–13. They will need paper and a pen to do so. If you have never done a storyboard, it is what is used in film and television to communicate the story before it has all the details filled in. Think similar to a cartoon, with frames drawn telling the story. It doesn't need to be funny, rather it forces students to consider what exactly is being communicated, and match words and images.

Ask the groups to explain what they have just read.

LIFE APPLICATION: *Ask:* How can you tell when certain people have been together? Do you know anyone who just makes you feel better by being in their presence?

Teacher's Note: Think of a story to tell here. It will be much more effective if you share one that is from your life. If I were there, I would talk about spending time with my grandfather. He always has stories that seem magical, is unconditionally loving and is willing to have silly conversations as well as share heart to heart. You can tell when I have been with him. Who does that for you?

Jesus offers a few principles we can follow. When He is going up the mountain, He includes His friends. He could have just gone alone. He could have told them about it later. But He includes them; He is surrounded by community. Jesus also allowed His friends to see His glory.

Scripture tells us that we, too, are called friends of Jesus.

Ask: How does Jesus want to include us in where He goes?

How can we experience His glory today?

MAKING IT PERSONAL: In the Bible, mountains are often places of revelation. Think of where you have experienced or had God revealed to you in the past. This may be on a walk in the park, in the midst of the city, by a lake or the sound or wherever!

Ask: What was it like for you after being in the presence of God?

While God can come when He wants, where He wants, there are ways for us to prepare ourselves to hear Him. Plan a time to go where

God has revealed Himself to you in the past. Set a date with God. It is easy to get busy, and knowing that God is with us all of the time we forget to be intentional about acknowledging Him.

SONG: "Are You Real" by KJ52 on the CD *Behind the Musik*

Q U O T A B L E   Q U O T E S :

There is nothing like returning to a place that remains unchanged, to find the ways in which you yourself have altered.

—Nelson Mandela, *A Long Walk to Freedom*

Transformation—Midweek

MEMORY VERSE:
I no longer call you servants, because a servant does not know what his master is doing. But I call you friends, because I have made known to you everything I heard from my Father.—John 15:15 (NCV)

SCRIPTURE: Ecclesiastes 4:7–12

LESSON IN A SENTENCE: Authentic friendship from God always leaves its mark on our lives.

FOCUS

Imitation *is* the best form of flattery

Enlist a few students beforehand to come up with impersonations of some of the leaders in your group, other church leaders, or students you know can take it well. Give each a chance to offer their "performance" and then a chance for the group to guess who they were supposed to be. You may end up with a few improv additions. Have fun!

Imitation is a form of flattery. It is amazing that just by being with someone you can not only recognize the quirky things they do, but often you start to imitate one another without realizing it.

Have your students list all the phrases they use in common, or ones they have realized they have picked up from others. We don't think about it—it just happens! This even works broadly for different parts of the country. If you are in the south, at a restaurant it is not unusual to be asked what kind of coke you want. In the southwest you would be asked what kind of soda. We all rub off on one another.

Write your list on a dry erase board for a visual of just how many there are!

DISCOVERY

In groups of four, read Ecclesiastes 4:7–12.
Give the following questions to each group as they read.
Are we supposed to have other people in our lives?
Does having other people in our lives make work easier or harder?
What does it mean when it talks about vanity?
Why are two better than one?
Why does the cord mentioned have three strands and not two?

Have each group rewrite the main ideas of this passage as a story. Encourage them to be creative. Have each group either tell their story or act it out.

LIFE APPLICATION: Friendship is precious. We are not meant to live alone. In fact, so much so that the Bible says it is vanity to work so hard if only for ourselves.

Ask: What makes a good friend? Do we ever have friends for the wrong reasons? Why do we do this? How hard is it to change friends when we realize they are not good for us or that we are not good for them? Do we even need to do this?

Did you know that God does not want for you to be alone?

We have all been impacted or changed by other people. Many of us are blessed with friends. Some people are not. As much as God does not want for you to be alone, He does not want for anyone to be alone.

It is easy to become self-absorbed and consumed with what we have or do not have. Often, the biggest blessings come when we lift our eyes and look beyond ourselves. Think of someone you know who could use a friend. How might God work through you to befriend this person? Pray for that person right now and ask direction for what you should do in this process.

AUGUST 13, 2006

Going for the Gold (Christian Disciplines)

By Anna Aven

MEMORY VERSE:
Brothers and sisters, I know that I have not yet reached that goal, but there is one thing I always do. Forgetting the past and straining toward what is ahead, I keep trying to reach the goal and get the prize for which God called me through Christ to the life above.—Philippians 3:13–14 (NCV)

SCRIPTURE: Philippians 3:12–17; 1 Corinthians 9:24–27

LESSON IN A SENTENCE: Being a Christian is like being an athlete: it's not just a one-time decision, so much as it is a lifestyle.

THE BIG PICTURE (OR WHAT YOU'RE TRYING TO GET ACROSS):
   All of us have goals that we want to attain. There are two elements to getting to the goal: 1) Forgetting what is behind. Our pasts often seem like weights that hold us back and prevent us from feeling like we can move forward. 2) Straining toward what is ahead. In this day of instant gratification, it is important to remember that none of our big goals in life come without effort, and none of them come instantly.

IN THIS LESSON STUDENTS SHOULD:

- Understand that their past record—no matter what it is—is wiped clean, and since God doesn't remember it anymore, why should they?
- Realize that there's no such thing as a Christian who has "arrived," we're all still on a journey.

STUFF YOU NEED:

- Clips/pictures/interviews of an athlete who has recently been in the spotlight. Since the 2006 Winter Olympic games were in Turin in February, note if a particular athlete stood out (like Michael Phelps in the 2004 Olympics in Athens http://www.michaelphelps.com).

○ Copies of a goals sheet. Can just be a piece of paper with "goals" at the top, and then spaced out evenly, underneath the headings: "Spiritual," "Family and Friends," "Education and Career," and "Recreation."

See options under the Discovery section for additional materials needed.

FOCUS

When we have a major sporting event and you see the athletes walk out in all their glory, often a thought will pass briefly through our minds: "I wish. . ." and we'll fill in the blank with some great athletic goal or something like that. But what we usually don't think about is the fact that the person is doing what they're doing not as the result of simply deciding a few minutes before the game that they were going to play. *Here you can substitute the information on Michael Phelps with another athlete that's been in the spotlight more recently. Putting up pictures while you talk, if available, will help to illustrate the point.* Swimmer Michael Phelps from the 2004 Olympics in Athens has arms that are slightly disproportionate to his body. They are longer than average, giving him a slightly longer reach. That, combined with the fact that he is 6'4" gives him an advantage over other swimmers, in that he can go further with one pull. However, while he was gifted with those two things at birth, he wouldn't have become the best swimmer in the world at age nineteen unless he had devoted his life to it. He eats, drinks, and sleeps swimming. He practices rigorously, eats properly, and in short, gears his entire life toward being the best that he can be. His genetics wouldn't matter if he sat around on the couch all day, eating junk food, or whatever. *Read 1 Corinthians 9:2–27.*

Often we say, "I wish I was a better Christian," or we idolize someone whom we perceive to have "arrived" in their spiritual walk. The first thing we need to realize is that no one has arrived. The second thing is that if you see someone whom you admire because of their walk with the Lord, you need to realize they didn't get there by accident.

DISCOVERY

OPTION 1:
Discussion of Movie Clip (better for high school)
Needed: *Lord of the Rings: Return of the King*

You can break into small groups at this point if it would make discussion easier for your group.

Read or have a student read Philippians 3:12–17. Show the clip from *Return of the King*. Have students reflect on parallels between the scene in the movie and the Scripture passage.

You could wrap up the discussion by saying something such as: In this scene, Frodo is walking into Shelob's lair, but he keeps looking back. As he looks back, he can't see where he's going and ends up tangled in a web. In the same way, we cannot make progress forward in our Christian walks if we continue to look behind us. *Continue on with the Discovery section below Option 2.*

OPTION 2:

Backwards/Forwards Race (better for middle school/junior high group)

For a younger group or simply because you know there's a guest speaker that's going to go long and you need to use up more time, you can use this option to get to the discovery part.

Materials needed: Masking tape for the floor to form the starting line and finish line. Four or five volunteers with stop watches to time the fastest students.

Space on the floor of your youth room/hallway/gym/parking lot to run a short race.

The point of this exercise is merely to have your group run a race backwards, and then run the same race forwards, to show that it's easier to run when you're facing forward. IMPORTANT: Make sure you instruct them to look where they are going even when they are running backwards. This doesn't make quite as good of an illustration (because they are looking forward—but it's a lot safer).

Read or have a student read Philippians 3:1–17. Ask them to find the parallels between the race they just ran and the Scripture passage.

You can wrap it up by saying something such as: As we all knew, and just proved, it's oh so much easier to run when you're looking forward. In the same way, continuing to look back at times we've messed up will only hold us back.

There are three parts to running the race, or living a disciplined Christian life: 1) forgetting what is behind, 2) pressing toward what is ahead, and 3) doing the first two in the context of realizing that we have not yet attained nor are we perfect yet, but since Christ has finished the work, we can go forward in faith to lay hold of and grow in that perfection. The other thing that is important about all three of these is that they are a simultaneous, ongoing process. Paul says, "forgetting those things which are behind." This very sentence structure itself implies that this is an ongoing process. If he had said, "Now that I've forgotten the mistakes of my past, I am free to press forward. . ." this would be an entirely different story, but because of this verb usage, "forgetting," we can rephrase it something like this: "I have a goal in front of me: to get what Jesus has already gotten for me. To get to this goal, I am both forgetting the mistakes of my past, and I am running forward with all my energy, pushing through whatever hardships may come because I know what is in front of me is so much better than I can imagine."

There's a goal that we're trying to get to, and choosing to run forward means choosing not to look back, nor turn back. As was illustrated by our example (*Refer back to the Option you chose to introduce the Discovery time*), looking back doesn't get you very far. Both running forward and choosing not to look back are ongoing processes. This is why Paul words the sentence like this. He begins it all with the realization that "I have not attained perfection" or "I don't have it all together yet, but I can do this one thing: press on." That's what a disciplined Christian life looks like. It's not perfection. It's not a higher spiritual plane that some have gotten to and the rest of us can only hope to get to someday. It's a journey, a process. It's ongoing and it will never be completed until we graduate to heaven.

LIFE APPLICATION: *Options for this section:* If you want to introduce actual spiritual disciplines, read at least chapter nine of Dallas Willard's *Spirit of the Disciplines* or some such work that introduces spiritual disciplines so that you can touch on them and explain what they are for, especially if you want to do a series on them, or a book study with some of your older students, etc. Space is limited here, so the Option 2 is to continue a discussion of discipline in the Christian life in general.

Okay, so now that we have this great realization that it's an ongoing process what do we do about it? We've discussed how to realize that the Christian discipline thing is an ongoing process, and we touched briefly at the beginning about how it takes discipline and focus on the goal. Let's look back at 1 Corinthians 9:24–27 for a minute. *Read passage.* If an athlete wants to achieve a goal, he or she has to bring their desires, their focus, and their entire lives into discipline to reach that goal. It doesn't sound like fun at first, but you can't be a great athlete in a moment's time. You can't get in shape in a week. You can't get straight A's without studying—well, at least, most of us can't. You can't have a relationship without work.

You can personalize the story that follows, or generalize it. I was talking to a friend recently and he was telling me how many changes he had made for his girlfriend. As the relationship has gotten further along (they've been dating for almost a year at this point), and has gotten more serious, he has increasingly rearranged his schedule. Now, when one of you is dating someone, I don't hear you complaining about the amount of time you spend with that person. You're willing to arrange your entire life for the purpose of getting to know that special someone.

And yet we sit and complain at times about how our relationship with Christ isn't as meaningful as some of our human relationships, and I'd ask, how much do you put into it? Because if you only put a fraction of the time into your relationship with Christ as you do into your human relationships, you're only going to get a fraction of the meaning out of it.

MAKING IT PERSONAL: *Ask:* How many of you have goals? If you have time, you can actually hear examples of these, write them up on a whiteboard/overhead/PowerPoint slide, etc. Pass out the goals sheet that you prepared. A lot of times we have goals in some areas of our lives, but what I want to do right now is encourage you to make goals in all areas of your life, starting with your spiritual goals—your Jesus-relationship goals. Think about where you want this to go. And then later on this week, as you have time, fill in the other categories as well. I'd encourage you also to pray through these goals, or pray for God to give you goals if you don't feel like you have any big ones at the moment. These range from goals for your family and friend relationships, to what mountain you want to climb someday, or whatever. But think about this. If you want a better relationship with one of your siblings, think about how to make that happen on your side, and then take steps toward being the kind of sibling you would want to have, and see if it doesn't produce some better results in your relationship. If you've always wanted to do something as a career, or a recreational goal or whatever, put that down and think about how to get to it.

Leader, if you have examples of things that you planned for and then achieved, or wanted to do, but didn't plan for, and so you didn't get there, you could mention them here. Also, you can turn this into a time of reflection while the kids think through their spiritual goals. You could have them go off into separate parts of the room, turn the lights down, and play a contemplative song such as Dave Crowder's "Only You" from the *Illuminate* CD. If you are doing the mid-week lesson as a follow-up to this one, you can have them bring their goals sheets back to discuss them in small groups.

SONGS: "Only You" on *Illuminate* David Crowder Band.
"Cry of the Disciple" by John Chan

(chords for this song can be found at
http://www.praisearchive.com/songwindow.php?id=50).

EXTRA! EXTRA!: And in this truth lies the secret of the easy yoke:
The secret involves living as he [Jesus] did in the entirety of his life.
Following 'in his steps' cannot be equated with behaving as he did when
he was 'on the spot.' To live as Christ lived is to live as he did *all* his
life." Dallas Willard, *The Spirit of the Disciplines*, p. 5.

Going for the Gold (Christian Disciplines)—Midweek

MEMORY VERSE:
Brothers and sisters, I know that I have not yet reached that goal, but there is one thing I always do. Forgetting the past and straining toward what is ahead. I keep trying to reach the goal and get the prize for which God called me through Christ to the life above.—Philippians 3:13–14 (NCV)

SCRIPTURE: Philippians 3:7–17

LESSON IN A SENTENCE: Being a Christian is like being an athlete: it's not just a one-time decision so much as it is a lifestyle.

STUFF YOU NEED:

○ Options for this service include discussing goal sheets from Sunday in small groups, and/or bringing something that represents things that hold you back and destroying them (wastebasket, bonfire, or whatever is feasible on your property).

FOCUS

Discuss: What do you count as accomplishments in life? If you accomplished all the goals on your goal sheet, would you think you had arrived? The point of this discussion is not to negate Sunday's point that we need to "press on" in our walks with Christ. It is important to have goals and to press on in our walk with Christ, however, our relationship with Christ—knowing Christ—is the ultimate goal, and no matter what we are striving for, no matter how worthy that cause may be, we need to be willing to count it as nothing to gain Christ. You don't need to say all of this—hopefully your students will be able to pull some of this out for themselves in the Discovery part.

DISCOVERY

Read Philippians 3:7–11. *Connections:* Paul says that everything that was his gain he now counts as loss, because he wants to know Christ so badly. Other places in his letters, Paul tells us that he was a

Jew of Jews and a Pharisee of Pharisees. This means that Paul was at the top of his game. He was the son of a Pharisee, and one of the rising stars of Judaism. So "all this" that he counts as loss is quite a bit. What do you think Paul is trying to say here by "counting it all as loss?"

Being a Pharisee meant that Paul was one of the religious leaders of his day. He knew the Old Testament (the Hebrew Scriptures) very well, and would have been a scholar of many people's commentary on the Scripture. In light of all that, what is the significance of Paul saying "not having my own righteousness?" You may want to explain that righteousness means that God has granted us "right-standing" with Him. If anyone could have been said to be righteous from works, Paul would have been a good candidate. Paul declared that only knowing Jesus can give us right-standing with God, because Jesus gave us His perfect record when He died in our place.

In v. 10, Paul says he wants to know Christ. At this point, Paul has been a Christian for a while. What is the significance of him saying that he wants to know Christ? The answers should hone in on the idea that we can always get to know Christ better.

LIFE APPLICATION: What accomplishments of ours do we sometimes turn over in our heads to convince ourselves of our good standing in life? Give plenty of time for silent reflection. Probably getting students to list them out loud won't be productive as it could turn into a bragging session, which would detract from the point. It's not that accomplishments are bad things, but in comparison with knowing Christ, Paul counts all these as rubbish, or dung, as it says in the old King James. Use your imagination here. . .Paul might possibly have been using a stronger word. Well, just maybe. All of our accomplishments or goals should be nothing in comparison with the desire to know Christ.

MAKING IT PERSONAL: Knowing Christ is a holistic pursuit, in that it doesn't mean that we're supposed to go sit out in the desert and meditate on God. We can know Christ better as we go through our life and let Him teach us what it means to follow Him. That's where this lesson ties in with Sunday's lesson on Christian disciplines. By seeing our entire lives—not just Sundays or times when we're reading our Bibles—as a training session for following Christ and living as He lived, then knowing Christ suddenly becomes the focus of everything we do. In what ways can you choose to follow Christ better in various spheres of your lives?

AUGUST 20, 2006

More than a Ceasefire (Reconciliation)

By Amy Jacober

MEMORY VERSE:
If possible, so far as it depends on you, live peaceably with all.—Romans 12:18 (NRSV)

SCRIPTURE: Genesis 30:22–24; Genesis 37:3–17; Genesis 37:18–36; Genesis 39:1–6; 41:38–44; Genesis 42:1–28; Genesis 45:1–18

LESSON IN A SENTENCE: God desires true reconciliation.

THE BIG PICTURE (OR WHAT YOU'RE TRYING TO GET ACROSS):
Reconciliation is indeed more than a ceasefire in an argument. It restores the relationship, often to a stronger place than in the past. This takes time, humility, forgiveness, and an open heart. Have you ever noticed how beginning at a very young age we are taught to say sorry and ask for forgiveness? When done correctly, this is good and healthy. Often, however, it is manipulative and simply empty words. Here's a simple example: Person A spreads a mean rumor about person B. Person B is really hurt. Person A goes to person B, says sorry and asks for forgiveness. If person B is still hurt, then they have not only been hurt, but they look like a jerk if they are not ready to forgive. If person A simply says sorry and lets person B have the space he needs, the path has been paved for true reconciliation. Our job as adults is to encourage students to indeed open their hearts to forgiveness, even when the worst has been done. This is patterned after God Himself. In our sin we are like person A, needing to acknowledge that we have hurt God. The big difference is that God is always ready to forgive us. Our repentance is a response to this amazing love.

IN THIS LESSON STUDENTS SHOULD:

- Define reconciliation.
- Understand that forgiveness is a choice.
- Learn that no matter how many wrong or bad things have been done to you or you have done to others, reconciliation is still possible.

STUFF YOU NEED:

○ Chairs (Option 1)
○ A large blanket (Option 1)
○ *Mean Girls* video or DVD (Option 2)

FOCUS

Heads up! There is a lot of Scripture to cover today. Be certain to leave the majority of your time for the Discovery section. This is a great story and with so many good points. You are already going to cover a lot of territory; keep focused on the main point of reconciliation at the end. There will be other days where you can look to other principles offered.

OPTION 1:

Before you set this up, have three guys step outside the room. Quietly take two chairs and cover them with a blanket. Be certain to leave space between the two chairs so it looks more like a bench. Have two of your girls, one in each chair sit to hold the blanket in place. Be certain to pull it tight to continue the illusion of a bench. While all of this is being set up, tell the guys the object of the game is to try and come up with the best pick-up line. The girls will invite him to sit down if they like his line. Meanwhile, tell the students in the room to not give away the secret. The girls are to refuse the first two guys and invite the third to sit. Of course as he sits, there is no chair beneath the blanket and he will fall to the floor! Don't worry, it's not a far fall and with the blanket pulled taught, the fall gets cushioned. He may be a little embarrassed and the room will certainly be laughing!

In the big picture of things, this is not that big a deal; maybe a little embarrassing, but not that big a deal. Think of other times when you have been embarrassed and did not want to forgive the person for what was done.

OPTION 2:

Show a clip from *Mean Girls*. If you haven't seen this movie, view it beforehand to be certain you and your leadership find this appropriate. It is the story of a girl raised in Africa and her first year in the United States at a public high school. There are many great clips in this film from which you can choose. If you need a hint, go to the clip that shows the "burn book" being shown to the principal.

Ask for reactions to the clip. Could you ever forgive someone for doing something like that?

DISCOVERY

Break into six groups. Hand each group an index card with the following instructions.

Read your passage and retell the story in 3–5 sentences, no more!! If you are feeling really clever, see if you can make it rhyme!

Group 1: Genesis 37:3–17
Group 2: Genesis 37:18–36
Group 3: Genesis 39:1–6; 41:38–44
Group 4: Genesis 42:1–28
Group 5: Genesis 45:1–18

Teacher's Note: This is the story of Joseph. Many of us know about Joseph and the coat of many colors. Before your students begin, set up the story of Joseph. You will need to read through Genesis 29–31. Ask your students to think of the most messed up, dysfunctional family they can imagine. . .DO NOT have them say this out loud.

Say: So let me tell you about a guy named Joseph. To understand Joseph, you have to know about his parents and family. Joseph's dad was Jacob. Jacob fell in love with Rachel. Jacob asked Rachel's dad, Laban, for her hand in marriage. Laban said they could get married IF Jacob was willing to serve for seven years. After seven years, Jacob was ready. The morning after the marriage, he realized it was not Rachel with whom he had been, but her older sister, Leah. Laban said if Jacob still wanted Rachel, he would have to give another seven years. Jacob openly loved Rachel more so he worked another seven years. Once he finally married Rachel as well, it turned out she was unable to have children. Leah, on the other hand, was very fertile. Rachel was heartbroken and gave her maidservant, Bilhah, to Jacob. Bilhah gave two sons. Leah was jealous and gave her maidservant, Zilpah, to Jacob; she bore two sons. So let's do a little check—Jacob now has children from three different women and is in love with a fourth and all of them live in the same household. Leah continued having sons and daughters as well. Finally—after many years, Rachel was pregnant. She bore a son and he was named Joseph. So here is Joseph, with many brothers and sisters—but he was the favored son, as he was from the wife Jacob loved most. If you've ever thought your parents played favorites—this family takes the cake! After some time, Rachel became pregnant again. She named her second son Benjamin, just before dying after a hard labor.

So there's the set up—Joseph's family was a little complicated, to say the least!

Just in case your students spend more time on being creative and clever than actually communicating a concept, have a quick summary of each section ready.

Group 1: *Genesis 37:3–17* Joseph told his brothers about a dream he had in which he was the ruler, and they and their father bowed at his feet. Needless to say, the brothers hated him. Jacob sent Joseph after his brothers, who were tending their father's flocks.

Group 2: *Genesis 37:18–36* Joseph's brothers saw him coming. They decided to kill him. Once they captured him, instead of killing him they decided to sell him and make a profit. They went back to their father and lied, saying Joseph was dead.

Group 3: *Genesis 39:1–6; 41:38–44* Joseph was sold again to Potiphar's household, an Egyptian officer of the Pharaoh. Potiphar liked and trusted Joseph. He put Joseph in charge of everything he owned. Joseph also ended up finding favor with Pharaoh and was eventually put in charge of all that Pharaoh ruled.

Teacher's Note: You may want to add in here that while you aren't actually reading it, Joseph met Pharaoh after being seduced, wrongly accused and then sent to prison, where he thought he was going to die. It wasn't exactly a smooth transition for him.

Group 4: *Genesis 42:1–28* A famine came to the land where Jacob and his sons lived. The only place nearby to obtain food was Egypt. Jacob sent his sons to buy food for the family. Joseph recognized his brothers, but did not let them know who he was.

Group 5: *Genesis 45:1–18* Joseph finally tells his brothers who he is. Instead of having them killed or refusing to help them, he blesses them, provides for them and tells them to move close so that he may care for them from that point on. His forgiveness moves far beyond words and brings about reconciliation and a stronger relationship than they had before.

LIFE APPLICATION: Still in groups, ask how realistic they think it is that Joseph would have forgiven his brothers? Keep in mind that he was dropped in a pit, sold twice, forced to work in a foreign land, and put in prison. This wasn't exactly a minor spat between siblings.

Can you think of a time when you have hurt someone and they chose to forgive you? What was the relationship like after that?

God calls us to reconciliation. Joseph wasn't ready the minute he saw his brothers for the first time, but his heart was already moving in that direction. He could have been bitter and taken revenge. Instead he chose to forgive and ended up with restored relationships with his family.

Why do we choose to stay angry or to take our own revenge, instead of trying to reconcile?

MAKING IT PERSONAL: Ask each person to think of one person who has wronged them or hurt them recently. Invite each person to consider forgiving that person and to seek a restored relationship. Close, asking God to provide ways for conversations to take place to restore broken relationships.

Teacher's Note: Some of your students will not take this very seriously, but others will. You may want to give a warning that although what God desires is reconciliation, there are some people who, even when forgiven, will choose to reject that person. There are many reasons why this happens. Tell your students that the response of the other person is not their responsibility. Their own actions and attitudes are.

LOOKING AHEAD: In just under one month See You At The Pole (SYATP) will take place. This is a student initiated time to pray for your schools, community, and country. It is the third Wednesday of September every year. Take the time to begin discussing this with your students. Check out the website at www.syatp.com.

SONG: "Heaven" by Salvador, on the album *So Natural*

QUOTABLE   QUOTES :

In an argument, leave room for a reconciliation.
—Russian Proverb

More Than a Ceasefire (Reconciliation)—Midweek

MEMORY VERSE:
If possible, so far as it depends on you, live peaceably with all.
—Romans 12:18 (NRSV)

SCRIPTURE: Luke 23:33–43

LESSON IN A SENTENCE: God desires true reconciliation.

FOCUS

This one will take a little preparation several days before you meet. Get in touch with the parents or guardians of several of your students. Ask for a short story of a time when their child did something for which they got in trouble, and the consequence they earned. While you may gather many stories, only use the ones that you know will not embarrass or make any of your students angry. What you are looking for are stories such as: one of your 11th graders ran away from home at the age of five, and after being walked back home, had to ask to be let back in the house. Or when one of your 9th graders destroyed her mom's dress by making a parachute for her stuffed animals, and was given the job of doing the family laundry for two weeks.

This can be done several ways. You can simply collect stories and read them out, asking your students to guess which person goes with the story. Another option would be to take a camera and record the parents telling their stories. You don't need fancy editing, just record them and play them at your meeting.

We've all done things for which we deserve punishment. Some of the things we have done or tried to get away with are funnier than others!

DISCOVERY

As the laughter dies down, have someone from the back of the room read Luke 23:33–44.

Have your students read this passage again in pairs. Have each pair look at the passage and discuss the following:

Have you ever realized that Jesus was forgiving those who crucified Him, even though they never acknowledged that what they were doing was wrong?

Do you think Jesus still does this today?

What do you think of the two criminals?

God's desire is so strong to be reconciled with His creation, that He stepped out of heaven and gave Himself as the ultimate sacrifice, offering forgiveness even when it was not requested.

LIFE APPLICATION: *Ask:* Which criminal do you think you are like?

What does this tell you about the way you receive and offer forgiveness?

Close, praying that every person is able to accept the forgiveness God offers and walk daily with Him. Reconciliation is not a one time event—it is an ongoing, growing relationship that grows deeper and stronger with time.

In the World and Not Afraid

By Rick & Kristi Bennett

MEMORY VERSE:

"I am not asking you to take them out of the world but to keep them safe from the Evil One. They don't belong to the world, just as I don't belong to the world."—John 17:15–16 (NCV)

SCRIPTURE: Daniel 1

LESSON IN A SENTENCE: We need to approach the culture of this world as missionaries, with a message to change it, bold and not frightened.

THE BIG PICTURE (OR WHAT YOU'RE TRYING TO GET ACROSS):

Daniel and his friends were taken, as young teenagers, from a place of relative comfort and safety to a pagan world. Through their strong belief in God and strong bond of community with each other, they were able make good decisions which kept them from becoming "defiled" by the pagan world of Babylonia. Because of their discernment, they were undefiled, though they learned from the pagan teachers (witchcraft and sorcery) and took Babylonian names, because they knew that not eating defiled meat was the most important decision. God used them to teach their leaders and change the hearts of their captors.

IN THIS LESSON STUDENTS SHOULD:

- Know the story of Daniel and his friends.
- Understand the difference between being "in" the world and "of" the world.
- Make a decision to take a risk to reach someone for Christ.

STUFF YOU NEED:

- Index cards for memory verse

OPTION 1: paper/pencils/markers

OPTION 2: enough blindfolds for everyone in the group

Pieces of paper with different colors (no more than four of each color) written on them (don't use colored paper, because then it will be easier for students to identify who is in their group just by looking around before they are blindfolded).

A container for the paper

FOCUS

Choose either Option 1 or 2.

OPTION 1: High School

Have a sheet of paper or chalkboard to write down the answers to the questions asked.

As a group, discuss the following: Think about some people you know who live the kind of lives you don't agree with. What do they do that makes you afraid to be around them? Where do they go, who do they hang out with, what do they do, what do you think motivates them to do these things, and so forth?

What about the surrounding culture (nation, school, city or town, television, etc.) scares you? What about the surrounding culture bothers you the most? What about the surrounding culture do you think is not as bad as others tell you? What about the surrounding culture entices you? What about the surrounding culture could be changed to become good?

When you hear about life in your parents' day, does it sound easier to be a Christian then or now? What about in the days of your grandparents? Why?

Do you think it is harder to be a Christian now or in biblical times? (The point of this question is to lead them to see that the world of Daniel and his friends was no less pagan and scary than today.)

OPTION 2: Junior High (Active Group)

**Note: Tailor the amount of people in each group according to how big/small your group is. If you have a small group, you would want to pair up students, whereas in a large group, you could have four in a group. The point is to make it as difficult as possible for students to find each other.

Have students draw a color out of a hat. Then have students put on blindfolds and try to find the others in their group by shouting out their color. The goal is for students to group up according to color, so that at the end of the exercise, they have made a group of four (symbolic of Daniel and his group of friends). Then have everyone remove their blindfolds and ask: How did it feel when you were trying to find the others in your group? What made it difficult?

Is it difficult to know which voices to pay attention to? Do you think it is difficult to listen to the right voices in the world that you live? How do you decide which voices to listen to?

DISCOVERY

Ask students to read Daniel 1.

Explain to the students that Judah was a world in which everyone worshiped the same God, learned the same things about God, and everyone believed the same thing about God.

However, God delivered these people to a pagan king. Why did He do that? Does the world God delivered them to sound any scarier than the world today? Why?

It is imperative for the students to understand that Babylonia was a wicked kingdom, which was pagan. It practiced sorcery and witch-craft. It was the polar opposite of Judah, the home of the Jews.

Look at vv. 4–5. What age do you think these men were? (Point out they were likely teenagers). Point out that they were taken from the idyllic world and forced to live in a pagan society, learn its language, its customs, eat the non-kosher food (Jews lived according to strict dietary laws, which were broken by the Babylonians), learn the pagan customs of the day (vv. 17, 20) and even change their names to Babylonian names (vv. 6–7).

How would you feel if this was forced upon you? Would it frighten you? Why? What would you do? Would it help to have friends going through the same thing? Why?

They made some difficult decisions and risked their lives, but were always respectful of their captors. Can you find an example of the humility and respect they practiced towards their captors? (vv. 8, 9, 12, 20)

These young men continued to respect their captors and leaders (Daniel and the lion's den, the fiery furnace, etc.). Why was it impor-tant to not eat the meat and drink the wine? Notice what they did when they chose not to defile themselves. How did they win the right to not eat the meat?

What happened when they were tested? How did God protect them? How did God use them? (vv. 15–20)

Were these young men missionaries?

Teacher's Note: So many of us learned the phrase "garbage in/ garbage out" as a teenager. It is imperative to help the students under-stand that this does not need to be the case. Since Daniel and his friends were undefiled in other areas of their lives, God protected them when they learned from the Babylonians (knowing their purpose was as missionaries). In fact, they understood the pagan concepts better than those who believed them (think of such a concept when we look at evolution in school).

Concerning the defilement, make sure the students understand that eating the meat and drinking the wine would have broken their oaths as young Jewish men.

LIFE APPLICATION: As teenagers navigating a pagan culture in school, on television and in all areas of life, today's students need to understand that they are missionaries and are given an opportunity to make decisions that will not impact *them*, but those around them.

It's not where we go that defines us, it's what our mission is. And that's what is important. It's not where we are, it's what we are doing there. The world needs these students (at work, at school, in clubs, on sports teams, etc.).

Ask these questions:

1. Do you have a place that is like Babylon to you?

2. What impresses you about Daniel and his friends? How are they examples?

3. Do they seem to have anything in common with you? What?

4. What things did they do that you could learn from and put into action?

5. How could God use you like God used them? Where can He use you?

MAKING IT PERSONAL: Think of one person you encounter on a daily basis (at school, work, etc.) that you try to stay away from because of the choices that person makes in her or his own life. Then write down on your index card some practical ways you could make a conscious decision to become friends with that person, and try to "be Christ" to them.

Finish by reading Jesus' prayer for His disciples (John 17:6–19) together as a group. Make it a prayer for your group (you can personalize it and pray it together).

MEMORY VERSE ACTIVITY

Upon praying this prayer together, have them write the Memory Verses down on an index card as a personal prayer. Have them write the ways they need to be "in the world" but not "of the world" on the other side of the card.

CONNECTIONS: It is important to make your prayer for the students in your care the same as that of Jesus for His disciples in John 17:15–19; that they stay in the world, but protected from the Evil One.

This concept which connects directly to Daniel and his friends is imperative. None of this can be done without prayer and community. There are many examples related to Daniel and his friends throughout the Book of Acts and in church history. Romans 12:2 is another verse to relate to this.

EXTRA EXTRA!!: Sitting in a seminar, I heard our leader make a pronouncement that confused me. He said, "the church is of the world, but not in it." I thought he said it wrong. And then I realized he said it right. Too often we in the church act just like the world, but in the safety of our own cocoon. We treat each other with disrespect. We gossip. We backbite. However, we do this in church.

Another mistake we make is to be outside of the world when not of it. We may behave correctly and do many of the things the world needs us to do to be good witnesses. But we choose to do these good things in the confines of our Christian ghetto. This has very little impact upon the world around us.

Only when we do the difficult thing (in the world/not of the world) do we have the impact. Jesus knew this. That is why He prayed for God to protect the disciples but keep them in the world. To have impact, they had to be there. As 1 Peter 2:12 (NIV) says, "live such good lives AMONG THE PAGANS that, though they accuse you of doing wrong, they may see your good deeds and glorify God on the day he visits us."

QUOTABLE QUOTES:

A man who puts aside his religion because he is going into society is like one taking off his shoes because he is about to walk on thorns.

—Richard Cecil

In the World and Not Afraid—Midweek

MEMORY VERSE:
"I am not asking you to take them out of the world but to keep them safe from the Evil One. They don't belong to the world, just as I don't belong to the world."—John 17:15–16 (NCV)

SCRIPTURE: Matthew 5:13–16

LESSON IN A SENTENCE: How can we influence the world around us if we refuse to engage it?

STUFF YOU NEED:

- ○ 2–4 blindfolds
- ○ Saltines (salted and unsalted)
- ○ Pretzels or potato chips (salted and unsalted)
- ○ Nuts (salted and unsalted) or any other food that comes salted and unsalted
- ○ Water

FOCUS

To illustrate the flavoring capabilities of salt on the world, a simple game can be played. Before the game, you must gather a few resources, listed above.

Invite 2–4 players to play a blind taste test. Give each of them a blindfold. After blindfolding, give each of them a different food example. Give each person two samples of the same food, one salted and one unsalted.

Simply ask them which one tasted better and why. This simply illustrates the wonders of salt as a flavoring agent. Make sure you pick things that people are used to eating with salt. Have something to drink close by.

DISCOVERY

If possible, bring some salt to the class, along with a lamp or flashlight—so students can see the metaphors.

Concerning salt, ask them what they know about salt. Point out that this is an important metaphor to the world in which Jesus lived.

Some things to point out regarding salt include:

1. Before refrigeration, salt was used to cure meat as a preservative (to keep it from going bad and causing sickness). Think of its importance in such a hot climate. Salt is a transforming agent. It actually changes the meat when it is put on it.

2. Salt was a valuable currency in the ancient Middle East. It was valuable, like silver or gold—because it was so needed.

3. Even today, salt is the most important flavoring to dishes. Jesus understood that salt must be put on the meat to make the meat taste good and to preserve it. It must penetrate the meat (it is active, not passive).

Ask how these things about salt apply to the church.

Ask the students what they know about light. Point out that this was another important metaphor for the gathered people (especially since Israel was considered the light of the world).

Some things to point out regarding light include:

1. Light causes growth.

2. A little light allows a child to sleep, even when scared of the dark.

3. The thing that makes horror movies scary is the lack of light. We do not see many horror movies or thrillers that take place in the daylight.

4. As we see in movies, darkness hides things (such as truth), while light opens things up.

Ask students how these things about light apply to the church.

Ask these questions:

(1) What is light? Some answers to emphasize include that it is an instrument (it is not to be noticed, but to put the focus on something else).

(2) Why is light needed? Some things to look for could be that the world is in the dark, there is not enough light, even by the church. It is the opposite of darkness, where bad things happen.

Point out that for light to be useful, it must be in a room. To be useful to the world, Christians (as light) must be in the same world as non-Christians to point them to Jesus. They are of no use if they are separate from those needing the light, since light is conspicuous.

Also, for salt to be useful, it must be on the food we want flavored. Salt does not preserve meat or make it taste better if the salt is not at the table or if it is poured on a different plate. To be useful to the world, we must be poured out on the world.

Ask students for specific ways the church has been salt and light to the world around it (much like Daniel and his friends in Babylon). There are many great answers, but help them see things such as the abolition of slavery, the Civil Rights movement, Great Awakenings in the past, etc.

LIFE APPLICATION: Ask the students—if they are SALT and LIGHT, how that changes their outlook on the world, school, jobs, etc.

Some specific questions include:

1. How has the church hidden its light? (by not being in the room, by hiding ourselves from others) How do you hide your light from the world surrounding you?

2. How has the church lost its saltiness? How have you?

3. Is light needed by the world? In what ways can we be light to the world?

4. How can your light be seen by your friends and enemies?

5. In what specific ways can you change to the culture surrounding you?

6. If you are the salt and light of the world, should you be afraid of the surrounding culture? How have you been afraid of the world around you? What steps can you take to not be afraid, but be confident in your role as salt and light to your school or work?

Read 2 Peter 2:12 as a benediction.

CONNECTIONS AND TEACHER'S NOTES: Isaiah 49:6 tells us of God's servant who is the light to the nations. Jews saw Israel as light of the world. This band of weak, tiny, ragtag disciples was now light.

Understand Jesus is the light of the world (John 1:4–5; 8:12). In the New Testament we are told to walk in the light (1 John 1). Light is a constant Scriptural image.

"We can't see light itself. We can only see what light lights up, like a little circle of night where the candle flickers."— Fredrick Buechner

SEPTEMBER 3, 2006

Mercy

By Amy Jacober

MEMORY VERSE:
And from far away the Lord appeared to his people and said, "I love you people with a love that will last forever. That is why I have continued showing you kindness."—Jeremiah 31:3 (NCV)

"Show mercy, just as your Father shows mercy."—Luke 6:36 (NCV)

SCRIPTURE: Lamentations 3:19–25; Micah 7:14–20

LESSON IN A SENTENCE: As God extends mercy to His followers, we are required to extend mercy to others.

THE BIG PICTURE (OR WHAT YOU'RE TRYING TO GET ACROSS):
Mercy is one of those amazing things that is both an action and a characteristic. Just when you think you have pushed God to His limit, he extends His hand of mercy. This is not to say that there are no consequences to sin, there are. Mercy does not remove consequences. It does bring into reality longsuffering compassion. God does not cast us aside just because we are slow to learn. He does not turn His back on us even after we have treated Him like dirt. He loves us, and His forbearance is beyond our imagination. Our world is much more about an eye for an eye, than turn the other cheek. We not only want what is due to us, but we believe we have a right to it. In God's mercy, He does not give us what is due. Instead He offers eternal life. While we are amazingly blessed to have a God who in the end does not forget us, we are thus charged with responsibility. Just as we receive mercy, we are to offer mercy. It is easy to be like the servant who borrows money, is forgiven, and turns right around to punish one who owes him. We are short sighted and forget how much we have been given. God calls us to keep this in mind, so that we too may give freely. Mercy does not fit in with most plans in this world to get ahead. We, however, were not called to get ahead, but to live as followers and imitators of Christ.

IN THIS LESSON STUDENTS SHOULD:

- ○ Discuss the difference between mercy and consent.
- ○ Be comforted that God's mercy does not fail.
- ○ Find hope in God's mercy.

STUFF YOU NEED:

○ Blindfolds (Option 1)
○ Sour and bitter items (Option 2)
○ 2 buckets (Option 2)
○ Water (Option 2)

FOCUS

OPTION 1: Taste test

Ask for at least three people to volunteer for a taste test! On a table have several sour or bitter items on separate plates covered with napkins. Blindfold each person. Use a variety of objects like lemons, pickles, unsweetened chocolate, salt and vinegar potato chips, and gummi sours.

Without letting them look, feed each person these items. As they taste, ask each person to identify the item. Have them keep going until they cannot take the sour or bitter items anymore.

You may want to pass out lemon drops or some other sour item to the entire group.

Things that are bitter or sour are hard to bear for long and even at that, only in small amounts. We do things all of the time that taste bitter or sour to God. He has an immeasurable ability to not only handle the bitterness we offer, but to extend mercy beyond what any of us deserve.

OPTION 2:

Choose two teams of four. Have the team lie on their backs in a circle with their feet raised to meet in the middle, balancing a bucket of water on their feet. Each team member must remove his/her shoes without spilling the water.

Life can bring about some pretty tough things. Some of them may even seem impossible to survive. Amazingly enough, the worst that happened in this game was that some of you got wet. In life, even after heartbreaking difficult circumstances, God's mercy comes and given patience, and in time, we can survive.

DISCOVERY

Read Lamentations 3:19–25.

Reread and ask the following questions:

Why would anyone ask God to remember their afflictions or wanderings?

What do you think it means to have your soul bowed down?

The passage says God's loving-kindness never ceases and compassion never fails. Do you think this is really true, or is there a limit?

Say: We have all done wrong things. We all have things we have done that grieve the heart of God. Even more, we all have things we have done that deserve a harsh judgment from God. And yet, God offers mercy.

In pairs, have your students write a letter to God asking Him to extend mercy to our world.

Have each pair read Micah 7:14–20.

Ask: How does your letter compare with this passage?

LIFE APPLICATION: Have each pair make a list of things they think we need to confess to God—ways we have ignored His commandments and desires. After a few minutes, have each pair offer their list. You may want to write these on a dry erase board where everyone can see.

Ask: Why is it so hard for a group of people to do the right thing?

How can we recognize God's mercy in this world?

What makes it difficult to think God is merciful? Or at least that His mercy is unending?

Spend some time in prayer asking God's mercy for all people.

MAKING IT PERSONAL: It is easy to point out ways that we as a society go against God in this world.

It is another thing to think through the places in our lives where we need to ask for God's mercy. Some of us focus so much on what we have done wrong, that we assume that we have already blown it too much for God to forgive us, and if we can't be forgiven, why bother?

God's loving-kindness never ends. His mercies are new every morning.

Invite your students to choose one place in their lives that they repeatedly struggle. Just as we think we have worn out God's patience and we continue in the same sin, He offers mercy again. Give a few moments for each person to pray asking God to extend mercy and to help in the place where they are struggling. Close, thanking God that He does love us and forgives each time we repent.

SONG: "Heaven Help Us All" by Ray Charles and Gladys Knight, on the CD *Genius Loves Company*

ANCIENT PRACTICES: The *kyrie eleison* was practiced by the ancient church. It is a prayer used in worship asking for God's mercy, and thus is to invoke the practice of mercy in life. It is a simple prayer that may be repeated in worship as a group. You may want to take a few moments and discuss the meaning. Make note of its use of communal language. It does not say have mercy on me. Have mercy upon *us* is another reminder that Jesus is Lord of all, not just one of many options. Likewise, we as a Christian community have corporate responsibilities, not just that we individually are merciful.

Lord, have mercy upon us
Christ, have mercy upon us
Lord, have mercy upon us

QUOTABLE QUOTE:

All great things are simple, and many can be expressed in single words: freedom, justice, honor, duty, mercy and hope.

—Sir Winston Churchill

Mercy—Midweek

MEMORY VERSE:
And from far away the Lord appeared to his people and said, "I love you people with a love that will last forever. That is why I have continued showing you kindness."—Jeremiah 31:3 (NCV)

Show mercy, just as your Father shows mercy.—Luke 6:36 (NCV)

SCRIPTURE: Matthew 5:7; James 2:13

LESSON IN A SENTENCE: As God extends mercy to His followers, we are required to extend mercy to others.

FOCUS

Get two or three couples. (If possible get tall guys and short girls). Tie the boy's right wrist to the girl's left wrist. Blindfold the girls first, then boys. After the boys are blindfolded, remove the girls' blindfolds. Give each a rolled newspaper and tell them on the signal to "smash" each other. The boys can't understand why they are getting smashed, but have a hard time trying to find the target.

This is not exactly a game where much mercy is shown. In fact, not only is mercy not shown, but there are different rules for different people. Most of us wouldn't say this is how we want to live, but functionally, this is exactly what we do.

DISCOVERY

Read Matthew 5:7 and James 2:13.
   Ask: How do these two verses relate to one another?
   What is the relationship between giving and receiving mercy?
   How seriously do you think Jesus takes the concept of mercy?

LIFE APPLICATION: *Ask:* When is a time you were shown mercy? Think through times when you should have been grounded or in serious trouble at home or school. What did it feel like to receive mercy?

For some, mercy is almost more difficult to receive than a punishment. In our minds, it simply does not make sense to not have to pay when we have messed up. We want to earn our way back into a right relationship.

   Ask: Why do you think this is? This is yet another reminder that God's ways are not our ways.

Now think of someone who has wronged you.

Ask: How can you show mercy to this person?

When Scripture says that you are to show mercy as you've been shown mercy, how serious do you think this is?

We are to be imitators of Christ (Ephesians 5:1). As Christ offers mercy, so should we. It is a commandment and a privilege to be able to extend mercy to others. Imagine what the world would be like if we indeed lived under this new covenant.

EXTRA! EXTRA!: The daily prayer of the Missionaries of Charity, Calcutta.

Mother Teresa and the Sisters of Charity worked with the least of the least. They chose to work with the dirty, the unattractive and irritable. They also chose to imitate Christ by centering their lives around offering mercy. The following is their daily prayer:

"Dearest Lord, may I see you today and every day in the person of your sick, and whilst nursing, minister to you. Though you hide yourself behind the unattractive disguise of the irritable, the exacting, the unreasonable, may I still recognize you and say: 'Jesus, my patient, how sweet it is to serve you.' Lord, give me this seeing faith, then my work will never be monotonous. I will ever find joy in humoring the fancies and gratifying the wishes of all poor sufferers. O beloved sick, how doubly dear you are to me, when you personify Christ; and what a privilege is mine to be allowed to tend you. Sweetest Lord, make me appreciative of the dignity of my high vocation, and its many responsibilities. Never permit me to disgrace it by giving way to coldness, unkindness, or impatience. And, O God, while you are Jesus, my patient, deign also to be to me a patient Jesus, bearing with my faults, looking only to my intention, which is to love and serve you in the person of each of your sick. Lord, increase my faith, bless my efforts and work, now and for evermore."

THEY NEED WHAT YOU'VE GOT!

By Chris Renzelman
N.W. REGIONAL COORDINATOR,
NATIONAL NETWORK OF YOUTH MINISTRIES

"I have no greater joy, than seeing my children walk in the truth."

—3 John 4 (NIV)

Many a parent, teacher, club leader and youth leader know the joy of seeing those invested in, move forward in life making solid, healthy decisions and living productive lives. This is especially true when life is lived according to the truth of Scripture. Nationally adopted phrases—"It takes a village to raise a kid" or "No child left behind"— hold many a challenge in today's adolescent culture. But working together we can make a difference. None of us can do the total job, but if each one of us mentors another, then an impact on this generation of young people will be felt. Here are some principles that I have found helpful in seeking to help children, of whatever age, walk in truth.

First you need to: Know what you want to see happen.

All good planning clearly articulates the anticipated outcome. What will the final product look like? A good architect will ask plenty of questions before putting pen to paper. Fortunately for the Christian we have been given a guide from which to gather our design. Jesus' earthly life is often spoken of as a twofold mission. Yes, His death on the Cross, but also His life lived daily before those who walked and watched how He lived.

Mark 1:17 (NIV) *"Come, follow me,"* Jesus said, *"and I will make you fishers of men."* And later in Mark 3:13–15, when selecting the Twelve it was said, *". . . He appointed twelve— designating them apostles—that they might be with him. . ."* There is a lot that can be unpacked in these verses, however our focus here is the relational imperative. Jesus knew the importance of being in community. He knew that more is visually caught than will ever be audibly taught and the two of them together are of great value. This was also an obvious pattern in Paul's ministry. 1 Thessalonians 1:5 (NIV) is one place where this is captured when it says, *"because our gospel came to you not simply with words, but also with power, with the Holy Spirit and with deep conviction. You know how we lived among you for your sake. v. 6 You became imitators of us and of the Lord. . . And so you became a model to all the believers. . ."* 2:8 *"We loved you so much that we were delighted to share with you not only the gospel of God but our lives as well, because you had become so dear to us."* (emphasis added) There is no substitute for relational connections and visual learning that happens as we are going about living life.

In today's culture we often use the terms: coaching, mentoring, discipling, or modeling interchangeably. The idea is being in context, observing, understanding and making it our own. Seemingly in life we are bound to live as we have observed, unless we develop convictions that tell us otherwise. Jesus' own life, Scripture tells us, experienced growth in four areas. Luke 2:52 (NIV) says, *". . . Jesus grew in wisdom and stature, and in favor with God and men."* This verse is a great place to start when giving focus to investing in the lives of others. Ask the question, what could or should their life look like at the end of my time with them in at least these four areas. Write out a profile defining elements of measured growth in these four areas:

Wisdom is knowledge and its application.

Stature represents not just physical growth, but health and care.

Favor with God is the spiritual dimension of our lives; our time in the Word, Prayer, Worship, Witness, Service and Fellowship.

The favor with men represents our social—relational connections.

You can add family, finances, skills, etc. as additional areas of profiled growth goals if you want. This approach to determining what you want to see happen allows you to aim for measured results.

A prominent Ivy League university tracked a number of their graduates over several years, in the area of strategic planning. Their findings said 87% lived life as it came, not giving much thought to goal planning. Ten percent of their graduates established goals but did not make plans to accomplish them. The remaining 3% not only set goals but also directed their daily affairs to focus on achieving them. The result was that the 3% had accomplished more than the other 97% combined. Wow! Jesus' life reflected the pattern of this 3% and He was able to say at the end of His earthly life *". . . it is finished"*. Jesus came and completed what He intended to do. Not just His atoning death on the Cross and Resurrection, but also training those who became His disciples, to live in His ways, so that future generations might also be followers of Christ. (2 Timothy 2:2)

Often the phrase is quoted, "If you fail to plan you plan to fail." When teaching parenting classes I call this "Premeditated Parenting." Anticipating a needed direction often allows for good planning with enough lead time and the right resources to mentor toward favorable results. Good planning allows one to spend more time interacting and less time emotionally reacting. Defining what you want to see happen leads you to the next step.

Understanding the Process

In Exodus chapters 3—10 we observe God coaching Moses toward personal growth. God's method provides a good example with value to our own ministries. This chart might help you visualize the process.

B. What are they Now Like?   *C. Steps to Achievement*
A. Reality at Desired Goal

Paralysis (NO WAY!)
Comfort Zone (Easy)   Fear Frontier   (Hard)

Always develop the "A" column first. What do I want to see true at the fulfillment of my goal? The profile items talked about earlier from Luke 2:52 go here. If you have a class, it would be your goal for the students by the end of that class. If a parent, it might be what qualities, understandings, skills, do you want to see your son or daughter reflect by the time they leave your home. In a discipleship relationship it would be what you want to have true in the student's life when they leave your nurturing care. As a youth worker, it would be the details of your goals that students would achieve before they leave your focused area of ministry.

In Exodus 3:3 we begin to see the unfolding of God's goal for Moses. God picked Moses to lead the Israelite children from Egypt to the Promised Land. But for Moses his response was "NO WAY", paralysis, excuses, disbelief, it was too much of a stretch. One defining description of a leader is that they clearly see the goal before others are even ready to follow. That's definitely God, so what does God do next? Move to column "B"... this is the familiar area, the comfort zone. It answers the question "What are they now like?" For Moses in Exodus 4:2–4 (NIV) "...the LORD said to him, 'What is that in your hand?' 'A staff,' he replied. The LORD said, 'Throw it on the ground.' Moses threw it on the ground and it became a snake, and he ran from it. Then the LORD said to him, 'Reach out your hand and take it by the tail.' So Moses reached out and took hold of the snake and it turned back into a staff in his hand."* Here we see Moses stepping back and forth on the line between the Comfort Zone and the Fear Frontier. All growth takes place when we are just outside our comfort zone and that is where God is pushing Moses, albeit stubbornly.

The heart of growth happens in column "C"; this is also where some good thinking and planning needs to take place. This is where the progressive steps of development happen. Remember that growth is always moving from the known to the unknown. Taken too fast, fear and resistance set in; this is a fine line to walk. One individual's pace may be different from another's pace. When working with a group, discern the steps of growth to be taken together and what you might need to work individually on with others. This column "C" is where calendar and the resources of curriculum, budget, and other people come to bear on what it's going to take for the growth process to happen. Read through these chapters of Exodus 3—10 and see how all these growth steps unfold in shaping Moses into a leader who gets the job done. Observe how Moses' staff is visually used as a reminder of what God has already done. It's as if God is saying, Moses remember what I did with this staff? I can also do this next thing. Ultimately Moses grows and gets the job done. The Israelite children make it to the Promised Land. Even Moses eventually gets there as noted in the Mount of Transfiguration records.

Ready to give it a try? Start by reflecting on how God has brought about growth in your own life. Who around you, parents, other leaders, or organizations is modeling premeditated development of others? Engage with them to discuss their learning and ways. (See www.mentoryouth.com) Then start where you are. Identify those God would have you begin to invest your life with, even in the smallest of ways. The length of time may be known or not. Whether you have five minutes or five years, you can make a difference. Don't forget to look at Scripture (i.e. Luke 2:52) and build a profile of what your individual or group of focus might ideally look like when they leave your touch. Now go for it! Using what you have, either personally or from others in the way of experiences, training and resources. Doing what you can, be it great or small. Begin the nurturing process and experience the joy of watching them grow in truth. May you say with Paul. . . "*Be imitators of me as I am of Christ.*" And someday you may hear God say "*Well done thou good and faithful servant.*"

SEPTEMBER 10, 2006

Building a Bridge

By Whitney Prosperi

MEMORY VERSE: I have not stopped giving thanks to God for you. I always remember you in my prayers.—Ephesians 1:16 (NCV)

SCRIPTURE: Psalm 78:1–8

LESSON IN A SENTENCE: Although generations and miles may separate us from our grandparents, we can be purposeful about building and deepening our relationships with them.

THE BIG PICTURE (OR WHAT YOU'RE TRYING TO GET ACROSS):

Our culture places a high value on youth. That's why people pay millions of dollars each year to keep a young appearance, even as they are growing older. It's easy to overlook grandparents, because they are from a different generation and are often very different than we are. But God gave them to us so we could learn from them and they could be encouraged by us. You will learn a lot if you take some time to listen to some stories from your grandparents' younger days. They will share with you their wisdom, and you will show them that you value them. Practice gratitude for the ways your grandparents have invested in your life.

IN THIS LESSON STUDENTS SHOULD:

- Recognize the investment their grandparents have made in their lives.
- Identify some ways to deepen their relationships with their grandparents.
- Plan some ways they will encourage and thank their grandparents this week.

STUFF YOU NEED:

- Pens
- Stationery appropriate for both males and females to use
- Envelopes
- Blank paper
- Current newspaper article (described below)

FOCUS

Show students an interesting newspaper story about a person who would be approximately the same age as many of the students' grandparents. Tell some of the highlights of the article. Now ask them to think of some interesting things about their own grandparents and share them with the group. Examples would be that they fought in a war, have a special talent, or live in an interesting place. Encourage several students to share.

DISCOVERY

Read Psalm 78:1–8 as a group.

Ask students to think about the way God has set up family. Explain that He has given us generations before so that we could learn from them.

Ask: What life lessons have you learned from your parents? Your grandparents? Have you learned any lessons about God from your grandparents?

Reread v. 7.

Ask: Why is it so important to share with our family members the ways that God has moved in our lives?

Now read v. 4.

Ask: What does this verse teach that we can learn from those who have lived before us?

Now ask students to draw a "family tree" that goes back to their grandparents on both sides. Ask them to put a symbol next to the name of each grandparent, that symbolizes something important about their life. For example, next to a grandmother's name you might place a music note if she especially loved music, or a cross if she had a strong faith in Jesus. Encourage students to be as creative as they can.

Say: Maybe you have heard a story that one of your grandparents told about a miracle that occurred in their lives. This story should be passed on to you and then to your children someday, so that you have a record of the ways God has moved in your family. Do you take the time to really listen to the stories of your grandparents? Sitting down with your grandma or grandpa to listen to them tell you about their lives may not seem like the most exciting thing you've ever done; but you will be amazed at what you will learn. Ask your grandmother about her "first love" and watch her gush. Or ask your grandfather when and how he learned to drive, or what his growing up years were like, and you will be in for more than a few laughs.

Grandparents are a gift from God. Do you take them for granted?

LIFE APPLICATION: *Read 1 Thessalonians 3:9.*

Ask: When was the last time you thanked your grandparents for the way they have invested in your life?

Say: Take some time to think of the ways they have positively influenced you. They raised your parent, they may pray for you, and they probably make holidays more fun.

Take some time to write them a letter on the stationery provided, that thanks them for the way they have loved you. It won't take you very long, but you can be sure it will be something that they will treasure.

Teacher's Note: There may be a student in the group who has no living grandparents. If this is the case, ask them to use this lesson to think about an older friend or relative that they know, like an aunt or uncle. Some students may have grandparents who are sick or who have recently died. Be sensitive to how these students feel during this lesson.

MAKING IT PERSONAL: What kind of legacy do you want to leave for the children and grandchildren who will come behind you? That may seem like a very long way off, but it will be here before you know it.

Ask rhetorically: Are you living the kind of life that you would want a child or grandchild to imitate years down the road? If there are some changes you would make, why not make them today? You are building your legacy by the daily choices you make each day.

If someone follows in your footsteps, will they be led to Christ?

CONNECTIONS: Read verses that talk about the brevity of life and stress with students that each day is important. Are they living lives of gratefulness and godliness? Some verses are: James 4:13–15; Job 7:16; Psalm 39:5

SONG: "Who am I" by Casting Crowns

MEMORY VERSE ACTIVITY

Encourage students to find a picture of one of their grandparents and attach it to a piece of paper with the Memory Verse on it. When they work on their memory verse they can also be reminded to pray for their grandparent.

Grandparents—Midweek

MEMORY VERSE:
I have not stopped giving thanks to God for you. I always remember you in my prayers.—Ephesians 1:16 (NCV)

SCRIPTURE: Proverbs 19:20

LESSON IN A SENTENCE: Although generations and miles may separate us from our grandparents, we can be purposeful about building and deepening our relationships with them.

FOCUS

Ask students to share about their favorite memory with a grandparent. What did they do? Why was it special? When and where was it? Be sensitive, as some students may have never known their grandparents or may have lost them to death.

Now ask them to tell you their favorite thing about one of their grandparents. Maybe it's the way their grandpa always took them fishing, or the way their grandmother so patiently taught them multiplication tables.

Now ask students to share what they think one of their grandparent's favorite things about them is. You may want to share first to get the conversation started.

DISCOVERY

Ask a student to read aloud Proverbs 19:20. Ask the following questions:

Who is the wisest person you know? How do you think they got that way?

Why is it so important that we listen to what those wiser than us say?

Have you ever gone against the advice of a parent or grandparent and then later realized you had made a mistake? If so, share that experience and what you learned.

How can you take advantage of the wisdom of your grandparents?

LIFE APPLICATION: God has placed us in the family He wants us in. Acts 17:26 (NCV) says, "God began by making one person, and from him came all the different people who live everywhere in the world. God decided exactly when and where they must live."

That also means that He placed you in the family He wanted you in. You have the grandparents He has chosen for you.

In what way will you choose to honor and learn from them this week? Ask them to share some of their wisdom with you. You will have it for the rest of your days.

Talking with God

By Amy Jacober

MEMORY VERSE:
Call to Me and I will answer you and tell you great and wondrous things you do not know.—Jeremiah 33:3 (HCSB)

SCRIPTURE: 2 Chronicles 7:11–22

LESSON IN A SENTENCE: God does not want to be disregarded.

THE BIG PICTURE (OR WHAT YOU'RE TRYING TO GET ACROSS):

God is jealous. He does not want our divided attention, let alone to be an afterthought when we find it convenient. He wants to be in touch with us on a regular basis. He wants to hear about our daily needs and the concerns of our hearts. He wants to hear about His world from His people. It seems that we often take for granted that the creator of the universe allows us to talk directly to Him. Even more He wants for us to talk with Him!! Prayer is a privilege and a blessing.

IN THIS LESSON STUDENTS SHOULD:

- Be made aware of God's desire to hear from us.
- Know that God will not stand to be ignored.
- Discover ways to pray that fit their personality.

STUFF YOU NEED:

- Strips of paper (Option 1)
- Copies of a list of 15–20 lines from current songs (Option 2)
- Pens or pencils
- Sheets of paper for each group
- Dry erase board
- Materials for stations around the room (see Making It Personal)

FOCUS

OPTION 1: Thesaurus

Break into teams of 4–6 and then pair teams against one another. Pass out two or three strips of paper to each person. Have each person write a word on each strip. Place the strips of paper for each opposing team in a cup. Take turns drawing a strip of paper. The person who has drawn the paper must get their teammates to guess the word, by describing it without ever saying the word or any variation of the word. For example—if the word is cookbook, you cannot say cook nor book. You can say recipes, papers collected, pictures of food, etc. Give each person 30 seconds to try to get their team to guess. If this time does not work for you, add or subtract time.

There is always more than one way to say something. This game proves even when you don't think you can or when it is not straight-forward, you are able to communicate.

OPTION 2:

Recruit a few students to help you with this one ahead of time. Create a list of 15–20 lines from songs that are currently popular. Type these out and create a worksheet. Either individually or in pairs, ask your students to identify the song from which the line comes. If you are able, create a CD with a medley of the lines from the songs. It's amazing how many of the songs will be familiar once the lines are heard with the music!

Many of us can sing right along with the radio, but once the music is gone, the lines are totally foreign. So often we don't even pay attention to what we are singing, it is meaningless to us, but through repetition comes out without our thinking. Sadly, this can also be the way we approach talking with God.

DISCOVERY

Ask: Do you think God cares if you pray or not? Does this matter to you? Why or why not?

Give a piece of paper to every four students. On one side, have them write what God wants. On the other side, have them write what God will do. Give each group time to read 2 Chronicles 7:11–22.

There are many things that could be listed in either side. When it comes down to it, God wants us to communicate with Him and Him alone, and He promises to listen.

Teacher's Note: Prayer is one of the more difficult parts of the Christian life for many. This passage could easily lead you to talk about God causing natural catastrophes (v. 13), being chosen (v. 12, 16) or even God's punishment (v. 20). Try as best as you can to focus on God wanting a relationship with us, but not in a pathetic way. Rather, He is jealous and demands all of our attention. In return, He promises to listen and forgive.

LIFE APPLICATION: On a dry erase board, make a list of all the things you can think of that need prayer right now. Include everything—tests coming up, broken relationships, illness, your church, missionaries around the world, the President, Hollywood stars, whatever!!!

MAKING IT PERSONAL: Prayer does not happen in just one way. Think of all the ways we communicate with one another today. Some direct, like talking in person, on the phone, e-mail, or even notes and cards. We might also communicate thoughts in journals, blogs, or our own web page or space. Then there are non-verbal communications like gifts or time, touch or presence. All of these communicate volumes! Why is it that we think there is one way to pray to God?

Set up stations around your room that offer/explain different ways to pray. Spend a few moments explaining these. DO NOT panic!!! This needn't be a stressful, difficult task. There are a few suggestions listed here. Feel free to add, delete, or adapt as you see fit!

Provide a card with the letters ACTS in large letters. On the back of the card write this as an acronym with

A–Adoration, meaning to say what you love about God;
C–Confession, meaning to confess sins in your life and a need for God;
T–Thanksgiving, meaning to thank God for what He has provided and what He will provide;
S–Supplication, meaning to ask God on behalf of others.

Have a Bible open to Matthew 6:9–13. If need be, write on a Post-it the verses to read, to be certain they know what to do.

Set out papers and crayons with the simple instruction to draw a picture for God when you cannot find words.

Set out tea lights and matches. Write the instructions to choose one thing about which they want to pray, and offer this to God as you light the candle.

Provide a card with all of the names for God you can find. Father, Lord, King, Prince of Peace, Creator, Redeemer, Sustainer, Lover, Judge, etc. Instruct the student to choose one word and tell God why this word stands out to him or her at this time.

Set out a journal and a pen. Invite each person to write a note to God. You choose whether to make it anonymous or not.

LOOKING AHEAD THIS WEEK: This week is See You At The Pole (SYATP). This is a student-initiated time to pray for your schools, community and country. It is the third Wednesday of September every year. By now you should have been talking about this with your students. Just in case, it's still not too late! All it takes is a little conversation and meeting before school to pray. As you do this, you will be joining thousands of other teenagers all across this country and even around the world! Check out their website at www.syatp.com.

SONG: "We Acknowledge You" by Karen Clark-Sheard on the *2005 WOW* Gospel CD

QUOTABLE QUOTES:

He that is not jealous is not in love.

—Augustine

See You at the Pole Day—Midweek

MEMORY VERSE:
Call to Me and I will answer you and tell you great and wondrous things you do not know.—Jeremiah 33:3 (HCSB)

SCRIPTURE: Matthew 10:24–33

LESSON IN A SENTENCE: God does not want to be disregarded.

FOCUS

If your students participated in SYATP, ask for a report of how that went. You may want to offer a few of the stories from the website to remind them of the connection with so many others all over the world. For those of you who were able, you stood up in front of your classmates and all the world. This pleases God.

Have poster board or construction paper and markers on hand. As a group, create a list of all the hopes and dreams you have for the new school year, both in school and in your group. After a few moments, refine this brainstorming time to discussing hopes and dreams for spiritual growth and service. You may need to get the group started. Create a youth worship team, adopt a needy child, commit to pray for seniors in your church, a once-a-month prayer night, etc. Choose five of these as goals for the year. Use the construction paper or poster board to create visual reminders of the goals you have set. Be certain to choose ones that are realistic. Take a few more moments in smaller groups and create a plan to follow through. Feel free to choose more or less goals, as you see fit. If you have students who really seem excited for one or more of these, go with those and let them take the lead!

DISCOVERY

Find one of your students or leaders who is theatrical. Gather your students around as though it is an intimate story time. Have the "storyteller" sit in a chair or stool in the group, with the others either on the floor or on lower chairs. Have him or her recite the passage. (If you do not have anyone who is able to memorize a passage this long, type it up *readers theatre* style. Have reader #1 read v. 24, reader #2 read v. 25, reader #1 read v. 26 and so on.)

Finish by repeating vv. 32–33.

LIFE APPLICATION: For the most part Matthew 10: 24–31 are words of instruction, encouragement and endearment. Verses 32–33 take a sharp turn. Jesus states clearly that if you acknowledge Him before other people, He will acknowledge you in heaven. If, however, you deny Him, He will deny you.

What do we do with a verse like this?

Can you think of ways in your own life right now where you are denying the presence of Christ?

Today was a day where many prayed for their school, for this country, and others. Spend a few moments asking God to reveal to you the places where you deny Him, and for help to fully acknowledge Him in all your ways!!

CONNECTIONS: Proverbs 3:5 is an excellent verse for an additional memory verse or further discussion.

LOOKING AHEAD: You had a reminder a few months ago but just in case—In November we observe another day of prayer. It is the International Day of Prayer for the Persecuted Church. Check out these websites to find downloads, maps, newsletters, videos, devotionals, and a number of resources that will help for your lesson. www.persecuted-church.org and www.idop.org. Images offer an understanding often missed when simply discussing the struggles of believers in the world. There are free videos to either download or order. Take advantage of these resources as you seek to lead your group.

Who Am I?—Identity in Christ

By Michelle Hicks

MEMORY VERSE:
God has made us what we are. In Christ Jesus, God made us to do good works, which God planned in advance for us to live our lives doing. —Ephesians 2:10 (NCV)

SCRIPTURE: 2 Corinthians 5:16–21

LESSON IN A SENTENCE: We are created in God's image and are new creations in Jesus Christ.

THE BIG PICTURE (OR WHAT YOU'RE TRYING TO GET ACROSS):
So often we base our identity on outer physical characteristics or activities. We describe ourselves according to eye color, hair color, family lineage, education, age, and so forth. However, even though most of us know who we are on the outside, many of us wonder who we are on the inside. We take personality profile tests, spiritual gift inventories, or answer any other number of questions in our quest to discover who we really are on the inside. True identity is about one's essential self and the characteristics that make one unique. Being created in God's image leaves a longing within us to be reconciled to our Creator and

IN THIS LESSON STUDENTS SHOULD:

- Recognize the uniqueness of each individual.
- Discover what it means to be reconciled to God through Christ.
- Identify positive things in themselves that reflect their identity in Christ.

STUFF YOU NEED:

- Variety of identity items for Option 2
- Paper
- Markers
- Pencils

STUFF YOU NEED:

○ Colored construction paper
○ String or yarn
○ Plastic or real ring
○ Art supplies for Memory Verse Activity

to identify with Him. This study examines the deepest part of one's being, who you are in Jesus Christ.

FOCUS

Choose either Option 1 or 2. Be sure to watch your time and not get carried away with this part of the lesson.

OPTION 1: Junior High

Instruct students to sit in a circle. Ask one volunteer to stand in the center of the circle. The volunteer will say one thing he or she wants in life. For example, "I want to travel to Austria" or "I want to become a dentist." Anyone in the circle who would also like to have or do that same thing stands up and moves to a new chair. Those who do not want that particular thing may remain seated. The person left standing must say one thing that he or she wants from life, and the game continues. Play this game, allowing everyone to move around the circle.

Explain that sometimes we want the same things in life as others and sometimes we do not. It is a lot of fun to dream about all the things we may do someday. Many of you may still be trying to figure out what your dreams are and who you are. Today we will look more at who we are in Christ and discover our true identity.

OPTION 2: Extra Supplies

Before students arrive, collect a variety of items. For example, a mirror, a driver's license, an ID bracelet, any jewelry with a personal name on it, and so forth. Try to stay with items that would relate to the identity theme. However, try to include some items that would be difficult for students to identify. Cover the items with a towel or blanket.

As students arrive, direct them to the covered items. Instruct students one-at-a-time to reach under the blanket and try to identify an item, without removing it from under the blanket. As students call out their answers, write them on a large sheet of paper with marker. To conclude, remove the blanket and identify any remaining items. Explain that although students could not see the items, they were able to identify many of them correctly. Explain that today's Bible study is about being created in Christ and what that looks like. Although we may not be able to see everything clearly, God does give us some instructions and ideas of what a life looks like when a person is living with Jesus as the center and purpose of his or her life. Today we will look at who we are in Christ and discover our true identity.

DISCOVERY

Distribute paper and pencils. Instruct students to quickly draw a self-portrait. Encourage them to reflect on the things they see about themselves that no one else knows or sees. Explain that in today's Bible study, students will discover more about what it means to be created in Christ and in His image. They will understand more about the new life they have when Jesus is their life.

Call on a volunteer to read 2 Corinthians 5:16–21 aloud. Discuss the passage by using the following questions:

What does reconciliation mean?

What does God do through Jesus? Through us? For us?

What does it mean that we are Christ's ambassadors?

Explain that as we remain in Jesus and His Holy Spirit fills us, we are reconciled to God. No matter what we have done in the past, we are a new creation in Jesus. His love and forgiveness cover us. When we make Jesus our life He continues to fill us fully and completely. He displaces the old life with our new life in Him.

Instruct students to take their self-portrait and tear around it to form a cross. Continue by explaining that no matter how we may see ourselves, when we trust in Jesus and become a new creation, from that point forward we are seen in the shadow of Christ and the Cross.

LIFE APPLICATION: Place various colors of paper in the center of the group. Encourage students to look at the various colors and then choose a color that is their favorite. Invite students to share their favorite colors and why they like them.

Explain how looking at these colors of paper and seeing the spectrum of color can be a totally different experience for someone who is color-blind. Both people see the same sheets of paper, however, the person who is color-blind may only see in tones of black, white, or gray. The person who can see all the colors experiences a richer, deeper, more exciting view. This person is able to see many brilliant colors. The person who is color-blind knows and understands that there is something more there but cannot fully see it. Sometimes we can become like someone who is color-blind if we do not view ourselves the way Jesus does. We can only see a part of who God has created us to be, and not the full picture.

Ask: What would help you to see yourself more the way God sees you? What continues to hinder you from seeing yourself as a new creation in Christ?

Arrange students into groups of three. Instruct each group to develop a modern day role-play that would relate to the Scripture today and focus on becoming a new creation in Christ. Guide students to display the life-change that takes place when one is reconciled to God through Jesus. Allow small groups to perform their role-plays for the large group. Discuss their presentations and the insights they gained from this activity.

MAKING IT PERSONAL: Instruct students to sit in a circle. Take a piece of string or yarn and have every person hold the string with both hands, except for one person who stands in the middle. Tie the string at both ends to make it one big circle, with a ring on the string that is able to slide all the way around. Use a ring of yours or one of the students. Instruct students to pass the ring along, keeping it hidden in their hands from the person in the middle. This person will try to guess who has the ring by tapping different people's hands. When a student's hand is tapped, he or she opens his or her hand to reveal whether the ring is there. When the student in the middle taps someone's hand that is holding the ring, the person with the ring says one positive thing they see in the other student and they switch places. If the student guesses incorrectly, the student in the center of the circle must say one positive thing about him or herself.

After playing the game, *ask:* Why did we sometimes hesitate to guess who was holding the ring? What risk do you take if you guess incorrectly in this game? *Say:* Like this game we often hesitate because we do not want to hear the positive things said about us or we do not want to sound conceited by saying positive things about ourselves. Also, another problem is that often people do not really believe the good things others say about them. We need to continue to focus on our identity in Christ. That means instead of seeing ourselves, our weakness, and our failures, we see Jesus standing in our place.

Close in prayer, asking students to pray silently. Guide students to look at the palm of their hands and to study their fingerprints as they continue their prayer time. Pray that students will live as God's creations and in His image during this week. Remind students how special they are to God as you close the prayer time.

MEMORY VERSE ACTIVITY

Provide various art supplies (Play-Doh®, foil, craft sticks, glue, scissors, and so forth) and instruct students to create something that relates to being God's creation. Somewhere on their creation students will write the verse from Ephesians 2:10, or the reference, to help them remember their memory verse this week when they see their creation.

SONG: "Who Am I" by Casting Crowns

Q U O T A B L E   Q U O T E S :

Define yourself radically as one beloved by God. God's love for you and His choice of you constitute your worth. Accept that, and let it become the most important thing in your life.

—Brennan Manning

[Brennan Manning, *Abba's Child: The Cry of the Heart for Intimate Belonging* (Colorado Springs: Navpress, 1994) p. 49.]

Teacher's Note: It is OK to let students realize that even as adults we sometimes struggle with our identity and our worth. Remember that students and adults need affirmation and encouragement to help them in their journey, as they become all that God desires for them to be. Be a cheerleader and encourager for the people you find in your sphere of influence. Allow God to use you to be an example of someone who not only identifies with Christ, but finds his or her identity in Christ.

Who Am I?—Identity in Christ—Midweek

MEMORY VERSE:
God has made us what we are. In Christ Jesus, God made us to do good works, which God planned in advance for us to live our lives doing.
—Ephesians 2:10 (NCV)

SCRIPTURE: Ephesians 2:8–10

LESSON IN A SENTENCE: God created students for a purpose, and good works for them to accomplish.

STUFF YOU NEED:

- Balloons (one per student)
- Markers
- Pin to pop selected balloons
- CD player
- Contemporary Christian music

FOCUS

Divide the large group into two smaller groups. Explain that one group will form an outside circle. Then instruct the second group to form an inside circle by facing someone from the outer circle. Every student needs to have a partner to face. Explain that this activity is like a musical chairs game, but no one leaves the game. When the music is played, the outer group will move in a circle to the right. At the same time the inner group will move in a circle to their left. When the music stops, students will share with their partner one way they are created in God's image and with a purpose. Then start and stop the music again to continue allowing students to share ideas with several other students.

Remind students of the lesson on Sunday about how each person is created in God's image and that we are new creations reconciled to God through Jesus. Explain that today's Bible study will continue our focus on being God's creations.

DISCOVERY

Distribute balloons and instruct students to blow up the balloons and tie them. Instruct students to write on their balloons various good works that people do for God. Explain that all of us have good works that God prepared in advance for us to do during our lives. Call on a volunteer to read Ephesians 2:8–10. Instruct certain students to draw faces on their balloons, while other students draw a cross on their balloons. Take a pin and randomly pop several of the balloons with the faces. Explain that many of us do good works, but those good works are accomplished by our own power. We may work hard to accomplish things for God without ever seeking His direction or discovering the purpose that He has for us. Sometimes those "good works" pop or fall apart in the end, especially when they are done by our own power. Point to the balloons with good works and crosses drawn on them. Explain that when the good works we do are accomplished by the power of the Holy Spirit and our dependence upon Christ, they do not deflate. Although we may not see or understand the expanse of those good works like we see a balloon inflate, we can trust that Christ is accomplishing His purpose through us. Remind students of their identity in Christ, and to trust Him to accomplish great things in their lives.

LIFE APPLICATION: Create three groups. Assign each group one of the case studies below. Write each case study on a separate 3 x 5 card or make copies of them to distribute to the small groups.

Case Study 1: Erica noticed Maria crying and went to sit down beside her. Maria continued crying and began to share with Erica how she hates herself. Maria is not the most popular person in school and actually is not really that nice to most people. What might Erica say to Maria to help her?

Case Study 2: Ashley couldn't believe these people had just walked into her church. Other people were starting to turn and stare at them. Ashley almost felt embarrassed for them. They obviously had not been to church in a long time or at least they were not dressed to come to this church. How would these people ever fit in here? What should Ashley do? What would you most likely do in this situation in real life?

Case Study 3: Jason just stood by and watched the group of guys making fun of Nick. Nick never said anything back to them—he just stood there and took it. Jason felt sick and frustrated. Why wouldn't Nick stand up for himself? Had he done something to deserve this harassment? Should Jason get involved or stay out of it?

Suggest the groups present their case studies and how they would reflect and live out the Ephesians 2:8–10 passage. After each case study is presented, discuss and allow students to recall similar situations they have been in. To close, read Ephesians 2:8–10 again and then pray that students will live as God's creations daily.

OCTOBER 1, 2006

I AM

By Amy Jacober

MEMORY VERSE:
The Lord God says, "I am the Alpha and the Omega. I am the One who is and was and is coming. I am the Almighty."—Revelation 1:8 (NCV)

SCRIPTURE: Exodus 3:10–15; John 4:26; 6:35; 8:23; 9:5; 10:7, 11, 14, 36; 11:25; 13:13; 14:6, 16, 26; 15:1; 16:7–8, 13; Acts 1:8; Romans 8:26; Revelation 1:8, 17

LESSON IN A SENTENCE: God wants us to know Him.

THE BIG PICTURE (OR WHAT YOU'RE TRYING TO GET ACROSS):
Understanding God can seem far off and mysterious. To our human finite mind, we simply will never be able to take all of Him in. That doesn't mean that He doesn't want us to know Him. He is no longer a pillar of cloud or fire. He came and walked this earth as a man. He also left the Bible for us. God reveals Himself to us all throughout Scripture. We also have the Holy Spirit active and present with us. God says "I AM." We can look to other statements where God offers a little more insight into who He is. While we may not be able to fully understand God this side of heaven, we do not have to be as clueless as many of us are. He has revealed Himself and is revealing Himself *everyday.*

IN THIS LESSON STUDENTS SHOULD:

- Recognize that God functions as the Father, Son, and Holy Spirit.
- Learn several descriptions God gives to Himself in Scripture.
- Identify how he or she has viewed God and be open to broadening this perspective.

STUFF YOU NEED:

- Close up pictures and a way to show these (Option 1)
- Magazines (Option 2)
- Scissors (Option 2)
- Construction paper (Option 2)
- Glue (Option 2)

FOCUS

OPTION 1: Up close and personal

This may take a little advance preparation, depending on what kind of camera you use. If you need to take pictures and get them developed, be certain to do this several days in advance. If you are using a Polaroid or digital camera, this can be done on shorter notice. Take pictures of common everyday objects, but really up close! Take the pictures up so close that it is difficult, if not impossible, to tell what it is. Take pictures of things like the knob on the stereo in your car, the bristles on a toothbrush or the carpet in the room where you meet. Display these pictures in your room, or run a power point slide presentation with the pictures if you used a digital camera. Give your students time to try and guess what the pictures are.

All of these pictures were of common everyday items.

Ask: What made knowing what they were so hard?

Do you ever look at God with such a close up focus? As in, do you think of God as savior but not as the One who convicts? Or as judge, but not loving?

OPTION 2: Morphing

Have several magazines that your students might read available. (You may want to call them before this meeting and ask them to bring any old copies that they wouldn't mind getting ruined.) Break into groups of four. Give each group a piece of paper, scissors and glue. Their task is to morph people from the magazine into one person. Use the eyes of one, the nose of another, the ears of someone else.

After they have created their morph, have them trade papers and try to identify the people the other groups used to make their new person.

Ask: How is this like what we do to God?

Some people have very distinct features. Even with those distinct features, when taken away from the whole, they become difficult to recognize. We do this all the time with God. We look to one part of Him, on description. While we will probably never know Him in full this side of heaven, we can have a fuller understanding by looking at what He says about Himself in Scripture.

DISCOVERY

Read Exodus 3:10–15 as a group.

Ask: What do we learn about God in this passage?

What is Moses instructed to say to the Israelites?

Well, now we know His name is I AM. That doesn't exactly help us a whole lot. This is one close-up look at God.

Give each student a strip of paper with the following verse written on it. If you have a larger group, pair people up, if you have a smaller group, give more than one verse to a student. Instruct them to look up their verse, find out something else about God—and write it on the strip of paper. While the main idea is written here for your benefit, DO NOT write the description on the strip of paper. Rather, simply write the passage they are to look up.

Teacher's Note: Many of these passages state titles directly like: I Am the Messiah, I am the Good Shepherd, etc. This is simply a sample list. There are many more verses you could include. Feel free to add if you need.

John 4:25–26 Messiah
John 6:35 Bread of Life
John 8:23 From Above
John 9:5 Light of the world
John 10:7 Door of the sheep
John 10:11 The Good Shepherd
John 10:14 The Good Shepherd
John 11:25 The Resurrection and the Life
John 13:13 Teacher and Lord
John 14:6 The Way, the Truth and the Life
John 14:16 Helper
John 14:26 Teacher, helps you remember
John 15:1 The True Vine
John 16:7–8 The One who Convicts
John 16:13 Guide
Acts 1:8 Giver of Power
Romans 8:26 Intercessor
Revelation 1:8 Alpha and Omega, the Almighty
Revelation 1:17 The First and the Last

After a few minutes (this shouldn't take long, each person or team only has one verse!) ask what they learned about God. Be certain each person shares. Tape all of the strips of paper on the wall close together.

LIFE APPLICATION: Look at the wall with all of the descriptive words for God.

Ask: Did you learn anything new today about who God is?

Why do you think we so often forget to consider the big picture of who God is?

How do you think the world might be different if everyone knew all of this about God?

How do you think the world might be different if believers actually lived like they believed?

What other names or descriptions of God do you know? Add these to the wall.

Even with all of these words, all of these descriptions, and with knowing God personally, He is so big, so beyond what we can understand here on earth, that we are still only getting a distorted partial view of Him. He is greater than, bigger than, mightier than anyone or anything we know. And yet, He is still extraordinarily interested in you!

MAKING IT PERSONAL: We all focus on God in particular ways. Some of us understand what it is to be in fear of the Lord, but barely comprehend that He is love. Some of us focus so much on love that we forget He actually requires that we live by His commandments.

Look at all the descriptions we have placed on the wall. Choose one you favor, one way you already understand God. Choose another that is either a new concept to you or one you most often ignore.

Thank God for how you already understand Him. Ask Him to teach you about other parts of His character.

Close, by reflecting on what this says about you. Play the song "I Am a Child Of God" by Anna Maria Pasley. Knowing what you do now about who God is, think through what it means to be His child, made in His image.

SONG: "I Am" by Anna Maria Pasley on the CD *I AM*
       See www.ampasley.com to purchase this CD

QUOTABLE   QUOTES:

Dear God, I do not think anybody could be a better God. Well I just want you to know that I am not just saying that because you are God.

—Charles
Children's Letters to God

October 4, 2006

I AM—Midweek

MEMORY VERSE:
The Lord God says, "I am the Alpha and the Omega. I am the One who is and was and is coming. I am the Almighty."—Revelation 1:8 (NCV)

SCRIPTURE: Mark 8:27–30

LESSON IN A SENTENCE: God wants us to know Him.

FOCUS

Name That Person!
These must be prepared ahead of time. You will need a few sheets of construction paper (3–5), scissors, several magazines your students might read, and glue for this project. Cut out the faces of at least ten people from the magazines for each sheet of construction paper (it's fine if you repeat some). Glue the faces to the sheets of paper and write a number next to each. Break your students into the same number of teams as sheets of construction paper that you prepared. Hand one of the sheets, a blank piece of paper and a pen to each team. Give them 45 seconds to try and write down the names of all the people on their sheet. Call time and pass the sheets to another group. Keep doing this until the groups have seen all the sheets. At the end, go over the responses and tally up which team had the most correct answers. Offer that team a small prize.

DISCOVERY

Read Mark 8:27–30.
After you have read this, break into four groups. Have each group take one of the following and learn as much as they can: John the Baptist, Elijah, the prophets, the Christ.

Teacher's Note: You may need to help on these. If they need, show your students how to use the concordance. Talk to your pastor and see if you may borrow a Bible dictionary or Bible encyclopedia to help explain these. John and Elijah were real people. Prophets served a specific function. Christ is a title, not a part of Jesus' name, though we barely notice the difference today. In Hebrew it is the Messiah. In Greek, it is the Anointed. The title moved from being a confession— Jesus who is the Messiah— to a statement: Jesus Messiah. A weak analogy but the closest we have, might be Queen Elizabeth. When someone mentions the Queen today, no one asks who or which one. The title and the name of the person can become interchangeable.

Ask: How does understanding these people or descriptions help us understand God more?

LIFE APPLICATION: Jesus asked Peter a direct question. He asked "But who do *you* say I am?"

Imagine for a moment that Jesus were here right now asking you that same question. Turn in partners and talk about how you might respond.

What are some of the ways we understand Jesus to be?

We live in a world that says almost anything goes. We live in a time that says there is more than one way to truth. Being a follower of Jesus can come across as exclusive and judgmental.

Ask: How does it strike you that Jesus says He is THE Christ?

How do we balance this with all of the other religions and claims being offered today? What might Jesus say when looking at other beliefs?

Being a follower of Jesus does not leave room for other saviors. He is not interested in sharing the limelight. Over and over again, God is quite clear that He is *The* way, *The* light, *The* truth, *The* Christ, *The* Savior. . .not one among many. This can be a tough concept to swallow.

Close in prayer, thanking God for who He is. Ask God to reveal Himself to those who still do not know Him. Ask God to help you understand Him for who He is, and not whom we choose to understand Him to be.

OCTOBER 8, 2006

Journey to the Light (Follower of Christ)

By Anna Aven

MEMORY VERSE: But if we live in the light, as God is in the light, we can share fellowship with each other. Then the blood of Jesus, God's Son, cleanses us from every sin.—1 John 1:7 (NCV)

SCRIPTURE: 1 John 1:5—2:2; Mark 8:34

LESSON IN A SENTENCE: Following Jesus is not a list of "dos" and "don'ts;" rather, it is about walking where Jesus walks, and not walking where He won't walk.

THE BIG PICTURE (OR WHAT YOU'RE TRYING TO GET ACROSS):

Because following Jesus yields a holy lifestyle, it is easy in many ways to turn Christianity into a bunch of rules for holy living. However, if God had wanted us to follow a bunch of rules, He could have handed down an extended version of the Ten Commandments— a twenty-page list of do's and don'ts or something like that. Instead, He left us with a two-thousand-page love letter. Clearly, holy living is supposed to come from our relationship with God—and with God-in-the-flesh, Jesus—rather than from following rules.

IN THIS LESSON STUDENTS SHOULD:

- ○ Realize that Jesus is calling them into a relationship because He loves them and desperately wants to be in a relationship with them.
- ○ Understand that holy living comes from following Jesus—going where He goes, living as He lived, not from following arbitrary rules.

STUFF YOU NEED:

- ○ See materials for sketch under Focus
- ○ See Service Options

SERVICE OPTIONS: If you have the time, setting up stations for the personal application time could be very effective. The reflection for that time is Jesus' invitation to "Come follow me." Possible stations include:

Art station: "Where I am." Instruct students to create an artistic representation of where they were when they first heard the call of Jesus to "come and follow." Things they can represent include their attitude, thoughts, physical location, posture, and so forth. Easy materials for this station would be crayons and/or Crayola® markers and blank paper from the copier. You can get as elaborate as you'd like if you have more time/resources with pastels, chalk, paint, modeling clay, and so forth.

Journaling station: "Where I need to go." Following Jesus is about walking where He walks and not walking where He doesn't walk. *Part 1:* Have students reflect on where they tend to go, literally and figuratively (as in places they go they shouldn't, thoughts they think, things they do, websites they visit, etc), where they know that Jesus wouldn't go. *Part 2:* Have students reflect on places they know that Jesus would like them to go. Encourage them to avoid the obvious responses such as "church," and have them think about places like sitting next to the loner kid at lunch, or perhaps some ministry (soup kitchen, mission trips, tutoring younger kids) that has touched them but they're afraid to get involved in for various reasons. Materials needed for this station: you could encourage kids to bring their journals in advance, but also provide pens/markers/pencils and paper.

FOCUS

Sketch:

Needed: One male and one female actor, and a sheet of paper with the "rules" that the girl reads (see below). One pen. One bench, or two chairs pushed together so the actors can sit side by side. Guy starts out with paper and pen in his pocket.

Guy: (*slowly, like he's scared*) "So you wanna be my girlfriend?"

Girl: (*slightly breathless*) "Okay!"

(*Guy puts his arm around the girl and he looks blissfully content for a minute*)

Guy: "Well, if you're going to be my girlfriend, there're some things I need you to do." (*Pulls out a folded sheet of paper from his back pocket and hands it to girl*).

Girl: (*Reads out loud*) 1. Remind me often how great I am. 2. Call me every other day, no more unless in case of emergency, and at the end of every conversation say "I love you." 3. Every 4–6 weeks surprise me (*sound incredulous here*) with a spontaneous gift. . ." What is this!!!

Guy: (*leans over*) "Keep going, I need you to sign at the bottom" (*pulls out pen and hands to girl*)

Girl: (*makes exasperated sound, and reads*) " 4. Leave me notes. . ." "What on earth?? You can't do a relationship like this. . .it isn't, well, it's just not RELATIONAL if there's all these rules!!" (*Stands up, crumples paper, throws back at guy and walks away*).

Leader, you can then transition into the next segment by saying something like, "Well, that was a short lived relationship or was it a relationship at all?" Or, you could break your group up into smaller groups and pose this as a question. You could also discuss in a large group setting if your students are comfortable with answering and you want to keep the transition shorter.

DISCOVERY

Read 1 John 1:5–10.

This passage is pretty clear. You can't have fellowship with God in the light and walk in darkness. To come into relationship with God is to come into the light because "in him there is no darkness at all." Thus we cannot walk in darkness. This seems like it should be obvious, and yet how often do we try to somehow do both, or run back and forth from the light to the darkness. After all, as long as we're in the light "most of the time" we should be okay, right? Or not. If God is light in whom there is no darkness, then any time that we run back into the darkness, or flirt with the darkness, is choosing to not be where God is. And if we want to be in relationship with Him, then it helps to be where He is.

The second part of this passage talks about how we all have sinned, and if we say we haven't, then we're lying. To paraphrase this with the part before it, it would sound something like this: "God is light, and if you want to be with Him, you have to walk in the light. Now, we've all sinned, there's no denying that, so you might as well not, because you're not only lying, you're making God out to be a liar, and clearly there's no truth in you." So we still sin, we have sinned, and we will sin. The key is continuing to walk into the light. See, the light brings sin to the surface, that's why a lot of people aren't comfortable with the light—they'd rather their sins be hidden in the darkness. And yet, to continue to grow, we need to get past these sins that pull us back, but first, we have to be aware that they are there. The only way to do that is to come into the light.

The philosopher Soren Kierkegaard broke off his engagement to a young lady because he realized that to marry her and have a real relationship, he was going to have to let her into his life and let her see all of him, even the things he struggled with and kept hidden from the rest of the world. He was afraid that she would reject him if he really showed her everything that was in him—his fears, his struggles, his bad relationship with his father, and so forth. But the beautiful thing about a real relationship is that amazing feeling you get when someone really knows you—and I mean really knows you—and yet still loves you, and you know that even if you do something stupid in front of them, or say the wrong thing or whatever, they will love you. It's an amazing relief and it lets you be yourself.

We have the opportunity for that kind of relationship. See, God already knows all about you. He's already seen all of your most embarrassing moments. He's seen your failures, knows your fears (the ones you're afraid to voice for fear people will laugh at you, yeah, those fears), and sees you, just as you are, the good and the bad, and guess what? He loves you. In fact, He loved you before you were born, and knowing all the kinds of mistakes and dumb things you would do, died for you. He knows you completely, and wants to make you whole again. That's the purpose of asking you to come into the light. It's not so you can squirm as He accuses you of all the stuff you've ever done wrong. He wants to help you not do that stuff anymore because that stuff hurts you, and He doesn't want to see you hurt.

LIFE APPLICATION: Okay, so John is saying here, "Come walk in the light and have fellowship with God and a bunch of other people who are on this journey into the light. I know you sin, don't bother denying it." But God wants to make us whole again. Read 1 John 2:1–2. John is writing this so that we won't sin. But if we do sin we have an advocate. What's an advocate? Well, if you were ever charged with a crime, you would have a lawyer who would argue your case for you. That's being an advocate. But Jesus did far more than argue your case. He looked at your case, knew you were guilty, saw what your punishment would be and paid it Himself. Now, if anyone wants to look at your record, He'll hold it up gladly and show that it's gone. That's what propitiation means. He paid it. It's all done. What you need to do know is walk into the light and accept that gift.

Now this may sound like an invitation to come meet Jesus, and it is. If you've never met Him, consider yourself invited and we'll give you an opportunity in a little bit to respond. And for those of you who have already met Jesus, this is an invitation to you as well. Live in the light. And don't be bogged down by guilt or wondering how God could ever love you 'cause of whatever junk you might have in your life. Realize that He loves you, has always loved you, and will always love you. Also realize that as you ask for forgiveness for the bad stuff you do along the way, God wipes it away. He doesn't remember it anymore, so you don't have to ever think about it again. Learn from whatever mistake it was, and then put it behind you and move on.

MAKING IT PERSONAL: *Read Mark 8:34.* Jesus calls His disciples to (*Emphasize these words*) Come, Follow, Me. The call to come involves movement. If I ask you to come to me, you have to first get up from where you are, and then move to where I am. There are actually movements in this meeting between Jesus and us. He made the biggest one, moving from His location in heaven, to earth in human flesh. What remains is for us to take the last step to Him, because while He comes all the way to us, He leaves the last step up to us so that we can choose to enter into relationship with Him. Lastly, the call is to follow HIM. This is an invitation into a relationship, a lifestyle, not a rigid set of rules and regulations.

You have a couple of options here: you could have your kids reflect on what it means to take that last step in their lives and/or you can do the stations described above under service options. Whatever you choose to do, make sure you give some opportunity for kids to respond to the gospel in whatever fashion you're used to doing it at your church. If you haven't done this with your students before, you could:

1. add a response station to the three above, have materials and people ready to talk to students,

2. you could have everyone bow their heads and close their eyes and ask people who want to accept Jesus to look up at you (or raise their hands), then lead the entire group in a prayer of salvation, and have volunteers standing around the room who pay attention to who raised their hands so that they can go talk with them quietly after the service.

CONNECTIONS: Matthew 16:24–27; Luke 9:23–26

QUOTABLE   QUOTES:

Above all, measure your progress by your experience of the love of God and its exercise before men.
—William Wilberforce

Journey to the Light (Follower of Christ)—Midweek

MEMORY VERSE:
But if we live in the light, as God is in the light, we can share fellowship with each other. Then the blood of Jesus, God's Son, cleanses us from every sin.—1 John 1:7 (NCV)

SCRIPTURE: Romans 8:38–39; 1 Corinthians 1:9

LESSON IN A SENTENCE: Following Jesus is not a list of "do's" and "don'ts;" rather, it is about walking where Jesus walks, and not walking where He won't walk.

STUFF YOU NEED:

◯ Movie: *Bruce Almighty*

FOCUS

You can either have a movie night where you watch the entire movie and discuss it, or you can show pertinent clips from the movie as you go through the discussion questions. Synopsis of the film: Bruce Nolan (Jim Carrey) is convinced that God is out to get him. He can't get the promotion that he wants, and after a day when things go from bad to worse, he yells at God saying: "the gloves are off." God then proceeds to page him to get him to come to a mysterious building where God is the janitor, the maintenance man, and the boss (the Trinity, anyone?). God offers Bruce a chance to "be god" for a while to understand what it's like. The stipulation is that he cannot mess with free will. Eventually, Bruce realizes that God has reasons for what He does, even though people cannot always see why. He also discovers the pain of wanting someone to love him so badly—his girlfriend who's left him—that he'd do anything to win her back, but since he can't mess with her free will, there's nothing he can do to make her love him. By the end of the film, he realizes that God has a plan for his life, that he was made for a purpose, and if he just gets in line with God's plan and lives out his purpose, he'll find the peace he's looking for. So he surrenders his life to God, and after getting run over by a semi-truck, gets his life on the right track.

DISCOVERY

Read Romans 8:38–39. Put this in your own words. How much does God love us? What lengths will He go to stay in relationship with us?

Clip: START (chapter 5) 00:17:21 END: 00:32:21 (partway into chapter 8). Here Bruce's life has gotten completely messed up, and he blames God for it. What is the significance of Bruce yelling at God? Does God answer him? Do you think that God answers this kind of prayer, even if you're mad at what He's doing? You could mention that God never gets mad at Bruce, even when Bruce is being sarcastic. Clearly, what God wants is a relationship with Bruce, which really starts when Bruce stops trying to be God and surrenders his life to God's will.

LIFE APPLICATION: *Clip: START: 1:13:05 (chapter 15) END: 1:16:47.* This is the result of Bruce trying to be God. It's not a pretty picture. What happens when you try to play God in your life? Is it a pretty picture?

MAKING IT PERSONAL: *Clip: START: 1:25:39 (chapter 18) END: 1:32:35 (end of movie).* Bruce surrenders to God's will after realizing that he's no good at running his own life. Ultimately, this movie serves as a great metaphor for us trying to be "god" in our life. While we don't have the opportunity to experiment with God's powers, we do often try to run our own lives and figure out what's best for us, instead of surrendering to the One who made us. What is the result of Bruce surrendering? In what ways do we need to surrender in our lives? Most of us know that trusting God with our lives is a smart idea, but will we? What steps will you take this week to trust God with your life?

OCTOBER 15, 2006

Your Body Is a Gift from God to You

By Amy Jacober

MEMORY VERSE:
My darling, everything about you is beautiful, and there is nothing at all wrong with you.—Song of Solomon 4:7 (NCV)

He heals the brokenhearted and binds up their wounds.—Psalm 147:3 (NIV)

SCRIPTURE: 1 Thessalonians 4:1–5; 1 Corinthians 7:1–3; Hebrews 13:4

LESSON IN A SENTENCE: God's desire is that we remain sexually pure.

THE BIG PICTURE (OR WHAT YOU'RE TRYING TO GET ACROSS):
Sexually pure is not puritanical. Christians often work so hard to be different from the world, that we create a community that is afraid to deal with sexuality in a healthy way. God created sex. We needn't be ashamed that we have been created as sexual beings. That said, neither should this be the only thing to define us. Offering sound biblical perspectives and honest conversation within the Christian community can go a long way in creating a healthy identity. Our students are flooded with messages about sex. If the church does not discuss this openly, her voice will be lost. This requires much more than a commandment set down that sex is bad before marriage. It requires dialogue and guidance. There are also those who have been violated in sexual ways. If the only message sent is that sex is bad and those who have had sex are by default bad, we re-victimize the victim. The Christian community must speak up. Sex is a part of our lives. Viewing sex from God's perspective will help us to be more authentically who He has created us to be.

IN THIS LESSON STUDENTS SHOULD:

- See clearly that Scripture does address sexual immorality.
- Define sexual immorality.

○ Know that God desires only the best for us.
○ Become more comfortable discussing sex within a
   Christian context.
○ God's mercy even covers sexual sin.

STUFF YOU NEED:

○ Frozen mayonnaise (Option 1)
○ Sundae toppings (Option 1)
○ Spoons (Option 1)
○ Tape (Option 2)
○ Two roses (Option 3)
○ Aretha Franklin's "A Rose Is Just a Rose" (Option 3)

FOCUS

OPTION 1: Sundaes

Ask who likes ice cream?! After this one question, do not mention ice cream again. Call it a sundae. You will need to have the "ice cream" scoops prepared ahead of time. Freeze mayonnaise and scoop it into bowls to look like vanilla ice cream. Explain that you have three sundaes and are wondering who could eat this the quickest. Choose three volunteers for the sundae eating contest. You may want to make this quite dramatic by having the scoops in the bowl on a table and allow each person to choose their topping! Hand each person the spoon and sundae. Ready, set, go!!

After a few bites they will realize that these are not bowls of vanilla ice cream. Be certain to have a waste basket nearby as they realize they are eating mayonnaise and want to spit this out!

Ask the students what made them think it was ice cream? Remind them that you never said they were ice cream sundaes. You simply asked if they liked ice cream and then offered sundaes. Sometimes we think we are getting something really good. It looks like what we have been told, it seems like it is going to be good, but that is not always the case. This can often end up disgusting and making us feel a little sick. Even when we have some say in the matter, just like choosing the topping, it becomes more than we bargained for. Sex is a lot like this. We are told it is going to be great. We may even want it. Even if it feels good in that moment, it is changing who we are and going against what God intended.

OPTION 2: Stuck on you

Tear off two strips of tape. Tape these on the sleeves of one guy and one girl in your group. They need to pass this on, boy to girl and girl to boy until everyone in your group has had this same piece of tape placed on them at least once. This may require the same person to have the tape more than once, depending on how many girls and guys you have. Once the last two people have been taped, try to stick the two pieces together. With all of the lint, fingerprints, and being passed around, the tape won't stick. Tear off two brand new strips of tape. Hand one to a male student and one to a female student. Have your students stick the two pieces of tape together. Now, try to pull the tape apart. You will not be able to do this.

Ask: How do these two illustrate God's ideal for sex in our lives?

OPTION 3: A rose is a rose

Play the song "A Rose is Just a Rose" by Aretha Franklin. As you do this, pass around a rose. Tell your students to inspect the rose. Have them look at it, touch it, and smell it.

At the end of the song ask how the rose you passed around is doing. Hold up a second brand new rose.

Ask: If I were going to give a rose to you, which one would you want?

Roses are fragile. They can easily wilt and look ruined. God wants us to save ourselves for one person and one person only. For some, decisions have already been made, where they have passed around their own bodies to someone other than their marriage partner. God wants to renew each of us to become brand new.

DISCOVERY

Break into groups of three, preferably all girls or all guys in each group.

Have each group read 1 Thessalonians 4:1–5.

Ask: Is this a suggestion or a commandment from God?

What is sexual immorality?

What does it mean to be responsible for your own body and not give into lust?

Read 1 Corinthians 7:1–3.

Paul says it is good for a man to not touch a woman or a woman to touch a man. Now we know this is simply not going to happen for most people. So did Paul.

Ask: Who does Paul say a man is to have? Who did he say a woman is to have?

If you avoid immorality by being with your husband or wife, this implies you avoid immorality by being with the one you have married.

Read Hebrews 13:4.

Ask: What does it mean to defile the marriage bed?

Teacher's Note: Some of your students may need guidance with regard to this passage. We live in a world that does not like to give clear-cut boundaries. Even Scripture does not address the often asked question "how far is too far"? Is it alright to hold hands but not kiss? Is it alright to kiss but nothing more? These are difficult questions. Where Scripture is clear is that sexual morality is related to the marriage bed. We are not to have sex before marriage. The messages sent to students through peers and popular culture is primarily that as long as you love this person, or feel ready, this is a natural progression. The implication is that if you do not have sex, you are unnatural. Speak plainly and clearly with your students as they wrestle with God's Word on this subject.

LIFE APPLICATION: Many topics are handled well with activities and games. This topic is such a serious one that students appreciate a more grown-up discussion. You may consider separating into male and female groups for this discussion.

Discuss the truth just presented in Scripture. Ask your students if they have any questions.

Avoiding sex can be very difficult. Discuss why this is so difficult at this time. Brainstorm ways to be certain you uphold God's commandments with regard to sex.

Teacher's Note: Pay attention to your students. You may have a group with several students who have been or currently are sexually active. God still loves them. Be certain to set forth truth and remind them of the forgiveness God offers. Allow your discussion to flow in a direction that best suits your group.

MAKING IT PERSONAL: Invite each student to thank God for their sexuality.

Read Song of Solomon 4:7 together. This is the way God sees each person. Give each person a small mirror. Tell them this is a reminder that the person they see in the mirror is the one God calls beautiful.

SONG: "Befriended" by Matt Redman, on the CD *Where Angels Fear to Tread*

EXTRA! EXTRA!: Be certain to check out True Love Waits. This program offers a yearly option for committing or recommitting to sexual purity. http://www.lifeway.com/tlw/

QUOTABLE   QUOTE:

It is with our passions, as it is with fire and water, they are good servants but bad masters.

—Aesop

Your Body Is a Gift from God to You—Midweek

MEMORY VERSE:
My darling, everything about you is beautiful, and there is nothing at all wrong with you.—Song of Solomon 4:7 (NCV)

He heals the brokenhearted and binds up their wounds.—Psalm 147:3 (NIV)

SCRIPTURE: Psalm 22; 147:1–3

LESSON IN A SENTENCE: God's desire is that we remain sexually pure.

FOCUS

Digital Scavenger Hunt

Teacher's Note: Prepare a Power Point slide show in advance. Create a slide show with current statistics relating to sexual abuse. These may be found in a variety of places including www.ucr.gov, www.cpyu.org, www.youthbuilders.com or by doing a search through Google. These may be shocking for you and your students. This information is difficult but important for the church to address. You may also find many resources from www.faithtrustinstitute.org.

Create a scavenger hunt that can be easily accomplished close to where you meet. You can make this about finding items in your community such as jack-o-lanterns or a particular street sign or by having each team create pictures like a pyramid or letter of the alphabet with their bodies. Another option is to hide items on your property, and they must find them and take a picture of at least one team member and the item. Have 5–10 items on your list.

Be certain to have several digital cameras available to be used by groups. Break into the number of groups for which you have cameras. Don't forget to check for batteries before you send your students out!

Have a memory card reader, computer and projector set up waiting for their return. As each team returns, download the pictures and create a slide show. Offer bottled water to each team as they return.

Take a few minutes to show the entire slide show once everyone is back. Set a time limit that will work for your schedule. You may want to blow a whistle to call them back.

Ask: What was the hardest thing to find? What was the most frustrating? Which picture(s) did you like best?

You were each just sent out looking for different things. When you returned, you were given purified water. Any guess as to why?

Tell your students you are going to look at a serious subject this meeting. Last time you talked about sexual purity. Today, you will be looking at sexual abuse.

Show the slide show you created.

Ask: What statistics stood out to you?

How hard is this to consider?

Do you think God can make someone pure again after experiencing such abuse?

DISCOVERY

Being angry is a very natural reaction. Many want to know where God was during such horrific things. In the Christian community, we are not often encouraged to cry out to God.

Read Psalm 22:1-21.

Ask: What did you hear the psalmist saying? (This is a psalm of crying out to God. Of yelling and anger and calling out to God in extreme pain.)

Have your students re-write this psalm keeping sexual abuse in mind. Tell them to be brutally honest as they cry out in anguish for those who have been hurt.

Share their versions of Psalm 22 with each other.

Read Psalm 147:1–3.

Verse 2 talks of God gathering the outcasts. Surely those who have experienced sexual violence feel like outcasts. God does not abandon them.

Read v. 3 aloud and together.

What does this verse mean?

Teacher's Note: You will need to be sensitive during this lesson. It may be (in fact it is likely) that one or more of your students will have experienced sexual assault at some point in their life. If this is the case, be sensitive to the Holy Spirit and move the time together in a way that will be most beneficial for the group.

LIFE APPLICATION: God does want to bind wounds of the broken-hearted. It was never His design that they be violated in the first place. He weeps with you and wants to offer healing.

Most students know very little of sexual abuse. Spend a few moments defining sexual violence, it includes the following:

○ rape
○ forced participation in sexual acts

- forced participation in sexual acts that are degrading or humiliating
- flaunted cheating
- forced prostitution
- pornography
- unwanted humiliating touch in public
- forcing pregnancy/miscarriage/abortion

Every day there are things we can do to avoid and prevent sexual violence.

Brainstorm ways you can do such a thing. Be certain to include:

- report abuse if you know it exists.
- watch jokes, comments and stories that may put girls or guys down for their sexuality (this includes slang and jokes that are "just in fun".
- listen when someone says no to a sexual advance.
- don't put up with this kind of behavior from or around your friends.

This is a problem that is prominent and for the present time is not only not going away, but is actually growing. Sometimes your students may have to risk a friendship, when they tell an adult in order to keep their friend safe. What has been offered here is barely enough for the beginning of a discussion. It will, however, create awareness and hopefully protect some of your students.

Be certain to end with an emphasis on Psalm 147:3.

EXTRA! EXTRA!: This is a tremendously complex and difficult subject. Some leaders will want to shy away from this with younger or less mature groups. Please consider modifying rather than ignoring this very serious matter. Go to www.faithtrustinstitute.org for help with curriculum and ideas regarding abuse of several types dealt with from a Christian perspective. October is National Abuse Awareness month. This is a good time to speak up as the Christian body. While abuse happens to both males and females, the vast majority are females. You may want to consider setting a hotline number or brochures regarding abuse in the women's restrooms of your church. These offer a safe place for a woman to learn of help. The National Network Hotline for Rape/Abuse/Incest is 1-800-656-HOPE (4673). Several denominations have specific stances or resources as well. Talk with your pastor to see if yours is one of these.

REACHING OUT TO KIDS WITH DISABILITIES THROUGH CARING FRIENDSHIPS

By Blaine C. Clyde
AREA DIRECTOR, YOUNG LIFE

We all long for a place to belong, a place of love and acceptance. Now imagine going through your teen years without the opportunity to find this place. Fifteen per cent of the teen population in America faces this dilemma daily. Many are without the opportunity for friendship, fun, and adventure. For the teen with a disability, this exclusion from mainstream life, combined with a struggle to come to terms with his or her disability, leaves a teen confused and discouraged, with nowhere to go and no one to turn to. Teens with disabilities struggle with isolation and unfulfilled potential. Other than life at school, these teens often agonize through one long, lonely day at home after another. For example, Elizabeth has cerebral palsy and is confined to a wheelchair. After coming to Young Life for a few weeks, she said, "I am so bored at home. At Young Life, I get the chance to get out of the house and make new friends."

How many churches do you know that have a ministry, or plan to have a ministry, to people with disabilities in the community? The fact is that less than 5% of churches outreach to people with disabilities. However, one cannot read the Gospels without being overwhelmed by how much of Jesus' ministry was among people with disabilities. We see in Luke 14:15–24 in the Parable of the Great Banquet, Jesus quotes the master as commanding his servants to *"go out quickly into the streets and alleys of the town and bring in the poor, the crippled, the blind and the lame."* Why these particular people? Jesus knew they would respond. In fact, the servant came back and said they had come once invited. People with disabilities are so often forgotten and ignored. They are hungry for love and acceptance. If we will only take the time to *go* and *bring,* then they will surely respond.

Nowhere in the Gospels do we see this more beautifully than, in Mark 2:1–12, when four loving friends bring their disabled friend to the feet of Jesus at great cost. As the paralyzed man is lowered at the feet of Jesus, He sees *their* faith says to the paralytic, "*My son, your sins are forgiven.*" Jesus affirmed the faith of those who would *go* out and *bring* their disabled friend to Him.

A love for Christ and a sincerity to love all people is all that is needed to begin working with people with disabilities; no "special gifting" is required. Jesus said "what you do to the least of these you do to me." (Matthew 25:40) So when we step out of our comfort zone and are a friend to a person with a disability, we are being a friend to Jesus. A general rule of thumb is to treat a person with a disability the same way that you would want to be treated. Take the time to look through a person's disability and you will soon find out that they are a person who happens to have a disability.

A few years ago my wife and I took two students from our Young Life group on a double date. For my wife, Susan, it was one of the first experiences with people with disabilities. Annie and Dana, aged 16 at the time, were dating, but due to lack of transportation for their wheelchairs had never been on a date. We took them out to dinner and then to a park. Annie said that she wanted to have some time for girl talk with my wife. What you should know about Annie is that in addition to being in a wheelchair, she is also unable to talk and must communicate through a computer that sits attached to her electric chair. So "talking" with Annie takes time and patience as she types her end of the conversation. While Susan and Annie had some "girl talk" time, Dana and I took a walk. Later my wife shared with me her experience. Susan said, "When I look at Annie in her wheelchair I see a young gal that I have nothing in common with. She drools continually, needs help to eat and use the bathroom, and she must communicate through a computer. But after our time of girl talk I quickly learned how much Annie and I have in common. She asked me about getting dressed up and going on another date; she asked me about kissing boys, and she told me she wanted to go to the mall together. Annie is a girl after my own heart; she likes to get dressed up and go out, she wants to be loved, and she likes to shop!" I share this story because it is a great example of someone who took the time to get to know a young lady who outwardly seemed so different, but is really so much the same. This is a truth I have found over and over again as I spend time building friendships with kids with disabilities.

I have found in our Young Life ministry to teens with disabilities that I actually receive far more than I ever give away, and I have a lot to learn from these amazing kids! These kids are so accepting and non-judgmental; they do not care about the clothes I wear, my degree or job. They simply love me for who I am. In fact, one kid that I pick up every week for club never fails to ask me about my wife and kids. "How's your wife? Tell her hi for me," is what he says to me each week. When I take him home he always says "Blaine, thank you for picking me up." There is such a simple sincerity in him that I could learn so much from.

I am also confronted and challenged in my own values—what do I deem worthy? Society tells us that it's the people with the most money, biggest homes, best clothes that are rewarded. God's Word tells us in I Corinthians 1:27–29 (NIV) what God chooses as worthy: "*But God chose the foolish things of the world to shame the wise; God chose the weak things of the world to shame the strong. He chose the lowly things of the world and despised things—and the things that are not— to nullify the things that are, so that no one may boast before him.*" What we deem as weak, inadequate, and worthless, God sees as supremely valuable. This alone should motivate us to reach out to the lonely and forgotten people in our world—people with disabilities.

In the Old Testament in 2 Samuel 9, we have a tremendous picture of God's inclusiveness of disabled people around the Great Banquet Table. In honor of Jonathan, David takes Jonathan's son Mephibosheth, who is crippled in both feet, to live in his house and dine with the king daily. When Mephibosheth heard David's invitation he said, "What is your servant that you should notice a dead dog like me?" But David treats him as royalty. Is this not a parable and call for us to treat those who are like "dead dogs" in our culture as royalty and bring them to Jesus the King to dine at His table with us?

But perhaps the greatest motivation for disabled ministry comes in the very nature of God Himself as revealed in Jesus Christ. We see this in Philippians 2:5–8 (NIV): "*Your attitude should be the same as that of Christ Jesus; who, being in very nature God, did not consider equality with God something to be grasped, but made himself nothing, taking the very nature of a servant, being made in human likeness. And being found in appearance as a man, he humbled himself and became obedient to death—even death on a cross!*" God stripped Himself of the privileges of being God and became human. In other words, God put limits on Himself, and this is what it means to be disabled. It is to be limited. God became disabled and He identified with us all in becoming human, but especially with people who are limited all their lives. Yet in these very limits His power was grandly revealed, and this is the great hope for people with disabilities: "*Power perfected in weakness.*" We are to emulate God's downward mobility to reach out and identify with people who have disabilities.

OCTOBER 22, 2006

Justice

By Rick & Kristi Bennett

MEMORY VERSE:
Religion that God our father accepts as pure and faultless is this: to look after orphans and widows in their distress and to keep oneself from being polluted by the world.—James 1:27 (NIV)

SCRIPTURE: Matthew 25:31–46

LESSON IN A SENTENCE: As followers of a Christ who was committed to those oppressed by the powers of the world, we must take the time to love and serve those He cared for.

THE BIG PICTURE (OR WHAT YOU'RE TRYING TO GET ACROSS):
Christ spent much of His time with the outcasts of society. He cared deeply for those that society had turned its back on. He taught us, through this passage and His parables on the Sermon on the Mount, that as His followers we must serve those who are outcasts. Not only does God bring justice to those who have suffered in this world, He expects *us* to bring justice to those people and spend our time with them, teaching and learning. When we spend time with the "least of these" we are serving Christ and loving Christ. By giving us the examples of taking care of prisoners, sick, naked and hungry people (along with the widows and orphans), we know that we are to take care of those that cannot take care of themselves.

IN THIS LESSON STUDENTS SHOULD:

- Know the story of the sheep and the goats.
- Evaluate who they are in light of this passage (sheep or goat) and make practical steps to be faithful sheep.

STUFF YOU NEED:

- Chalkboard or other large writing surface
- Pens
- Index cards
- Sheet of paper with "Prayer of St. Francis" written (or it can be on a chalkboard)

OPTION 1: Potato chips, popcorn, other snacks (more than enough for entire group)

OPTION 2: Monopoly® game

FOCUS

Choose either Option 1 or 2.

OPTION 1: Short Period/ Larger Group

This is a hunger simulation game. Sit the students in a circle. By yourself or with an assistant, walk around the circle handing out potato chips, popcorn and/or other snacks. Do not give each person the same amount of the snack; in fact, give some a lot, some very little, and some students none (be careful to not hurt the feelings of very sensitive students, though). As they ask why they are not getting some, tell them there is just not enough to go around, but still maintain the high level which you have given other students (pick an affluent student to go without). As they sit and finish their snacks, have them process their thoughts, drawing parallels between the game and real life.

Point out how this shows the injustice in the world. Some of us can have a lot of resources, money, things, freedom, safety, family, etc. while some of the world has very little or none.

Is this fair? What would you do about it? Does God care?

OPTION 2: Longer Time Period/ Small Group

Bring in the game Monopoly®. Instead of evenly splitting the money and resources (property), give each student a different share. Give one student almost nothing, while others have little and a few have a lot. Give a couple of students a lot of property at the beginning. Play until someone loses or wins (if a student decides to share his resources, let him—but do not encourage it).

Ask about the fairness of this game. *Ask:* Do you like playing a game when someone has all the money or property and someone else has none? Point out the same lessons and questions as Option 1.

DISCOVERY

In Israel, sheep and goats regularly graze together during the day, according to commentators, however they need to be separated at the end of the day because goats require extra care to be kept warm. In the evening it is difficult to tell them apart, because they are similar in color and size. A shepherd knows the small differences between the two and has no problem separating them.

In deciding who is a sheep and who is a goat, we must remember the words of Jesus (Matthew 12:50), that those who do the will of God are his brothers and sisters.

What does this tell us about belief vs. actions?

What does this tell us about the will of God that we should follow?

Regarding the prisoners, ask why Jesus mentions them? How do you feel about them?

By caring for the needy and undeserved, what are we doing for Christ?

What do you think this means?

Why is Christ concerned for the poor, homeless, prisoners, etc?

Who are the needy? They include single parents, working poor, uninsured or underinsured, elderly, disabled, homeless, mentally unstable, permanently hospitalized, and the prisoners, to name but a few.

For each group Jesus mentions (hungry, thirsty, stranger, naked, sick, prisoner):

Who are the _____ Jesus is speaking of?

Why is it important to take care of them?

Why do they need our help?

How can we help them?

How serious does Jesus take the helping of the needy? How do we know this?

Teacher's Note: According to N. T. Wright,

"Justice is one of the most profound longings of the human race. If there is no justice, then deep within ourselves we know that something is out of joint. Justice is hard to define and harder still to put into practice; but that has never stopped human beings and societies seeking it, praying for it, and working to find ways of doing it better. And 'justice' doesn't simply mean 'punishing wickedness,' though that is regularly involved. It means bringing the world back into balance.

"Central to the Jewish and Christian traditions. . .is the belief that this passionate longing for justice comes from the creator God himself, Jews and Christians believe that he will eventually do justice on a worldwide scale, in a way that the International Court can only dream of. God's judgment will be seen to be just. The world will be put to rights."

How did the needy become needy? According to pastor and author Steve Sjogren, it is because of many factors, including oppression by the Evil One (Luke 4:18), bad choices, or oppression by unfair social political systems.

LIFE APPLICATION: When you think of a person or people in need, who comes to your mind first?

Why?

Is there something the church, this youth group, or you could do for that person or people?

At this time, it will be good to have a few practical concrete ideas of what the youth group can do to help those in need, and serve those who are victims of injustice. Resources and books will be listed below.

If the church has projects or needy people already, a suggestion is to create a project for the students or bring in a speaker who works in this area.

Continue to brainstorm ideas for the youth group and individuals. Pick one or two projects to focus on. Appoint a student to gather information or resources on each project.

MAKING IT PERSONAL: Discuss with the students practical ways they can serve those in need. Ask each student to come up with one way they can individually (or with another student) serve one of the groups Jesus and Paul mentioned.

Ask them to pray for that person or group throughout the week. Ask them to commit to coming Wednesday with a practical idea of how they will serve that person or group in the next week.

Pass out 3 x 5 index cards to write down whom they are committed to serve.

Read the Prayer of St. Francis ("Make Me an Instrument") as a benediction. The prayer is at the end of this lesson. Either have it written on a chalkboard or printed on a sheet of paper for each student.

MEMORY VERSE ACTIVITY

On the back of the index card, ask them to write down the Memory Verse. Ask them to picture a widow and orphan this week (maybe one in South East Asia) as they read the verse.

SONGS: "Man in Black" by Johnny Cash
"Folsom County Blues" or "San Quentin" by Johnny Cash
"Peace on Earth" by U2

CONNECTIONS: The Book of Amos is primarily about social justice.

EXTRA! EXTRA!: Mother Teresa said: "At the end of our lives, we will not be judged by how many diplomas we have received, how much money we have made or how many great things we have done. We will be judged by 'I was hungry and you gave me something to eat. I was homeless and you took me in.'

"Hungry not only for bread—but hungry for love.

"Naked not only for clothing—but naked of human dignity and respect.

"Homeless not only for want of a room of bricks—but homeless because of rejection.

"This is Christ in distressing disguise."

"If every church or synagogue in the United States took in ten families who are on welfare, we would eliminate welfare."

—Reverend Billy Graham

Q U O T A B L E   Q U O T E S :

The great thing about serving the poor is that there is no competition.

—Eugene Rivers

The Cross provides a real stimulus to alleviate the suffering of others because the suffering of any of God's people grieves his heart. By seeking to relieve the hardship of others, we are working to ease the suffering and the pain of God. As we meet the practical needs of those who suffer, we demonstrate to them the message of the Cross. Our presence with and provision for the needs of those who are hurting assure them that God has not abandoned them in their misery and pain. Any assistance that we extend to them speaks of God's presence and identification with them in their suffering.

—Isaiah Majok Dau, Sudanese Minister and author of "Suffering and God: A Theological Reflection on the War in Sudan."

There is such an enormous gap between our words and deeds! Everyone talks about freedom, democracy, justice, human rights, and peace; but at the same time, everyone, more or less consciously or unconsciously, serves those values and ideals only to the extent necessary to defend and serve his own interests, and those of his group or his state. Who should break this vicious circle? Responsibility cannot be preached: it can only be borne, and the only possible place to begin is with oneself.

—Vaclav Havel

Justice—Midweek

MEMORY VERSE:
Religion that God our father accepts as pure and faultless is this: to look after orphans and widows in their distress and to keep oneself from being polluted by the world.—James 1:27 (NIV)

SCRIPTURE: Luke 4:16–21

LESSON IN A SENTENCE: We need to do something to help those in need, not just study about the importance of helping them.

FOCUS

OPTION 1:
Both of these options take some planning. Option 1 is to have a guest speaker come in to give his or her testimony regarding service to those suffering from injustice, or those who are needy.

Another, riskier idea, is to ask someone who has been a victim of injustice or needy to come speak to your students and share with them how it feels to be an outsider.

Either person would help a student put a practical face on the issue of justice and see a need to take action.

OPTION 2:
Option 2 would be a service project. Since you studied justice on Sunday, you can serve someone today. If you are bound to staying in the church, please consider either (1) taking this time to plan a mission experience with the students or (2) do something for one of the groups mentioned in Matthew 25.

Some ideas for you to consider (this is not exhaustive—see the Internet or books for more ideas)

1. Write letters to prisoners.
2. Make care packages for the homeless.
3. Collect food, toys, or clothes from church members (warn them in advance).
4. Give bags to each church member that night with instructions to bring back the bag on Sunday full of a needed item.
5. Wash the cars of passers-by for free that evening.
6. Visit a nursing home, shelter, or another place with needy people (just to talk and befriend those people).

There are a number of ideas. A student may have an idea on Sunday. Be prepared for an exciting time that may become a regular event.

DISCOVERY

Because the bulk of the time will be taken by the special speaker or project, read Luke 4:16–21 together and simply ask the students:

1. What did Jesus say He was anointed to do? Four things.

2. Can you think of examples from Jesus' life where He did this?

3. If we are to be followers of Jesus, what does this mean for you?

4. How can this be done?

LIFE APPLICATION: This entire lesson is about application. Ask students to come up with ways they can make this a regular part of their lives. Ask how it can become a part of the youth group's life. Put students in charge of taking lead in this area.

Books and Resources for Further Study and Projects:
101 Ways to Help People in Need by Steve and Janie Sjogren
101 Ways to Reach Your Community by Steve and Janie Sjogren
Churches That Make a Difference by Ronald Sider, Philip Olson and Heidi Unruh
Good News About Injustice: A Witness of Courage in a Hurting World—Youth Edition by Gary Haugen
The Justice Mission curriculum by Youth Specialties
Ideas: Camps, Retreats, Missions, & Service Ideas by Youth Specialties
Compassion International, World Vision or World Relief all have curriculum and projects for youth.

WEB CONNECT

www.ijm.org International Justice Mission
www.servlife.org ServLife (a mission organization)
If you are member of a denomination, use their site on missions or service.
www.network935.org network of churches committed to serving the poor.
www.missionyear.org
www.bread.org Bread for the World
www.servantevangelism.org site with great project ideas
www.compassion.com Compassion International

Some of these sites are updated periodically with the latest statistics and stories on hunger, poverty, etc.

Prayer of St. Francis

Lord, Make Me an Instrument of Your Peace;
Where there is hatred, let me sow love;
Where there is injury, let me sow pardon;
Where there is doubt, let me sow faith;
Where there is despair, let me sow hope;
Where there is darkness, let me sow light;
Where there is sadness, let me sow joy.

Oh God, grant that I may not so much seek
To be consoled, as to console,
To be understood as to understand,
To be loved as to love.

For it is in giving that we receive;
It is in pardoning that we are pardoned;
And it is in dying that we are born to eternal life.

AMEN

OCTOBER 29, 2006

Standing Up for What You Believe

By Amy Jacober

MEMORY VERSE:
If you throw us into the blazing furnace, the God we serve is able to save us from the furnace. He will save us from your power, O king. But even if God does not save us, we want you, O king, to know this: We will not serve your gods or worship the gold statue you have set up. —Daniel 3:17–18 (NCV)

Our fight is not against people on earth but against the rulers and authorities and the powers of this world's darkness, against the spiritual powers of evil in the heavenly world.—Ephesians 6:12 (NCV)

SCRIPTURE: Daniel 3:13–30

LESSON IN A SENTENCE: Even against the worst of odds, you can stand up for what you believe.

THE BIG PICTURE (OR WHAT YOU'RE TRYING TO GET ACROSS):
It is no secret that there are evil powers in this world. Simply being a follower of Christ can make a person a prime target for attacks. These attacks often come in quiet, subtle ways. They come through parents who tease their child for choosing to go to church with a friend, they come through teammates who think you are lame if you won't give yourself an extra edge to help the team, they come through friends thinking it would be fun to go to a palm reader and a movie for someone's birthday. Attacks, temptations, and deception are all around us. It can be a pretty scary world. Followers of Christ are called to stand up for what they believe. This need not be in an arrogant or obnoxious way. There are also those who wear T-shirts saying things like "I'm going to heaven and you're not" and call it an attack when others are offended. This is not what this lesson is about. This is about those "real-life, where does your faith fit in" kind of situations, when you are indeed at risk and may have something to lose.

○ Find comfort knowing that they are not the first, nor will they be the last, to have to stand up for their faith.
○ Learn that just because they may be going through a hard time does not mean that God is not with them.
○ Understand that it is not other people who are the enemy, rather Satan and his principalities.

STUFF YOU NEED:

○ Bowling pins of some sort (Option 1)
○ Pumpkins, lots of them (Option 1)
○ Caramel apples (Option 2)
○ Caramel onions (Option 2)

FOCUS

OPTION 1: Pumpkin Bowling

Go to a local bowling alley and ask for any pins they are going to be throwing away. You may need to go to a couple of alleys to gather several. If you cannot get old bowling pins, use empty soda bottles, empty tin cans, or whatever creative items you can find. Set up a "bowling alley" with several lanes for your students. You may need to set down garbage bags to protect carpet and/or furniture. The catch is instead of bowling balls, you've got pumpkins! Hold a bowling tournament complete with manual setup and score keeping! Tell your students to be careful with the pumpkins; each team gets one and only one. Know that a mess is coming, but this might hold it off for a few minutes. Chances are the pumpkins will be destroyed long before the tournament is finished. . . this is fine! It's really just about having fun.

OPTION 2: Caramel Apples?

It's time for a little fall festivity! Have caramel apples ready as a snack for the whole group. Before passing them out, tell your students you are going to have an eating contest to see who can eat their apple the fastest! Call three or four volunteers up front. Hand each their "apple". Instead of an apple, however, give each person a caramel onion. (You will need to have these prepared ahead of time. Find onions which are roughly the same size as the apples you've made.) Your students will be so focused on winning, that for the first few bites they won't even notice. Be certain to have a trash can close by! Once the discovery has been made, let them finish and offer the real apples to everyone.

Give your students a few minutes to wash out their mouths. Ask the volunteers how they felt when they realized they were not eating an apple?

It can be so easy to be deceived. What may look fine on the surface really ends up being harmful. While this was an unpleasant trick, Satan uses the same methods. It looks great on the outside but what he offers on the inside isn't what we think.

DISCOVERY

Teacher's Note: Read over Daniel 1—3:12. Help your students understand the background of this story. Nebuchadnezzar was now king. He chose the finest of young men and offered them choice food, drink, and education. Daniel was one of those chosen. He, however, did not want to eat the rich food nor drink the wine, and asked permission to have an alternative diet. Daniel and his friends were given permission and they lived on vegetables and water. To everyone's surprise, they turned out healthier and smarter than all the others. Daniel's friends were Shadrach, Meshach and Abed-Nego. Nebuchadnezzar was so impressed that he promoted Daniel's friends as rulers in Babylon. A little while later, Nebuchadnezzar built a golden image to be worshiped as an idol in Babylon. He never checked with the rulers he placed there, and once again they refused to defile themselves. This is where we pick up the story.

Read Daniel 3:13–30.

Have the following questions written on a dry erase board for everyone to see.

Who was Nebuchadnezzar?

Who are Shadrach, Meshach and Abed-Nego?

What did Nebuchadnezzar want them to do?

What happened to Shadrach, Meshach and Abed-Nego when they refused?

How did this story end?

This is a great passage!! There are so many lessons to be learned here. Once you've covered the overall passage, spend some time on specifics.

Verse 25 says a fourth man was in the fire with them. Who was this?

What does this say to you about spiritual warfare?

Here were three friends placing all of their faith in God, so much so that they were willing to give their lives for it. Have you ever thought that God protects you, fights for you, even when you cannot see it?

If God is fighting for you, who is He fighting?

What does *this* say to you about spiritual warfare?

LIFE APPLICATION: Halloween is in just a few days. While for many families and communities, Halloween is about harvest festivals and innocent costumes, there is a darker side. Spiritual warfare is real. It, however, does not only happen on Halloween. Even more, it is not always vampires and demons with pitchforks. Spiritual warfare is most often subtle and seemingly harmless.

Verses 17–18 have the three friends declaring that they trust that God will deliver them, but even if He does not, they refuse to give in.

Ask: Why do you think Shadrach, Meshach and Abed-Nego refused to bow down instead of just going through the motions and not really believing it? What could possibly make them think it was worth it to risk a painful death, when they could have pretended and remained in power?

Ask: What is the worst or most difficult thing you have ever risked by standing up for what you have believed?

In small groups discuss the following questions. After they have had time in their small groups, have each group offer a response. Really encourage your students to think through these questions and offer honest answers.

What ways do we as Christians choose to stand up for what we believe today?

This may be in the way we dress, or the parties we choose to attend or not attend. There is no one right or wrong way to do this.

What ways do we choose to go through the motions that make us look like we fit in with the world, even when we know it is not what God would want?

Sadly, this is all too common for Christians today. We make choices that benefit us financially rather than helping others, we choose friends because they make us look good, not because they need a friend. Even actions that seem like they would be godly, can be sinful when done with the wrong attitude or heart. Satan will take any foothold and try to turn us from following Jesus.

Why is this so difficult? What can we do to be followers of Jesus who stand up for what we believe?

MAKING IT PERSONAL: We all have places where we struggle. Spiritual warfare is not always a big dramatic horror film kind of an experience. In fact, it is often simply what is expected in society, but that we know runs counter to what God would want. It may even look good on the outside, but once we realize what is just below the surface, our perspective changes. Giving a discount to friends at work, intentionally not inviting someone to go out with your group on the weekend, giving answers to someone on homework when you are only supposed to be helping. We all know right from wrong, but there are many wrongs we decide are socially acceptable.

Pray and ask God to show one thing in your life that you know needs to be changed. Ask Him to reveal this clearly and to give you the courage to stand up for what you believe. This isn't to earn God's love, rather it is in response to His love. The conviction comes as you are open to Him transforming you from the inside!

Teacher's Note: While this lesson is on spiritual warfare, it may not be in the way you have seen in the past. Satan, demons, and spiritual struggles are real. As followers of Christ we experience every day struggles that keep us from following Jesus as we should. It is easy to talk of extreme cases of spiritual warfare, and forget that every day we can combat the powers of darkness. When we know the ways of Christ, we can recognize deception and know when to stand up for what we believe.

SONG: "You're Worthy of My Praise" by Big Daddy Weave and Barlowgirl, on the CD *Absolute Modern Worship*

CONNECTIONS: Henri Nouwen has a wonderful little book that explores the temptation of Christ called *In the Name of Jesus*. It looks at the devil as he tempts Jesus. It also explores major principles and how Jesus responded. Jesus sets the model for how we can stand up for what we believe, and even more how we can avoid some pitfalls that come with the deceptions of the devil.

QUOTABLE QUOTES:

The devil hath power to assume a pleasing shape.
—William Shakespeare *Hamlet*, Act 2 scene 2

Standing Up for What You Believe—Midweek

MEMORY VERSE:
If you throw us into the blazing furnace, the God we serve is able to save us from the furnace. He will save us from your power, O king. But even if God does not save us, we want you, O king, to know this: We will not serve your gods or worship the gold statue you have set up. —Daniel 3:17–18 (NCV)

Our fight is not against people on earth but against the rulers and authorities and the powers of this world's darkness, against the spiritual powers of evil in the heavenly world.—Ephesians 6:12 (NCV)

SCRIPTURE: Ephesians 4:26–28 (NIV); 1 Peter 5:8–9

LESSON IN A SENTENCE: Even against the worst of odds, you can stand up for what you believe.

FOCUS

Play a simple game of hide and go seek. You may want to have a whistle to blow to bring everyone back at the end. Once you have chosen "It", invite that person to choose two more people as his or her helpers. In total you will have three people being "It." Adjust the number of people being "It" to work best with your size of group. Be certain you always have at least two. Establish the room or area where you meet to be home base.

Let them tell stories of the game. Is there anyone who was never found? Any good chases that happened? Anyone who was really easy to find? What was it like for the multiple "It" people?

We are talking about spiritual warfare. Satan is not sitting back waiting for you to come to him. He is coming after you! Even more, he has a strategy to get you. It is important to realize that while we don't need to be living in fear, neither do we need to be naïve.

DISCOVERY

Read through Ephesians 4:26–28 in the NIV.
Ask: How does this passage tie together sin, anger, and a foothold for the devil?

Teacher's Note: The NIV offers the phrase "Do not give the devil a foothold." Other translations use the word 'opportunity' or 'room.' All of these are helpful and useful. Within many Christian writings, however, that phrase foothold is common.

Keep this in mind and turn to 1 Peter 5:8–9, read this aloud.
Ask: What is the devil doing in this passage?
What are you to do according to this passage?

LIFE APPLICATION: You've played Hide and Seek and you've just read about the devil being on the prowl for you. You are being pursued. God also is pursuing, but make no mistake, the devil cares what you are up to and will try to keep you from building the kingdom.

Go back and look at the first passage.
Ask: What is a foothold? How do we give the devil footholds in our lives?

Why would this be so dangerous?

This is easy to blow off or think it's antiquated or silly.

The next passage you read tells of the devil prowling like a roaring lion ready to devour someone.

What do we do with this?

Brainstorm how the devil prowling about can take hold of a little tiny foothold and turn it into a huge issue. What begins as jealousy, turns into bitterness. What begins as the silent treatment, turns into gossip and lying about friends. What begins as trying a cigarette, turns into a smoking addiction. Come up with as many of these as you can. You may even want to write them on a dry erase board or on papers that you can tape on the walls. The devil does not tempt you on places of strength, he tempts you in your weaknesses.

Read 1 Peter 5:9.

This passage says that we are to resist the devil, being firm in our faith. It's great to suggest resisting the devil! In fact you'd be hard pressed to find many people who would say they'd like to be taken over and devoured by Satan.

Ask: What does this verse teach about what allows us to resist the devil? (being firm in our faith)

We aren't told exactly how to resist the devil. We do, however, have a lot of information on how to be firm in our faith. Being firm in our faith means being able to stand up for what we believe. It means spending so much time with God, that we recognize something that is not of Him.

Look back at the footholds we mentioned earlier. Identify ways you can choose to resist the devil and not allow those to be taken over by Satan.

Close, asking for God's protection and discipline as you seek to grow more firm in your faith.

NOVEMBER 5, 2006

God Pursues You!

By Whitney Prosperi

MEMORY VERSE:
The time is coming when the true worshipers will worship the Father in spirit and truth, and that time is here already. You see, the Father too is actively seeking such people to worship Him.—John 4:23 (NCV)

SCRIPTURE: John 4:1–26

LESSON IN A SENTENCE: The God of the universe pursues a personal, intimate relationship with us.

THE BIG PICTURE (OR WHAT YOU'RE TRYING TO GET ACROSS):
While students pursue many things and people, they must be reminded of the most important "pursuit" they can ever have—Jesus Christ. They seek Him because He sought them first. He chose to come to the earth to die for our sins so that we could have a personal relationship with Him. He wants us to respond to Him with our choices, our affection, and our time.

IN THIS LESSON STUDENTS SHOULD:

- Evaluate whether or not they have received God's gift of salvation.
- Recognize the amazing fact that God seeks them out each day in personal relationship.
- Prioritize time spent deepening their relationship with Jesus Christ.

STUFF YOU NEED:

- Pens
- Paper
- Newspaper personal ads
- Personal planner or palm pilot

FOCUS

Begin by reading to the group several personal ads from the newspaper. You will need to make sure to choose the clean ones that won't have any offensive or suggestive language in them. Ask students to share with you some common denominators in all of the ads.

DISCOVERY

Read John 4:1–26 as a whole group. Point out that v. 4 says that Jesus *had* to pass through Samaria. He passed through this region for a divine appointment with this woman.

Say: She was definitely in pursuit to get her needs met in life. We can tell this from the conversation she had with Jesus.

Ask: Where was this woman looking to get her emotional needs met?

Ask: Where do you go to get your own emotional needs met?

Say: Jesus responds to her with grace and truth. He doesn't offer judgment, but He does tell her the truth. He shares with her that the end of her search is standing in front of her. She looked to men to get her needs met, although they would never fill the nagging emptiness inside of her. God created her for Himself and He alone could offer the fulfillment she was looking for.

Now read Luke 19:10 as a group.

Ask: What does this verse teach that God is seeking?

Ask: What about you? Have you ever come to Jesus asking Him to forgive you and come into your life? He offers salvation through His death and resurrection. Have you ever received that gift?

Break students into groups of 2–3. Now ask the groups to write a personal ad from God that might appear in their local paper. Ask them to be as creative as they want. When they finish, have them share their ads with the whole group.

Ask: What do we learn about God's heart through the story in John 4?

Ask: How should we respond to this truth?

Teacher's Note: Be mindful of the spiritual pulse of your group. If there are some students whose salvation you are not sure about, you may want to stress that aspect of the lesson more. If you are fairly sure that most of the group has a personal relationship with Christ, you may want to stress that God is seeking to deepen their relationship through time spent with Him in His Word and in prayer.

LIFE APPLICATION: Hold up a personal planner or palm pilot. Now ask students to think about the way they spend their time each day. Ask them to draw twenty-four boxes on a piece of paper, with each box representing one hour. Now ask them to fill in each box with how they spend a corresponding hour of an average day. If they spend eight hours sleeping, have them fill in eight boxes with a picture of them asleep or the word "sleep." Now ask them to label the boxes they spend in school and doing different activities. Ask students to make sure they show the time represented in deepening their relationship with Jesus. It may be represented by a whole box, half box, or even none at all. Lastly, ask students to look over their days and determine if there are some ways to rearrange their schedules so they can spend more time alone with God.

MAKING IT PERSONAL: As we saw in the above exercise, our lives are filled with many activities. In what ways can we make sure that we take time to learn about God each day?

Ask: Will you schedule time alone with Jesus for the coming week? Decide on the time when you and He will be alone together. Now schedule this time like a real date. You may want to go somewhere special or you might just stay in your room alone. Maybe you will put on some music or light a candle. Whatever you do, don't let anything else come in the way of your date with God.

CONNECTIONS: Ask students to read Jeremiah 29:13 and Hebrews 11:6. Discuss the conditions for seeking God. Now discuss the rewards.

MEMORY VERSE ACTIVITY

Write up this verse in a way that looks like a personal ad. Now attach it to your mirror or locker. You will be reminded each time you see it that God is seeking you today. It will prompt you to spend time in prayer and worship each day.

EXTRA! EXTRA!: Leader, be reminded as you prepare that God is seeking a deeper relationship with you. Don't let this study time be simply that, *study time.* Instead, let it be a time when you dedicate yourself to knowing God more and responding to Who He Is. He longs for you to draw close to Him today. James 4:8 (NCV) says, "Come near to God, and God will come near to you." Let the incredible truth of that promise wash over your heart today.

God Pursues You!—Midweek

MEMORY VERSE:
The time is coming when the true worshipers will worship the Father in spirit and truth, and that time is already here. You see, the Father is actively seeking such people to worship Him.—John 4:23 (NCV)

SCRIPTURE: Isaiah 30:18–19

LESSON IN A SENTENCE: The God of the universe pursues a personal, intimate relationship with us.

FOCUS

If you could spend one hour with anyone in the world, who would it be? It would be totally uninterrupted time with just you and that other person. Maybe you would choose a celebrity, singer, or world leader. Have each student share with the group whom they would choose.

Now ask them what they think the chances are of ever getting to actually meet that person—let alone spend time with them. Probably the chances are pretty slim of most of us meeting that one person we would love to spend an hour with. The circumstances would have to be pretty remarkable. Celebrities don't just "hang out" with ordinary folks everyday.

But guess what? God, who made the whole earth and everything in it, longs to spend time with you. He actually looks forward to hearing from you. And He thinks you are marvelous. Why wouldn't He? You're His one-of-a-kind creation!

Most of us would jump at the chance to meet Brad Pitt, J-Lo, or Usher. We would actually "drop everything" and spend time with them. But what do you do when faced with the chance to spend time with God? Is He a priority? Or do you tend to put Him after everyone else?

DISCOVERY

In pairs, read Isaiah 30:18–19. Answer the following questions.

Have you ever thought about the fact that God "waits" for you? How does that make you feel?

How would prioritizing time alone with God each day change your life?

If you're like me, you may feel that there are times when no one hears you or "gets" you. What difference does it make for you to know that God always hears you and understands exactly where you're coming from?

LIFE APPLICATION: Think of some of the things you will pursue over the course of your life. Maybe you will pursue getting into a certain club or making a particular team. Or maybe you will pursue a college degree or a certain goal. Make a list of the top five things you will pursue in the next ten years. Is a relationship with Jesus Christ on that list? If not, you may want to rethink it. Remember—He is waiting for you.

NOVEMBER 12, 2006

The Persecuted Church

By Amy Jacober

MEMORY VERSE:
"And indeed, all who desire to live godly in Christ Jesus will be persecuted."—2 Timothy 3:12 (NASB)

SCRIPTURE: Acts 2:43–47; 28:16–22

LESSON IN A SENTENCE: We were never promised an easier life through following Jesus.

THE BIG PICTURE (OR WHAT YOU'RE TRYING TO GET ACROSS):
No one likes to go through difficulties. And yet, here we are, choosing to follow Jesus, knowing we have been warned that we will be misunderstood at best, and persecuted at worst. This is often a difficult concept to understand when we live in such a privileged part of the world. While struggles in daily life are very real, encourage your students to begin realizing the difference from being teased, overlooked, or misunderstood, and actual persecution. In the body of Christ, when one part hurts, we all hurt (1 Corinthians 12:26). We needn't just sit by. Awareness of the persecuted church connects us with the greater Christian body and reminds us to be involved in the lives of not only those we personally know, but those around the world. This lesson refers to web research more than others. This is to ensure that the information you are presenting to your students is the most current possible.

IN THIS LESSON STUDENTS SHOULD:

- Be reminded that following Jesus does not mean life gets easier.
- Learn more of the lives of Christians worldwide.
- Pray for those being persecuted around the world.

STUFF YOU NEED:

- Video on the persecuted church (This should have been ordered prior to this week. See suggested websites. If not, check with your pastor and/or church library.)

FOCUS

OPTION 1: Video

Open with a video that explains and/or explores the current situation of those being persecuted for their faith. There are many available for free or at a nominal cost through several websites (see www.persecuted-church.org).

OPTION 2: Step into the shoes of...

Before the night of your meeting, collect the stories of several (4–5) people or people groups currently being persecuted (see www.perse-cutedchurch.org, Voices of the Martyrs). Have these typed out all set to be read aloud when you cue. Recruit a few students and/or leaders as readers. They will be interrupting the activity of writing on the banner, so be certain the person you choose to begin has a loud and command-ing voice. (Summarize these stories and rewrite them in first person. It will help to keep the stories between ⅓ to ½ page and no longer.)

Have the word PERSECUTION written in large letters on a piece of butcher paper (like a banner if possible). Make the letters large, but leave enough room to either write around the letters or to fill in the let-ters with words. As your students walk in the room, draw attention to the banner. Ask them to begin talking about ways they know people are persecuted today. Once everyone has arrived and they have had a few minutes to discuss, ask your students what it means to be persecuted. Take volunteers and have them write around the word "persecution" ways that persecution takes place in their world and daily life.

Midway through, have the interruption begin as your readers share the stories of those persecuted around the world. (Depending on the setup of your room, you may want to have all the readers lined up in the front or scattered around the edges of the room. Be creative!)

Ask: After hearing these stories, how would you define persecu-tion?

DISCOVERY

Split into groups of 3–4. Ask each group to read first Acts 2:43–47 and then Acts 28:16–22.

What is happening in each passage? What is said about the church as a whole?

Pay particular attention to Acts 2:47 and Acts 28:22.

In Acts chapter 2 it says the church was finding favor with all the people (this includes those who were not currently believers). By the end of Acts however, chapter 28:22 tells us that followers of Christ were spoken against everywhere. This is quite a turnaround in a very short time.

Ask: What do you think would bring about such a change?

LIFE APPLICATION: *Ask:* What is the church doing today that could bring about persecution? Is this the same or different from what was happening in the first-century church?

Can we legitimately call the misunderstandings and being overlooked "persecution?" If yes, why? If no, why not? (Also, if no, what then is it?)

Say: Today is the International Day of Prayer for the Persecuted Church. (See more details at www.idop.org .) You've heard the stories of several people and we've now read in Scripture that being persecuted is no surprise. Changes happen quickly and where Christians were once viewed favorably, in many places the opposite is now true.

Walk your students through a guided prayer. This means that you will offer a topic about which they will pray for a minute or two, and then move to the next topic. If you have never led a guided prayer, do not be nervous! This is simply a way to allow each person to act as an intercessor for those in need. Many students struggle with prayer and claim they do not know what to pray about. This eliminates that anxiety. Encourage them to take this seriously, and even for those who may not feel comfortable, ask them to not distract the others.

Dear Lord—

We call out to you today on behalf of Christians everywhere who are persecuted.

Pray for Christians in jails or prisons because of their faith. (pause)

Pray for Christians who are hurting. (pause)

Pray for Christians being tortured because of their faith. (pause)

Pray for the families, the loved ones, of those being persecuted. (pause)

Pray for the churches and communities where those being persecuted serve. (pause)

Pray for entire communities where following Christ costs their dignity and lives. (pause)

Pray for those who persecute followers of Jesus. (pause)

Pray for anyone you may know who is being put down or overlooked because of their faith in Christ. (pause)

Pray that we who follow Christ do not persecute others. (pause)

God we thank You for the protection and blessings You give to us. Help us to not take them for granted nor to judge others as unworthy who are less fortunate.

Amen.

MAKING IT PERSONAL: Tell your students about the websites you have been using to research. Invite them to do their own research and learn more about the persecuted church.

MEMORY VERSE ACTIVITY

Pass out 3 x 5 cards with the name and country of someone who is currently being persecuted for being a follower of Jesus. Have each student write the Memory Verse on the back of the card. Invite them to discuss what it means to be persecuted. (The obvious question, if they are not being persecuted, is. . .are they really living a godly life?) Allow your students to lead where this discussion goes.

SONG: "He Will Carry Me" by Mark Schultz, on the album *Songs and Stories*

QUOTABLE   QUOTES :

Christ is a substitute for everything, but nothing is a substitute for Christ.

—Henry Allan Ironside (1876–1951)

Worry does not empty tomorrow of its sorrow; it empties today of its strength.

—Corrie Ten Boom

The Persecuted Church—Midweek

MEMORY VERSE:
"And indeed, all who desire to live godly in Christ Jesus will be persecuted."—2 Timothy 3:12 (NASB)

SCRIPTURE: Matthew 10:16–23

LESSON IN A SENTENCE: We were never promised an easier life through following Jesus.

FOCUS

All tangled up! Have all the guys in your group take off their shoes (I know. . .it may smell a bit, but better than someone getting kicked accidentally with a shoe!) Clear a large area in the center of the room. Tell the guys to link arms and hang on for dear life! The girls get to try to pry them apart. They can pull, tickle, or drag them away from one another.

Ask: How was this like what happens to followers of Jesus? (There is no right or wrong answer, this is just to get them thinking!)

DISCOVERY

Read Matthew 10:16–23.
Ask: Who is speaking?
How are followers of Jesus supposed to behave?
What response will they receive?
How long does this bad treatment last?

LIFE APPLICATION: This seems like a thoroughly depressing perspective on following Jesus. What happened to the life of abundance? To peace and joy? To eternal salvation? Realistically, things do happen to those wonderful aspects of the Christian faith. Being a follower of Christ is not all wrapped in sunshine and flowers. In fact, it is often hard.

Ask: How many of you have ever felt like you have been hated? What was this like?

Did you ever dream that Scripture talks about this as well?

There are things that we can do as people that will just make others mad, and we've all met someone who was simply not a nice person. There are, however, some people who will simply never accept you for who you are as a Christian. You will be ridiculed, laughed at, left out, and misunderstood. You are not alone!!!

There are others around the world much more isolated than you currently trying to live a life faithful to God.

Close with a time to write letters for protection and/or release of those in the persecuted church. (You can find resources on the website for Voice of the Martyrs.)

NOVEMBER 19, 2006

Honoring Your Body

By Christine Kern

MEMORY VERSE:
Or do you not know that your body is the temple of the Holy Spirit who is in you, whom you have from God, and you are not your own? For you were bought at a price; therefore glorify God in your body and in your spirit, which are God's.—1 Corinthians 6:19–20 (NKJV)

SCRIPTURES: Matthew 12:1: Jesus and the disciples pick grain to eat.

John 4:6: Jesus is weary from His journey and rests by the well while His disciples get food.

Matthew 14:12–13: Jesus goes off by Himself after learning of the beheading of John the Baptist.

Matthew 14:14: Jesus has compassion on the crowd and heals their sick.

Matthew 14:15–16: The disciples and Jesus recognize the crowd's need for food (and Jesus feeds them miraculously).

LESSON IN A SENTENCE: Christianity teaches that the body is good and important and worth our care. Care includes not just sexual purity or keeping away from bodily sins, but active care for it.

THE BIG PICTURE (OR WHAT YOU'RE TRYING TO GET ACROSS):
God created and saves the whole person of you, including your body. Honoring God in your body includes not only sexual purity, but also care for the body's health. This includes exercise, sleep, and eating well. When we are tired or run down, it is hard to have any relationships. Of course, there will be things that are out of our control, but there are many others things that are in our control. Looks are discussed more often in this world than health. God wants us to be healthy and honor the bodies He has given.

IN THIS LESSON STUDENTS SHOULD:

- Realize or be reminded that God honors the body, and so we should treat it with respect.
- Identify the culture's attitudes toward the body.
- Identify their family's attitudes toward the body.
- Set a measurable goal of action or attitude toward care of the body.

OPTION 1:

A picture or printout of Michelangelo's painting *Last Judgment—the Resurrection of the Dead* from the Sistine Chapel. You can find this online, or find a copy in an art book at your public library.

OPTION 2:

Paper and pens, and a prize for the winning team (something good for the body, like fruit, not junk food). Since the lesson is about care for the body, choosing a healthy prize will be as memorable as the game itself. Here are some ideas:

STUFF YOU NEED:

- ○ an assortment of exotic fruits from a nicer grocery store, like star fruit or globe grapes or figs
- ○ bottled water drinks with vitamins added, in different flavors
- ○ healthy juice drinks like Naked juice

FOCUS

OPTION 1:

Using Michelangelo's *The Resurrection of the Dead,* have each student pick one of the persons depicted and come up with a zany caption that the person might be saying at the moment they are raised from the grave in the bodily resurrection. This can be silly and fun.

OPTION 2:

Divide the group into two teams. Have each team think of as many contemporary advertising or bumper sticker slogans which portray either a positive or negative view of care of the body. For example, the phrase "I'll sleep when I'm dead" devalues taking care of the body's need for sleep. Give each group three minutes to get as many slogans as they can. As they read their slogans, they should interpret how the slogan views caring for the body. Whichever team comes up with the most slogans wins the prizes. The prizes should also be an important part of the lesson: somehow the prizes should relate to healthy care of the body.

DISCOVERY

Depending on which activity you did, use the following as jumping-off places:

OPTION 1:

If you did the Michelangelo exercise, note that the resurrection of the body demonstrates that God values the body. God saves the whole person, not just the soul. Our current bodies are raised from the dead, and we get a new body at the final judgment.

When God resurrected Jesus, He didn't resurrect just His soul, but the body He lived in. When He is called the "firstfruits" (1 Corinthians 15:23) of the resurrection, that means that just as His body was raised from the dead, ours will be too. (A fun aside: Lauren Winner, in her memoir *Girl Meets God*, ponders whether our resurrection bodies will still have tattoos!)

OPTION 2:

If you get the slogan exercise, transition right into talking about the messages we get about our bodies from our culture. Help students see the link between the pressure to look perfect, and the desire for us to simply use our bodies rather than honoring them.

SCRIPTURE: Have different students read the verses about Jesus' actions that demonstrate that Jesus stopped His ministry to care for His body. Even though ultimately He sacrificed His body, He honored its needs during His life. Have students identify what action of caring for His body each verse illustrates. If you have time, and a group of students that knows the Bible fairly well, ask them for more examples that show Jesus took care of His body. You might also ask how the Creation relates to our respect for the body. (Since God created humans in His image, clearly He valued our creation.) Or the Incarnation. Read Hebrews 2:17 and ask what Jesus would not have understood about our lives if He had been sent to earth as an adult, and never had to live in a body from the beginning.

For a discussion question, ask what are ways that we as Christians overlook God's esteem and care for the body? Even if we don't share all of the world's values about the body, what are ways that we might disrespect the body. Students might name things like eating junk food at youth group events, always focusing fellowship around times for eating, or not respecting the need for those in ministry to take time off and rest.

LIFE APPLICATION: Ask each student to think about how care for the body is treated in his or her family. As they look for ideas, read aloud prompts for them to consider: what is your family's attitude about rest? Getting enough sleep? Setting boundaries with other obligations? What is your family's attitude about eating? About healthy food? About weight? What is your family's attitude about sexual purity? About the use of alcohol?

MAKING IT PERSONAL: Ask each student to make one decision about caring for their body in the next week. It might be a health resolution like giving up soda for a week, or eating a piece of fruit every day for a week. Or it might be a resolution to seek help about an eating disorder. It might be giving up television after a certain time of night if they're not getting enough sleep. Don't make the students say their decisions out loud, although you might give each student a 3 x 5 card to record their decision and take with them.

If you as the leader have time, you might warn students that you'll call them mid-week to see if they are following through with their resolution (but that you won't pry into what it was!). If sensitive issues are raised through this discussion, that might allow students to open up about problems they're struggling with.

Teacher's Note: Some other religions teach that the body traps the soul, as though the soul is pure and good, and physical existence is bad. The Gnostics heretics were convinced that Jesus couldn't really have been a human with a physical body (since they believed matter was evil), so that if Jesus walked on a beach, He wouldn't leave footprints! Some contemporary religions similarly teach that the body is not good.

Honoring Your Body—Midweek

MEMORY VERSE:
For you were bought at a price; therefore glorify God in your body.
—1 Corinthians 6:20 (NKJV)

SCRIPTURES: Hebrews 13:4; Ephesians 5:29–31; Genesis 2:24–25

LESSON IN A SENTENCE: Honoring your God-given sexuality will be reflected in your general care of your body. God invented sex!

THE BIG PICTURE (OR WHAT YOU'RE TRYING TO GET ACROSS):
   It's easy to fall into extremes: either despising the body or obsessing about it. Sometimes we even do both! The goal is for each student to start to identify ways in which they don't care for and value their body, as well as ways in which they may over-emphasize the body for their self-worth.

STUFF YOU NEED:

   ○ A stack of youth magazines, ideally both Christian and secular (Option 1)
   ○ A pair of scissors for each student
   ○ Poster board or piece of paper
   ○ Glue sticks

FOCUS

OPTION 1:
   Have everyone volunteer to tell embarrassing moments from their lives. This should be entertaining and fun. They can choose to tell bigger embarrassing moments and smaller ones.
   Afterwards, make the connection that some of the most embarrassing moments—and that we can feel the most shame about—aren't things that are wrong at all, like when you trip in front of everyone. Sometimes we experience the most powerful shame in our understanding of our bodies, which God made and called good.

OPTION 2:
   Give everyone a magazine and a pair of scissors. Have each student cut out pictures of bodies in magazines. Just the bodies! Glue them up on a poster. What message does each body give? Have each person comment

on the body they cut out. You may have to model how to answer this, so that the group doesn't fall into the very problem that the lesson is trying to address—of valuing only "perfect" bodies, or thinking that all sexuality is somehow ungodly.

DISCOVERY

Have different people read each of the following passages: Hebrews 13:4; Ephesians 5:29–31; Genesis 2:24–25.

For each passage or verse, answer the question, does God approve of sex (within marriage)?

Does God think sex is something to be ashamed of?

If not, what does God seem to think?

LIFE APPLICATION: Many times the way that we respect or mistreat our bodies relates to what we think about our bodies. Eating disorders are often linked to a sense of shame about having a body that is becoming sexualized as it matures. But God made your body and honors your body. Just think: God invented sex!

Ask each student to think of a way in which they might not value their body enough. This could include anything from thinking it's ugly, being promiscuous, abusing substances, not getting exercise. Have them think of their own life, and not answer out loud.

Encourage students who think that their body is "bad" to get help from a trusted therapist or counselor (and don't assume that those with attractive bodies have a positive view of their bodies). Then have everyone read the Memory Verse out loud, in unison.

Give several fill-in-the-blank statements for students to complete in their minds:

What one thing would God like for me to act differently in caring for my body?

What one think would God like for me to think differently about my body?

MAKING IT PERSONAL: Caring for our body and honoring our sexuality go together. Ask each student to imagine that if God calls them to marriage, and it's their wedding day, what kind of gift do they want to give to the love of their life?

EXTRA! EXTRA!: A nice additional reading for this lesson is an excerpt from *The Screwtape Letters*, which is written from the viewpoint of a devil trying to train his nephew to tempt Christians. The devil understands reality better than the Christian, though the devil is evil. The devil explains that all pleasures were invented by God, and only when the devils pervert good pleasures are they bad. Hence gluttony is a perverted pleasure of eating, and sexual promiscuity is a perversion of the pleasure of marital sex.

REFLECTIONS OF A FIRST TIME ADULT VOLUNTEER

By Steffen Nelson
PRESIDENT, OBJECTIVE MEDICAL ASSESSMENTS CORP.;
YOUTH LIFE VOLUNTEER

You'll be great!" she exclaimed, as we finished up our initial meeting. "The kids will love you. Just show up at the church on Monday night and you'll figure out what to do." Armed with those instructions, I arrived as a new urban youth group volunteer and I was suddenly very nervous. In my work life as a business manager I routinely face potentially intimidating challenges, but working with urban youth was something completely new and it was way outside of my comfort zone. I had prayed that God would give me a ministry, however, and urban youth work was where He was leading. Heading into the church, I prayed for confidence, grabbed a plate of food and headed over to a table of high school boys. "What's up?" I nodded as I sat down. "I'm Steffen." The boys nodded back, took one more bite, stood up and walked away. Alone at the table, I remembered for a moment what it felt like to actually be a high school kid walking through the lunch room with a plate of food, desperately hoping to spot a friend in the crowd. I had no idea what to expect or what to do next.

As a casual observer of youth ministry prior to taking the plunge myself, I always admired the boisterous, energetic interaction between youth leaders and kids. I tend to get along easily with a broad range of people and I assumed my own interaction with kids would look pretty much like the youth ministers and volunteers I had observed from afar. After a month or more of consistent participation, however, the kids still barely acknowledged my presence at our meetings. Despite my barrage of open-ended conversation-starting questions, I could not get more than two words out of anyone! I soon entered a period of serious self-doubt. "These kids won't even talk to me," I thought. "What do I really have to offer?" Based primarily on the conviction that God really did call me to work with these kids, I just kept showing up. Three or four months rolled by until one week one of our boys got in a fight, told off another leader, and stormed out of the meeting. I followed him outside and found him sitting, fuming in the car. I let myself in and sat with him in silence for a very long 10 or 15 minutes. Eventually I simply asked him what was going on and to my surprise he decided to open up with me. Four months of my own self-doubt suddenly seemed so insignificant. I was there at the right time and had a chance to be a voice in his life, trying to reflect Christ's love. This was the youth ministry experience I had envisioned, but I had no idea it would take so long.

Prior to this, my youth ministry resume included being a student in my high school youth group and a week at Young Life camp nearly twenty years ago. I can certainly recall some of the pains and joys of my own adolescence, but when I walked into a room full of high school kids I was suddenly struck by the realization that I had completely forgotten what high school kids do with themselves. What types of things could I do with them? What the heck is "youth culture" all about these days anyway? I needed some training!

As an adult with a busy work, church, and volunteer schedule, I often find that my time with friends is very deliberate and planned. "Movie, Friday, 7:00?" "Dinner, Wednesday, 6:30?" We meet *somewhere* to do *something*. Monday morning workplace conversations always seem to revolve around the question "what did you do this weekend?" When I asked this same question of the kids, however, the response was typically a shrugged "I don't know. Just kicked it with some of my boys I guess." "But did you *do* anything fun?" I would ask. Another shrug. I had forgotten that high school kids spend a tremendous amount of time simply hanging out with their friends. While I was trying to plan specific times or events with kids, tremendous amounts of time that could have been spent just hanging out and developing relationships was passing us by. Over time, I came to understand that I really didn't need to worry about finding the perfect thing to do with kids. Any time is better than no time and this realization set the stage for some of my best interactions.

One Saturday I had made plans to spend time with one of my guys, but that day was also my only chance to make a much needed trip to the city dump. Why not combine these events? I picked up my guy with a full trailer of junk in tow and announced, "Today we're going to the dump." "That's cool," he said and we headed off for what turned out to be a great day of hanging out together. On our way home his cell phone rang. "Nothing," I heard him say. "Just kickin' it with my youth leader, Steffen." "Yep," I thought and smiled, "Just kickin' it at the dump."

In addition to finding myself unsure how to interact and engage with kids, a second major frustration of my first year as an adult volunteer was that I did not really understand the big picture mission and vision of the ministry with which I was working. I knew the goal was ultimately to reach kids for Christ, but I just didn't quite grasp how the games and meetings and messages all fit together. I was doing my best to establish meaningful relationships, but our often-stated objective of "just lovin' on kids" seemed so nebulous. Weekly leader meetings were entirely focused on planning for the upcoming week—brainstorming games and mixers, choosing the right music, and praying for kids. Our senior leader gave a talk each week, but I wasn't seeing how each week was building on the previous week's message. What made this ministry unique? What was the point? How was it different from other youth groups or other para-church ministries targeted at high school kids? Beyond a call to share Christ with kids, I lacked the framework in which to direct my activities.

The real moment of clarity for me finally came after my first time at camp. The week was truly amazing! I saw that all the talks throughout the year were building and reinforcing the message that was delivered at camp. The time we had spent developing relationships with kids throughout the year gave us an opportunity to have honest and meaningful conversations and to truly come alongside as they wrestled with the truth of the gospel. The crazy games we played each week were designed to let kids have fun, but also to push them outside of their comfort zone; to let them take a risk and succeed. Having taken many small risks, they were better prepared to take the risk of accepting Christ. It all made sense and I was tremendously excited about starting the next year with the whole goal in mind.

Now comfortably into my second year as a leader, I must confess I have not always been the ideal volunteer. I'm busy, my schedule is difficult to work around and I'm not always completely reliable. Unfortunately, that also makes me pretty typical. I need to plan my schedule several months in advance to ensure I don't end up with a conflict. Particularly when it comes to something like planning a week away at camp, having my whole year scheduled out ahead of time is tremendously helpful for coordinating vacation schedules at work. I also like to receive communication about schedules and events in writing, even if I've also had a phone conversation or a live brainstorming session about an event. The chances of my showing up on time and thoughtfully prepared are greatly enhanced by one or two e-mails in the months and weeks leading up to something. For me, seeing a youth ministry item on my calendar also triggers me to think about the details of the event. If I have to say something, what will it be? If I have to bring something, what will I bring?

Ultimately, what I value the most from the professional youth ministry staff with whom I work, are the words of encouragement and guidance. Although I may be ten years older and an accomplished professional in my work life, I'm still just a beginner in the world of youth ministry and sometimes all I really need is a pat on the back. When I was at my lowest points, I was really sustained by timely comments letting me know that we are all in this together, that I was doing the right things, and that ultimately it's all up to the Lord anyway. We are simply vessels through which He may choose to work. "You're doing great!" she said, "Just keep doing what you are doing. The kids love you!"

NOVEMBER 26, 2006

Loneliness

By Christine Kern

MEMORY VERSE:
Now faith is the substance of things hoped for, the evidence of things not seen.—Hebrews 11:1 (NKJV)

SCRIPTURE: Psalm 13 (especially vv. 1, 5)

LESSON IN A SENTENCE: Having *faith* in Jesus for your eternal salvation is sometimes easier than having faith that He will see you through a crisis of loneliness. Trust God for what most concerns you, even when you have to go through the middle of pain alone.

THE BIG PICTURE (OR WHAT YOU'RE TRYING TO GET ACROSS):

God cares when we suffer from loneliness, and we should take our loneliness to Him even when we don't experience immediate relief when we do turn to Him. Faith in God involves more than just trusting Him for our future salvation; faith includes trusting Him for sometimes the most difficult things, like hope for a way out of loneliness.

Loneliness can hurt more if you're also judging yourself for suffering it. Remember all the biblical models of those who suffered the pain of feeling separated from everyone—from the writers of the Psalms, to Job, to Jesus Himself. God didn't immediately stop their experience of separation and loneliness. When it says that Jesus experienced every hardship we have (Hebrews 4:15), we know that included loneliness, so experiencing the pain of loneliness and not experiencing an immediate answer from God doesn't mean you're a bad Christian.

Deciding what to do about loneliness is difficult. The first part is easy: cry for help to God. For the times where God doesn't send immediate relief, the hard part is figuring out what do next. Participate in God's help by reaching for good help. But don't "medicate" your loneliness yourself, acting as though the current struggle will last forever, so that you give yourself permission to *use* comforts to insulate yourself from pain.

IN THIS LESSON STUDENTS SHOULD:

- ○ Apply their faith in God to whatever they're currently experiencing or worrying about.
- ○ Let go of false assumptions that a good Christian won't suffer loneliness. Jesus did.
- ○ Practice their trust in God.

STUFF YOU NEED:

○ Paper and pens, or 3 x 5 cards
○ A divider, like a sheet or a room divider.

FOCUS

OPTION 1:

Acting option: Give some students verses from Psalm 13 for them to read as passionately as possible. Have four students stand on the other side of some sort of barrier (like a hanging sheet, or a moveable divider) to act out possible emotions in God's response. Make sure that the rest of the students can see both sides, but the supplicants cannot see the representations of God's emotion. For the students acting out God's emotional response, give them 3 x 5 cards telling them which option to act out—caring but waiting, judging and mean, indifferent and unfazed, or busy with more important things.

Have the students in the "audience" first try to name what different emotional responses of God are being acted out. Then have a discussion about which emotional response is most scriptural, and which ones they've imagined God's response to be. This can allow them to share (or at least think about) the common fear that He doesn't seem to care about their current concerns.

OPTION 2:

Drawing option: Give each student a sheet of paper and ask them to draw a situation where the only way out is through it. You may need to help them brainstorm. . .things like getting through school, getting a driver's license, your first heartache, etc. Let them be as silly or serious as they need to be. The point is that some things just don't disappear, you have to go through them to get to the other side.

DISCOVERY

If you didn't read Psalm 13 for the activity, read it now, out loud, together. (Even if you did, you might want to read it together anyway.)

Ask everyone to think of a time when they felt completely lonely. Ask if they remembered to turn those feelings and that experience over to God, and if they did, what it felt like if there was no immediate answer. Share a story from your life when you felt lonely—either lonely in general, or especially lonely and feeling cut off from a connection with God.

Describe the problem of deep loneliness, how the deeper into loneliness you get, the harder it seems to reach out effectively to other people. You reach out too hard, like a drowning person, and scare people away. The worst part of loneliness is the perspective on time. When you're in the depths of loneliness, there's some part of you that is completely convinced that this feeling will never, ever go away. (Or that if it will, it will only go away after it's far too late to help you.) Ask if anyone has ever been in a situation that they thought would never end, but actually did.

Have someone read Hebrews 11:1. Talk about how we normally think we have such a strong faith in God for our salvation, but we have a harder time trusting Him for the pain we're currently experiencing. Most of us can more easily believe that God took a dead, spoiling body and made it alive, than we can believe that He can or will touch our loneliness. But faith is not only about heaven or hell. Faith in Christ is a relationship that starts from the moment you accept it. So trusting God with your current struggles is part of your faith.

Here's the hard part: once you do turn your loneliness over to God in prayer, there's no guarantee that God will immediately stop the experience. The Bible is full of references to ongoing suffering in the lives of Christians.

Ask someone to read Romans 8:22–25. Look especially at the word "groans"—this passage talks about the agony of separation from wholeness. Even though this verse may seem less connected to the personal experience of loneliness, it actually places that loneliness in context: we're experiencing the pain of separation. As long as the whole is separated from complete union with God, we'll experience separation in other ways, too. And read vv. 24–25 out loud again: "For we were saved in this hope, but hope that is seen is not hope; for why does one still hope for what he sees? But if we hope for what we do not see, we eagerly wait for it with perseverance." (NKJV)

Point out that Paul is openly teaching that going through the pain of separation is part of the deal with Christianity, and the tough answer given is perseverance: going on through the pain.

LIFE APPLICATION: Explain that when we're actually experiencing emotional pain like loneliness, every one of us is tempted to act like an alcoholic. Really. Inside, we are so convinced that the current pain is going to outlast what we can stand. We don't believe 1 Corinthians 10:13a, which says that we won't be subjected to more than we can stand. So what do we do? We self-medicate. It's pretty obvious when people deal with stress and insecurity with lots of alcohol. People who are intimidated by connecting with strangers at parties sometimes treat that insecurity with drunkenness. But we can abuse other "substances" for the same spiritual purpose without even realizing it. Sure, there's a place for the occasional consolation of Ben and Jerry's, but food itself can be an emotional crutch to drown emotional pain. Or hyperactivity in sports, or studying, or even church involvement. Or indulging in negative thinking, as though getting deeper into emotional pain would help somehow—allowing yourself self-pity and picturing things even worse. The word alcoholics and drug addicts have is "using," and we can "use" anything if we want to be in charge of our own pain, instead of facing it.

Instead of "using," Christians are called to relating. Relying on God in faith, holding onto a person instead of using substances or relationships or emotions.

Go around the group and have students name something that people their age can use to try to shortcut around pain. Encourage them not just to name things that "the world" uses, like drugs, but more subtle ways that even Christians *use*, rather than trusting God.

MAKING IT PERSONAL: In a moment of quietness (maybe with everyone with their eyes closed) have each person think of one thing that they use to try to "shortcut" through emotional pain in their lives. Ask them to pray silently for help in trusting God when they don't yet feel this answer.

EXTRA! EXTRA!: In the Harrison Ford version of the movie *Sabrina*, there's a short scene where the lonely heroine, who has gone off to Paris, is given advice by an older woman who tells her to learn how to accept her current loneliness. That scene was very comforting to me when I saw it during an excruciatingly lonely time of my life. You might show this short clip to students during the middle of the lesson.

Loneliness—Midweek

MEMORY VERSE:
No temptation has overtaken you except such as is common to man; but God is faithful, who will not allow you to be tempted beyond what you are able, but with the temptation will also make the way of escape, that you may be able to bear it.—Corinthians 10:13 (NKJV)

SCRIPTURE: Psalm 22:1b–5, 22–24; Matthew 27:46; 2 Peter 1:5–7; Romans 8:25

LESSON IN A SENTENCE: Loneliness will come, and persevering in times when we feel isolated will build our faith, even if we don't feel it immediately. Watch out for temptations while you feel lonely. Cry out to God by reading the Psalms aloud.

THE BIG PICTURE (OR WHAT YOU'RE TRYING TO GET ACROSS):
    This lesson has two main points: (1) Express your feeling of emotional abandonment to God Himself, as the Psalmists did, and as Jesus did. (2) Persevere. Even by praying your complaints to God, you are staying connected to Him even while you don't feel it.
    Loneliness is twice as hard if you aren't expecting it. Read the Psalms as a prayer to God whenever you're feeling bad—connecting in that way with others who have felt abandoned and yet had faith in God, will strengthen your faith. It also puts your current crisis in perspective with God's past faithfulness.
    The trick in loneliness is that your emotions don't seem to correspond with your beliefs or your understanding. The experience of the current moment of time seems to cancel out any hope for the future. But do what Jesus and the Psalmists did: cry to God.

IN THIS LESSON STUDENTS SHOULD:

○ Recognize (again) that the Christian life can and does include loneliness.
○ Learn to turn to God during their loneliness, even without immediate relief.

STUFF YOU NEED:

○ For the less-active option, printouts of optical illusion games

◑ Handouts of the three questions in the Discovery section, if you don't have a board to write on
◑ Letter-writing paper and simple envelopes for the Making It Personal lesson.

FOCUS

For an active group: Play sardines, where one person starts out hiding, and everyone else in the group must try to find the person who's "it." When each person finds the person who is "it," they join that person in the hiding place. Eventually everyone is in a huge group, and only one person is left searching for the whole large group.

LIFE APPLICATION: Talk about what it feels like to be alone, and how it feels when everyone else is with other people while you're alone.

For a less-active group: Optical illusion games. Find optical illusion games on the web at sites such as www.eyetricks.com. Print these and hand them out. They're fun and memorable.

Be sure to make the point afterwards that our perception of our experience isn't always accurate, though we certainly feel it is. (Don't, however, make it seem like it's stupid to feel what we're experiencing. Remember that Jesus wept at Lazarus' death, even though He was about to resurrect him from the dead! Also, Jesus cried out from the Cross, asking why God abandoned Him, so clearly, it can't be wrong to *feel* abandoned.)

DISCOVERY

Write these three questions on a board or on handouts:

Does God let us feel lonely and abandoned at times?

Should we feel guilty or like our faith isn't real if we feel completely alone and abandoned by God?

Are we really abandoned and alone when we feel abandoned and alone?

Divide up the students into small groups, have them read the Scripture passages from Psalm 22 and Matthew 27:46 and answer each of the three questions using the verses. Hopefully, they will realize that feeling separated from God is part of a life of faith. Since the kingdom of God is already here but not fully realized on earth, we have the Holy

Spirit and yet "groan with all creation" (see previous lesson) while we wait for God to make everything right.

LIFE APPLICATION: What does it mean to persevere? Ask students to give physical examples of perseverance—whether from sports, or travel, or scholarship, etc. Then ask students how perseverance applies to internal things.

Have students read aloud 1 Peter 1:5–7 and Romans 8:25. Ask students to connect the call to perseverance to the feeling of loneliness in the Discovery section. In the next section, they will take some of these ideas, and write them in a letter to themselves, to use during a lonely time of their life.

Remind students also that reaching out to the body of Christ is necessary! If students are facing more than just loneliness, and are experiencing depression or suicidal thoughts, they need to get professional help right away. You might have every student write down the phone number of a suicide prevention phone number in their Bible so that they have it in case someone needs it someday.

MAKING IT PERSONAL: Write a letter to yourself to save for a lonely time. Start with "Dear me,"

Then include whatever point most stuck out to you from this lesson. Don't be fake! Be sure to include a Bible verse from the lesson. Label the outside of the envelope: *Open when lonely!*

Stick your letter in your Bible, or, when you get home, put it wherever you'll find it when you're having a lonely time (in your CD collection?). You might end the evening on a storytelling note by letting students tell where they would need their letter to be.

EXTRA! EXTRA!: Consider reading aloud a portion of John Bunyan's *The Pilgrim's Progress,* which is an allegory of the Christian life as "Pilgrim's" journey. Especially look at the chapter on the "Slough of Despond"(you'll have to explain that a slough is like a bog you get stuck in). You might make the application that it's easier for us to picture moving on physically, than when the problem seems so internal— but that's why Bunyan wrote the book!

Advent: Hope

By Amy Jacober

MEMORY VERSE:
The Light shines in the darkness, and the darkness has not overpowered it.—John 1:5 (NCV)

SCRIPTURE: Romans 4:13–21

LESSON IN A SENTENCE: Hope is a choice to eagerly anticipate what we do not see.

THE BIG PICTURE (OR WHAT YOU'RE TRYING TO GET ACROSS):
Hope is a difficult subject at this time in history. On one hand, we have more than we have ever had. We are not in a feudal system, most of us have food and clothes, opportunities seem to abound. Yet we find that we are often without hope. Teenagers in particular have more opportunities than at any other point in our history. So many, in fact, that they can drown in the sea of choices. It is hard to hold to hope when you are struggling just to survive. For some students, it seems like life is just stacked against them. From divorce to a death in the family, illness and poverty. . .they see the choices all around them and they seem out of reach. Hope enters in to extend a lifeline. It offers peace and rest, it offers respite from daily struggles. When the hope is from God it offers not only a temporary break, but the assurance of His blessing in the end.

IN THIS LESSON STUDENTS SHOULD:

- Realize they are not the only ones to struggle.
- Find encouragement from the life of Abraham .
- Learn that hope can be a choice.

STUFF YOU NEED:

- Green paper
- Scissors
- Markers
- Tape
- An Advent wreath (with candles)
- Matches
- Precut holly leaves, one per student (for Discovery and Memory Verse)

FOCUS

OPTION 1: Hanging of the Green

This is the official beginning of the Christmas season! As each student arrives direct them to a table with green paper, scissors, markers, and any other decorative items you may have around the church. Ask each to make some manner of Christmas decoration—a holly leaf, a green chain, pine branch. Encourage them to be creative as they work individually or in teams. As they are working on the decorations, explain that tradition has us hang green during the Christmas season to remind us of the evergreens God has placed in the world. Those evergreens are a symbol of the everlasting life offered through Jesus Christ. It is only fitting that as we celebrate His birth, we remind ourselves of the blessing He brings!

OPTION 2: Advent Wreath

Today is the first Sunday of Advent. Advent means 'coming' or 'arrival.' Each week we will be focusing on the arrival of Jesus as we await and celebrate His birth! The wreath is evergreen to remind us of the everlasting life God offers. It is in a circle to remind us of the eternal nature of His love; there is no beginning and no end. The first candle is purple to remind us of Jesus as king, purple is the color of royalty.

This first Sunday is the Sunday of *hope*. The prophets hoped for a Savior. We hope for what the Lord is doing in the world today as well as for His Second Coming. Have one of your students read Isaiah 9:2, 6–7. Isaiah was a prophet full of hope. Light the first candle on your wreath and allow it to burn during the remainder of the lesson. Pray, thanking God that what had been promised, what had been prophesied, indeed came to fulfillment.

DISCOVERY

Break into groups of four. Give each group the following list of questions.

What is the difference between being through the law and through righteousness that comes by faith?

Why was it so unlikely that Abraham and Sarah would become parents?

How did Abraham handle what God had promised?

Read through Romans 4:13–21 with the above questions in mind.

After you have read and discussed the questions, give each group a few moments to state v. 21 in their own words.

Teacher's Note: Read over Genesis 18 for a reminder of the story of Abraham and Sarah as they become pregnant in old age and give birth to Isaac. They believed in God's promise. Through years of heartache, they held on to hope, sometimes well and sometimes they struggled, but hope was present.

LIFE APPLICATION: *Ask the entire group:*

1. Should you rely on your own skills and strength to accomplish things?

How do you explain when you have done everything right and something still does not work?

How do you handle it when you have done everything right and it still does not work out as you wished?

What can you learn from Abraham when it comes to facing what seem to be impossible situations?

Abraham was indeed a man of faith. He believed that God would fulfill what had been promised. Because he believed, in the end, he was able to live through the hard times, eagerly expecting a good ending. Verse 21 says that he was able to perform, he was able to go on, because he was so sure of what had been promised. The struggle was that Abraham was old and getting older. It seemed not only like he had been hoping for a long time, but that even by all logic he and Sarah should have been biologically prohibited from being able to have children. And yet he chose to believe, he chose to hope.

Why is it so hard to hold to hope today?

Abraham waited until he was an old man to see the fulfillment of a promise in which he believed.

How long do you think is reasonable to hold on to hope?

When do you need to give up and move on?

How is this impacted by the place in which you place your hope? The place from which the promise has come?

Teacher's Note: You know your group best! This can be a fairly simple discussion that looks at Abraham and his amazing hope as we relate it to the hope for the birth of Jesus. This can also be a deeply personal conversation where you look at Abraham clinging to hope beyond what was reasonable, through heartache and hurt, knowing that God had promised to make him the father of nations. Many of us think promises come from God—promises for good parents, for a happy home, for dreams fulfilled. While God does want for us to have an abundant life, He wants us to see the blessings in our midst instead of always longing for what we don't have. He has made a clear promise to His children, that we will one day be with Him. This is a far cry from those who follow the letter of the law and gain material wealth or seem to have life together.

Christmas is full of happiness and celebration, it can also be full of heartache, as what we don't have is magnified. If your group is struggling with what they do not have, remind them they have the promise of God, the promise that He stepped out of heaven to come as the infant Jesus, in order that they may be saved. Life here on earth is hard, we have mansions waiting for us in heaven. When all else fails here and now, we can hope in this.

MAKING IT PERSONAL: Have each person choose one place where they struggle with having hope.

Remind them that they do have a promise from God that there is a better time and place to come.

Pass out a precut holly leaf. Have each student write the Memory Verse on this leaf.

When we get caught up in the darkness, when we fail to have hope or lose hope, we forget the light. The great thing about light is that it pierces the darkness. You will never find a "darklight". . .something that shines a beam of darkness in a light place (as opposed to a flashlight). Even the tiniest spark, even the most dimly lit wick, will light up a darkened room. Jesus is the light to shine in the dark corners of their hearts. Hope is what we can choose in response to this light.

SONG: "Someday" by The Katinas, on the CD *Roots and Christmas EP*

QUOTABLE   QUOTES :

There has been only one Christmas—the rest are anniversaries.

—W. J. Cameron

December 6, 2006

Hope—Midweek

MEMORY VERSE:
The Light shines in the darkness, and the darkness has not overpowered it.—John 1:5 (NCV)

SCRIPTURE: Romans 8:18–25

LESSON IN A SENTENCE: Hope is a choice to eagerly anticipate what we do not see.

FOCUS

Concentration

Set up several games of concentration around the room. There are many ways to go about this—some elaborate, some simple. Let your personality dictate how you want to do this. The most simple, take a deck of cards and spread them out upside down. Play in groups of 4–5. Have each student take a turn where they turn two cards over. If they match, he gets to keep the match (number and color). For example, if he turns over a 3 of hearts and a 3 of diamonds (3 and red), it is a match. If however he turns over a 3 of hearts and a 3 of clubs, it is not a match (3's but one red and one black). When it is not a match, have your student turn the cards back face down and the play moves to the next person. Keep playing until all of the matches have been made. Keep track of the one who has the most matches and offer a prize! (If you have the budget, make the prize something they really want—something they will hope to win. Examples would be a gift certificate to a local coffee shop, a CD, or movie tickets.

If you want to make this more seasonal, play the same game but create your own cards. These can be simple stick figure type drawings or elaborate ones. Be creative and have fun! Make two of each of the following (feel free to replace or add to the list):

Star
Candle
Manger
Gold
Frankincense
Myrrh
Wreath

Holly
Tree
Wise Men
Crown
Angel
Inn

Ask: Was the game difficult or easy? (Typically they will say difficult at first but as cards were eliminated, it became easier.)

For many of us, we go through situations and it seems impossible. Matching 52 cards face down may have seemed impossible at first. With a little experience, from paying attention to both your moves and the moves of others around you, each person learns. With each experience, hope can increase, knowing that there is a prize in the end.

DISCOVERY

In partners have your students read Romans 8:18–25.

What is this passage saying?

What do you like about this passage? What do you not like or not believe?

What themes do you see that arise?

Two themes are clearly evident in this passage. The first is that of suffering and struggles, the second is that of hope. The two just seem to go hand in hand.

For many of your students (and many of us adults for that matter!) we long for the glory at the end but do not want to go through the struggle. We question why God allows our hearts to hurt so much, and forget to see what He has revealed. The idea of hope will be very difficult for some of your students. Especially as it relates to them considering their present sufferings as worthy. You may need to help them see the connection and to realize that while suffering is a part of life in a fallen world, even in that God provides comfort.

LIFE APPLICATION: Still in partners, make a list of every place where you think teenagers struggle today. Compile the entire list on a dry erase board up front as each set of partners share.

We all struggle in different places. Look over this list. Praise God we do not all struggle with all of these, but many of us struggle with several! If you focus on that, life can just be overwhelming!

What struggles can you think of from your past that have been resolved?

Did any of you want a later bedtime? A certain outfit? Thought you would never stop fighting with your brother or sister? Did you pay any attention to when that stopped being a struggle?

Think back about things you have been through—with every struggle it can indeed feel like your world is falling apart in that moment. God, however, does not call us to be so caught up in the present time. (This is not to say you shouldn't stop and smell the roses once in awhile, rather that both the good and the bad only last for a season and then we move to something new.) Just when you think you can't take any more, you can. Life changes, it gets better and worse, but never stays the same for long. Glory is awaiting us all!

Look at the list on the dry erase board. Ask each person to mentally choose one.

What do you hope for? What keeps you from living a life of hope?

Ask if anyone can recall the Memory Verse. . .Light does pierce the darkness. Pray, asking God to pierce the darkness that hopelessness can bring and to reveal the glory which we eagerly await!

DECEMBER 10, 2006

Advent: Peace

By Amy Jacober

MEMORY VERSE:
The Lord is my light and the one who saves me. I fear no one. The Lord protects my life; I am afraid of no one.—Psalm 27:1 (NCV)

SCRIPTURE: Isaiah 9:6; Philippians 4:4–9

LESSON IN A SENTENCE: Jesus brings peace to the world.

THE BIG PICTURE (OR WHAT YOU'RE TRYING TO GET ACROSS):
Jesus is the Prince of Peace. He is the Prince of Peace for all the world and for each person in the world. We have much to be thankful for and much to eagerly expect. As you consider this second Sunday of Advent, consider the idea of peace. Each student experiences some level of turmoil in their everyday life. God is concerned, and seeks to be the peace we each need in this chaotic world. At the same time, Jesus is the peace of the world. He is equally as concerned for individuals as He is for the community. It is His desire that the world dwells in peace. As you look to the birth of Christ, focus today on Jesus' role as the Prince of Peace. Encourage your students to take comfort in the peace offered to them. Encourage them also to participate in the peace God desires for the world.

IN THIS LESSON STUDENTS SHOULD:

- Identify Jesus Christ as the Prince of Peace.
- Think about the meaning of peace.
- Find comfort in the peace God provides for them.
- Consider their role with God in the process of peace in this world.

STUFF YOU NEED:

- Advent wreath and candles (Option 1)
- Matches (Option 1)
- Headlines from the paper that week or check the *Washington Post* online for news from around the world (Option 1)
- Puzzle of the world (Option 2)
- Map of the world

FOCUS

OPTION 1: Advent Wreath

Today is the second Sunday of Advent. Before you begin, hand a few headlines from struggles around the world to your students. (The Focus this week is peace. Our world is full of turmoil. Choose a few headlines of places that need peace today.) Light the candle of hope. Last Sunday hope was the Focus. The hope that only the Savior of the world could bring. Hope for what we cannot yet see. Hope brings with it the ability to let go of anxiety and worry. Hope brings peace. This Sunday the Focus is peace. Have one of your students read Micah 4:3–5. Ask the students with the headlines to read those headlines out loud. Pray for God to bring peace to this struggling and war-torn world.

OPTION 2: Pieces of the world

Buy a puzzle—if possible, find one that shows a picture of the world, a map, or a globe. Depending on the size of your group, give each student at least one piece of the puzzle. If your group is large, buy more than one puzzle. If you use more than one, be certain to distinguish the puzzles by placing a purple dot on the pieces of one, and red dots on the pieces of the other, and so on. Have a large area to work on the puzzles. Encourage each student to participate.

Ask: What was necessary for the puzzles to be completed?

(Answers will range from someone actually putting it together, to each person giving their piece.) Each of us will participate in life and community in different ways. Some will take a very active role, others will observe and offer only when necessary. Regardless of the role to which you feel called, we are all to participate. All of us must participate or the puzzle could not have been made. God calls all of His children to participate in bringing peace to the world. Even if it is just a little bit, everything put together makes a big difference. As Jesus brings peace to the world, we can participate in this peace with each way we join in this work.

DISCOVERY

You will want to recruit two readers before this time begins. Choose two people who can read loudly and are not shy about breaking into the discussion of a group and grabbing their attention. If you do not have any students able to do this, it is fine to have a leader.

Have someone read Isaiah 9:6 as you end your Focus activity. Don't announce that 'now is the time to read Scripture,' rather, have the person read it as a declaration. Have them read this loudly so as to interrupt and draw everyone's attention to the same place. Tell them this passage can be found in Isaiah 9:6 if they want to look at it for themselves.

Ask: What do you think it means to be the Prince of Peace? How do we see this being lived out in the world today? How have followers of Jesus denied this in the past or the present?

End the time of question and answer with another declarative reading. (Think of the angels coming before the shepherds to declare the birth of Christ!) This time have someone stand up and read Philippians 4:4–9. You may also consider having two readers, one on either side of the room, alternating verses as they read.

Ask: What did you just hear? (Give your students space to simply state what they picked up on in the initial declaration.)

Did any of you hear a specific message for you today?

Turn in your Bibles and read Philippians 4:4–9 again.

Ask: What is this passage saying? Do you think it is possible to know the peace of God so much that you no longer worry? That you are no longer anxious and your mind is able to dwell only on those things that are honorable, pure, and excellent? How can we possibly ever do such a thing? What would this look like?

LIFE APPLICATION: Our world contains so many beautiful wonderful reflections of God! It also contains many distortions and fragments of what was to be.

Ask: In such a broken world, in a world torn by conflict, how can we find God's peace? What, if any, is our role with joining God in bringing about peace on this earth? Verse 4 says that we are to rejoice always— how can we rejoice when there are children dying in the world? How can we rejoice when we are fighting with our closest friends, or a parent has lost her job? What on earth was God thinking, asking us to rejoice always?

Most of the world is not as well off as even the poorest in the U.S.. We are blessed beyond what most of us realize. There are those around the world who rejoice in spite of their circumstances, not because of them. There are also those who are so badly off that rejoicing seems impossible. As we look to the hope, let the promise of Christ be the hope that produces peace in us and through us. There are many places all throughout the world where anxiety is the norm. Verse 6 tells us to make these known to God in prayer. Verse 7 tells of the peace God wants to give.

Look at the map on the wall.

Ask for suggestions of places where you know conflict is occurring presently. (You may want to do a little research on this before coming to the group this day.)

Regardless of how you personally understand peace, spend a few moments interceding for peace around the world. Place a dot or push-pin in each location for which you will be praying specifically. If any of your students have family members in the military, be certain to include those locations on your map.

MAKING IT PERSONAL: You've spent a few moments praying for others around the world. At times, it is actually easier to focus on the big picture of peace, as it is removed from our immediate circumstances.

Reread Philippians 4:4–9. Ask each person to name one thing for which they are anxious. (We all have them!! This is actually a pretty tough question. Encourage your students to be as honest as possible, but do not chastise them if they offer silly examples—they will still hear what you have to say. Pray that the Holy Spirit is at work in their hearts, even if their maturity hides the fact.)

Just like we prayed for the anxieties of the world, asking God to let His peace cover all, we, too, can pray about our own anxieties. God wants us to be at peace. He wants us to truly let go, to not just say the words, but to replace anxious worries in our hearts and mind with things that are pure and good. Think of the one thing that you named that makes you anxious. Pray, asking for God to give peace to you surrounding this one thing. Remind your students that prayer is not a magic trick. They can pray and still choose to dwell on the anxiety-provoking things. They can also choose to follow God's advice and seek to fill their minds with things that are true and lovely.

MEMORY VERSE ACTIVITY

Go over the Memory Verse, Psalm 27:1. Give each person a piece of the puzzle. Have each person write the passage address on the back of the puzzle piece as a reminder to look it up when they get home.

SONG: "Do You Hear What I Hear?" by Out of Eden, on *City on a Hill; It's Christmas Time*

Q U O T A B L E   Q U O T E :

May Peace be your gift at Christmas and your blessing all year through!

—Author Unknown

Peace—Midweek

MEMORY VERSE:
The Lord is my light and the one who saves me. I fear no one. The Lord protects my life; I am afraid of no one.—Psalm 27:1 (NCV)

SCRIPTURE: John 14:25–27

LESSON IN A SENTENCE: Jesus brings peace to the world.

FOCUS

Cover your room with small signs that read Merry Christmas in a variety of languages. (See list below.) The more the better! This should be very obvious so don't skimp. You will refer to this later in the lesson.

Afrikaans: Gesëende Kersfees
Afrikander: Een Plesierige Kerfees
African/ Eritrean/ Tigrinja: Rehus-Beal-Ledeats
Albanian: Gezur Krislinjden
Arabic: Idah Saidan Wa Sanah Jadidah
Argentine: Feliz Navidad
Armenian: Shenoraavor Nor Dari yev Pari Gaghand
Bahasa Malaysia: Selamat Hari Natal
Basque: Zorionak eta Urte Berri On!
Bengali: Shuvo Naba Barsha
Bohemian: Vesele Vanoce
Brazilian: Boas Festas e Feliz Ano Novo
Bulgarian: Tchestita Koleda; Tchestito Rojdestvo Hristovo
Catalan: Bon Nadal i un Bon Any Nou!
Chile: Feliz Navidad
Chinese: (Cantonese) Gun Tso Sun Tan'Gung Haw Sun
Chinese: (Mandarin) Kung His Hsin Nien bing Chu Shen Tan
Choctaw: Yukpa, Nitak Hollo Chito
Columbia: Feliz Navidad y Próspero Año Nuevo
Cornish: Nadelik looan na looan blethen noweth
Crazanian: Rot Yikji Dol La Roo
Cree: Mitho Makosi Kesikansi
Croatian: Sretan Bozic
Czech: Prejeme Vam Vesele Vanoce a stastny Novy Rok
Danish: Glædelig Jul

Dutch: Vrolijk Kerstfeest en een Gelukkig Nieuwjaar!
or Zalig Kerstfeast
Eskimo: (inupik) Jutdlime pivdluarit ukiortame pivdluaritlo!
Esperanto: Gajan Kristnaskon
Estonian: Ruumsaid juulup|hi
Farsi: Cristmas-e-shoma mobarak bashad
Finnish: Hyvaa joulua
Flemish: Zalig Kerstfeest en Gelukkig nieuw jaar
French: Joyeux Noel
Frisian: Noflike Krystdagen en in protte Lok en Seine yn it Nije Jier!
Galician: Bo Nada
Gaelic: Nollaig chridheil agus Bliadhna mhath ùr! German:
Froehliche Weihnachten
Greek: Kala Christouyenna!
Hawaiian: Mele Kalikimaka
Hebrew: Mo'adim Lesimkha. Chena tova
Hindi: Shub Naya Baras
Hawaian: Mele Kalikimaka ame Hauoli Makahiki Hou!
Hungarian: Kellemes Karacsonyi unnepeket
Icelandic: Gledileg Jol
Indonesian: Selamat Hari Natal
Iraqi: Idah Saidan Wa Sanah Jadidah
Irish: Nollaig Shona Dhuit, or Nodlaig mhaith chugnat
Iroquois: Ojenyunyat Sungwiyadeson honungradon nagwutut.
Ojenyunyat osrasay.
Italian: Buone Feste Natalizie
Japanese: Shinnen omedeto. Kurisumasu Omedeto
Korean: Sung Tan Chuk Ha
Latin: Natale hilare et Annum Faustum!
Latvian: Prieci'gus Ziemsve'tkus un Laimi'gu Jauno Gadu!
Lithuanian: Linksmu Kaledu
Low Saxon: Heughliche Winachten un 'n moi Nijaar
Macedonian: Sreken Bozhik
Maltese: LL Milied Lt-tajjeb
Manx: Nollick ghennal as blein vie noa
Maori: Meri Kirihimete
Navajo: Merry Keshmish
Norwegian: God Jul, or Gledelig Jul
Papua New Guinea: Bikpela hamamas blong dispela Krismas na
Nupela yia i go long yu
Pennsylvania German: En frehlicher Grischtdaag un en hallich Nei
Yaahr!
Peru: Feliz Navidad y un Venturoso Año Nuevo

Polish: Wesolych Swiat Bozego Narodzenia or Boze Narodzenie
Portuguese:Feliz Natal
Pushto: Christmas Aao Ne-way Kaal Mo Mobarak Sha
Rapa-Nui (Easter Island): Mata-Ki-Te-Rangi. Te-Pito-O-Te-Henua
Rumanian: Sarbatori vesele
Russian: Pozdrevlyayu s prazdnikom Rozhdestva is Novim Godom
Samoan: La Maunia Le Kilisimasi Ma Le Tausaga Fou
Sardinian: Bonu nadale e prosperu annu nou
Serbian: Hristos se rodi
Slovakian: Sretan Bozic or Vesele vianoce
Scots Gaelic: Nollaig chridheil huibh
Serb-Croatian: Sretam Bozic. Vesela Nova Godina
Spanish: Feliz Navidad
Swedish: God Jul and (Och) Ett Gott Nytt År
Tagalog: Maligayang Pasko at Manigong Bagong Taon
Trukeese: (Micronesian) Neekiriisimas annim oo iyer seefe feyiy-eech!
Thai: Sawadee Pee Mai
Turkish: Noeliniz Ve Yeni Yiliniz Kutlu Olsun
Ukrainian: Srozhdestvom Kristovym
Urdu: Naya Saal Mubarak Ho
Vietnamese: Chung Mung Giang Sinh
Welsh: Nadolig Llawen
Yugoslavian: Cestitamo Bozic
Yoruba: E ku odun, e ku iye'dun!

Prepare a list of eleven common Christmas songs ahead of time. Split your group into two teams. Have each team send up a representative to receive the song title. They are to go back to their team and hum the song. The first team to guess the song wins that round. Work through all eleven songs, offering a prize to the winning team at the end.

So humming may not be your typical way of communicating with others, but we all do communicate in ways other than just talking. Non-verbal language, the choices we make, what we offer to the community, all communicate what is important to us.

DISCOVERY

Read John 14:25–27.
   Ask: What do you think Jesus was talking about here?
   What kind of peace do you think the world offers?
   What is the difference in the kind of peace that Jesus offers?

Of all the things Jesus could have mentioned leaving, why do you think He chose to mention peace specifically?

Teacher's Note: Jesus is talking to His disciples here. This is not a random speech nor one intended for a generalized audience. It is specific. He is telling those who are His followers, those who are close to Him, that He will give peace to them.

LIFE APPLICATION: How does peace play out in the world today? Have the group spend some time thinking through their lives—where is peace experienced and where is chaos experienced? (Take this as personally or globally as you believe will be best for your group.)

Look around the room. There is a map of the world, there are signs everywhere that say Merry Christmas in more languages than most of us even knew existed. God came to this world as a baby to bring peace, and when He left, His desire was to leave peace. It may not always feel like it, especially as with each passing day we hear of some new place where the world seems to be falling apart, but God longs to have peace in this world. He longs for His children to know peace. We are invited to join in this process.

Merry Christmas is really a phrase that comes from Merry Christ's Mass, or Celebration of Christ. All over the world, the celebration of the birth of Jesus is happening. It's a good reminder that just as the birth of Christ is celebrated all over the world, so also did Jesus promise His peace for all of His followers all over the world. Close in prayer, thanking God for the community of believers that extends far beyond our borders.

DECEMBER 17, 2006

Advent: Joy

By Amy Jacober

MEMORY VERSE: The angel said to them, "Do not be afraid. I am bringing you good news that will be a great joy to all the people." —Luke 2:10 (NCV)

SCRIPTURE: John 15:1–11

LESSON IN A SENTENCE: Jesus desires that we follow Him, not to limit our lives, but to be full of joy!

THE BIG PICTURE (OR WHAT YOU'RE TRYING TO GET ACROSS):

God stepped out of heaven in order to reconcile Himself to us. The Christian life gets distorted when we are so consumed with the rules that we miss the relationship. It was never God's intent that we beat ourselves up for not being perfect, for there is only One who is perfect. It is not God's intent that we get caught up in legalism or trying to look the perfect part. It was and is His intent that we are in relationship with Him. That we may not feel bound or limited, but that we actually experience freedom! We are free from having to fit in, from having to get caught up in material wealth, from having good grades, or the right clothes, or all of the other things the world tells us are important. We are free to receive what God offers— life, hope, peace, and joy!

IN THIS LESSON STUDENTS SHOULD:

- Discover connections between living as Christ instructs and the joy that follows.
- Be reminded that God loves them.
- Define joy.

STUFF YOU NEED:

- Video (made ahead of time, Option 1)
- Karaoke (borrow this ahead of time, Option 2)
- CD's for the karaoke machine
- Jingle Bells (Memory Verse Activity)
- Ribbon (Memory Verse Activity)

FOCUS

OPTION 1: Advent Wreath

Today is the third Sunday of Advent. Ask someone to lead your group in the Christmas Carol, *Joy to the World.* Do you really believe this? Is the birth of Christ really a joyous occasion for all the world? Do you sometimes forget that you, too, are a part of the world? God wants you to be full of joy and offers this to you! Last Sunday, peace was the Focus. We first looked at hope. Light the first candle for hope. Hope leads to peace. Light the second candle for peace. When we are at peace, we are free to experience joy! Have one of your students read Luke 2:8–11. Offer a popcorn prayer to the Lord of what brings joy to you. This means to invite your students to say out loud in just a word or two, things that bring joy to them. Close, thanking God for so many things that bring joy to us!

OPTION 2:

Enlist some students to help out with this one! Before you meet, head to the local mall or somewhere with a lot of people. (If you go to a mall, let them know what you would like to do and ask permission to be taping!) With the shopping frenzy in full swing, many people get caught up in what will bring joy! Make a tape asking people about joy. Create your own questions or use some of the following:

What does the word joy mean to you?

What brings joy to you?

How do you find joy?

Keep it simple. The end product doesn't need to be any longer than five minutes or so. If you have someone who is really creative with video, go crazy! If not, don't worry, simple camera editing and a hand-ful of responses will be enough. You may want to spend some time at the mall, then ask a few of your students or other members of your church these same questions!

Show the video and let the responses be a springboard for discussion.

OPTION 3: Karaoke

Ahead of time, ask around and see if there is anyone in your church, or a friend, who has a karaoke machine that you can borrow. Be certain you have several karaoke CD's from which to choose. Once you have this in place, there is not a whole lot of setup. Pick a song and get ready to impress one another, or perhaps just get to laugh a whole lot with one another! The great thing about karaoke is that you don't really have to be able to sing to enjoy it. Feel free to set the tone for your students if they are feeling shy. While students are sometimes reticent at first, they often warm up to the idea and then you have a hard time getting them to stop! (Don't forget to send a thank you note to the person from whom you've borrowed the karaoke machine.)

Joy comes in the strangest of places. Most often we associate it with laughter and having a good time. While this is part of it, it's not the whole story. You may not be the best singer in the world, but singing can still be fun! Perfection is not required, living as a child of God is.

DISCOVERY

Break into groups of three. Ask each group to come up with why they think God wants us to keep His commandments. Write these on a dry erase board so that everyone can clearly see them.

Have each group read through John 15:1–11.

What was Jesus saying in this passage?

Verse 8 talks of bearing fruit, what does this mean?

Did you catch the reason behind this whole passage? Why does God want us to keep His commandments?

Teacher's Note: This is a fairly common passage. It will not be unusual if your students have read this several times before in the past. Most often the focus is put on what it means to abide in Christ and to have Christ abide in you. Feel free to talk about this and unpack this passage as you see fit for your group. Try, however, to not have this become the final focus of the day.

LIFE APPLICATION: Most of us do not associate joy with keeping commandments, with following rules. Doing what someone else says is not our first choice. We like to make our own decisions. We live in a society that communicates in many ways that everything is my own choice and my own right.

Ask: Can you think of any commandments that you are glad most people keep today? (Think rules, laws—things like stopping at red lights, or that other people are not supposed to just come in your house and take your things) Why are you glad these rules are followed?

While these laws are helpful, God has His commandments as well. God never says we are to be on our own. He wants us to abide in Him and to have Him abide in us. He wants to have a relationship with us. He wants us to be full of joy!

The passage says that God wants us to keep His commandments so that we will know joy and our joy may be full. This is no passing emotion or short time happiness. It is full joy, all of the time, regardless of what is happening. This is a pretty lofty goal. So much so, that it can seem unrealistic.

Ask: What keeps us from joy? Do you really think this kind of joy is possible in a world that has so many bad things happening?

As a group, come up with a definition of joy.

Teacher's Note: There are many ways to understand joy. Most often it is confused with happiness, the feeling of being happy at the situation or circumstance. Jesus is offering something more than this, but it can be very hard to understand. Joy comes regardless of circumstances. Joy is a constant in a very unstable world. Joy is a contentment that transcends the situation. This is a very hard concept for most students, for most adults as well. Think of families in third world countries where life is filled with poverty, struggles, and disease, and yet they smile and laugh; they are full of joy. Let this be a guide as you seek to define joy with your group.

Ask: What keeps us from experiencing joy?

MAKING IT PERSONAL: We all have crummy days. We all have times when a bad mood or tough circumstances get us down. Joy is not saying that we are to lead a fake, super sweet Christian existence. Joy is experiencing God even when our worlds are falling apart. Joy may come in the form of laughter or great fun with friends. Joy may also be present as life falls in around you, but hope is still recognized, bringing peace, which gives way to joy even in the toughest of circumstances.

Ask: What brings great joy to you? How can you ensure that you have joy instead of being consumed by the roller coaster of events in your life?

MEMORY VERSE ACTIVITY

Read Luke 2:10 as a group. This passage tells of angels declaring good news of great joy for all the people! Have a pile of bells, as in the jingle bells that are at any craft store this time of year, ready to be used. Be certain to have at least two bells per person, if not three or four. Also have ribbon that is wide enough to write on, but narrow enough to thread through the top of the bell. Have each student write Luke 2:10 in the ribbon and tie it to the bell. The passage says that it is good news for all the people! Invite your students to join in sharing the good news with others. They may keep one bell and give away the others.

SERVICE ACTIVITY: Serving others impacts us in many ways. Simply putting someone else first for a change can help us to feel good. Serving others can also make us aware of how much we have. Often, those we are serving may lack resources, but they have a spirit, a hope that many of us are lacking. Arrange a time to serve at a soup kitchen, a shelter, or assisted living home with your students. Be certain to plan for time at the end to discuss what you have just experienced. It may take you pointing out the joy that others, who seem to have so little, actually possess. Encourage your students to consider joy as a state of mind not dependent on the circumstances of their lives. Rather, joy is produced with the realization that God loves them and they are able to accept love.

LOOKING AHEAD: For your mid-week lesson this week throw a party! This doesn't need to be expensive, rather be creative in your decorations and have your students bring a wrapped, white elephant gift! You will need to tell them of this today and perhaps a reminder phone call the day before you meet. If you've never done a white elephant gift exchange, it is simple. Ask each student to bring a gift from home that is recycled. This can be anything—a silly statue, an old book, one of those singing fish—think of things that would most likely end up in the Goodwill pile. They needn't spend any money. The goofier the better! The day of the party, have your students draw numbers. The #1 chooses the first gift from a pile in the center, #2 the next gift and so on. Be certain to bring a few extras yourself, as students always show up who either forgot or did not know.

SONG: "Angels We Have Heard On High" by Chris Rice, on the CD *The Living Room Sessions: Christmas*

QUOTABLE   QUOTE:

The joy of brightening other lives, bearing each other's burdens, easing other's loads and supplanting empty hearts and lives with generous gifts, becomes for us the magic of Christmas.

—W. C. Jones

Joy—Midweek

MEMORY VERSE:
The angel said to them, "Do not be afraid. I am bringing you good news that will be a great joy to all the people."—Luke 2:10 (NCV)

SCRIPTURE: Matthew 2:1–12

LESSON IN A SENTENCE: Jesus desires that we follow Him, not to limit our lives, but to be full of joy!

FOCUS

Make this time a white elephant gift exchange.

Create a scavenger hunt. This can be simple, but the more elaborate the better! You will want to be in at least two teams and possibly several, depending on the size of your group. This can be done with clues around your building, the entire property, the neighborhood, or even by placing people in key locations in a large mall or town square. If you are able, have a person at each station to give the next clue. At that station, they must earn their clue by singing *Jingle Bells,* saying the Memory Verse, building a pyramid, whatever. Be creative!! The object is to really make your students search. In other words, do not make this too easy!

At the end of your scavenger hunt, hand the students an invitation to a party—a party for the birth of Christ! This means that back at the room where you meet, while your students are on the scavenger hunt, you decorate, set out snacks, have a table with party favors—horns to blow, confetti, party music, balloons, etc.

DISCOVERY

Once all of your students have returned, begin the production. Ahead of time, enlist some volunteers to act out Matthew 2:1–12. (This is a great time to pull in adults who do not normally volunteer with the students. While they may not become regular volunteers, it is always a good idea to make connections between your students and others in the church!) Feel free to be creative in costuming and staging—ideally do not just read this, but really ham it up as it is acted out!

Narrator off to the side, magi entering the stage area...

Narrator: Now after Jesus was born in Bethlehem of Judea in the days of Herod the king, behold, magi from the east arrived in Jerusalem saying,

Magi #1:   Where is He who has been born King of the Jews? For we saw His star in the east, and we have come to worship Him.

Herod with a few people representing the chief priests, scribes, and people around him. . .they pantomime what the narrator is saying as the narrator says it. You may want to choose three people. On each, respectively, pin a sign that reads, priest, scribe, and people.

Narrator: And when Herod the king heard it, he was troubled, and all Jerusalem with him. And gathering together all the chief priests and scribes of the people, he began to inquire of them where the Christ was to be born. And they said to him,

Scribe: In Bethlehem of Judea, for so it has been written by the prophet,

Priest: And you land of Bethlehem, land of Judah, are by no means least among the leaders of Judah; for out of you shall come forth a ruler, who will shepherd My people Israel.

Priest, scribe, and people walk away. Magi walk up to Herod.

Narrator: Then Herod secretly called the magi, and ascertained from them the time the star appeared. And he sent them to Bethlehem, and said,

Herod: Go and make careful search for the Child; and when you have found Him, report to me, that I, too, may come and worship Him.

Have Herod move away. Have the magi pretend to walk. . .following the star.

Narrator: And having heard the king, they went their way; and lo, the star, which they had seen in the east, went on before them, until it came and stood over where the Child was. And when they saw the star, they rejoiced exceedingly with great joy.

Magi rejoice. . .shout, dance whatever!

And they came into the house and saw the Child with Mary His mother; and they fell down and worshiped Him;

Have Mary off to one side holding a baby, have the magi approach Jesus and Mary and fall to the ground.

And opening their treasures they presented to Him gifts of gold and frankincense and myrrh.

Have the magi present Jesus with their gifts.

And having been warned by God in a dream not to return to Herod, they departed for their own country by another way.

Have the magi slip away in the opposite direction.

LIFE APPLICATION: Have your magi return for a little Q & A.

Begin the time by telling your students that the magi have agreed to return for an exclusive interview. Create a mock talk show feel. Have questions on 3 x 5 cards prepared. Begin with the following questions. You can improv the answers, but try to get across the main ideas offered below.

What was it like to meet Herod? *While he was powerful, there was just something wrong, something he was lacking.*

Did you ever think you were really going to find the baby Jesus by following a star? *It seemed crazy, but when God offers something to follow, you just have to trust.*

Why did you rejoice so much when you found Jesus? *Are you kidding?! This was the greatest experience of our lives!!! There is nothing more worthy of a celebration than meeting God!*

Were you always planning on offering gifts or was that spontaneous? *We brought the gifts with us intending to give them, but honestly, just being in His presence made us want to give everything we have in response to the love He gives.*

How did you know not to go back to Herod where it was dangerous? *Herod is still powerful. It really would be tempting, but once you experience Jesus, temptations don't disappear, so you have to make choices to not place yourself in a position to be tempted.*

Ask your students if they have any questions for the magi?

Ask: What parallels can you see from the responses of the magi to your own lives?

It's now time for the white elephant exchange! Just like the magi, your response at the birth of Christ is a party! While you are exchanging gifts, remind your students that while we exchange gifts with one another, we respond to the love of Jesus with love in return.

Enjoy the party!!

DECEMBER 24, 2006

Christmas Eve: Love

By Amy Jacober

MEMORY VERSE:
I pray that Christ will live in your hearts by faith and that your life will be strong in love and be built on love. And I pray that you and all God's holy people will have the power to understand the greatness of Christ's love—how wide and how long and how high and how deep that love is. Christ's love is greater than anyone can ever know, but I pray that you will be able to know that love. Then you can be filled with the fullness of God.—Ephesians 3:17–19 (NCV)

God loved the world so much that he gave his one and only Son so that whoever believes in him may not be lost, but have eternal life.—John 3:16 (NCV)

SCRIPTURE: 1 John 3:1–3; 4:7–21

LESSON IN A SENTENCE: When we truly understand and receive the love of God, we in turn can truly love others.

THE BIG PICTURE (OR WHAT YOU'RE TRYING TO GET ACROSS):
Christmas is all about gifts. There is nothing like being around a bunch of children at Christmas. Their eyes light up, they are filled with wonder, and they haven't grown out of being able to openly express that they like to receive presents. A new doll, a new game, a new bike—each of these brings delight for the day. You will often even see children showing their new toys, sharing with others. The problem is that three months later, with rare exception, kids don't even remember what they were given. There is a Christmas gift that is not only amazing the day it is received, but every day, for the rest of our lives, for the rest of eternity. This is the gift of Jesus. He offers love unconditionally. Just as parents like to shower their children with presents, Jesus showers His children with love. This love is in such abundance that we needn't be stingy with it. He wants us to share it with others. In a world that focuses on hoarding and material gain, it is hard to imagine anything that would be encouraged to be given away freely. Love is such a thing. Thanks be to God for His indescribable gift!

IN THIS LESSON STUDENTS SHOULD:

○ Understand that the baby Jesus came as a gift of love.
○ Realize that followers of Jesus are children of the King.
○ Be exposed to the truth that God is love.
○ Consider that God loves them.
○ Make a connection between the privilege of being loved and their response to living as one who is loved.

STUFF YOU NEED:

○ Advent wreath (Option 1)
○ Matches (Option 1)
○ Clear glass ball ornaments (Option 2)
○ Paint pens (Option 2)
○ Tinsel and/or confetti (Option 2)
○ Dry erase board and markers
○ Candy canes

FOCUS :

OPTION 1: Advent Wreath

Today is the final Sunday of Advent. Today is Christmas Eve! This is as close as we get to Advent, to looking forward to the coming of the baby Jesus, to the coming of God incarnate before the day we celebrate His birth. The motivation, the entire reason God stepped out of heaven, can be summed up in one word, love. He loves us. He has always loved us. He loves those who were on earth 2,000 years ago, He loves those of us who are here today and He loves those who will be coming. He loves us so much that He was willing to step out of heaven and walk on this earth. He walked to His death out of love. This love is what offers hope. *Light the first candle for hope.* In the hope that comes from Christ we find peace. *Light the second candle for peace.* Understanding peace that comes only from Jesus, we are able to experience full joy. *Light the third candle for joy.* Have one of your students read John 15:13. Hope, peace and joy are wonderful but they pale in comparison to love. God loves us! Thank Him for loving us long before we loved Him.

OPTION 2: Simple gifts of love

When you experience love, it is natural to want to give love. While each student may not be into the real reason for the season, you can still offer tokens of love to others. Have your student decorate ornaments for others. This is a quick turn around project. Tell them they will decorate an ornament with the express purpose of giving it away before they leave that day. Buy clear glass ball ornaments. (It's the end of the season, you should be able to find these on sale.) Be certain that you have at least one per student. Spread out tinsel, paint pens, confetti, and any other items you think may make for good decorations. Give each student a glass ball. Invite them to decorate their ornament with the paint pens and tinsel. You can gently remove the top of the ornament and stuff tinsel or confetti inside. It won't take long for these ornaments to dry.

Everyone loves a surprise! One of the greatest surprises of all was God coming to earth because He loves us! This is the season when we are reminded that as we experience His love, we in turn can be motivated to give love.

DISCOVERY

Split into two distinct teams. If you have a large group, you may split into smaller groups within the teams.

The first team is going to deal with 1 John 3:1–3.

Have them read the passage and identify the main message of this passage. Next, have them create a sketch that explains the message.

The second team is going to deal with 1 John 4:7–21.

Have them read the passage and identify the main message of this passage. Next, have them create a sketch that explains the message.

Have the first group share their sketch. (Be certain the point of being loved by God so much that we are indeed considered as His children, comes across clearly.)

Have the second group share their sketch. (Be certain that the point is emphasized that along with being loved, comes the privilege and responsibility that we, too, will genuinely love others.)

While sketches can be great fun, if you need, read both passages aloud before moving on.

Ask: How do these two passages relate?

The passage in chapter 3 talks of being children of God, of being beloved. Most of us can say that, but figuring out what this means and how it can change our lives is another thing.

Have everyone reread 1 John 4:7–21 in light of 1 John 3:1–3.

Ask: What sticks out to you? What do you like? What seems unrealistic?

LIFE APPLICATION: Today is Christmas Eve. It's also the last Sunday of Advent. We have already heard about the love God gives through Himself in the baby Jesus. This is the whole reason Jesus was born, because He loved us so much and wanted to be reconciled.

Ask: Do you really think John meant that God is love? If this is true, can you have love apart from God?

Ask: What would the world look like if Christians actually did love one another? What if Christians loved others, regardless of what they believed?

This passage says that God loved us first. This means that God already loves us. Nowhere does it say that our enemies will love us, even after we love them. But we are still called to do that very thing.

Screaming parents, unfair teachers, back-stabbing friends, racist coaches, money-hungry corporations, and a community that expects you to look and act a certain way, are the worlds in which most of us live. If these are not your experiences, what are? Ask your students to come up with a list of people and/or things that function as the enemy for them. Write these on the dry erase board.

So how do we love others when they do us so wrong? Check out verse 19—this is really hard!

God loved us so much that He stepped out of heaven! He loved us first. We celebrate Christmas not because we all love babies, but because God Almighty Himself declared His love by coming and putting our interests first, knowing full well many of us would reject Him, and those of us who do follow would do so by stumbling and making mistakes all along the journey. He loved us and still loves us!

MAKING IT PERSONAL: Give each person a candy cane. There are many stories that go along with candy canes and their origin. Among those is that candy canes were created by a candy maker as a multi-sensual reminder of all that Jesus is to us and for us. The shape, if held one way, is that of a 'J,' when held the other way, that of a shepherd's crook. Jesus is the Good Shepherd. The candy cane is sweet and minty to remind us of the sweet refreshment that comes from God. It is striped red and white to be sure we never forget the lashes He took in our place. The colors are red and white, red for the blood He shed, and white for the purity He offers. This simple little candy cane is a reminder of the real gift of Christmas.

Each person has been offered this gift. We love because He first loved us. Close, thanking God for the gift of His Son and that each person present may find the courage to respond in kind.

SONG: "Love Came Down" by Stacie Orrico, on the CD *Christmas Wish*

QUOTABLE QUOTE:

Blessed is the season which engages the whole world in a conspiracy of love.

—Hamilton Wright Mabi

Love—Midweek

MEMORY VERSE:
I pray that Christ will live in your hearts by faith and that your life will be strong in love and be built on love. And I pray that you and all God's holy people will have the power to understand the greatness of Christ's love—how wide and how long and how high and how deep that love is. Christ's love is greater than anyone can ever know, but I pray that you will be able to know that love. Then you can be filled with the fullness of God.—Ephesians 3:17–19 (NCV)

God loved the world so much that he gave his one and only Son so that whoever believes in him may not be lost, but have eternal life.—John 3:16 (NCV)

SCRIPTURE: Deuteronomy 6:5; 10:12–13

LESSON IN A SENTENCE: When we truly understand and receive the love of God, we in turn can truly love others.

FOCUS

It's after Christmas now. While we never tire of celebrating the birth of Jesus, all of the things that go with Christmas can become tiresome. Ask a few of your students to volunteer for one last Christmas activity. (It may be best to recruit these students ahead of time. You will need students who are not shy for this one.) You are going to have a contest to see who can offer the best Christmas carol, *American Idol* style. Have three of your leaders seated at a table as the judges. The rest of the group is the audience. When the first person begins, she has already been given a helium balloon. Let her sing one verse of the Christmas carol of her choice. Do this for each volunteer you have recruited. At the end, close the "contest" by inviting the helium choir to sing *Jingle Bells!*

Do a little check-in with your students. What has gone well over Christmas? What was hard over Christmas? Spend a little time sharing stories, hearing what they did, what gifts they received or gave, how they experienced Christmas.

DISCOVERY

Before your students arrive, write the following on the top of separate pieces of construction paper:

To love God with all your heart
To love God with all your soul
To love God with all your might
Fear the Lord
Walk in all His ways
To serve Him with all your heart
To serve Him with all your soul

Read through Deuteronomy 6:5 and Deuteronomy 10:12–13.
Verse 12 says that God requires this. . .
Ask: According to this passage what are we supposed to do?
Have your students read through the passage and list the requirements God sets forth. Pull out your premade papers only after they have read for themselves.

LIFE APPLICATION: God doesn't seem to leave a lot of room for halfway commitments. Even the language used—it's not *God would like,* or *God requests that you try*—it is that *God requires!*

There are many questions where you could focus. Choose one or two from these passages and focus your conversation around these. While they are all good, chances are your students will lose interest if you try to cover them all. If your group is engaged, however, keep going! Let the discussion fit the needs and maturity of your group.
Ask questions like:
What does it mean to love God with all of your heart?
What does it mean to walk in all of His ways?
Write some of their responses on the pieces of construction paper. Keep these in front of you as tangible reminders that while they may seem impossible, you have already brainstormed some concrete ways to keep His commandments. Learning from and supporting one another as we seek to follow His ways, is one more reason to remain in a community of believers.
Do you think this is realistic?
How do we handle such difficult requirements?
Spend some time talking about all that God requires. Let your students be open and honest if they feel overwhelmed or frustrated. Wherever the discussion goes, be certain to end reminding them of the love God offered first. He never requires more than He has already given.

MEMORY VERSE ACTIVITY
Close, asking if anyone knows the Memory Verse. If not, read over Ephesians 3:17–19. All of the requirements you learned about tonight seem impossible and would be impossible, were it not for Christ

dwelling in your heart. Being rooted and grounded in love, God offers His all to you!

Say the Memory Verse again as a prayer thanking God for all He has given.

DECEMBER 31, 2006

Favorites—Christmas Reflections—Christian Symbols

By Joyce Del Rosario

MEMORY VERSE:
You did not choose me, but I chose you and appointed you to go and bear fruit—fruit that will last.—John 15:16a (NIV)

SCRIPTURE: Luke 1:26–38

LESSON IN A SENTENCE: You are highly favored, watcha gonna do now?

THE BIG PICTURE (OR WHAT YOU'RE TRYING TO GET ACROSS):

We all have our favorites. Maybe it's a favorite ice cream flavor or a favorite color. Sometimes it's a favorite band or music group. What makes something a "favorite" is that we set it apart from the rest. It may not look very different from the other choices, but for some reason we choose our "favorites" to stand apart from everything else.

When the angel Gabriel appeared to Mary he said, "Greetings you who are highly favored." Mary was chosen to stand apart from all the rest. She was one of God's favorites! The Bible doesn't say that she was the prettiest or the smartest or the most athletic in all the land. In fact, Mary was a lot like us. She was a young teenage girl. She probably went through the same emotions with her boyfriend Joseph. She probably stressed out at the sight of a pimple. She probably freaked out when she saw an angel in the sky talk to her. But nonetheless she was highly favored. She was chosen by God to deliver Jesus Christ into the world. What an awesome task.

Her heart must have been pounding and her thoughts swarming, "You want ME to be the mother of Jesus Christ?" Did she have doubts? Did she feel up to the challenge? What would her family think? What would her friends think?

This was Mary's response, "I am the Lord's servant. May it be to me as you have said." (Luke 1:38) Why would God set her apart for such a great task? What made her so highly favored? She may not have known the answers to those questions, but what she did know was that if she obeyed, God would use her in mighty ways. God would use her to change the world.

As a child of God you also are highly favored. You are also set apart from the rest. The Lord may be giving you a different way to bring Christ into the world. Are you up for the challenge?

IN THIS LESSON STUDENTS SHOULD:

O Reflect on how they would feel if they were Mary or Joseph.
O Reflect on what God may be calling them to do now.
O Consider what they think and feel about such a call.

STUFF YOU NEED:

O Paper (preferably a notebook that can serve as a journal)
O Pen
O Colored pencils or other drawing implements

FOCUS

Play Corners.

Have the students go to the corner that represents their "favorites." Begin by having four corners labeled red, blue, green, and yellow. This is to start the game out with a simple choice. Each corner should be assigned a different color and then the students move to the color/corner they like the best. Once they get the idea, move on to ice cream flavors, music genres, music groups, children's books, cartoon characters, etc.

Ask: How did you decide something was your favorite?

(While you will get a bunch of different responses, favorites come down to not what is earned—rather, what is simply chosen for what it is. This is the point you are trying to make.)

DISCOVERY

Read Luke 1:26–38 out loud and allow the students to feel like a part of the account. Have the students write a journal entry in their own language as if they were Mary or Joseph.

Ask: If an angel came to you right now and said that you were highly favored and that you were about to have a son who would change the world, what would you write in your journal?

What thoughts would you have?

What questions would go through your mind?
What would you be excited about?
What would you be afraid of?

LIFE APPLICATION: God has chosen people to bring Jesus Christ into the world. It's a big task. Sometimes we may feel like we don't know enough, or we're not old enough to tell someone about Jesus. God used a young teenage girl to bring hope into the world.

Ask: Have you ever thought about God choosing us to share Him with others?

What ways do you think teenagers are perfect for bringing Jesus to the world?

What ways do you think teenagers need to grow in order to being Jesus to the world?

MAKING IT PERSONAL: How is God calling you to bring Christ into the world? Maybe God is calling you to a mission trip with your youth group. Or maybe to serve people in need in your own community. God may be calling you to use your gifts and talents to share Christ's love with others. Maybe you are being called to be a leader.

Whatever God is calling you to, write a journal entry about how you feel and think about this task. Can you answer the way Mary did and say, "I am the Lord's servant, may it be to me as you have said?" Write down why or why not. Pray about this answer and how God might use you to change the world.

Favorites—Midweek

MEMORY VERSE:
You did not choose me, but I chose you and appointed you to go and bear fruit—fruit that will last.—John 15: 16 (NIV)

SCRIPTURE: Joshua 1:6–9

LESSON IN A SENTENCE: You are highly favored, watcha gonna do now?

STUFF YOU NEED:

- ○ The same journal from last Sunday or a new notebook
- ○ Pens and pencils

FOCUS

Draw a picture in your journal of what you think you will look like in ten years. This may be literally what you will look like or small pictures that represent what you want your life to look like. Include what your favorite hobbies will be, who will be around you (friends and family), and what you will be doing as a job/career/call. Share your drawing. Now do the same for the next thirty years. Share drawings. Then forty years and share drawings.

DISCOVERY

Think about what you will need to enter into the future.

In groups of three, evaluate each other's drawings and decide what tools are needed for that person to reach the ten year goals, thirty and forty year goals.

Ask:

Will you need a college education or other training?

Will you need a hammer or a pencil?

Will you need special equipment or clothing to reach these goals?

What Scriptures might help in each stage?

Teacher's Note: If your students are unfamiliar with finding verses, this is a great chance to teach them about concordances. Many Bibles have these in the back or you can purchase them separately. If you don't have one, check with your pastor or church library.

Look up Scriptures of encouragement, strength, inspiration, and hope.

What kinds of things/people would help that student be strong and courageous in reaching their goals?

What would you say to Joshua before entering a new land? How could you encourage him?

Teacher's Note: As you enter into the New Year, be strong and courageous "for the Lord your God will be with you wherever you go." Like Mary, God calls us "highly favored." We're one of God's favorites! But being set apart and called by God is not always easy.

Joshua was about to lead the Israelites into the Promised Land. It was a new place with an unknown future, but he was chosen for the job. The Lord gave Joshua the tools that he would need to make it through this new land in his new role:

"Be strong and courageous, because you will lead these people. . ."

"Do not let this Book of the Law depart from your mouth; meditate on it day and night, so that you may be careful to do everything written in it. Then you will be prosperous and successful."

"...the Lord your God will be with you wherever you go."

In order to be the leader God was calling Joshua to be, he had to know three things: who he was in Christ (strong and courageous), what the Word says, and that God would be with him wherever he went. These are the same three things we need to pursue whatever it is God is asking us to do. These three tools will help us on our journey as we enter into the New Year and into new places and an unknown future.

LIFE APPLICATION: Take the same journal you used on Sunday. This time write in it as if you were Joshua. Read Joshua 1 out loud. Then write down what your thoughts and feelings would be if you were the one leading the Israelites into the Promised Land. Would you be nervous? Do you think you could do the job? What would inspire you at this time? If Joshua had a Discman (or MP3 player) what songs would be playing in his headset as he leads the people?

EXTRA! EXTRA!: Martin Luther King, Jr. entered a new land when he led an entire movement to help end racial segregation.

> "This faith can give us courage to face the uncertainties of the future. It will give our tired feet new strength as we continue our forward stride toward the city of freedom."
> —Dr. King's Nobel Peace Prize acceptance speech.

CONNECTIONS: Read the accounts of Moses, Rahab, David, Abraham, and Esther. Do you think they were set apart by God? What risks did they need to take? What came out of their willingness to be strong and courageous?

YOUTH MINISTRY WEB RESOURCES

Curriculum Resources these are the web addresses for publishers who offer dated and undated curriculum.

www.augsburgfortress.org
www.Cokesbury.com
www.cookministries.com
www.grouppublishing.com
www.helwys.com
www.lifeway.com
www.standardpub.com
www.studentlife.net
www.thomasnelson.com
www.tyndale.com
www.upperroom.org
www.urbanministries.com
www.wjkbooks.com
www.youthspecialties.com
www.zondervan.com

Games
www.egadideas.com—Offers a directory of indoor and outdoor games for your youth group to play.
wwwfunattic.com—A site dedicated to games of all sorts, for all age groups.
www.ferryhalim.com/orisinal—A whole host of silly Internet games.
www.thesource4ym.com—Provides a huge collection of games for youth groups, ranging from mixers to swimming pool games.
www.youthministry.com—Offers games that are just for fun, for large and small groups, noncompetitive, and that illustrate a point.

Human Social Resources
www.adopting.org—Adopting is a website designed to offer assistance, information, and support for adoption.
www.amnesty.org—A worldwide group seeking to end human rights violations.
www.aspenyouth.com—This is a website that provides information about Aspen Youth Ranches, which provide education, treatment, and rehabilitation to at-risk youth.
www.behindthelabel.com— A site that offers information about name brands and the conditions under which the products were made.
www.bread.org—Bread for the World. A lobbying group to Congress which provides study materials for high schoolers.

www.breakawayoutreach.com—Breakaway Youth is a ministry that reaches troubled youth through juvenile justice ministries, sports, and multimedia productions.

www.childrensdefense.org—Children's Defense Fund. They offer materials on the needs of American children, in particular the poor, for use in churches.

www.faithtrustinstitute.org/index.html—Formerly the Center for the Prevention of Sexual and Domestic Violence, now the FaithTrust Institute. This organization seeks to educate and prevent sexual and domestic violence and is the only one of its kind in the country looking at this from a faith perspective.

www.esa-online.org—Evangelicals for Social Action. Publishers of a wide array of Bible-based materials on social justice.

www.goshen.net/directory/Teens/—Provides numerous links for youth pastors and youth who are struggling with crisis issues such as suicide, drugs, and alcohol, and much more.

www.jmpf.org—John Perkins Foundation. Social justice and service.

www.mcc.org—Mennonite Central Committee. The relief and development agency of the Mennonite and Brethren in Christ churches.

www.rainn.org—Rainn is the website to a confidential 24-hour rape hotline.

www.tamethemonster.com—An organization that offers information and practical advice for combating poverty beginning with prayer.

www.vpp.com/teenhelp—VPP provides a national toll-free hotline designed to assist parents, childcare professionals, and others in finding resources for the treatment of struggling youth.

Magazines

www.briomag.com—Brio is a magazine for teenage girls that strives to teach, entertain, and challenge girls, while encouraging them to grow in a closer relationship with Christ.

www.gp4teens.com—*Guideposts for Teens* is similar to the original *Guideposts* magazine for adults. *Guideposts for Teens* tackles real issues such as sex, dating, faith, and spirituality.

www.theotherjournal.com—An online journal looking at the intersection of theology and culture. It is only in an online formula, with updates during the month of the initial release. There are also interactive portions.

www.pluggedinonline.com—Plugged In is designed to help parents, youth leaders, ministers, and teens to both understand and impact the culture they live in. Plugged In offers reviews and discussions regarding entertainment and its effects on youth and families.

www.relevantmagazine.com—A magazine for considering God and progressive culture.

www.youthspecialties.com—*Youthworker Journal*—A thematic magazine aimed bi-monthly at youth workers. Practical articles, devotional articles, resources, and a whole host of information regarding thoughts and trends within youth ministry.

Missions and Service

www.amor.org—A missions agency specializing in trips to northern Mexico.

www.apu.edu/iom/mexout—Mexico Outreach. A ministry based out of Azusa Pacific University taking high school and young adult groups into northern Mexico for service.

www.agrm.org—Association of Gospel Rescue Missions. An associational website that links to local missions. Missions typically provide shelter, kitchens, community development, and community centers.

www.asphome.org—Appalachia Service Project, a ministry that takes other groups on week-long mission trips to Kentucky and Tennessee to repair homes for the poor.

www.calebproject.org—An organization offering information and resources for global missions.

www.christiansurfers.net—An organization that helps students form a Christian organization of surfers, and offer the possibility of missions in the surfing community.

www.compassion.com—Compassion International. World Relief organization with programs that can educate and involve junior and senior high students.

www.crm.org—Church Resources Ministries—CRM exists to develop leaders in the church and to provide resources worldwide.

www.empoweringlives.org—An organization seeking to address spiritual and physical needs in struggling countries, primarily in Africa. They seek outreach and leadership development and child sponsorship opportunities.

www.gospelcom.net/csm—Center for Student Missions. A ministry offering customized mission trips to large cities for junior and senior high students.

www.habitat.org—Habitat for Humanity. Provides housing for low-income families with many service opportunities.

www.joniandfriends.org—An excellent (and one of the only) resource for ministry with those with disabilities.

www.larche.org, www.larcheusa.org, www.larche.org.uk, www.larche-canada.org—L'Arche is an organization begun in France which has spread to much of the world. They provide communities for those with and without physical or mental disabilities. Henri Nouwen is probably the best known participant associated with the organization.

www.newadventures.org—Missions organization providing trips for junior and senior high school students.

www.oneliferevolution.org—A focused ministry encouraging youth groups to not only raise awareness regarding the AIDS pandemic, but also a way for your group to fight this problem.

www.servlife.org—A missions organization which seeks to develop and empower indigenous workers in difficult areas. This is an organization that has taken innovation and heart to share Christ in places others are not going.

www.worldvision.org—World Vision is an organization that provides relief to third world countries by reaching out to the poor, and staying aware of current worldwide events.

Music Resources

www.acaza.com—Offers current news on Christian artists.

www.ccmcom.com—Provides up-to-date news on today's hottest contemporary Christian musicians.

www.christianitytoday.com/music/—Reviews new Christian music and provides interviews with the artists.

www.cmcentral.com—Christian Music Central offers visitors the chance to view editorials on music and artists, shows album and artist reviews, lists tour dates, and offers MP3 downloads.

www.christianradio.com—Christian Radio gives a list of over 2,000 Christian radio stations as well as over 500 Christian artists.

www.christianrock.net—Christian Rock is a 24-hour radio show broadcast on the internet. Christian Rock has two sister stations:

http://www.christianhardrock.net/

http://www.christian-hiphop.net/

www.rockrebel.com/—Christianity and spirituality in secular music (articles)

www.wellwatermusic.com—A resource for and about new artists.

www.worshiptogether.com—Provides a great overview of what is hot in Christian music by offering top ten lists, free song downloads, and more.

www.youthfire.com/music/compare.html—Youth Fire is a great website to refer to when looking for Christian music that is comparable to that played daily on mainstream radio.

Pop Culture

www.christianitytoday.com—Provides a good way to identify with Christian youth and their beliefs, by giving current detailed reviews on movies and music, and provides discussion questions.

www.cmli.org—Christian Media Literacy Institute

www.cpyu.org—Center for Parent and Youth Understanding. A comprehensive site with constant updates covering youth culture from many angles.

www.dickstaub.com—Pop culture review from a Christian perspective.

www.commonsensemedia.org—Family oriented media reviews (philosophy is sanity not censorship).

www.gracehillmedia.com—This is a company which holds major Hollywood studios as clients to find points of connection with the Christian community.

www.hollywoodjesus.com—A source that offers Christian perspectives of today's pop culture. You'll find reviews for today's newest movies, music, and much more.

www.medialit.org/focus/rel—articles.html—Center for Media Literacy (has some faith-based articles on media discernment.)

www.rollingstone.com—Update yourself on what youth are watching and hearing in today's secular media. This source reviews movies and particularly secular music, providing CD reviews, photos, and videos of today's pop stars.

www.screenit.com—Screen It offers reviews on all sorts of entertainment.

www.textweek.com—Gives sermon topics stemming from current and past movies.

www.tollbooth.org—An online magazine that provides reviews of Christian music, concerts, and books. Also provides reviews of past movies.

Spiritual Disciplines

www.contemplativeoutreach.org—An offering of both information as well as connection with other sites and groups interested in exploring the contemplative side of faith.

www.labyrinth.co.uk—Connected with Jonny Baker, the most commonly known labyrinth among youth workers.

www.princeofpeaceonline.org/psalms/lectio.html—offering articles and explanations into the practice of lectio devina.

www.sdiworld.org—The directory of Spiritual Directors International.

www.princeofpeaceonline.org/psalms/lectio.html

www.sfts.edu—San Francisco Theological Seminary has a Lilly-endowed program called the Youth Ministry and Spirituality Project. Many insights and resources available.

www.taize.fr—Site for the Taize community in France.

T-Shirts etc.

www.mcduck.com—A company familiar with youth ministry, offering embroidery and screen printing on a variety of items.

www.zazzle.com—A site that allows you to create your design and have it printed on multiple variations of shirts at a relatively low cost.

Worship Resources

www.audiblefaith.com—Audible Faith offers downloadable worship music, and sheet music can be ordered from this website in any key.

www.ccli.com—CCLI is a strong communication network that allows the dispensing of comprehensive and valuable informational resources about worship.

www.christianguitar.org—Christian Guitar is a fantastic Christian guitar resource page with over 7,000 tabs. Christian Guitar also offers lessons, PowerPoint slides, and message boards.

www.worshiptogether.com—Worship Together features Bible insights and other resources for worship and worship leaders.

www.integritymusic.com—Integrity Music offers a number of different worship resources that include information on artists, albums, and much more.

www.maranathamusic.com—Maranatha Music offers a number of resources for worship and worship leaders.

www.pastornet.net.au/inside—Inside Out offers free downloadable contemporary and evangelical worship music for non-commercial use.

www.songs4worship.com—Songs 4 Worship offers numerous worship resources including music, community, freebies, and more.

www.worshipmusic.com—Worship Music is a Christian music resource with CDs, cassettes, sheet/print music, videos, software, and more   for sale.

Youth Activities

www.30hourfamine.org—30 Hour Famine is a movement led by World Vision that fights world hunger with the help of youth and churches all around the world.

www.adventures.org—Adventures in Missions is an interdenominational short-term missions organization that offers programs for youth, college, and adults.

www.bigworld.org—Big World Ventures offers customized short-term mission trips for youth, adults, individuals, groups, church networks, and Christian organizations. This website provides information regarding all trips and destinations.

www.thejeremiahproject.org—The Jeremiah Project offers missions trips that are planned specifically for junior high youth.

www.noahsark.com—Noah's Ark is located in Colorado, offering a uniquely Christian perspective on whitewater rafting, rock climbing, rappelling, and a whole lot more!

www.syatp.org—See You At The Pole. Once a year in September it has become a youth ministry tradition in the States and around the world for students to gather around the flag pole at school and to pray.

www.ywam.org—YWAM Urban Ministries is an organization that attempts to bring safe and exciting events to communities in need, through innovative ministries and living with the people in the community.

Youth Pastor Emergent

www.emergentvillage.com—Resources and links for missional Christians across generations.

www.emergingchurch.org—Connecting point for intentionally postmodern thinking churches.

www.churchnext.net/index.shtml—Tribal Generation. A loose look at many topics from a Christian perspective.

www.theooze.com—Online magazine that looks to any and all issues, bringing them into a conversation within a Christian community.

Youth Pastor Resources

www.americanapparel.net—A Los Angeles-based company that ensures fair wages and good working conditions from production to distribution. This is a socially responsible resource for those plain shirts you want printed for camp or your retreat.

www.biblegateway.com—A collection of several translations of the Bible online.

www.buwc.ca/youthline—Youthline is a youth ministry resource page with events located primarily in Canada.

www.capernaumministries.org—A division of Young Life which focuses on ministry for adolescents with special needs.

www.crosswalk.com—Many different resources from articles and advice to online translations of the Bible.

www.discipleshipresources.org/downloads.asp—Free discipleship downloads from the United Methodist Church.

www.family.org—Provides articles that help parents know how to better deal with their growing children and changing families. Offers advice and wisdom for the ups and downs of family life.

www.highwayvideo.com—Highway video offers culturally relevant videos to be used in ministry and worship.

www.hmconline.org—A resource for urban youth leaders provides information on up-coming training sessions that help youth leaders become more efficient in their ministry with urban youth.

www.ileadyouth.com—A site offering articles, trainings, resources, and events for youth workers.

www.nwgs.edu—Northwest Graduate School. A unique accredited school offering a global perspective and experience to theological education. Because those attending are in ministry, the classes are offered in intensives and through cohorts, allowing the person to remain in ministry while training.

www.parentministry.org—Provides youth workers with articles that help build a stronger family-based ministry, and offers parents helpful articles for understanding their adolescent children.

www.persecution.com—A site offering updates and prayer requests regarding the persecuted church around the world.

www.reach-out.org—A resource for youth leaders that presents, finds books, articles, Bible studies, illustrations, ideas for training volunteers, and insight into leading a successful missions trip.

www.teamce.com—A website from Christian Endeavor, often credited with founding youth ministry in the U.S. An offering of philosophy and training for simplified youth ministry.

www.uywi.org—A ministry offering training for those specifically working in urban settings.

www.yfc.org—Provides current information on youth ministries for youth pastors, youth, and parents.

www.younglife.org—Offers information about young life and its work with today's youth.

www.youthbuilders.com—A resource for parents and youth leaders offering articles and answered questions that help parents and youth leaders better understand how to work with and relate to the youth in their lives.

www.youth-ministry.info—Great site with tons of information, both practical and philosophical, and links to just about everything connected with youth ministry that you can imagine.

www.youthpastor.com—Provides youth pastors with articles, games, youth group names, recommended reading, topical music resources, and more.

www.youthspecialties.com/links—This website offers thousands of links to websites on leadership, missions, skit ideas, crisis hotlines, and much more.

www.youthworkers.net—A resource that allows youth workers to be able to connect with each other by region. Also provides links to activities that youth nation-wide participate in.